The Goodheart-Willcox home economics series

The Food Book

Lynn Newberry
Home Economist
Ossining, New York

M. Frances Fisher
Home Economist
Croton-on-Hudson, New York

The Goodheart-Willcox Company, Inc.
South Holland, Illinois

Library of Congress Cataloging in Publication Data

Newberry, Lynn
  The food book.

  Includes index.
  SUMMARY: Presents information about food
and nutrition and discusses such topics as
kitchen equipment, shopping for food, basic
cooking techniques, planning and serving meals,
and career opportunities in the food industry.
    1. Food.   2. Nutrition.
I. Fisher, M. Frances, joint author.   II. Title.
TX355.C74   641   80-19009
ISBN 0-87006-299-9

Introduction

The Food Book introduces you to the fascinating world of foods. You will explore many different aspects of food, ranging from your own food choices to a worldwide look at the future of food.

Since you eat every day, you will be able to apply the knowledge you gain to your daily life. The facts you learn about nutrition will help you make wise food decisions. Your knowledge of appliances and cooking terms will help you gain confidence as you work in the kitchen. Your shopping skills will help you get the most for your money at the grocery store.

As you read this book, you will learn both the "how" and "why" of cooking. You will learn to manage meals, serve foods and plan parties. In addition, you will become familiar with various food-related careers.

The Food Book is easy to read and understand. It includes many interesting illustrations and charts to help you learn important concepts and skills. Each chapter begins with a list of learning objectives and ends with key words, review questions and related activities. These materials are designed to help you increase your understanding of foods.

Contents

4

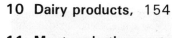

part three **Working with food**

6

part five

Widening food horizons

Food and people

*All people need food. Food is the
basis of life. A variety of foods
will provide good nutrition.*

Exploring your food choices

Why do you eat the foods you eat? After reading this chapter, you will be able to explain how eating habits develop. You will also be able to identify some of the factors that affect food choices and customs.

Many influences shape your eating habits and food choices.

What does food mean to you? That's a silly question, you may say. Everyone knows you need food to stay alive. Most people also know that good food is related to good health. But do you choose all the foods you eat just to be healthy?

No, food choices are influenced by many things besides health. Many cultural traditions center around food. Some religions restrict the foods their followers are allowed to eat. Social and psychological factors also affect food choices.

Many of your food choices are made by habit. A habit is something you have done so often in the past that you continue to do it without thinking. Habits make life simpler. Without habits, you would have to make hundreds of separate little decisions every day.

People begin to form food habits very early in life. Eating is one of the first happy experiences babies have. As babies are fed, they also receive love and attention, as shown in 1-1. Before long, they learn to associate food with comfort and security. Thus, we learn that food does more than just satisfy hunger.

Research shows that most of us could use some improvements in our food choices in terms of our health and well-being. But even when we know this, it is very difficult to change food habits. The fact that we are often not aware of them makes them especially hard to change. If you want to change your eating habits and food choices, it helps to know what they are and how you have formed them.

CULTURAL INFLUENCES

A *culture* includes the knowledge, beliefs, customs and traditions shared by a group of people. These are passed down from generation to generation. The traditions and customs survive because they tend to produce feelings of security—of having roots and identity. Many factors have created the differences in food habits, customs and traditions found in the world today.

Different cultures, different foods

Many factors influence the development of food customs. Two of the most important factors are climate and geography. For instance, people living near the sea often rely on fishing for much of their food supply. Likewise, the type of soil and weather conditions affect what crops will grow in a region. Foods that can be obtained in the largest amounts with the least effort usually become a culture's most important foods.

Rice is a good example of this principle. Much of the land in the Orient has poor soil. The good land that is available must therefore be farmed very carefully. Because rice produces a high yield, it has become the most important *staple food* for most Orientals. (Staple food is food which is produced and eaten on a regular basis.)

Fuel for cooking has always been rather limited in the Orient. Therefore, the most popular cooking methods are ones that use little fuel such as *steaming* and *stir-frying*. Orientals have developed a system of steaming several foods at one time. Bamboo baskets of food are stacked one on top of another over the rice pan. As the rice cooks, the steam rises through the baskets to cook the other foods.

Stir-frying is a popular cooking method in China and Japan. Stir-frying is done in a *wok*, a special kind of pan with sides that slope down toward the middle. See 1-2. The heat is concentrated at the bottom, in the middle of the wok. Foods to be stir-fried are cut into small pieces for fast cooking. As foods are quickly stirred and fried, they are pushed up the sides of the wok to expose uncooked food to the heat.

In Japan, the *hibachi* grill is widely used. The hibachi uses small amounts of charcoal. The Japanese also save fuel by eating many foods raw, including fish and seaweed.

In India, both rice and wheat are staple foods. More rice is eaten in southern India than in northern India. This is because the South has enough rain to grow rice. The North has a cooler and drier climate. Wheat grows better there.

Some people in India are *vegetarians*. Vegetarians are persons who do not eat meat, fish or poultry. Some vegetarians eat only plant foods. Others eat dairy foods and/or eggs in addition to plant foods. Many Indians are vegetarians because of their religion. The religious beliefs of most Indians forbid them to eat certain animal foods such as beef.

In the Middle East, sheep herding has been a way of life for centuries. It's not surprising to find that lamb and mutton (meat from mature sheep) are the bases for many favorite dishes. *Shish kebabs*—small chunks of lamb cooked on skewers over an open fire—originated in the Middle East. An American version of shish kebab is pictured in 1-3.

For centuries, Middle Eastern cities were important crossroads in the trade that developed between Europe and Asia. With so many traders and travelers passing through, the people in the cities developed many international food tastes. The world's first "fast food" places probably sprang up in this area. Barbecued meat, fried fish and dried fruits were sold from stands set up along main roads. Pita bread, a round bread slit to form a pocket to hold various fillings, may have been one of the world's first sandwiches. It is still popular today.

Climate made a major difference in the cooking styles that developed in northern and southern Europe. In northern Europe, people kept large home fires burning all the time through the long, cold winter. A large kettle was hung over the fire and was the main cooking pot. Whatever meat and vegetables were available went into the pot. This is probably the reason why hearty soups and stews have long been popular in northern Europe.

In southern Europe, such large home fires were not necessary because the climate was warmer. Nor were they practical because less wood was available for fuel. People in this area developed simple charcoal stoves for cooking.

Before refrigerators were invented, food preservation was a major problem. (To *preserve* food is to treat it so that it will not spoil.) In Europe, meats were often made into sausages and smoked. Foods were also salted to help preserve them. Smoked and salted

1-2 Stir-frying is an Oriental method of cooking. Before foods are stir-fried, they are cut into small pieces.

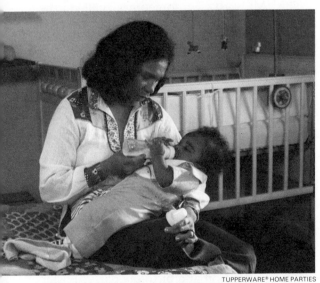

1-1 When babies are cuddled as they are fed, they learn to associate food with comfort and pleasure.

1-3 An "American" shish kebab is prepared by placing pieces of meat, vegetables and fruits on skewers.

foods are still popular in many areas. In Germany, for instance, sausages and sauerkraut (pickled cabbage) are national favorites. See 1-4.

On a continent as large and varied as Africa, it's not surprising that many varied cuisines developed. North African cooking reflects many Arab and European influences. As the spice trade developed, South Africa became a convenient stopping place for the traders who chose the sea route. Many European colonies sprang up along Africa's southern coastline. Laborers were brought in from the Orient. Each group of people brought their own ideas about food and cooking. Thus, the African cuisine today is full of rich variety, with many regional specialties.

Cultures and food customs in the United States

Food customs in the United States began with the American Indians and the first European colonists. One of the first "new" foods the Indians introduced to the colonists was corn. Corn was easy to plant, and it grew well. It could be eaten as a vegetable or used to make breads and puddings. Many other foods were also native to America. These included squashes, pumpkins, green and red peppers, turkeys and many kinds of beans and berries. The settlers had to adapt their old recipes to the new foods they found. This created a number of new dishes that became the basis of the American cuisine.

As time passed, more and more people from other countries came to America. These new Americans brought the customs of their native lands with them. As a result, the cultural heritage of America is rich and varied. It is a mixture of customs from many different countries.

Some Americans still follow the customs of their families' native lands. For instance, Italian-Americans are likely to eat Italian food more often than Americans of English or Chinese descent. Pasta dishes, antipasto (appetizers) and cannoli (cheese-filled pastries) are still an important part of the cultural heritage of many Italian-Americans. Mexican-Americans,

Polish-Americans and other ethnic groups feel the same way about their special foods.

Soul food is part of the cultural heritage of American Blacks. Soul food specialties such as black-eyed peas, collard greens, chitterlings (the cleaned intestines of hogs) and sweet potato pie developed in the rural South. Many of these foods used to cost very little. But increased demand for them has caused prices to rise. Spareribs are now among the most costly meats you can buy.

In the Louisiana area, *creole* cooking is popular. It combines the cooking traditions of the French, Spanish, African and American Indian. One famous creole dish is called jambalaya. It is a mixture of shellfish, poultry, sausage, spicy tomato sauce and rice.

People of the southwest have adopted many foods from their Mexican neighbors. Tacos, spicy sauces for vegetables, avocado dishes and flan (caramel custard) are some examples. See 1-5.

The Midwest is sometimes called the nation's breadbasket. Farmers in that region grow enough grain to feed the people of many countries. Foods of the Midwest are simple and hearty. Steaks, roasts, potatoes, corn, tomatoes and homemade cakes, cookies and pies are popular.

American cooking today is a unique blend of old and new, and of great cultural variety. It reflects the coming together of many different people from all over the world. Even today, as new immigrants arrive, the cuisine continues to evolve and grow.

Foods and special occasions

Every culture has food customs related to special occasions. A birthday cake is the center of attention at a birthday party. Easter is celebrated with egg hunts and baskets of treats. Picnics and barbecues are planned for the Fourth of July. Halloween would not be the same without carved pumpkins and trick-or-treating. Turkey with all the trimmings is associated with Thanksgiving, 1-6. Without food customs, special occasions might seem less special.

When you think of feasts, you probably

think of primitive societies or royalty. But many of today's wedding receptions and family reunions are feasts too. Church suppers and potluck dinners are feasts of a more casual style. In fact, food plays a part in most gatherings of people. This is true of club meetings, quick visits to friends and even coffee breaks at work.

UNITED DAIRY INDUSTRY ASSOC.

1-5 Many Mexican foods are popular in the Southwest. Pictured clockwise from top are: Mexican chocolate, flan (caramel custard), green beans and potatoes with spicy cheese sauce, tacos, tostados and chilled avocado soup.

NATIONAL KRAUT PACKERS ASSOC.

1-4 Sausages, sauerkraut and dumplings are eaten throughout Germany. Strudel (a pastry which often has a fruit filling) is a specialty in southern parts of the country.

NATIONAL TURKEY FEDERATION

1-6 Many families choose to celebrate Thanksgiving with a special turkey dinner.

People often have dinner parties to welcome new neighbors or to say good-bye to friends. Taking food to a family who is facing a crisis is a custom in some regions. And gifts of food at holidays such as Christmas are symbols of friendship and love, 1-7.

RELIGIOUS INFLUENCES

People of some religions have special food customs. Traditionally, Moslems and Jews have been forbidden to eat pork. Many theories surround the start of this taboo. Some people think it came from the belief that a hog was an unclean animal and a likely carrier of disease. Certainly pork did not keep well in the hot Middle Eastern climate. Other people believe that a prejudice against hogs started because hogs could not be herded like sheep. Herding was a way of life for the people of the Middle East.

In addition to the taboo against pork, Jews have many other dietary laws. Jews who follow all of these laws have a *kosher* home. According to the dietary laws, only animals which have split hooves and chew cud may be used for food. (This explains why beef is allowed and pork is forbidden.) The meat which is eaten must be kosher. This means animals must be killed according to ritual by a specially trained person. All blood must be carefully drained.

Seafood is also covered in the dietary laws. Jewish people may eat finfish. But shellfish are forbidden.

Other Jewish dietary laws state how food should be cooked and served. For instance, meat and dairy foods cannot be eaten in the same meal. Nor can these foods be eaten from the same plate. Kosher households keep one set of dishes and kitchen utensils for meat foods. They keep another set for dairy foods.

Pareve foods are foods which are neither meat nor dairy foods. Eggs, fruits, vegetables and baked products made with vegetable shortening are pareve foods. They can be eaten with either dairy or meat foods. Some Jewish foods are pictured in 1-8.

Passover is an important Jewish holiday. It pays tribute to the Jews' flight from ancient Egypt. A special meal, called the Seder, is prepared on the first two nights of the holiday. Each food that is served is a symbol of some part of the Passover. Matzo (unleavened bread) is an important symbol. Because the Jews needed to leave Egypt quickly, their bread had no time to rise. As a result, they had to make a simple bread with no leavening.

The Hindu faith has some special food customs. Hindus believe that all life is sacred. The cow is a particularly sacred animal. Therefore, most Hindus do not eat beef.

Hindus also have a taboo against pork. It began with the belief that hogs were unclean animals. The caste system in India supported the taboo. (The Indian caste system was a social system into which a person was born.) Only members of the lowest caste would eat pork. Today, the taboo against pork is losing strength. Some Hindus do eat pork occasionally.

Christians have some food restrictions. Until recent years, Roman Catholics were not allowed to eat meat on Fridays. This restriction paid tribute to the Friday on which Christ was crucified. This rule has been dropped (except for the Fridays during Lent). But many Catholics still do not eat meat on Fridays.

Fasting is practiced by some religious groups. For instance, many Christians fast on Ash Wednesday and Good Friday. (Ash Wednesday is the first day of the Lenten season. Good Friday is the anniversary of Christ's crucifixion.) During a fast, no food is eaten for a certain period of time. Fasting can also mean that a certain food, such as meat, is not eaten.

Some foods are deeply symbolic to Christians. The bread and wine served at a communion service are symbols of Christ's body and blood. Easter eggs are a symbol of rebirth. See 1-9.

Other religious groups also have restrictions. For instance, Seventh Day Adventists are not allowed to drink coffee, tea or alcohol. Christian Scientists are not allowed to drink alcohol. They are also discouraged from drinking coffee or tea.

SOCIAL INFLUENCES

A century ago, many people were involved with growing the food they ate. Today, most people simply drive to a supermarket or restaurant and buy it. Convenience foods have cut down the amount of time needed to prepare meals. Because people are less involved in producing the food they eat, they may attach less importance to it.

Nevertheless, eating is still a social activity. Most people prefer to eat with others than to eat alone. Children observe this early in their lives and reflect it in their play. You can often see children playing with toy dishes and imaginary food, serving their friends or dolls. They

THE POTATO BOARD AND THE CALIFORNIA RAISIN ADVISORY BOARD

1-8 Special foods are part of the religious heritage of Jews. Pictured clockwise from top are: chiffon cake, beef stew made with dried fruits, challah (braided bread) and potato latkes (potato pancakes).

WELCH FOODS, INC.

1-7 Gifts of homemade food are symbols of friendship and love.

STANDARD BRANDS, INC.

1-9 The colored eggs in Easter bread are a symbol of faith in a new life.

have learned that sharing food with others is fun, 1-10.

Food has social meanings for people of all ages. No matter how informal the occasion, food is nearly always involved. In fact, you would probably feel something was wrong with a get-together that didn't have something to eat or drink. And you would probably feel awkward if friends dropped by and you had nothing to offer them.

Dinner has traditionally been a family social experience. It has been a time for togetherness, a time to share the day's events. Many families still observe this tradition. But for others, this tradition is changing. Personal schedules may vary a great deal. Meals have to be planned around these busy schedules, 1-11. For some families, it is difficult to find times when they can all sit down and enjoy a meal together.

In many families, both parents work outside the home. This creates two major changes. One is an increase in income. The other is a decrease in time.

The increase in income allows the family to buy convenience foods and appliances that save time and effort in the kitchen. The higher income also allows the family to eat more meals away from home.

The decrease in time forces family members to share the tasks of grocery shopping, meal planning and cooking. Food-related companies are helping families meet these new demands. More convenience foods are being developed. More single-serving foods are being marketed. These foods can be prepared quickly and without waste. Also, new kitchen appliances are being made to reduce the time and effort needed to prepare meals.

PSYCHOLOGICAL INFLUENCES

What are your favorite foods? Why are they your favorites? If they were simply the best-tasting foods in the world, they would probably be everyone's favorites. Compare your list of favorite foods with those of your friends. You are likely to find that all of you have some favorite foods in common. You are also likely to find that you included a few foods that no one else listed.

Happiness and unhappiness

People often associate happy times with certain foods. This association of happy times and foods may determine your favorite foods. For instance, hamburgers, french fries and milk shakes are popular foods among teens. Thus, it is no surprise that local hamburger shops are often meeting places for teens.

Associations between happiness and certain foods can create problems. When people feel unhappy, frustrated or lonely, they often turn to food treats. Food treats tend to be associated with happier times. These treats are often rich desserts or party snacks. They tend to be high in kilojoules (Calories) but not very nutritious. If the unhappy feelings persist, some people may overeat. Overeating will make them gain weight, which makes them more unhappy. They may find themselves in an unhappy cycle.

Some children learn to think of certain foods as rewards for good behavior. See 1-12. Parents sometimes promise their children dessert if they eat all of the meat and vegetables. Perhaps you were promised candy, cookies or ice cream if you behaved well. Maybe you were told you could not have these treats if you misbehaved.

All of these experiences are fairly common. But they can create unhealthy attitudes about food. Food should not be used as a reward or punishment.

Guilt

Can you remember being told to clean your plate? Many children are taught that wasting food is wrong, especially with people in the world are starving. This produces the "clean plate syndrome." It makes people feel guilty if they leave any food on their plates. As a result, when they misjudge their appetites or are served too much food, they eat it all to avoid feeling guilty.

Food should not be wasted. But eating more than you need or want is also a waste of food. The best approach is to start with

1-10 *Children learn about the social meanings of food as they play.*

TUPPERWARE® HOME PARTIES

1-11 *People often eat quickly between their other activities.*

TUPPERWARE® HOME PARTIES

1-12 *Using candy as a reward may cause a child to develop unhealthy attitudes about food.*

smaller portions and enjoy a second helping later, if you wish.

Status

Food choices are sometimes affected by the desire for *status*. (A person who has a high status is respected and admired by others.) Many people would like to be more popular or to belong to an admired, respected social group. The image a person tries to create may involve eating certain foods or choosing certain brands. It may involve learning difficult or unusual cooking skills.

What image do you have of people who like to dine on imported caviar, fine champagne, and lobster? These are expensive foods associated with wealth and high status. This is an extreme example, of course. But the desire to have a high status image can also be seen in common situations. For instance, when company is coming for dinner, most people will serve something special.

Advertising often takes advantage of the desire for status. Sometimes people choose a product they feel is the popular choice because they don't want to feel left out. The problem is that the popular choice may not be the best product. It may just be the product with the best advertisement.

Being a gourmet cook is often associated with status. A *gourmet* is an expert judge of fine foods. The ability to prepare and serve unusual or elaborate dishes is a sign of refinement and status.

PERSONAL VALUES

People choose different foods for many reasons. You have read about the cultural, religious, social and psychological influences on food habits. The way these and other influences affect your food choices is related to your personal values. When you are faced with food decisions, your values help you make choices. Often you don't even think much about your values. Yet they play an important role in determining which foods you eat.

The chart in 1-13 lists may personal values that affect food choices. Health concerns (real or imaginary) are the most important value to some people. Others take health for granted. They may be more concerned about price or convenience. The importance you attach to each of these values is a personal matter.

FACTORS THAT AFFECT YOUR FOOD CHOICES

NUTRITION	Do you choose foods because you think you need them for growth, energy and good health?
ENJOYMENT	Do you choose foods because you like the way they look, smell and taste? Do you choose them because they are especially satisfying or refreshing?
PRICE	Are you concerned about getting your money's worth?
CONVENIENCE	Do you tend to choose foods that are easy to buy, to prepare and to eat?
SUITABILITY	Does the situation make a difference in your food choices? For example, would you fix different foods for a company meal than for a family meal? Do you eat certain foods because your friends eat them? Does your ethnic background or religion influence your food choices?
PERSONAL APPEARANCE	Do you eat certain foods because you think they will help you look the way you want to look? Is food related to your self-image? For example, do you think some foods will give you a good complexion or shiny hair, make you strong and athletic, or give you a lively personality?
SPECIAL HEALTH CONCERNS	Do you have a condition that limits your food choices (such as allergies, diabetes or hypertension)? Do you choose or avoid certain foods because of a weight problem?

1-13 Many factors affect your food choices.

*to*Define

creole . . . culture . . .
fasting . . . gourmet . . .
hibachi . . . kosher . . .
pareve . . . preserve . . .
shish kebab . . . soul food . . .
staple food . . . status . . .
steamer . . . stir-frying . . .
vegetarian . . . wok

*to*Discuss

1. What are habits? When are food habits formed?
2. What does an infant associate with food? Why?
3. Why do Orientals eat large amounts of rice?
4. Why do people from the Middle East eat large amounts of lamb?
5. Name five foods which are native to the United States.
6. Name three examples of soul food. From what culture did soul food originate?
7. List four holidays. Name several foods which are associated with each holiday.
8. Name two foods with symbolic meanings. What does each represent?
9. How have changing life-styles influenced people's food habits?
10. Name three foods which you associate with happy occasions.
11. Name seven factors which affect your daily food choices. Which ones are most important to you?

*to*Do

1. Sit down with your family and discuss your food likes and dislikes. Then answer the following questions. What were your eating habits as a child? Are many of your likes and dislikes similar to those of your parents? Do you dislike some foods because a family member or friend dislikes them? Does the part of the country in which you live affect what you eat? Does your culture or religion affect your food choices? Are there any changes you would like to make — or should make — in your food habits?
2. Divide a piece of paper vertically into columns. Head the columns as follows: name of food; time; place; alone or with others; reason for eating. For two days, keep a record of everything you eat or drink. Does the chart tell you anything about your eating habits? Summarize your findings in a short written report.
3. Choose a foreign country which interests you. Research the food customs of that country. Share your findings with the class in a short oral presentation. If possible, prepare one or two of the special foods you mention in your report.
4. Write a report describing the food specialties of a region of the United States. In your report, answer the following questions. What foods are native to the region? Which groups of immigrants settled in the area? How did they affect the development of food customs? Include five traditional recipes in your report.
5. In class, discuss the foods you enjoy during a special holiday. Do your classmates enjoy the same foods you do? Can you explain the similarities and differences? What special traditions does your family have? Compare your traditions with those of your friends.
6. Invite a rabbi to visit your class to discuss Jewish food customs.
7. Make a list of the foods you would serve if you were planning a special meal for a group of friends. Why do you think you chose those particular foods? Compare your menu with menus written by your friends. Do the menus have anything in common?
8. Use chart 1-13 to help you analyze your food choices. Decide which factors are most important when you choose foods:
   a. In the school cafeteria.
   b. At a fast food restaurant.
   c. At home.
   d. At a fancy restaurant.
   e. At the grocery store.
Summarize your findings in a short written report.

Based upon values of good health and nutrition, you might choose this citrus dessert rather than cookies or candy.

Nutrition matters

Why study nutrition? After reading this chapter, you will be able to explain how nutrition is related to health. You will be able to define carbohydrates, fats, proteins, vitamins and minerals and describe their importance to your diet. You will also be able to identify important food sources of these nutrient groups.

A famous French gourmet once said, "Tell me what you eat, and I shall tell you what you are." This remark refers to the relationship between eating habits and social status. But it applies to our nutritional status as well.

Your body is made up of trillions of cells. Each cell contains *nutrients.* (Nutrients are the chemical substances in food needed for life and health.) As cells wear out, your body depends on food you've eaten to make replacement cells. When you are growing, you have an extra need for the nutrients used in making new cells. In addition, certain nutrients provide the energy you need for life processes and for activities. The need for nutrients continues throughout life. See 2-1.

Nutrients also play an important role in the many processes which are always going on inside your body. For instance, what makes your heart keep beating? How does your body maintain a constant temperature of 37°C (98.6°F)? What tells your body to produce more energy when you are jogging? How and why are new blood cells produced when you are sick or injured?

You do not have to think about each activity that takes place inside your body. But you do influence what happens inside your body. You can make it possible for your body to function automatically by supplying it with the nutrients it needs. If you eat the right foods in the right amounts, your body works the way it should, 2-2. But if you do not give your body the nutrients it needs, it cannot work as well.

Over a period of time, nutrient shortages can create serious health problems. By having an understanding of *nutrition,* you can learn how nutrient shortages can be avoided. Nutrition is the science of food and how the nutrients from food are used in the body. It is a fascinating science because it is a study of you and how your body works.

THE FANTASTIC ENERGY MACHINE

Like a machine, your body needs energy to function. Many substances can be used to produce energy. Food is the source of energy for the body, 2-3. When you digest food, it is broken down into small molecules. In each cell of your body, some of these molecules combine with oxygen. When oxygen combines with a fuel substance, heat energy is produced. This process is called *oxidation*. Oxidation occurs, for example, when you burn gasoline in a car. Oxidation may be as rapid as a stick of dynamite exploding or as slow as a nail developing rust.

The oxidation that takes place in your cells is neither as rapid as dynamite nor as slow as rust, but somewhere in between. Oxidation makes it possible for you to obtain energy from your food. Without the process of oxidation, you would die.

The energy value of food is measured by the amount of heat produced when the food is oxidized. The unit that has traditionally been used to measure this heat is called a *Calorie*. A *kilojoule* is a metric unit for measuring energy. One Calorie equals about 4 kilojoules. Scientists prefer to use the kilojoule because it can be used to measure all kinds of energy, not just heat.

Your energy needs

People use energy from food for all kinds of activities. Except for very active athletes and people doing hard, physical labor, over half of the energy people use goes to support basic life functions. This is called *basal metabolism*. See 2-4.

Basal metabolism is the energy your body needs at rest, just to keep all the processes going that keep you alive. Your heart, for example, must have a constant supply of energy to keep beating. Every heartbeat means fresh nutrients and oxygen are being pumped to tissues throughout your body. You may be suprised to learn that your brain needs at least 20 percent of all the energy your body uses at rest. Basal metabolism also includes the energy needed to keep your body at its proper working temperature of about 37°C (98.6°F).

Basal metabolic activities are involuntary uses of energy. That means you have little or no control over them. Your body keeps on working to keep you alive whether you think about it or not. You also need energy for voluntary activities—the things you choose to do. See 2-5. The amount of energy needed for voluntary activities varies a great deal. It takes much more energy, for instance, to rake the yard than to sit and type for the same length of time. Chart 2-6 shows the differences in energy used in various activities.

TUPPERWARE® HOME PARTIES

2-1 Whether you are a child or an adult, your nutrition habits affect how you think, feel and act.

2-2 *Eating nutritious foods in the right amounts will keep your body healthy.*

2-4 *Basal metabolism is the energy a person needs just to maintain life processes. It is measured when a person is at rest.*

2-3 *Food provides the energy your body needs to function properly.*

2-5 *You need energy for everything you do, from quiet activities such as reading and thinking to active exercise such as bicycling.*

What happens if you eat more food in one day than you need to fuel all of your activities? Your body converts those extra, broken-down food particles to fat. Fat is a concentrated source of energy. Thus, it is an efficient way for your body to store extra food energy.

It may help you to think about your energy as if it were money to spend. You have to spend some money for necessities such as food, clothing and shelter. Likewise, you have to spend some energy for necessities (basal metabolism). You usually have some money to spend for extras such as entertainment. Likewise, you usually have some energy to spend for extras such as swimming and jogging. You save money that you don't spend in a savings account. You save energy that you don't spend as fat.

Everyone needs some fat reserves. Everyone (except for people on the verge of dying from starvation) has some fat reserves. These reserves are important because of the body's constant energy needs for basal metabolism. If your car runs out of gas, it will stop. You can fill up the tank later, and it will run again. If your body's energy reserves ever run out, your body will stop. But it will be too late to "fill up the tank."

CARBOHYDRATES FOR FUEL

Carbohydrates are a nutrient group that includes sugars, starches and fiber. Sugars and starches are important sources of energy for your body. In fact, half of the kilojoules (Calories) you eat every day should normally come from sugars and starches. The other kind of carbohydrate important to people is fiber. People can't digest fiber and use it for energy, but it is useful in other ways.

Sugars

Sugars are simple forms of carbohydrates. The most common sugar is *glucose*. Glucose occurs naturally in fruits, vegetables, honey, molasses and corn syrup. It is also formed in the body. Starches and complex sugars are broken down in the body mainly to produce this simple fuel. Proteins and fats can also be broken down and converted into glucose.

Glucose is carried in the bloodstream. It is always available as an energy source for all body cells. Glucose is used in hospitals to feed people who cannot eat normally. It is injected directly into their bloodstreams. This type of feeding is an efficient way to supply the patient with energy because the glucose can be used right away. No digestion is needed.

There are several other sugars. Sucrose ("table sugar") is made of glucose and fructose. Fructose is also found in ripe fruits and vegetables. Lactose is the sugar in milk and milk products.

The most common sources of concentrated sugar are foods which taste very sweet. Examples are candy, syrups, honey, molasses, jams and frostings. Most soft drinks, sweet snacks and desserts contain large amounts of sugar.

In recent years, sugar has developed a bad reputation. Many people blame obesity, tooth decay and many health problems on sugar. Is sugar really "bad" for you?

As with so many things, some is good for you, but a lot is not. The major cause of obesity is *overeating*. You overeat when you consume more kilojoules (Calories) than your body needs. Excess kilojoules (Calories) are stored as fat, whether they come from bread, meat or candy.

One complaint you may hear about most sweet foods is that they supply kilojoules (Calories) but little or nothing else your body needs. Nutritionists talk about the *nutrient density* of foods. Nutrient density refers to the kind and amount of nutrients that you get along with the kilojoules (Calories) in a certain food, 2-7. Milk, fruits and vegetables, for instance, are foods with a high nutrient density. That is, they supply a large amount of nutrients in relation to the number of kilojoules (Calories) they supply.

Gumdrops, however, have a very low nutrient density. They contain sugar but very little else. But this does not mean you have to

ENERGY USED IN VARIOUS ACTIVITIES

ACTIVITY	KILOJOULES PER HOUR	CALORIES PER HOUR
Sedentary—Activities that require little or no arm movement: watching television, reading, writing, sewing, playing cards.	330 — 420	80 — 100
Light—Activities that require some arm movement: preparing food, walking slowly, dusting, doing dishes.	460 — 670	110 — 160
Moderate—Activities that require moderate arm movement: sweeping, walking moderately fast, making beds, light carpentry work.	710 — 1000	170 — 240
Vigorous—Activities that require vigorous movement: bowling, gardening, walking fast, golfing.	1050 — 1470	250 — 350
Strenuous—Activities that require a great deal of movement: running, bicycling, dancing, skiing, swimming.	1470 and more	350 and more

2-6 Various activities require different amounts of energy.

TUPPERWARE® HOME PARTIES

2-7 These are low nutrient density foods. They provide kilojoules (Calories) but very little else.

go through life without gumdrops. If you choose foods carefully, you can fulfill your nutritional needs without getting too many kilojoules (Calories). You can then find a place for "extras" like gumdrops once in a while.

Tooth decay is often blamed on sugar. Certain bacteria in your mouth feed on sugars. These bacteria produce an acid waste which erodes tooth enamel and causes decay. The amount of sugar you eat is not the only factor that affects tooth decay. Other important factors are how often and how long the sugar is in your mouth where bacteria can reach it. Sticky foods and sweet snacks eaten between meals tend to lead to more decay. These foods provide the bacteria with more feeding time. This is why it is especially important to brush your teeth after eating sticky or sweet snacks, as well as after meals.

Starches

Starches are more complex carbohydrates. They consist of many sugar units joined together.

How do starches work in your body? Like sugars, starches supply energy to your body. Starch is broken down into glucose so that your body can use it as energy. If starch is not used as energy, it is stored in the body as fat.

We get starch mainly from grain products and from fruits and vegetables. Foods such as breads, cereals, beans, potatoes and corn are very high in starch, 2-8.

Some people believe that starchy foods are always fattening. This is not true. Most starchy foods are not especially high in kilojoules (Calories), and they supply important vitamins and minerals, 2-9. Some people overeat, and *that* is fattening. If you are trying to lose weight, do not cut all starchy foods from your diet. Instead, limit the amount of starchy foods you eat and watch how these foods are prepared. Consider potatoes, for example. Although they are high in starch, plain potatoes are fairly low in kilojoules (Calories). It's the way potatoes are prepared and served that can make potatoes "fattening." See 2-10. Butter or sour cream can add more kilojoules (Calories) than are in the potato itself.

Fiber

Fiber is another kind of complex carbohydrate. Your body does not have the enzymes needed to digest fiber. However, fiber is important in helping your body get rid of solid wastes.

Fiber has a great ability to absorb and hold water. This softens the solid wastes in your intestinal tract and helps them pass through easily. If your diet doesn't have enough fiber, your intestines have to strain to move the hard wastes. This is a common cause of constipation. Over many years, this kind of strain may produce problems such as diverticulosis (weak spots in the intestinal wall) and hemorrhoids (enlarged veins around the rectum).

What foods contain fiber? Fiber is part of the cell walls of plants, so fresh fruits and vegetables are good sources. *Bran* (the outer layer of grains) and whole grain breads and cereals also provide fiber. Many people eat bran cereals to prevent or cure constipation. Popcorn and nuts are also good sources of fiber.

FACTS ABOUT FAT

Like carbohydrates, *fats* are nutrients that supply energy. In fact, fat provides more than twice the energy as the same amount of sugar or starch. Fats have other jobs, too. Certain kinds of fats are needed to help your body grow normally. Some vitamins (A, D, E, K) are dissolved in food fats.

You need a certain amount of energy stored in your body. Body fat is the most efficient way to store it. As long as you have fat reserves, you will never completely run out of energy.

Fat protects parts of the body that get heavy use, such as the palms of the hands and the soles of the feet. It cushions and protects internal organs such as the heart, liver, and kidneys and helps keep them in place. Layers of fat under your skin help insulate your body. This makes it easier to maintain your

2-8 Breads are a good source
of starch.

PEPPERIDGE FARM, INC.

ENERGY VALUES OF COMMON "STARCHY" FOODS

1 ear fresh corn	295 kJ	70 Cal
125 mL (1/2 cup) canned green peas	350 kJ	83 Cal
1 medium baked potato	380 kJ	90 Cal
1 slice white bread	230 kJ	55 Cal
1 corn muffin	525 kJ	125 Cal
250 mL (1 cup) cooked spaghetti, plain	650 kJ	155 Cal
1 hamburger bun	505 kJ	120 Cal
250 mL (1 cup) plain popcorn	105 kJ	25 Cal

2-9 Most starchy foods are not
especially high in kilojoules
(Calories).

normal body temperature.

Eating would be rather dull without fats in your food. Fats make some foods—such as meat—more juicy and appetizing. Because fats take longer to digest, they keep you from feeling hungry again soon after a meal. Meats, nuts and egg yolks are foods high in fat. Foods prepared with a lot of oil, butter, margarine or cream are also high in fat, 2-11.

Types of fats

You have probably seen the terms "saturated," "unsaturated" and "polyunsaturated" in food advertisements and news stories. These terms are related to the hydrogen contained in the fat molecule. "Saturated" means a fat molecule has all the hydrogen it can hold. If it could hold more, it would be "unsaturated" or "polyunsaturated".

Saturated fats are usually solid at room temperature. Most come from animal sources such as meat, milk, and eggs. Fish and poultry, however, tend to have more unsaturated fats.

The fats in plants are usually *unsaturated* or *polyunsaturated*. Most often, these fats are liquid at room temperature. Vegetable oils—such as corn oil—are high in unsaturated fats. (Coconut oil, a saturated fat, is an exception.)

On the labels of many margarines and shortenings, you may see the words "hydrogenated vegetable oils," 2-12. This means the processor added hydrogen to the oils to make them more solid. The fat therefore becomes more "saturated" with hydrogen.

What about cholesterol?

In recent years, *cholesterol* has often been mentioned as a health hazard in articles about diet and heart disease. What is it? Cholesterol is a complex fat-like substance found in all types of animal tissues. Foods which contain saturated fats, such as eggs and meats, are rich in cholesterol. But the most important source of cholesterol is your own body, which produces large amounts.

Scientists do not yet know exactly how cholesterol works, nor everything it does. They do know that it helps the production of some hormones. Cholesterol is also important to functions of the brain and other parts of the nervous system.

If cholesterol is so useful in the body, how did it get such a bad reputation? A high level of cholesterol has been found in the blood of many people with heart disease. Eating foods with a lot of cholesterol tends to increase the amount of cholesterol in the blood. A person's blood cholesterol level can often be lowered by cutting down on food fats in the diet. The level can sometimes be reduced by shifting the *kinds* of fats eaten to include more unsaturated fats.

Should saturated fats be avoided?

This is not an easy question to answer. There is evidence that eating saturated fats tends to increase the level of blood cholesterol. But the question remains: Is a high cholesterol level a problem, or is it merely a sign of possible trouble? This leaves the real question unanswered: Does lowering blood cholesterol levels protect a person from heart disease?

The fact is that most of your cholesterol is probably produced right in your body. Even if you could completely avoid eating cholesterol, your body would still produce what it needed. Confused? You are not alone. Until research can answer these questions, what should you do?

First of all, keep in mind that cholesterol cannot be avoided entirely. If you tried to avoid eating all foods with cholesterol or saturated fats, you would have to cut out many foods that contain vital nutrients.

Second, remember that all fats, no matter how saturated or unsaturated, contain the same energy value. Being "polyunsaturated" does not mean that the fat is less fattening. Shifting to more unsaturated or polyunsaturated fats does not help you lose weight.

Third, eat a variety of foods. A diet that includes meats, fruits, vegetables, breads and milk products will provide you with a variety of fats—and other nutrients, too.

ENERGY VALUE COMPARISON OF POTATOES
PREPARED IN VARIOUS WAYS
(250 mL [1 cup] COOKED PORTION)

Boiled, plain	100 Cal 425 kJ
Mashed (with milk & butter)	195 Cal 825 kJ
French fries	215 Cal 900 kJ
Hash-browned	355 Cal 1490 kJ

2-10 Plain potatoes are not fattening. Extra kilojoules (Calories) are added by preparing them in various ways.

HAMILTON BEACH, DIVISION OF SCOVILL

2-11 Some foods are high in fat because of the way they are prepared.

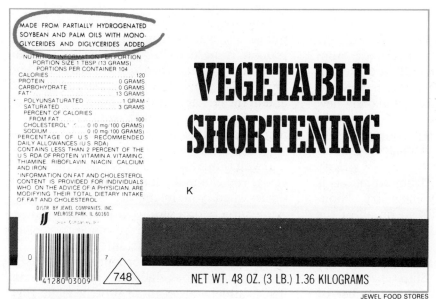

MADE FROM PARTIALLY HYDROGENATED SOYBEAN AND PALM OILS WITH MONO-GLYCERIDES AND DIGLYCERIDES ADDED

NUTRITION INFORMATION PER PORTION
PORTION SIZE 1 TBSP (13 GRAMS)
PORTIONS PER CONTAINER 104
CALORIES 120
PROTEIN .... 0 GRAMS
CARBOHYDRATE .... 0 GRAMS
FAT .... 13 GRAMS
POLYUNSATURATED .... 1 GRAM
SATURATED .... 3 GRAMS
PERCENT OF CALORIES
FROM FAT 100
CHOLESTEROL .... 0 (0 mg/100 GRAMS)
SODIUM .... 0 (0 mg/100 GRAMS)
PERCENTAGE OF U.S. RECOMMENDED
DAILY ALLOWANCES (U.S. RDA)
CONTAINS LESS THAN 2 PERCENT OF THE
U.S. RDA OF PROTEIN VITAMIN A VITAMIN C.
THIAMINE RIBOFLAVIN NIACIN CALCIUM
AND IRON
INFORMATION ON FAT AND CHOLESTEROL
CONTENT IS PROVIDED FOR INDIVIDUALS
WHO, ON THE ADVICE OF A PHYSICIAN, ARE
MODIFYING THEIR TOTAL DIETARY INTAKE
OF FAT AND CHOLESTEROL

DISTR. BY JEWEL COMPANIES, INC.
MELROSE PARK, IL 60160

VEGETABLE SHORTENING

K

NET WT. 48 OZ. (3 LB.) 1.36 KILOGRAMS

JEWEL FOOD STORES

2-12 Hydrogenated vegetable oils are solid at room temperature.

PROTEIN IS ESSENTIAL

The word *protein* comes from the Greek word "proto" which means "first" or "of primary importance." Every cell in your body is built mainly from protein. Most of what people see when they look at you (your skin, hair, etc.) is made of protein. Most of what goes on inside your body depends upon protein too.

Proteins are very large and complex molecules. They are made of smaller units called *amino acids*. About 22 amino acids have been identified in body and food proteins. The proteins we eat are broken down into amino acids during digestion. They can then be rearranged to form new molecules. Some are converted into different amino acids, depending on what your body needs at the moment. It is estimated that your body can make over 100,000 different compounds from amino acids.

Proteins have many uses

What does your body do with the thousands of compounds it makes from amino acids? Some compounds are used to build and maintain cells. No matter how old you are, your body is constantly making new cells for every part of your body. New cells are used for growth, for replacing worn-out cells and for repairing cells damaged by illness or injury.

Other compounds made from amino acids become part of your body chemistry. Thousands of chemical processes go on all of the time to keep you alive and healthy.

Enzymes, for instance, are complex substances that cause chemical changes. Each enzyme does just one thing. Since enzymes are so specialized, you need a huge number of them to handle all of the chemical changes going on in your body.

Your body also makes hormones from amino acids. Hormones are body messengers that set off and control many activities. For instance, a hormone made in your thyroid gland controls how fast you produce energy.

Amino acids are also used to make antibodies. Antibodies are part of your body's defense system against disease and infection.

Your body's buffer system also depends on compounds made from amino acids. This complex system keeps the tissues in your body in chemical balance.

Besides all of these special uses, protein can also be used to produce energy. Protein is used for energy when your diet does not supply enough carbohydrates and fats. After all, there is no reason to make new cells from protein if you don't have enough energy to stay alive. For this reason, your body has a priority system for using protein and other nutrients. The first priority is energy. Next is the maintenance of cells and body functions that are needed to live. Last comes the growth of new cells. Growth is generally possible only when needs for energy and basic maintenance are fulfilled.

Protein needs vary

Your need for protein depends on many things and varies from time to time. Since protein is needed to build new cells, your needs are greatest when you are growing. The most rapid growth occurs in early childhood and in the teenage years. Pregnancy is another time of rapid growth that requires extra protein. If a mother breast-feeds her infant, she will need extra protein to produce milk.

If you think about all of the uses for amino acids, you can make some good guesses about times when you might need extra protein. After surgery or a serious injury, for instance, many new cells have to be made to replace losses and to guard against infection.

Do athletes need more protein? Muscle development does increase protein needs. Thus, athletes need more protein while they are building up their muscles. See 2-13. But extra physical activity, no matter how vigorous, increases only the need for extra kilojoules (Calories).

What happens if you eat more protein than you need? Unfortunately, your body cannot store extra amino acids. Instead, they are converted to fat and stored.

Proteins have a certain "quality"

Your needs for protein are really needs for the amino acids in protein. Of the 22 or so amino acids important to humans, some are more important than others. You need different amounts of the different amino acids.

Some amino acids can be made in your body from other amino acids. Others must be obtained from the foods you eat. These are called *essential amino acids*. There are eight essential amino acids for adults. The quality of proteins in foods is based on how well they supply your needs for essential amino acids.

Complete proteins supply adequate amounts of all essential amino acids. We get complete proteins from meat, poultry, fish, seafood, eggs, milk and cheese.

Incomplete proteins lack one or more essential amino acids. Proteins from plants are generally incomplete. But not all plants lack the same amino acids. Corn, for instance, does not lack the same amino acid that rice does. When you eat combinations of in-complete proteins, you very often get all the essential amino acids. Combining complete and incomplete protein foods, such as cheese and macaroni, will also supply you with all the essential amino acids. See 2-14. Grain products and some vegetables contain some protein. The best plant sources are nuts and legumes. (Legumes are edible seeds that grow in a pod, such as beans and peas.) But remember, the best sources of protein are complete proteins such as meat, poultry, fish, eggs, milk and cheese.

You may hear some people talk about steak as if it were pure protein. It is not. Nearly everything we eat is a combination of nutrients. A good, juicy sirloin steak is about 25 percent protein and about 30 percent fat, measured by weight. (The rest is mainly water.) A plain hamburger is about 25 percent protein and 20 percent fat. The quality of the protein in the steak and hamburger is the same. The steak, of course, costs quite a bit more. Price is no guide to protein quality, 2-15.

TUPPERWARE® HOME PARTIES

2-13 Your body uses protein for growth. Athletes need protein to build muscles.

CEREAL INSTITUTE, INC.

2-14 Incomplete proteins from grain products can be supplemented by foods with complete proteins. Popular combinations include: macaroni and cheese, chicken and noodles, a ham sandwich and cereal with milk.

VITAMINS ARE VITAL

For many people, there is something almost magical about vitamins. They have been called cures or preventions for just about every illness and disease. Hardly a week goes by without some magazine article or television program discussing the need to take some vitamin in very large amounts. Some people believe that if a little of a vitamin is good for you, then a lot is even better. Most of these claims have not been proved true. Some claims have been proved false by research.

What are vitamins? *Vitamins* are chemical compounds that you need in very small amounts for life, growth and good health. Each vitamin has one or more specific functions to keep your body working properly.

Very little was known about vitamins before 1900. Today we know of at least 15 vitamins that are important to people. (Animals make many of their own vitamin supplies.) Vitamins themselves do not supply kilojoules (Calories). But we need them to convert the food we eat into energy.

Your body cannot make vitamins (at least in large enough amounts). Therefore, they must be supplied by food. Almost every food you eat contains some combination of vitamins. If you eat a balanced variety of foods, you will probably meet your daily needs for each vitamin, 2-16.

Sometimes you may get more vitamins than your body needs. Your body has no use for extra vitamins. Some may even cause health problems.

Vitamins A, D, E and K are *fat-soluble*; that is they dissolve in fat. Leftover amounts can be stored in your body fat. Very large doses of vitamin A or D sometimes create real problems. Excess amounts can build up in your body until they actually become poisonous.

Vitamin C and all of the B-vitamins are *water-soluble*. (They dissolve in water.) Extra amounts of these vitamins are not usually stored in your body. You get rid of excesses through your body wastes.

Vitamin A

Vitamin A is used to make new cells and to keep certain body tissues (especially skin) healthy. It is also involved in vision and is essential for seeing in dim light.

A shortage of vitamin A may lead to *night blindness*. People with night blindness do not see well at night or in dimly lit areas. (As you might guess, this makes driving at night hazardous, 2-17.) A lack of vitamin A may cause eyes to be sensitive to bright light and become irritated easily. Rough, dry skin that is easily infected may also be caused by a lack of vitamin A.

Carotene is a yellow pigment found in

2-15 *Price is no guide to protein quality. This steak contains the same amount of protein as a hamburger of the same size.*

NATIONAL LIVE STOCK AND MEAT BOARD

2-16 *You can meet your daily needs for vitamins by eating a balanced variety of foods every day.*

TUPPERWARE® HOME PARTIES

Both normal and vitamin A-deficient
persons see the headlights of an
approaching car.

After the car has passed, the person
with normal vision sees a wide stretch
of road.

THE UPJOHN CO.

The person with night blindness
(caused by a vitamin A deficiency) can
see only a short distance and cannot
see the road sign at all.

*2-17 This is an example of how night
blindness can affect vision.*

many fruits and vegetables. It can be converted to vitamin A in your body. Most deep yellow fruits and vegetables, such as apricots and carrots, are good sources of carotene. Carotene is also found in broccoli and dark green, leafy vegetables such as spinach. (The dark green of the chlorophyll hides the yellow carotene.) Other good sources of vitamin A are liver, egg yolks, butter, and whole milk. Low-fat milk and margarine are often fortified with vitamin A.

Because vitamin A can be stored in the body, too much of it can cause problems. Headaches, nausea and irritability are common signs of too much vitamin A. Very large doses of vitamin A can cause far more serious problems. These problems include hair loss and an enlarged liver and spleen. And in children, retarded growth and symptoms of brain tumors have been observed.

Unless you take vitamin A supplements, you are not likely to have an excess of vitamin A.

Vitamin D

The main job of *vitamin D* is to help the body use calcium and phosphorus. (Calcium and phosphorus are minerals which will be discussed later in this chapter.) Without vitamin D, we could not build bones and teeth, no matter how much calcium we had in our bodies.

Vitamin D is an unusual vitamin. It is found naturally in very few foods. Fish oil (such as cod liver oil) and fish eggs are very good sources. But most people do not eat these foods in large amounts. The vitamin D in our diets is found mainly in canned fish (such as tuna, sardines and herring) and in milk fortified with vitamin D.

Fortunately, we have one other source of this vitamin—sunlight. In fact, vitamin D is often called "the sunshine vitamin." Certain compounds in your skin are changed to vitamin D when they are exposed to sunlight. People living in tropical regions rarely have a shortage of this vitamin.

A shortage of vitamin D is critical during childhood. Severe shortages can stunt a child's growth. Bones become weak. The problem is easy to see in leg bones which tend to "bow" or bend from the weight of the body. (Bowlegs, however, are not always caused by lack of vitamin D.) In severe cases, lack of vitamin D can cause *rickets*, a bone disease. In the United States, fortified milk is so widely available that rickets is a rare disease.

It is possible to get too much vitamin D by taking too many vitamin pills. Vitamin D is a fat-soluble vitamin which can be stored in the body. Too much of it can cause weakness, nausea, weight loss and high blood pressure. Too much vitamin D can also lead to calcium deposits in "soft" tissues, such as blood vessels and kidneys.

Vitamin E

Many claims have been made about *vitamin E*. The claims range from curing skin problems, to slowing aging, to making hair grow. However, research over the last 50 years has failed to prove that people need to take extra vitamin E. In studies where animals have been fed diets lacking vitamin E, the animals have developed many problems. But the kind of problem varies a great deal from one animal to another. In guinea pigs, for instance, a deficiency attacks muscles. In rats, it affects the reproductive system. In calves, it causes heart damage. The variety of problems caused in different animals has made vitamin E difficult to study. We still do not know how a deficiency might affect humans.

No problem of a deficiency of vitamin E seems to exist among humans. Vitamin E is found in so many foods that shortages are not likely.

Some vitamin E can be lost when foods are processed. Even so, a well-balanced diet seems to provide plenty of vitamin E. Leafy green vegetables, whole grain foods, vegetable oils, fruits, eggs and beans are very good sources.

Vitamin E is an *antioxidant*. This means it helps to prevent oxidation—the breakdown of a molecule when it combines with oxygen. Vitamin E thus acts as a preservative in some foods, especially oils. It seems to protect some compounds in your body (such as unsaturated fats and vitamin A) the same way.

Since vitamin E is a fat-soluble vitamin, an excess could be harmful. However, research has not determined the effects of too much vitamin E.

Vitamin K

Vitamin K is needed for normal blood clotting. A shortage causes hemorrhaging, or severe bleeding. To prevent this, vitamin K is often given to patients after surgery or a serious injury.

Vitamin K is found in many foods, especially the leafy green vegetables. Also, certain bacteria in your intestines can make vitamin K. How do shortages occur? Some diseases and conditions can decrease your ability to absorb vitamin K from the foods you eat. Some laxatives, such as mineral oil, can also decrease your ability to absorb vitamin K. In other cases, shortages of vitamin K are caused by drugs which prevent the vitamin from being produced in the intestines. Antibiotics, for instance, may temporarily destroy all kinds of bacteria—good and bad—in your intestines. Without the necessary bacteria, vitamin K cannot be produced.

B-vitamins

At least eight different vitamins belong to the group we call *B-vitamins*. Three B-vitamins—*thiamin, riboflavin* and *niacin*—are part of the standard formula used to *enrich* grain products. (Enriched means that these vitamins and iron have been added in certain amounts set by law.) Other B-vitamins include *pyridoxine (B6), pantothenic acid, biotin, folacin* and *cobalamin (B12).*

All of the B-vitamins have at least one thing in common. In the body, they become parts of enzymes. This means they are needed for *metabolism*. Metabolism is a general term for all of the chemical changes that take place in the body. Food sources of some B-vitamins (thiamin, riboflavin and niacin) are pictured in 2-18. Specific jobs and food sources of the

B-vitamins are detailed in 2-19.

Some of the B-vitamins were discovered as people looked for cures to puzzling diseases. *Beriberi* was a common disease in the Far East in the late 1800's. The word means "I cannot." It reflects the fact that people with beriberi became paralyzed. For a long time, beriberi was blamed on germs. Finally, the trouble was traced to a diet of white rice. Poor people, who ate cheaper, unmilled brown rice, did not get beriberi. There seemed to be something in the brown outer layers of rice that prevented the disease. This "something" came to be known as thiamin.

In the early 1900's, *pellagra* was a leading cause of death in the southern United States. It was often called the disease of the four D's—dermatitis (inflamed skin), dementia (brain disorders), diarrhea and death. This sums up the fact that pellagra affects the skin, the nervous system and the digestive tract.

Around 1915, the U.S. Public Health Service sent Dr. Joseph Goldberger to the South to study pellagra. After months of work, he suspected poor diets caused the disease. He changed the diets of children in a Mississippi orphanage, 2-20. The children had been eating corn bread, salt pork, hominy (a corn product) and molasses. Dr. Goldberger added eggs, milk and meat to their diets. Pellagra

TUPPERWARE® HOME PARTIES

2-18 There are many food sources of thiamin (left), riboflavin (center), and niacin (right).

disappeared. The substance that cured or prevented pellagra was niacin.

Years later, when the amount of niacin in foods could be measured, scientists found another puzzle. They found that milk contained very little niacin. Yet infants, who lived on a milk diet, never got pellagra. Scientists finally discovered that a certain amino acid in milk could be changed to niacin in the body. Certain other vitamins are needed to make this change possible. This is a good example of the complex ways nutrients work together.

THE B-VITAMIN FAMILY

VITAMIN	MAIN FUNCTIONS	GOOD FOOD SOURCES
Thiamine (B₁)	essential for normal digestion; needed for growth, reproduction, and normal functioning of the nervous system	pork, beans, peas, nuts, enriched/whole grain breads and cereals, liver
Riboflavin (B₂)	needed to help body use carbohydrates and proteins	leafy vegetables, enriched/whole grain breads and cereals, liver, cheese, lean meat, milk, eggs
Niacin	needed to keep all body tissues in healthy condition	liver, lean meats, peas, nuts, beans, enriched/whole grain breads and cereals, fish
Pantothenic Acid	needed to support a variety of body functions, including proper growth and maintenance	liver, eggs, white potatoes, sweet potatoes, peas, peanuts
Folacin (Folic Acid)	helps body make red blood cells; essential in converting food into energy	liver, navy beans, dark green leafy vegetables, nuts, oranges, whole wheat products
Pyridoxine (B₆)	helps body use protein; needed for proper growth and to maintain body functions	liver, whole grain cereals, potatoes, red meat, green vegetables, corn
Cyanocobalamin (B₁₂)	needed for the normal development of red blood cells and for the healthy functioning of all cells (particularly in bone marrow, nervous system and intestinal tract)	organ meats, lean meats, fish, milk, shellfish
Biotin	needed to metabolize carbohydrates, fats and proteins	eggs, milk, meat

FOOD AND DRUG ADMINISTRATION

2-19 Each B-vitamin performs certain functions. B-vitamins are found in a wide variety of foods.

B-vitamins are water-soluble. Excess amounts usually become part of your body wastes.

Vitamin C

The most important function of *vitamin C* is to help in the production of *collagen*. You might think of collagen as a kind of glue or cement that binds cells together. A shortage of vitamin C will weaken all types of body tissues such as skin, blood vessels, cartilage and bones. A lack of vitamin C will make you more susceptible to infection. This is because the moist tissues that line your nose and throat are less able to protect you.

Suppose you had been a British sailor 300 years ago. Your chances of dying from *scurvy* would have been greater than your chances of dying from gunfire. Scurvy was a common disease among early explorers and sailors.

Scurvy victims were easy to recognize. Their skin was covered with sores and often looked badly bruised. Their gums became sore and spongy, and their teeth loosened. Their eyes looked as if they were sinking into their heads. Their bones broke easily. Their

joints were swollen and sore. Scurvy led to a very painful death.

In 1747, Dr. James Lind, a British medical officer, set out to find the cause of scurvy. He noticed that officers on ships rarely got the disease. But it was common among sailors. He also noticed that these two groups ate very differently. Sailors were fed cheaply. They ate dried beans, salted meat, cheese or butter that was often rancid, and breads that were often dry or moldy. Officers ate better foods and picked up fresh foods when they stopped in foreign ports.

Dr. Lind set up a famous nutrition experiment, 2-21. He took a dozen sailors with scurvy and divided them into six pairs. Something special was added to the diet of each pair. For instance, vinegar was added to one diet; a garlic mixture was added to another; and so on. At the end of a week, one pair was cured. They had been given citrus fruits. Dr. Lind ordered that lemon juice be

PARKE, DAVIS & COMPANY

2-20 In a study in a Mississippi orphanage, Dr. Joseph Goldberger proved that pellagra could be cured by adding foods with niacin to the children's diets.

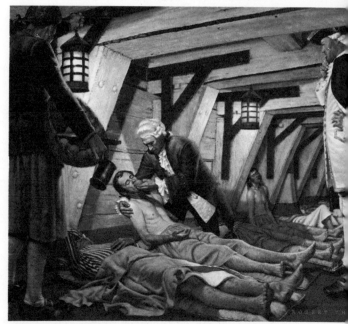

PARKE, DAVIS & COMPANY

2-21 Dr. James Lind discovered that adding citrus fruits to the diets of sailors would prevent and cure scurvy.

added to the sailors' diets. But most people could not believe that the cure to such an awful disease could be so simple. It was almost 50 years before the British navy added lemons to the sailors' diets. Once lemons were added, scurvy was no longer a problem. From this practice, British sailors got the nickname "limeys." (Lemons were often called limes at that time.)

Scurvy is not a disease you are likely to get today. It is the result of a very serious, prolonged lack of vitamin C. But people who have a slight shortage of this vitamin may have some problems. There are many stages between good health and scurvy. Bleeding gums are an early sign of a lack of vitamin C. Bruising easily is also a warning sign.

Because your body cannot store vitamin C, you need a good source every day. All citrus fruits are very good sources of vitamin C. Strawberries, cantaloupe, green peppers, tomatoes, green leafy vegetables and broccoli are good sources too. Vitamin C is easily lost by exposure to heat or air, and by being dissolved in steam or cooking water. To save the vitamin, cook fruits and vegetables as quickly as possible, in a covered pot, with as little water as possible. Cut them up no more than necessary. Pitchers of juice should be tightly covered and stored in the refrigerator. The sooner you use fresh vegetables and fruits, the more nutritious they will be.

Does vitamin C cure or prevent colds? Research does not show that large doses will prevent colds. But some studies do show that some extra vitamin C, taken when you are sick, may make colds and other infections less severe. One theory is that infections may increase your need for vitamin C.

A few studies point out dangers of taking large amounts of vitamin C. Excesses of the vitamin pass through the kidneys. This seems to increase the risk of developing kidney stones. High levels of vitamin C in the urine make it difficult to diagnose diabetes, liver disease and other health problems. Research suggests that large excesses may cause problems in pregnancy. Other possible negative effects are being studied.

Until more is known about the benefits and risks of large amounts of vitamin C, it is best to be cautious. The recommended daily allowances for vitamin C are based on careful, but generous, estimates of what most people need for good health.

MINERALS—SMALL BUT IMPORTANT

Unlike other nutrients, *minerals* are not complex molecules. Instead, they are basic elements. Over two dozen minerals have been found in the human body. Yet minerals make up only about four percent of your body weight.

Calcium and phosphorus account for most of the mineral content in your body. Potassium, sodium, chlorine and magnesium are other minerals you need in fairly large amounts. All of the other minerals are needed in such tiny amounts that they are often called *trace elements.* (Trace elements include iron, iodine, fluorine and many others.) Quantity is not a clue to importance. Deficiencies of any mineral can cause severe problems.

Although minerals are simple elements, their work in the body is complex. Minerals have many very important jobs. Their work always seems to depend on the presence of other nutrients. A shortage of one nutrient, therefore, affects the work of many others.

Scientists are not sure they know all the functions of minerals. Much research still needs to be done. The important thing for you to remember is that, in general, minerals have two main functions.

1. They join with other compounds to become part of your body's structure.
2. They are necessary for many activities that control what is going on in your body.

Calcium and phosphorus

Calcium and *phosphorus* are an example of nutrient teamwork. Almost all of the calcium and phosphorus in your body is found in bones and teeth. The teamwork of calcium and phosphorus makes bones and teeth rigid and strong. Shortages of calcium during the growing years may result in deformed bones or rickets. (Rickets, remember, can also be caused by a lack of vitamin D.)

Although your needs for calcium and phosphorus are greatest when you are growing, you need a steady supply throughout life. Bone cells are not like bricks. Once you have built a brick wall, it is finished. But bone cells wear out and need to be replaced. Many old people have fragile bones. Often this is because they have failed to include enough calcium and phosphorus in their diets through the years.

Bones are surprisingly strong for their weight. In a person weighing 75 kg (165 pounds), the skeleton accounts for only about 15 kg (30 pounds). Half of bone material is minerals—mainly calcium and phosphorus. About one-fourth is collagen, and the rest is mainly water. (Remember that collagen is a kind of protein "glue" that holds tissues together. Collagen depends on vitamin C. This is another instance of the complex ways nutrients depend on each other.) Together, minerals and collagen make a very strong bone structure.

Each year, about one-fifth of the bone calcium is replaced, just in routine maintenance. Repair work (for broken bones, for instance) takes extra calcium. Unfortunately, teeth cannot repair and maintain themselves in the same way.

Calcium is well known as a bone-building material. But it has other special jobs too. While the amount of calcium found in the rest of your body is small, it is very important. Every cell needs a tiny bit to function normally. This small amount is so important that calcium is often borrowed from the bones just to keep things running smoothly.

You need calcium for muscle action—from walking to writing. Your heart, a muscular organ, needs it to keep beating. Calcium helps your blood to clot when you are injured. It is involved in sending directions to nerve fibers. Calcium also plays a role in changing food to energy and in helping cells use vitamins.

Phosphorus helps the body produce energy and helps the body use nutrients. Phosphorus is also an important part of the many compounds found throughout the body.

The best food sources of calcium are milk and milk products, 2-22. It is difficult to meet your needs for calcium without these foods. Other foods with fair amounts of calcium are sardines and other canned fish, broccoli and most green leafy vegetables.

Good food sources of phosphorus are milk and milk products, whole grain breads and cereals, meat, fish, poultry and egg yolk.

Potassium, sodium and chlorine

Potassium, sodium and *chlorine* are another example of nutrient teamwork. These minerals make up your *body salts*. Body salts help to keep the fluid balance just right inside and outside each cell. These minerals help cells absorb nutrients from the blood. They also help the nervous system and muscles function properly.

Shortages of potassium, sodium and chlorine are rare. They usually occur only when you perspire heavily. This could happen during strenuous exercise or when temperatures are very warm.

Potassium, sodium and chlorine are found in most foods. Foods such as meats and bananas contain large amounts of potassium.

2-22 Yogurt is a nutritious snack that is a good source of calcium and phosphorus.

Table salt is an important source of sodium and chlorine.

Many doctors feel that people eat too much sodium. What happens when someone eats too much sodium? Usually it is removed by the body as waste. But, some people cannot get rid of extra sodium easily. Research has shown that there may be a relationship between sodium and high blood pressure. (High blood pressure can lead to strokes and heart attacks.) For this reason, people with high blood pressure are often put on *low-sodium* diets. People on low-sodium diets must limit the amount of salt they eat.

Magnesium

Magnesium keeps your nervous system and muscles working properly. Magnesium also helps your cells use carbohydrates, fats and proteins to produce energy.

Shortages of magnesium in the diet are rare. But alcoholics, drug addicts and others who do not eat enough food may have a shortage of magnesium. They may experience muscle tremors or shaking if they do not get enough of this mineral.

Magnesium is found in foods such as whole grain breads and cereals, nuts, legumes, dark green leafy vegetables and meat.

Iron

About 200 years ago, it was found that human blood contains *iron*. A scientist held a magnet over some dried blood. The magnet attracted part of the dried blood powder. This was *hemoglobin*, the iron-rich portion of red blood cells.

Although iron is found in every cell, about two-thirds of the iron in your body is found in your blood. It is used mainly to make hemoglobin. The iron in hemoglobin attracts oxygen and carries the oxygen throughout your body. A blood test that measures hemoglobin is the most common test for iron deficiency.

Your body tries to keep enough iron on hand. It stores quite a bit of iron in your liver, spleen and bone marrow. As red blood cells wear out, your body recycles most of the iron to make new hemoglobin. However, a little iron is lost every day in body wastes. Any blood loss (such as injury, surgery or menstruation) is also a loss of iron. Thus, women have greater iron needs during the years when they have monthly periods. The need for iron is also high during times of growth—such as infancy and teenage years. It is especially high during pregnancy.

Over time, a shortage of iron may lead to *iron-deficiency anemia.* Iron-deficiency anemia is the most common deficiency disease in the United States. Early symptoms are a tired, run-down feeling and a pale look. Later problems can be much more serious, including shortness of breath, chest pains, irregular heartbeat and an enlarged liver.

Iron is found in many foods, but few are very rich sources. Liver is an excellent source, but most people do not eat it very often. Other good sources are egg yolk, meats, green leafy vegetables and dried beans and peas. Enriched grain products and dried fruits have small, but useful, amounts of iron. Sources of iron are shown in 2-23.

Many women have iron deficiencies. Doctors often advise them to take iron supplements. These iron supplements often contain vitamin C, which helps the body absorb more iron.

Iodine

Iodine becomes part of a hormone produced by your thyroid gland. This hormone controls the rate of energy production in your body. A shortage of iodine results in a shortage of the

TUPPERWARE® HOME PARTIES

2-23 A wide variety of foods contain small, but useful, amounts of iron.

hormone. The thyroid gland then works harder and harder to make up for the shortage. This extra work makes the gland grow larger, making a large lump on the neck. This is called *goiter*.

Seafood and plants grown in soil near the sea are good sources of iodine. Before frozen foods became common, people in the Midwest region of the United States ate little (if any) seafood. Also, the soil that far inland lacked iodine. As a result, goiter used to be a serious problem in that part of the country.

To solve the problem, scientists wanted to add a small amount of iodine to something people ate every day. They finally decided on table salt. Since most people eat salt every day, goiter is now rare. *Iodized salt* may cost an extra penny or two a box. But it is very cheap "insurance" against goiter, 2-24. Iodized salt is now widely available.

Fluorine

Does your town have fluoridated water? Scientists have found that the mineral *fluorine* is very useful in preventing tooth decay. Fluorine seems to help teeth use calcium better. Because the teeth are stronger, they are better able to resist decay. Fluorine may also help make bones stronger.

Small amounts of fluorine are found in eggs, fish and milk. Fluorine is added to many toothpastes. But the best source is fluoridated water.

Some water supplies naturally contain helpful amounts of fluorine, but most do not. In regions where fluorine has been added, tooth decay in children has been reduced by 50 percent or more.

WATER IS A NUTRIENT TOO

Water is essential to your body, 2-25. You may be able to survive without food for weeks. But without water, you would die within a few days.

About two-thirds of your body weight is water. If you weigh 55 kg (120 pounds), you contain almost 40 L (10 gallons) of water. What does your body do with so much water?

Every cell in your body contains some water. The water helps cells keep their shape and size. The fluids inside and outside cells are kept in balance by body salts. This balance of fluid helps nutrients enter cells and helps wastes leave cells.

Water is your body's transportation system. When you eat food, it is broken down by digestive juices (mainly water). Nutrients

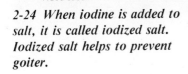

CONTENTS: SALT 98.95%, SODIUM SILICO ALUMINATE 1.0% HYPOSULPHATE OF SODA 0.04% AND 0.01% POTASGIUM IODIDE.

DISTR. BY JEWEL COMPANIES, INC. MELROSE PARK, IL 60160
© Jewel Companies, Inc.

IODIZED SALT

THIS SALT SUPPLIES IODIDE, A NECESSARY NUTRIENT

743

41280 03004

NET WT. 26 OZ. (1 LB. 10 OZ.) 737 GRAMS
JEWEL FOOD STORES

2-24 When iodine is added to salt, it is called iodized salt. Iodized salt helps to prevent goiter.

2-25 Water is an essential part of your diet.

from the food are absorbed into the blood (mainly water). The blood carries nutrients to the parts of the body where they are needed. The blood also picks up wastes from cells and takes the wastes to the lungs and kidneys for removal. The kidneys dump waste through urine (mainly water). And water helps solid wastes pass through your system easily.

Water is a cooling system for your body. Your body works well only within a narrow temperature range. All the chemical changes in your body produce heat. Water can absorb extra heat and carry it to your skin. At the skin, the heat and water are lost as perspiration. Usually, you are not even aware of this slight perspiration. Water also carries extra heat to your lungs for disposal. You have probably noticed that the air you exhale is warm and moist. You can see it on a cold day as your own small cloud.

Besides protecting you from too much heat, water is a kind of shock absorber. It helps protect your cells and tissues from sudden changes or jolts that could cause damage. It also lubricates your joints, helping them move easily with little wear and tear.

About half of the water in your body is replaced every week. That means you lose about 3 L (3 quarts) of water each day. How do you lose so much? Most of it is lost as urine and perspiration. When you perspire a lot, as in hot weather and after vigorous activity, you lose even more water. Large losses of water lead to *dehydration*. You will not completely dry up, but dehydration means your body is dangerously low on water.

If you need to replace so much water daily, how can you do it? No one normally drinks 3L (3 quarts) a day. Well, you get some water from the oxidation of food in your body. (Oxidation produces water and carbon dioxide in addition to heat energy.) You get quite a bit by drinking water, milk, fruit juice or other beverages. Eight or more glasses a day is the general recommendation. The rest of the water comes from foods you eat, 2-26.

THE PERCENTAGE OF WATER IN FOODS

Food	Approximate % water
whole milk	~88%
cheddar cheese	~37%
sirloin steak	~45%
lean ground beef	~60%
chicken	~70%
peanuts	~5%
corn	~85%
lettuce	~95%
baked potato	~75%
tomato	~90%
apple	~85%
banana	~75%
raisins	~18%
watermelon	~92%
white bread	~35%
cooked macaroni	~60%
pizza	~50%

2-26 Most foods contain a surprising amount of water.

THE HUMAN FACTORY

Earlier, we discussed the body as an amazing energy machine. By now, you have learned that making and using energy is only part of what your body does. When you think of all the work that is done in your body, you could compare it to a whole factory.

Your body "factory" needs many raw materials (nutrients in the foods you have eaten). These nutrients can then be used in the body's many production lines. Some nutrients become the materials for building or repairing body parts. Some become part of the conveyor system (the blood), that carries materials to the places where they will be used. Some nutrients become part of the working staff (hormones, enzymes, etc.) that supervise everything that happens in your factory. Nutrients control the on and off switch for many operations in the production line. All of this work needs energy. And energy is produced in this factory from the nutrient "fuel" you eat.

Your body is a very efficient factory. A few raw materials can be processed into others if supplies are low. Some nutrients, such as calcium and iron, are recycled. Energy is stored as fat so that the factory never has an energy shortage. Waste products are removed so they do not interfere with production.

There is really very little you have to do to keep the factory running smoothly. As manager, your main job is to provide all the raw materials that are needed. You can do this by eating nutritious foods.

What happens when a certain raw material is missing? Perhaps some needed part cannot be made. Or perhaps some important job is not finished. In any case, your factory simply does not work as well as it could. The key to good nutrition is to eat a wide variety of foods.

If you fail to eat a balanced diet, *malnutrition* can develop. Malnutrition occurs when the diet lacks the necessary quantity of any of the nutrients in relation to body needs. When there are not enough kilojoules (Calories) from fats and carbohydrates in the diet, protein cannot be used for its special functions. Instead, the protein is used for energy. Many people throughout the world suffer from this type of malnutrition, 2-27.

Malnutrition can result from a lack of any nutrient. Over time, this can seriously affect how you feel—both mentally and physically. The nutrition habits you develop while you are young, are likely to affect you for the rest of your life.

UNITED NATIONS FOOD AND AGRICULTURE ORGANIZATION

2-27 Food programs for children all over the world help to relieve and prevent malnutrition.

ₜₒDefine

amino acid . . .
basal metabolism . . .
beriberi . . . Calorie . . .
carbohydrate . . .
carotene . . . cholesterol . . .
collagen . . . dehydration . . .
essential amino acid . . .
fat . . .
fat-soluble vitamin . . .
fiber . . . glucose . . .
goiter . . .
iron-deficiency anemia . . .
kilojoule . . . malnutrition . . .
metabolism . . . mineral . . .
night blindness . . .
nutrient density . . .
nutrition . . . oxidation . . .
pellagra . . .
polyunsaturated fat . . .
protein . . . rickets . . .
saturated fat . . . scurvy . . .
starch . . . sugar . . .
trace element . . .
unsaturated fat . . .
vitamin . . . water . . .
water-soluble vitamin

ₜₒDiscuss

1. What is the unit used to measure energy?
2. List three examples of involuntary activities. List three voluntary activities. Which activities are included in your basal metabolism?
3. Name the three major types of carbohydrates that are important in nutrition. You should obtain half of the kilojoules (Calories) you eat every day from which two types of carbohydrates? Which carbohydrate can help prevent constipation?
4. List at least three reasons why fat is important in your diet.

5. Which foods contain saturated fats? Unsaturated? Do saturated fats contain more kilojoules (Calories) than unsaturated fats?
6. Name at least four functions of protein. Give two examples of times when a person might need more protein than usual.
7. What is the difference between complete and incomplete protein? Name three or more food sources of each.
8. Why is it dangerous to take large doses of vitamins A or D?
9. Why is vitamin K often given to patients after surgery?
10. What important function do the B-vitamins share?
11. Describe two early signs of vitamin C deficiency. How often do you need a good source of vitamin C? Why?
12. What are the two main functions of minerals?
13. Why do people need to include calcium sources in their diets throughout their lives?
14. How is iron used in the body?
15. Why was goiter once a problem in many inland areas of the United States? What was done to solve the problem?
16. How does water help your body maintain its proper temperature?
17. Why is it important that you get all of the nutrients in your diet?

ₜₒDo

1. Find an advertisement that makes nutrition claims for a product. Look for the product in a store, and copy the nutrition information panel. Write a short report analyzing the ad. Are the nutrition claims reasonable, or are they misleading? Does the ad try to educate consumers in a fair way? Discuss your findings in class.
2. Design a bulletin board or poster on carbohydrates, fats or protein. Include information about the important functions of the nutrient group. Cut out or draw pictures of the main food sources.
3. Prepare a short report on a vitamin or mineral of your choice. Include a list of the best food sources of the nutrient.
4. Invite a nutrition professional, such as a hospital dietitian, public health nutritionist or a college nutrition professor, to your class to answer questions about food and nutrition needs.

Food decisions

How do you make wise food decisions? After reading this chapter, you will know how to use the Basic Four Food Groups to plan your diet and how to use nutrition labeling information to help make food choices. You will be able to explain how to change a regular eating plan for some special diets. You will also be able to judge nutritional claims as either food facts or fallacies.

As you learned in the last chapter, nutrition is a complex science. Even nutrition experts have trouble remembering all the details.

For years, nutritionists have tried to find simple shortcuts to help people plan their diets. The best approach so far has been to group foods according to nutrient values. Putting foods into groups was not easy. No two foods are the same in nutrient values. So, experts looked for important similarities, such as good protein sources or good calcium sources. Finally, they devised the *Basic Four Food Groups.*

THE BASIC FOUR FOOD GROUPS

The "Basic Four" is an easy guide to follow in choosing the foods you eat every day. The Basic Four Food Groups are: milk, meats, fruits and vegetables, and breads and cereals. They are pictured in 3-1.

How do you use the Basic Four? You select the main part of your daily diet from the four food groups. You should eat a certain number of servings from each group. Your daily diet should then include the nutrients you need.

The milk group

The most important nutrient in the milk group is calcium, 3-2. Everyone needs some calcium, but the need varies at different times

3-1 The Basic Four Food Groups are milk, meats, fruits and vegetables, and breads and cereals. They are a guide to good eating.

MILK GROUP

EVAPORATED MILK ASSOC.

Foods:	Milk, cheese, yogurt, ice cream
Chief Nutrients:	Calcium, phosphorus, riboflavin, protein (Some foods in this group are fortified with vitamin D.)
Number of Recommended Servings:	Children under 9 . . . . 2-3 servings Children 9 to 12 . . . . 3 or more servings Teenagers . . . . 4 or more servings Adults . . . . 2 or more servings Pregnant women . . . . 3 or more servings Nursing mothers . . . . 4 or more servings
Typical Servings:	250 mL (1 cup) of whole fluid milk (Part or all of the milk may be fluid lowfat milk, fluid skim milk, buttermilk, evaporated milk or dry milk.) Cheese, ice cream and yogurt may replace part of the milk. The amount of these foods needed to replace a given amount of milk is figured on the basis of calcium content. Common portions of cheese, ice cream and yogurt and their milk equivalents in calcium are given below: 2.5 cm (1 in.) cube cheddar cheese = 125 mL (1/2 cup) milk 125 mL (1/2 cup) cottage cheese = 85 mL (1/3 cup) milk 125 mL (1/2 cup) ice cream = 85 mL (1/3 cup) milk 250 mL (1 cup) yogurt = 250 mL (1 cup) milk

3-2 Choose foods from the milk group to supply your body with calcium.

in life. Teens need more calcium than any other age group. They need at least four servings from the milk group every day.

Drinking milk is the easiest way to meet your needs for calcium. One 250 mL (8 ounce) glass of milk is considered one serving. Any type of milk—whole, lowfat skim or buttermilk—will provide the calcium you need. Other dairy products supply calcium too. But you may have to eat more of these foods to get the same amount of calcium found in a glass of milk, 3-3.

Milk and milk products are fine sources of high-quality protein and other nutrients too. But no other group of foods supplies important amounts of calcium. Meeting your needs for calcium is very difficult without dairy products. Milk can be included in your diet in many ways other than beverages. Dishes made with milk can help you meet your calcium needs. Examples are cream soups, custards, puddings and many frozen desserts.

The meat group

"Sources of protein" may be a better name for this group because it includes more than just meat. Poultry, fish, seafood, eggs, milk, cheese, nuts and legumes are also a part of this group. See 3-4. (Examples of legumes are kidney beans, navy beans, lima beans, black-eyed peas and lentils.)

Other sources of protein are *meat analogues*. These are imitation meats made from vegetable proteins, such as the protein in soybeans. Meat analogues are processed to resemble meats in flavor, texture and appearance.

What do all the foods in this group have in common? They all supply protein, along with important amounts of vitamins and minerals.

You should eat at least two servings from the meat group every day. About 60 to 90 g (2 to 3 ounces) of cooked lean meat, fish or poultry is one serving.

The fruit and vegetable group

We depend on the fruit and vegetable group mainly for vitamins, minerals and fiber. See 3-5. You need at least four servings from the fruit and vegetable group every day. A serving is about 125 mL (1/2 cup) of most fruits and vegetables.

Surveys have shown that many people do not eat enough fruits and vegetables. Moreover, many people are in a rut. They tend to eat the same ones all the time. Variety is important when choosing foods from this group. The kinds and amounts of nutrients vary a great deal from one fruit or vegetable to another.

You need one serving of vitamin C every day. Your body does not store this vitamin. For this reason, it isn't enough to get a lot one day and none for the next several days. Citrus fruits are good sources of vitamin C. But many other foods are fine sources too, 3-6.

Many people do not get enough vitamin A in their diets. You need a good source of this vitamin at least every other day, 3-7. Dark green leafy vegetables and orange or dark yellow fruits and vegetables are good sources of vitamin A. Generally, darker colors are a sign of higher vitamin A value.

CALCIUM EQUIVALENTS

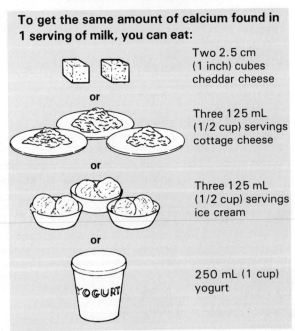

To get the same amount of calcium found in 1 serving of milk, you can eat:

Two 2.5 cm (1 inch) cubes cheddar cheese

or

Three 125 mL (1/2 cup) servings cottage cheese

or

Three 125 mL (1/2 cup) servings ice cream

or

250 mL (1 cup) yogurt

3-3 Different milk products contain different amounts of calcium.

MEAT GROUP

EVAPORATED MILK ASSOC.

Foods:	Beef, veal, pork, lamb, poultry, fish, seafood eggs, milk, cheese, nuts, legumes, meat analogues
Chief Nutrients:	Protein, thiamin, niacin, riboflavin, iron
Number of Recommended Servings:	2 or more servings every day
Typical Servings:	60 to 90 g (2 to 3 ounces) lean cooked meat, poultry or fish 2 eggs 250 mL (1 cup) cooked dried beans, dried peas or lentils 60 mL (4 tablespoons) peanut butter

3-4 Choose foods from the meat group to supply your body with protein.

FRUIT AND VEGETABLE GROUP

EVAPORATED MILK ASSOC.

Foods:	All fruits and vegetables
	Vitamin A sources: Dark green and deep yellow vegetables and fruits, such as carrots, spinach, apricots and cantaloupe.
	Vitamin C sources: Citrus fruits, such as oranges, grapefruit and lemons. Other fruits and vegetables, such as strawberries, watermelon, broccoli, Brussels sprouts, and cabbage.
Chief Nutrients:	Vitamin A, vitamin C, other vitamins, minerals (Fiber is also supplied by this group.)
Number of Recommended Servings:	4 or more servings every day, including: 1 serving of a good source of vitamin A at least every other day 1 serving of a good source of vitamin C every day
Typical Servings:	125 mL (1/2 cup) fruit or vegetable Ordinary portions, such as 1 medium apple, banana, potato or orange

3-5 Choose foods from the fruit and vegetable group to supply your body with vitamins, minerals and fiber.

SOURCES OF VITAMIN C

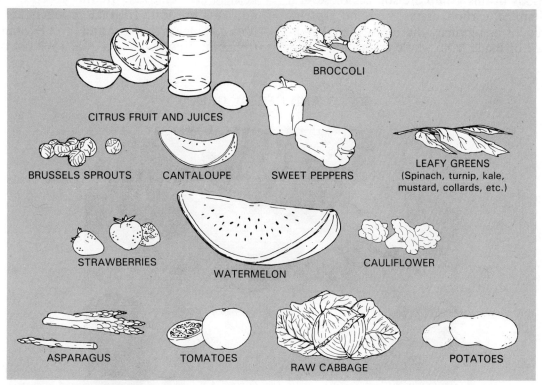

3-6 You need a good source of vitamin C every day.

SOURCES OF VITAMIN A

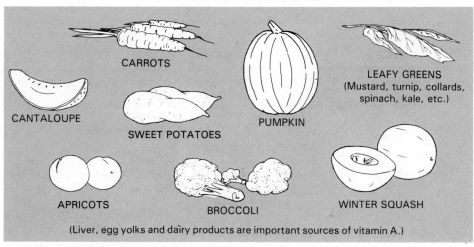

3-7 You need a good source of vitamin A every other day.

The bread and cereal group

Foods in this group are sources of several B-vitamins, carbohydrates, iron and protein. To count as servings, the foods must be enriched or made from whole grain, 3-8.

When grains are refined, parts of the kernels are removed. In the process, some nutrients are lost. If grain products are *enriched*, it means that iron and three B-vitamins (thiamin, riboflavin and niacin) have been

BREAD AND CEREAL GROUP

EVAPORATED MILK ASSOC.

Foods:	All whole grain or enriched breads and cereals.
Chief Nutrients:	Several B-vitamins, carbohydrates, iron, protein.
Number of Recommended Servings:	4 or more servings daily
Typical Servings:	1 slice bread 30 g (1 ounce) ready-to-eat cereal 125 mL (1/2 cup) cooked cereal, rice or pasta 1 muffin, biscuit or small roll 1 waffle 5 plain crackers 2 graham crackers 250 mL (1 cup) popcorn

3-8 Choose foods from the bread and cereal group to supply your body with B-vitamins, carbohydrates, iron and protein.

added. Look for this term on the labels of refined grain products.

Whole grain products contain the entire grain kernel. The nutrient values therefore remain intact. These products are also a good source of fiber.

Plain breads and cereals aren't the only foods in this group. All foods made from enriched or whole grain flour, such as pancakes, muffins or pasta, are a part of the bread and cereal group. You need at least four servings from this group every day.

What about other foods?

You may have noticed that several foods do not fit into any of the Basic Four Food Groups. Where, for instance, would you put salad oil? Candy? Soft drinks? Some nutritionists have suggested adding a fifth food group. This group would include a variety of foods with one thing in common. They supply food energy (kilojoules or Calories) and very little else, 3-9. Most people need to watch the amounts of these foods they eat to avoid unwanted weight.

There is no recommended number of servings for this "extra" group. Foods from this group are not essential to good health. But few people could give them up entirely. The important thing is to base your daily diet on the Basic Four Food Groups. Then add a few "extra" foods if the additional kilojoules (Calories) won't cause you to gain unwanted weight.

How to use the Basic Four

Almost everyone can use the Basic Four to plan meals and snacks. It is easy to remember and is fairly reliable if you use it properly. The Basic Four can be adapted to include the traditional foods of many ethnic groups, 3-10.

3-9 These foods have one thing in common. They supply food energy and very little else.

Remember two important guidelines when you use the Basic Four. First, do not try to do all your eating in one meal. Spread it over several meals. After all, your body uses nutrients continually—not all at once. Try to eat foods from various food groups at each meal.

Second, choose a different combination of foods every day. No two foods have the same nutrient values. If you choose the same foods day after day, you may be missing nutrients that you need.

Snacks can help you meet your nutrient needs, 3-11. If you are missing a good source of vitamin A, for instance, you might snack on carrot sticks, apricots or cantaloupe. If you are short on calcium, try a milk beverage, such as cocoa or a homemade milk shake, 3-12. Ice cream, yogurt, pudding and cheese also provide calcium. Getting enough iron is a problem for many people, especially women. Snacks with useful amounts of iron include nuts, tomato juice, apple juice, dates and raisins.

TRADITIONAL FOODS OF ETHNIC GROUPS					
	Milk (and milk products)	Meat (and meat substitutes)	Fruits and Vegetables	Breads and Cereal	Extras (fats, sweets, etc.)
Mexican	Milk (small amounts)	Beef Chicken Pork Fish Dried beans	Chili peppers Bananas Onions Tomatoes Citrus fruits	Cornmeal (tortilla) Wheat Noodles	Sugar Coffee
Italian	Cheese Milk	Beef Lamb Salami, sausage, etc. Fish Eggs Legumes	Broccoli Dandelion greens Green peppers Escarole Spinach Tomatoes Eggplant Zucchini Fruits in season	White bread Pasta Cornmeal	Olive oil Garlic
Chinese	Milk (small amounts)	Eggs Fish Meat Poultry	Native vegetables Bamboo shoots Soybeans (main source of calcium) Legumes	Rice Wheat	Sesame oil Lard
Middle Eastern	Fermented milk Yogurt Sour cream	Lamb Chicken Eggs Fish Legumes	Cucumbers Eggplant Leeks Okra Apricots Figs Melons	Cracked wheat and white bread	Ripe olives Lamb fat Seed oils Grape leaves Honey Herbs and spices Thick, sweet coffee

FORECAST FOR HOME ECONOMICS BY SCHOLASTIC MAGAZINES, INC.

3-10 Traditional foods of ethnic groups can be grouped into the Basic Four.

UNITED FRESH FRUIT AND VEGETABLE ASSOC.

3-11 Fruits and cheese can be nutritious snacks.

SWISS MISS HOT COCOA MIX

3-12 Snacks of dairy foods are delicious ways of helping you meet your calcium needs.

NUTRITION LABELING — A USEFUL TOOL

Nutrition information appears on the labels or packaging of many foods. It is a simple list of nutrient values found in a serving of a certain food. The format is set by law to make it easy for consumers to use.

Look at the sample label in 3-13. The serving size is listed first. You will also find out how many servings of that size are contained in the package.

Next, you will see the number of Calories supplied by one serving. After that, the protein, carbohydrate and fat contents are listed in grams. This helps you understand the basic composition of the food. Sometimes extra information is given to help people on special diets. You may see, for instance, how much of the fat is saturated and how much is polyunsaturated. The amount of sodium is sometimes listed to help people who have to limit the amount of salt they eat.

The next set of numbers lists the nutrient values for protein, five vitamins and two minerals. The nutrient values are given as percentages of the U.S. RDA's (United States Recommended Daily Allowances). The U.S. RDA's will be described later in this chapter.

Why are percentages used, rather than actual amounts? Suppose you were interested in knowing how much vitamin C you were getting in a glass of tomato juice. If you looked it up, you would find that 250 mL (1 cup) of tomato juice supplies about 40 mg of vitamin C. Is that a lot or a little? The information would not mean much to you unless you knew how much vitamin C you need each day. But suppose you read that 250 mL (1 cup) of tomato juice supplies about 85 percent of your daily need for vitamin C. You would know right a way that you were getting quite a bit of vitamin C.

Recommended dietary allowances

Who decides how much you need of each nutrient? A group of nutrition experts on the Food and Nutrition Board of the National Academy of Sciences make these decisions. These experts keep up with the most recent scientific research. About every five years, they publish a table called the *Recommended Dietary Allowances,* often called the RDA's. See the appendix in the back of this book.

As you will learn, the RDA table is fairly detailed. Because many nutrient needs vary with age, the table is broken down into age groups. From late childhood on, it also considers sex. This is because males tend to be larger and to have greater nutrient needs. Pregnancy and breast-feeding increase women's needs for most nutrients. Therefore, these two special situations are included.

People do not have identical needs for each nutrient. After all, each of us is unique. The RDA's are set high enough to meet the highest normal needs of almost all healthy people in the United States.

The U.S. RDA's *(United States Recommended Daily Allowances)* are based on the RDA table. They are set by the Food and Drug Administration. The U.S. RDA's are used to figure the information on nutrition

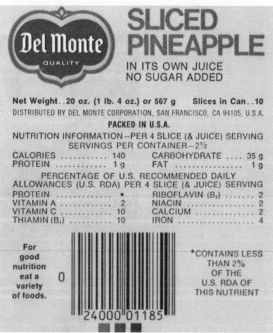

3-13 *You can learn a lot about the nutritional value of the foods you eat by reading labels.*

labels of foods. In most cases, the U.S. RDA for a nutrient is based on that nutrient's highest RDA for anyone. For instance, the highest RDA for iron is 18 mg. Therefore, the U.S. RDA for iron is 18 mg.

The table of U.S. RDA's generally used for nutrition labeling is shown in the appendix in the back of this book. (Keep in mind that these are not based on average needs. They are based on careful estimates of highest normal needs.)

How to use nutrition labels

Nutrition labels can help you learn more about the foods you eat. They can help you make wise decisions about buying and using food.

If you are watching your weight, for instance, you will be especially interested in Calories. Nutrition labels also tell you what nutrients you are getting with those Calories. Look at the labels in 3-14 (skim milk, cola and orange juice). You are getting a lot more than just Calories in some foods. Some foods contain more nutrients than others.

Compare food labels for a certain nutrient. For instance, suppose you were looking for a good source of vitamin A for tomorrow's dinner. You could compare the information on labels of different vegetables. You could choose a vegetable that would fill your need for vitamin A.

Compare the labels on different brands of the same food. Is a more expensive brand of canned corn any better for you than a cheaper brand? Probably not. Read the label on an expensive can of pineapple in the diet section. Does it have fewer kilojoules (Calories) than a can of ordinary pineapple packed in water? How does a "natural" cereal compare with presweetened corn flakes? What is the difference between apple drink and apple juice? These are questions that nutrition labels can help you answer.

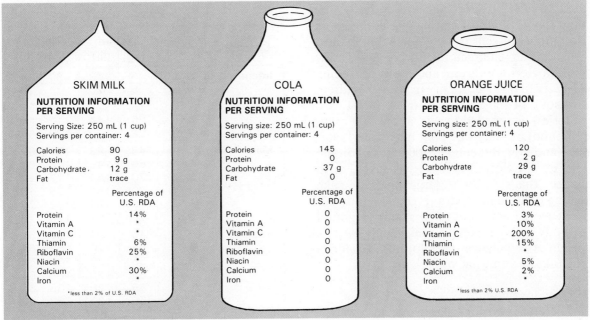

3-14 Read the label to find out how many nutrients and Calories are in foods.

THE UPS AND DOWNS OF
WEIGHT CONTROL

Most people are unhappy with their weight at one time or another. What makes some people fat and others thin? What is the best way to control your weight?

Your "ideal" weight

Height-weight tables can give you a general idea of how much you should weigh, based on your height. See 3-15. But your ideal weight is also related to your general body build. Some people have a small body frame. Others have a large body frame. Some people have a tendency to be lean. Others have a tendency to be heavy. Therefore, the "ideal" weights of two persons may vary, even if they are the same height.

Some obesity problems begin in infancy. (Obesity is a condition in which a person weighs at least 20 percent more than his or her ideal weight.) People used to think that fatness was a sign of good health in babies. Now we believe that fat babies are more likely to become fat adults. The reason is that they tend to develop more fat storage cells than they should. Fatness can be caused by an extra number of cells or by a normal number of cells that are enlarged by storing fat. Today, most doctors are careful about infant feeding. They try to prevent obesity in young children.

About 14 700 extra kilojoules (3500 extra Calories) are needed to add about 500 grams (1 pound) of body fat. That may sound like a lot — and it is. But eating 2100 extra kilojoules (500 extra Calories) every day is easy. For instance, that's just one large piece of cake. Eating that much extra every day for one week would add about 500 grams (1 pound) of body fat. The key to maintaining a good weight is to balance the kilojoules (Calories) you take in with what you use up.

How to lose weight

There are two logical ways to lose weight. One is to take in fewer kilojoules (Calories). This means eating fewer high-kilojoule (high-Calorie) foods such as sweets and fried foods. The other is to use up more kilojoules (Calories). This means getting more exercise such as walking and swimming. The best way is to do both.

Americans spend millions of dollars a year on books, pills, special foods and gadgets to help them lose weight. Many do lose some weight, but most gain it right back. Why is it so difficult to lose weight and keep it off? Which diet aids will really help you to lose weight and keep it off?

Diet pills, gadgets and gimmicks. Over the years, many kinds of diet pills have promised to make losing weight easy. Recently, *amphetamines* ("uppers") have been popular. These create health problems for many people, and they are addictive. Other diet aids promise to work by dulling the appetite. Typically, they include two main ingredients. One makes the mouth feel somewhat numb. The other is supposed to make the stomach feel full. These products have not proved to be very effective.

HEIGHT-WEIGHT TABLE

Category	Age	Weight (kg)	(lb)	Height (cm)	(in)
Infants	0.0-0.5	6	13	60	24
	0.5-1.0	9	20	71	28
Children	1-3	13	29	90	35
	4-6	20	44	112	44
	7-10	28	62	132	52
Males	11-14	45	99	157	62
	15-18	66	145	176	69
	19-22	70	154	177	70
	23-50	70	154	178	70
	51-75	70	154	178	70
	76 +	70	154	178	70
Females	11-14	46	101	157	62
	15-18	55	120	163	64
	19-22	55	120	163	64
	23-50	55	120	163	64
	51-75	55	120	163	64
	76 +	55	120	163	64

3-15 This table can tell you about how much you should weigh.

Some people claim that *diuretics* ("water pills") make them lose weight. Diuretics are substances that increase urine production. These pills can make people weigh less. But the loss is water, not fat, and it doesn't last. Diuretics can be dangerous. They should only be taken under a doctor's guidance.

You may have noticed magazine ads for reducing gadgets. They promise to take off kilograms (pounds) or centimetres (inches) magically. The truth is that there is no magic in losing weight. By law, advertising cannot be false. These ads are written carefully to avoid trouble. You will probably notice in the fine print that a special diet comes with the gadget. The diet is usually very low in kilojoules (Calories). This is the real "secret" to the reducing gadget. You can help the FTC (Federal Trade Commission) check fraudulent ads. Write and tell the FTC about claims and gimmicks which you feel are deceptive or misleading.

Diet foods. Most supermarkets contain a section of "diet foods." Some of these products are for people with specific diet problems, such as food allergies, diabetes or the need to avoid salt. Most items, however, are for people trying to lose weight. They offer kilojoule (Calorie) savings, but they often cost more than regular foods. Nutrition labels can help you compare "diet" foods, and "regular" foods. Look for products that offer you a worthwhile reduction in kilojoules (Calories) at little, if any, extra expense.

Diet books and articles. There is no shortage of diet books, 3-16. Many magazines regularly publish new diets. With so many people concerned about their weight, these diets boost magazine sales. Rarely are these diets really new or amazing. The best diets are well-balanced. They focus on limiting kilojoules (Calories) by eating less and avoiding certain foods, such as rich desserts. These diets work. Balanced, low-kilojoule (low-Calorie) diets have been around for decades.

On the other hand, *fad diets* come and go quickly. Fad diets look exciting. They tend to have something unusual about them to attract attention. Often they claim to be based on

some "secret" that has just come to light. Years ago, a diet based mainly on grapefruit and eggs was popular. The grapefruit supposedly contained something to make the body use up kilojoules (Calories) much faster. It did not, of course. It was a boring diet to follow, as most fad diets are. It worked for some people because it was low in kilojoules (Calories), not because of something special in the grapefruit.

Every several years, *fasting* becomes popular as a way of losing weight. You might call it a "no diet" diet, because no food is allowed. The real name for it is "starvation." What happens when you don't give your body any food? To conserve energy, the body shifts gears downward. Even the heart slows down. The fasting person loses not only fat, but also protein from body tissues and organs as the

TUPPERWARE® HOME PARTIES

3-16 Millions of dollars are spent on diet books every year. The buyers are looking for the secret of losing weight quickly and easily.

body looks for sources of energy. Large amounts of water are lost, which accounts for much of the early weight loss. When the water is lost, some important minerals, such as sodium and potassium, are lost too. Fasting causes great stress to the body. It is sometimes used for extremely obese people who stay in a hospital and are watched carefully during their fasts. For most people, it is a very poor way to lose weight.

There are many kinds of "high protein" diets. Some are low in carbohydrates; some are high. Most are rather high in fat. (Most animal sources of protein contain quite a bit of fat.) These diets should be used cautiously under a doctor's guidance. People tend to lose several kilograms (pounds) quickly at first. This is because digesting the extra protein causes the body to lose quite a bit of water. Thus, most of the early weight loss is water, not fat. These diets are usually not well-balanced. The stresses they cause the body can create serious health problems. This is especially true for people who tend to have kidney trouble or diabetes.

How can you tell if a diet plan is a good one? Ask yourself these questions:

- Does the diet include a variety of foods from all of the Basic Four Food Groups?
- Losing weight takes time, just as gaining weight does. You will not get tired of the diet as quickly if it includes many different foods. Besides, you run less risk of missing important nutrients. If the diet provides less than 4200 kJ (1000 Calories) a day, you should be under a doctor's guidance.
- Does the author claim magical results? No diet works like magic. And it is very unlikely that some "secret" has just been discovered. There are no tricks to dieting.
- What is the author's background? Is the person known and respected by nutrition experts? (Having a medical degree is not enough.) What proof does the author have that the diet works? Often the only proof is personal experience or observation. Any kind of new diet should be supported by careful research that involved many people and scientific controls. Beware of plans which promote a diet product. This may be a profitable plan for the author, but it may not be for you.

- What is the real "key" to the weight loss? Remember, kilojoules (Calories) are what count. You lose fat only by decreasing kilojoules (Calories) and/or increasing activity.

Diet clubs and groups. Some dieters find joining a diet club helpful. Some of these are businesses run for profit. You pay to attend meetings. Others are nonprofit groups. The cost of joining these groups is usually small. At group meetings you learn about dieting and nutrition. Longtime members share their diet tips and provide encouragement. If you need to lose weight, joining such a group may be a good idea.

Behavior modification. Behavior modification is a popular approach to losing weight. It means changing eating behavior. Usually, poor eating habits caused the weight gain. The person must change those habits to lose weight and keep it off. Dozens of books suggest ways to change eating habits.

Here are some behavior modification tips that you may find helpful:

- Identify your eating habits. For one week, make a list of everything you eat and when you eat it. How many times a day do you nibble or sip? Why do you eat? Are you bored? Nervous? Unhappy? You may be surprised to find that hunger is not always what drives you to eat. Figure out what habits or emotions are causing you to eat.
- Try to limit your eating to certain times of the day. Do not skip regular meals. (Research has never shown that skipping meals helps you lose weight.) Try to control your urge to eat until a scheduled eating time. This helps you avoid impulsive eating.
- Eat slowly. Take small bites and chew your food slowly. You will probably find the meal just as satisfying as one you gulped down, but with less food. Research shows that overweight people tend to be fast eaters.
- Serve yourself smaller portions than you would usually eat. Some people find that a smaller dish (such as a salad plate) helps

them feel as if they are getting more food. See 3-17.

- Remove temptations. If you have a weakness for candy and cookies, do not keep them in your home. Instead, keep low-kilojoule (low-Calorie) snacks handy and ready to eat. You are more likely to nibble on celery and carrot sticks if they are already washed and cut up, 3-18.
- Plan small rewards for yourself. After you've lost 1 kilogram (about 2 pounds), reward yourself. You might go to a movie or buy a new album. Do not reward yourself with food.
- Do things that use up kilojoules (Calories). Instead of sitting around talking to a friend, walk while you talk. Try to plan some kind of activity for mid-afternoons or after school. Many people find it hard to stay away from the kitchen at this time of day. What sports do you enjoy? Swimming? Tennis? Bicycling? Sports activities not only help you lose weight, they also help to shape, firm and tone your muscles.
- Do not cut out your favorite foods — just cut down on the amount you eat. If apple pie is your favorite dessert, dieting doesn't mean you can't touch it. Just eat a very small piece, and eat it slowly. Think about enjoying each bite. You may find you will enjoy it just as much as gulping down a large piece. Perhaps you will enjoy it even more, knowing that you have avoided a lot of kilojoules (Calories).

How to gain weight

People who have to fight fat tend to envy those who are *underweight*. But being underweight can be a very serious problem. It can lead to nervousness, lack of energy, lowered resistance to disease and other health problems. After all, underweight is a sign that the body is not getting all the nutrients it needs.

If being underweight is a problem for you, first see a doctor. A thorough checkup can tell you if the problem is caused by something other than your eating habits. Very often, however, eating habits are the cause. Under-

weight people often lack interest in eating. They sometimes have strong preferences for low-kilojoule (low-Calorie) foods over high-kilojoule (high-Calorie) foods.

In general, a person can gain weight by doing just the opposite of what people trying to

THE AMERICAN EGG BOARD

3-17 A smaller plate sometimes helps a dieter feel more satisfied with small portions of food.

'LEA & PERRINS, INC.

3-18 Keep low-kilojoule (low-Calorie) foods on hand and ready to nibble.

lose weight do. Eat more often (but not so much that you dull your appetite for the next meal). Give yourself larger servings. Look for high-kilojoule (high-Calorie) foods. Do not avoid exercise. Exercise can increase your appetite and help you tone up your muscles.

Exercise

Exercise does more than help you control your weight. It helps you feel good, healthy and full of energy, 3-19. Research shows that regular exercise makes you more alert. This is because it improves the supply of blood going to the brain. It also improves your strength and stamina. (Stamina means endurance or staying power.) Even though vigorous exercise can be tiring, it reduces a constant feeling of being worn out.

What is the best exercise? The best exercise for you is something that you enjoy and can do regularly. It should be an activity that exercises your heart and lungs. Cross-country skiing, jogging, running and swimming are among the most vigorous.

SPECIAL DIET CONSIDERATIONS

During a lifetime, nutritional needs vary a great deal. Infants and young children are busy growing. Their needs for nutrients are great, considering their small size. The teen years are also a time of rapid growth. A teen's needs for many key nutrients are higher than they will be later in life.

As people reach middle age, most tend to be less active. Yet they often keep eating the same amount of food. The result is "middle-aged spread." Extra weight gain during this stage of life may sometimes lead to poor health. It can aggravate many of the problems that often occur in later years, such as heart trouble and high blood pressure. Middle-aged people need to adjust their eating and exercise habits to avoid becoming overweight.

As people grow older, they generally become even less active. Their metabolism slows down. Thus, elderly people usually need even less food energy. See 3-20. On the other

hand, their needs for protein, vitamins and minerals decrease little, if any, with age. This calls for careful food planning. Poor nutrition in this stage of life makes many of the problems associated with old age even worse.

Elderly people often lose interest in eating. Poor teeth or dentures can make chewing difficult. Food may not taste as good as it once did. Loneliness and low incomes are common problems that affect eating. Many communities have set up food programs for their elderly citizens. In some cases, the people are picked up and taken to a central place for one or more meals a day. This kind of program recognizes the importance of mealtime as a social occasion.

Diets for athletes

Athletes, like other people, need a well-balanced diet. They need a variety of foods from all of the Basic Four Food Groups.

Physical activity requires energy, 3-21. More strenuous activities require greater amounts of energy. A swimmer, for instance, uses more energy than a bowler. People who are active in sports or who exercise a lot need more food energy.

Should athletes take extra vitamins? So far,

TUPPERWARE® HOME PARTIES

3-19 Exercise is fun with friends. Regular exercise can make you feel more energetic.

reliable studies have not found that taking vitamin pills improves athletic performance. (This assumes that the person eats a good diet and is in good health.) But very active people do need to eat more food. They also need more of the nutrients the body uses to process that food into energy (such as B-vitamins).

Athletes should have a well-balanced diet that includes a variety of foods. This will fulfill their increased nutrient needs.

Strenuous activity causes the body to lose a great deal of water and some salt in perspiration. Athletes, therefore, need to drink more liquids. In very hot weather, they may also need more salt. But usually the normal amount added to food is enough.

Diets for pregnancy

You may have heard people say that a pregnant woman is "eating for two." In some ways, this is true. During pregnancy, the woman needs nutrients for herself and for her developing baby. But some people think pregnant women need a lot more kilojoules (Calories). This is not true.

The average woman in her early twenties uses about 8800 kJ (2100 Calories) a day. During pregnancy, she needs only about 1250 extra kilojoules (300 extra Calories) a day. That's only 15 percent more food energy. But she needs about 65 percent more protein and quite a bit more of most vitamins and

3-21 Athletes need more food to meet their increased energy needs.

RECOMMENDED KILOJOULE (CALORIE) ALLOWANCE AT VARIOUS AGES

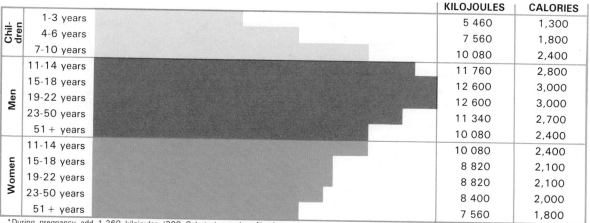

		KILOJOULES	CALORIES
Children	1-3 years	5 460	1,300
	4-6 years	7 560	1,800
	7-10 years	10 080	2,400
Men	11-14 years	11 760	2,800
	15-18 years	12 600	3,000
	19-22 years	12 600	3,000
	23-50 years	11 340	2,700
	51 + years	10 080	2,400
Women	11-14 years	10 080	2,400
	15-18 years	8 820	2,100
	19-22 years	8 820	2,100
	23-50 years	8 400	2,000
	51 + years	7 560	1,800

*During pregnancy add 1 260 kilojoules (300 Calories) per day. Nursing mothers should add 2 100 kilojoules (500 Calories) per day.

3-20 As you get older, your need for kilojoules (Calories) will decrease. But your need for nutrients will stay about the same.

minerals. The woman must make careful food choices to get all the nutrients she needs without too many kilojoules (Calories).

Preparing for a healthy pregnancy begins long before a woman becomes pregnant. It begins with her eating habits as a young girl. As she grows up, she needs a good supply of all the nutrients. Otherwise, her body may not be ready to handle the extra demands of pregnancy. The development of a healthy baby depends upon a well nourished mother.

Doctors are alarmed about the growing number of teenage mothers. Risks are much greater for them. It's hard for them to meet their own extra nutritional needs and those of a developing baby, too. If the mother is undernourished (as many teenage girls are), both mother and baby may be in for trouble. Malnutrition before birth and in infancy may mean the child will not reach his or her full potential. The child's mental or physical development may be affected.

Convalescence diets

People who are recovering from surgery or serious illness often need special diets. In a hospital, dietitians work with doctors to plan diets that meet each patient's needs. Sometimes these diets need to be continued at home.

You should not follow these special diets unless your doctor tells you to do so. They do not have the variety of a normal food plan. They also lack fiber, which helps your body eliminate wastes. The one exception is when you have a cold or mild flu. Since the flu often strikes without warning, it is wise to keep a few supplies on hand. Such supplies include broth, gelatin mixes, fruit juices, ginger ale and colas.

A *clear liquid diet* is prescribed for only a short time. It is low in protein, vitamins, minerals, fiber and kilojoules (Calories). The purpose of a clear liquid diet is to avoid irritating the digestive system. The diet creates no solid waste or gas. "Clear liquids" include water, coffee, tea, fat-free broth, soft drinks, fruit drinks and gelatin. A clear liquid diet is often prescribed right after surgery. This diet is also used when people have very serious illnesses or infection.

A *full liquid diet* is often a transition from clear liquids to a soft diet. It is based on foods which are liquid at body temperature. The diet includes all clear liquids. It also includes all forms of milk, strained soups, juices, soft custards and mushy cooked cereals. With very careful planning, liquid diets can be nutritionally adequate.

A *soft diet* consists of easy-to-digest foods with no fiber. It is used as a transition between liquid diets and regular diets. It's also good for people with chewing or digestive problems. Soft diets include all the foods allowed in a full liquid diet. They also include vegetables that have been cooked tender or pureed, and cooked fruits (without skins or seeds). Soft diets also include ground or minced meat, fish and poultry, mild cheeses, eggs, puddings and plain cake. Fried foods, rich or heavy foods, very spicy dishes, and raw fruits and vegetables are usually avoided.

Medically prescribed diets

People with health problems such as diabetes, ulcers, high blood pressure and heart trouble often have special diets. Their doctors prescribe these diets to help control the problems. Special diets vary in the kinds and amounts of foods recommended. Because they restrict food choices, they should only be used under a doctor's guidance.

Vegetarian diets

A *vegetarian diet* is based on foods which come from plants. There are many different kinds of vegetarian diets. Typically, they include vegetables, fruits, breads, cereals, nuts and some seeds. Some vegetarians also eat eggs and dairy products. A few eat fish. They all avoid meat and poultry.

People choose to be vegetarians for many reasons. Some religious groups, such as Seventh-Day Adventists, forbid eating meat. Some people do not believe animals should be killed for food. Some think a vegetarian diet helps them become more "pure" in mind and spirit. Still others believe eating foods from animal sources is unhealthy.

Are vegetarian diets safe? Some are, but many are not. Vegetarian diets that are planned with care can be nutritionally sound. Vegetarian diets should include a variety of plant foods. Diets that also include eggs and milk products are more likely to supply enough nutrients. On the other hand, some vegetarian diets are very restricted. A few extreme diets focus on only one or two foods. The "macrobiotic diet" was popular a few years ago. It was an example of such an extreme. Its followers gradually gave up more and more foods. Finally, they were eating only brown rice. At that point, they were supposed to enjoy total spiritual bliss and peace. What they really experienced were severe cases of malnutrition. Several even died.

A good vegetarian diet includes a variety of foods. As more foods are cut out, the diet becomes less likely to meet nutritional needs. Some nutrients are more likely to be lacking than others. Without some form of milk, getting enough calcium is very difficult. Vitamin D may be in short supply, too. Milk and meat are top riboflavin sources. Therefore, getting enough of this vitamin could be a problem for the vegetarian. Vitamin B_{12} is found naturally only in meat, fish eggs and dairy products. Strict vegetarians have to be careful. To avoid some nutrient deficiencies, they may need to eat fortified foods or rely on nutritional supplements.

Protein does not have to be a problem for the careful vegetarian. The proteins in plants are incomplete. (They lack one or more of the essential amino acids.) By combining different incomplete proteins, you can end up with complete protein. Legumes and grains are a good combination, 3-22. Examples include beans and rice or beans and corn. Peanuts and wheat (as in a peanut butter sandwich) are also a good combination. Vegetarians have more foods from which to choose today. This is because of the growing number of products made from textured vegetable protein.

Research has not shown that vegetarian diets make people healthier. Yet many vegetarians seem healthier. Why? They tend to be more careful about all aspects of good health. A serious vegetarian learns quite a bit about nutrition in order to make wise food choices. Vegetarians tend to avoid drinking and smoking. They also tend to be more interested in physical fitness.

FOOD FACTS AND FALLACIES

Which of the following statements are true?
- Eggs with brown shells are more nutritious than eggs with white shells.
- Fish is a brain food.
- Butter has more kilojoules (Calories) than margarine.
- Beets help to cleanse your body of waste products.
- Raw milk is better for you than pasteurized milk.
- Milk causes constipation.
- Starch is more fattening than sugar.
- If you crave a certain food, your body needs it.
- Natural vitamins from foods are better for

3-22 Combinations of incomplete proteins such as beans and rice, corn and beans, or peanut butter and bread can help vegetarians meet their protein needs.

you than synthetic vitamins from pills.

- Everyone should take vitamins to ensure good health.

These statements are not true. Yet many people believe they are. Many of these statements appear in books about health and nutrition. We tend to believe what we read in books and magazines. There is a vague feeling that false information would not be "allowed." But who would censor it? Our government stays out of such matters because of our right to "freedom of the press." The government has no power to insist on accuracy, except in cases such as advertising and labeling information.

How can you tell what is fact and what is fiction? How do you know whom to trust? Where can you get reliable information?

Some things are a matter of a little knowledge plus some common sense. What, for instance, makes eggshells different colors? The color of an eggshell depends on the breed of chicken that laid it. It has nothing to do with nutritive values.

What about vitamins in foods and pills? Vitamins are chemical compounds. Vitamin C, for instance, is a certain molecule made up of atoms. If the molecule were missing something or if it contained something extra, it would not be vitamin C. Your body does not know or care if the molecule came from a pill or from an orange. Yet nutrition experts recommend oranges rather than pills. Why? Because oranges also contain fiber and other nutrients. Eating a variety of foods is better than depending on pills. It gives you a better chance of meeting all your nutrition needs.

When you read about nutrition, beware of exaggerated claims and "miraculous" results. Also beware of broad generalizations such as, "sugar is bad for you." (In some cases it may be, but this is not always true.) Compare claims and statements with what you know about nutrition.

Home economics teachers can help you find information that sorts out facts from fallacies. Other professionals that can help you are hospital dietitians, public health nutritionists, extension home economists and your family doctor. The Food and Drug Administration has information specialists in its national and regional offices. Professional organizations such as the American Medical Association (A.M.A.), American Dietetic Association (A.D.A.), American Home Economics Association (A.H.E.A.) and Society for Nutrition Education (S.N.E.) are also reliable sources of information.

to Define

amphetamines . . .
Basic Four Food Groups . . .
behavior modification . . .
clear liquid diet . . .
diuretics . . . enriched . . .
fad diet . . . fasting . . .
full liquid diet . . .
lactating . . . obesity . . .
RDA's . . . soft diet . . .
underweight . . .
U.S. RDA's . . .
vegetarian diet

to Discuss

1. Name the Basic Four Food Groups. How many servings does a teenager need from each group daily?
2. List four foods you can eat as alternatives to meat.
3. How often should you eat a good source of vitamin C? Why?
4. How can you find out what nutrients are in the foods you plan to buy?
5. Which of the Basic Four Food Groups can you skip when you are trying to lose weight?
6. Why is being underweight often a serious problem?
7. Even if your weight is just right, why is exercise important?
8. Why do elderly people usually need fewer kilojoules (Calories) than they needed when they were younger? How do their needs for most nutrients change?
9. Name three types of convalescent diets. Why is medical guidance important?
10. What kinds of foods do all vegetarian diets include?
What foods are sometimes included?
11. Is it better to eat a variety of foods than to take a vitamin pill every day?

to Do

1. Keep a record of everything you eat for one week. List the foods under headings of the Basic Four Food Groups. At the end of each day, evaluate your diet. At the end of the week, evaluate your weekly diet. Did you eat a variety of foods from each group? Did you make any changes in your diet during the week? What are the strong and weak points of your food patterns?
2. Collect ten nutrition labels from various foods. Analyze the labels. Consider questions such as: Do any of the foods supply just a few nutrients along with lots of kilojoules (Calories)? Are any of the foods a particularly rich source of one or more nutrients? Does the cost of a food seem to be related to its nutritional value?
3. Clip or make a photocopy of a diet that has appeared in a magazine. Analyze the diet. Consider questions such as: Does the diet include all of the Basic Four Food Groups? About how many kilojoules (Calories) does the diet provide per day? What special claims are made for this diet? Do you judge this to be a good diet or not? Defend your judgment.
4. Invite a gym teacher, coach or other fitness expert to visit your class. Ask for a demonstration of exercises that will help you keep trim and physically fit.
5. Write a report about vegetarian diets. Include sample menus for one week. Do the menus meet your nutritional needs?
6. Invite a hospital dietitian to speak to your class about special diets and career opportunities in dietetics.
7. Make a collage of magazine articles and ads that promote miracle diets, reducing aids and gadgets of questionable value. Give your collage a title such as "Let the Dieter Beware."
8. Make four or more small posters on common food fallacies. Display the posters in your school lunchroom. Be sure to include facts to correct the fallacies.

SAVINGS WORTH

Tools of the trade

*Food preparation can be easy when
you use proper equipment and methods.
Shopping skills can help you to
select quality foods within your budget.*

4

Making appliances work for you

Why do you use appliances?
Appliances are designed to
make life easier. After reading
this chapter, you will be able to
select, use and care for large
and small kitchen appliances.
You will also be able to
describe ways of using
appliances to conserve energy.

As you learn to cook, you also need to learn how to use kitchen appliances. They can help make your work easier. A refrigerator, for instance, makes it possible to purchase food ahead of time. A dishwasher eliminates the need to wash most dishes by hand. And an electric mixer saves time when making a cake.

Appliances can save you time and energy in the kitchen. But no appliance will work the way it should unless you use and care for it properly.

REFRIGERATOR BASICS

The refrigerator is a food storage appliance. If you did not have a place to keep foods cold, you would have to shop every day. Foods that spoil very quickly, like fish or poultry, would have to be purchased just before mealtime. With a refrigerator, you can shop days or even a week ahead of time. If you also have a freezer, you can buy some foods weeks or even months before you use them.

Kinds of refrigerators
Refrigerators come in three basic styles: one-door, two-door and a compact-portable.
One-door refrigerators contain a small

compartment which is colder than the rest of the refrigerator. Ice cubes and foods which you buy already frozen can be stored in this compartment. The compartment is not cold enough to freeze foods which are not already frozen. Nor is it cold enough to store already frozen foods for a long time.

Two-door refrigerators are purchased by most people. They have a refrigerator and a separate freezer. The freezer may be located beside, above or below the refrigerator. See 4-1. Because the freezer maintains very low temperatures, it can be used to freeze foods.

Compact-portable refrigerators are much smaller than the other two styles. This makes them popular in recreation rooms, mobile homes and college dorms. They have a small compartment for ice cubes.

How a refrigerator works

A refrigerator has two basic systems. One system makes cold air. The other system circulates the cold air throughout the refrigerator. The circulating cold air is what cools the food in a refrigerator.

Have you ever covered a hot dish of food and set it on the counter to cool? As cool air came in contact with the hot dish, the steam inside turned to water droplets. The droplets collected on the inside of the cover. This process is called *condensation*.

When condensation occurs, the moisture which forms must go somewhere. If food is placed in the refrigerator in a covered container, moisture will collect inside the container, 4-2. If the food is not covered, the moisture will collect around the refrigerator's cooling system and turn into frost. When the frost builds up to about 0.5 cm (1/4 inch), you will need to *defrost* the refrigerator. If you do not remove the frost, your refrigerator will have to work harder to keep food cold and maintain the proper temperature.

Defrosting your refrigerator

Defrosting a refrigerator is not difficult. But it does take time. First you need to either turn the temperature control to the defrost

4-1 In this two-door refrigerator, the freezer is located above the refrigerator.

WHITE-WESTINGHOUSE

4-2 Storing foods in covered containers helps keep frost from forming.

EVAPORATED MILK ASSOC.

setting or turn the refrigerator off. Next, you need to remove the food. You can keep food cold by storing it in an insulated picnic basket.. Or you can wrap the food in several layers of newspaper. Place the wrapped food in a sturdy box and cover it with more newspapers.

Once the refrigerator and freezing compartments are completely empty, place shallow pans under the drain holes. The pans will collect the water which will form as the frost melts. To speed up the defrosting process, you can place pans of hot water inside the freezing compartment. Never try to remove built-up frost with a sharp object, such as a knife. If you do, you could damage your refrigerator permanently.

If you have a frost-free or automatically defrosting refrigerator, you will not need to defrost it. But refrigerators with a frost-free feature are more costly to buy and operate.

Cleaning your refrigerator

All refrigerators need to be cleaned often. A clean refrigerator helps keep food safe to eat. This is because bacteria are more likely to grow and multiply in a dirty refrigerator.

About once a week, you should wipe the shelves of your refrigerator with a damp cloth. Some refrigerators have special compartments for meat, fresh produce and butter. These should also be cleaned. If the special compartments can be removed, they are easier to wash and rinse at the sink. Use a soapy cloth to clean the outside of the refrigerator. Do not use abrasive cleansers because they can scratch the surface.

Once in a while, you will need to clean the refrigerator more thoroughly. The inside of the refrigerator should be cleaned with a baking soda and water solution. Baking soda is a good cleaning agent, and it absorbs odors. You can make the solution by mixing 30 mL (2 tablespoons) of baking soda with 1 L (1 quart) of warm water. Clean all inside surfaces with this solution. Then rinse with cool water and wipe dry. Clean all outside surfaces with a soapy cloth, rinse and dry. Remove the grill from the bottom of the refrigerator. It should be washed in soapy water, rinsed and dried. The drip pan, which is located behind the grill, needs to be emptied and washed.

At least twice a year, lint and dust should be removed from the back of the refrigerator. This is done so the refrigerator can work efficiently. First, pull the refrigerator away from the wall and unplug it. Then, use the vacuum cleaner to remove any dust or lint around the base of the refrigerator. Finally, vacuum the condenser coils. These coils usually are located on the back of the refrigerator.

Storing food in the refrigerator

Your refrigerator's job is to store foods which spoil easily. You can help your refrigerator do its job well. You can set the thermostat control and store foods properly.

The *thermostat* control in a refrigerator regulates the temperature. The control should be set so that the temperature inside the refrigerator is about 2 to 4°C (35 to 40°F). The bottom is usually the coldest part of a refrigerator. For this reason, perishable foods such as poultry, meat and fish should be stored there.

Many refrigerators have special compartments for storing certain foods. In some refrigerators, produce can be stored in a special drawer. This drawer is called a "hydrator" or "vegetable crisper." Its purpose is to keep fruits and vegetables from drying out. Most produce can be stored uncovered in the crisper. But leafy green vegetables and certain other produce which will be stored for more than one or two days should be wrapped. Some refrigerators have special compartments for meat and butter. The meat compartment is usually near the bottom of the refrigerator where the temperature is the coldest. Meats should be wrapped before they are stored. The butter compartment is usually in the door. It often has a separate temperature control so that butter and margarine will stay soft and spreadable.

Adjustable shelves make storing food easier. When large items such as turkeys need to be refrigerated, shelves can be adjusted or removed.

Many packaging materials can be used for refrigerator storage. Examples are aluminum foil, plastic wraps, plastic bowls and other containers with tight-fitting lids. All of these materials help keep food from drying out. They also keep odors from escaping into the refrigerator.

Food odors are undesirable for two reasons. They make the inside of the refrigerator smell bad. And mild-flavored foods, such as butter, absorb flavors from strong-flavored foods, such as onions. Besides wrapping foods carefully, some people also leave an open box of baking soda in the refrigerator. The baking soda absorbs odors.

Cooked foods should not be taken directly from the range or oven to the refrigerator. Hot foods will warm up the inside of the refrigerator. As a result, the motor must work harder to lower the temperature. Allow containers of hot food to cool a *short time* before putting them in the refrigerator.

FREEZER BASICS

Freezers are used to store foods for longer periods of time. The freezer space in a two-door refrigerator is not enough for some families. These families may be large, or they may choose to save money by buying large amounts of sale items and freezing them for later use. A separate freezer can provide the extra freezing space these families need.

Kinds of freezers

Freezers are available in two styles: chest and upright.

Chest freezers, 4-3, open from the top. They cost less to operate than upright freezers. This is because less warm air enters this type of freezer when it is opened. It is easy to store bulky packages in a chest freezer, but small packages can be difficult to organize.

Upright freezers look like one-door refrigerators, 4-4. They take up less floor space than chest freezers, but they cost more to

WHIRLPOOL

4-3 Chest freezers are more economical to operate than upright freezers.

AMANA

4-4 Upright freezers take up less floor space than chest freezers.

operate. It can be difficult to store bulky packages in an upright freezer, but small packages are easy to organize.

Using your freezer

Foods can be stored in a freezer longer than in a refrigerator. This is because freezer temperatures are much lower. A freezer should maintain a temperature of −18°C (0°F) or lower.

Packaging is very important when freezing foods. It must be air and moisture-proof so foods will not dry out. Aluminum foil, freezer paper and plastic containers with tight-fitting covers can be used. Some foods, such as casseroles, can be frozen in their baking dishes.

Not all foods can be frozen. Foods such as mayonnaise, sour cream, gelatin products, custard, hard-cooked egg white, lettuce and certain other raw vegetables do not freeze well.

Food will not keep forever in a freezer. Some foods can be stored frozen longer than others. Beef, for instance, can be stored in the freezer for six to 12 months. Cherries, on the other hand, should not be stored for more than one month. This is because food will lose some of its eating quality while it is frozen. Ice cream should be used within a month. A freezer chart for commonly frozen foods is given in 4-5.

COOKING WITH GAS, ELECTRICITY OR MICROWAVES

The range is the most frequently used appliance in most homes. Ranges are available in several different styles. Some come with special features. Consider your cooking and baking needs when buying a range. You can also purchase cook-tops and ovens separately.

Range styles

Ranges come in three basic styles: free-standing, slide-in and built-in. Each basic range style may be fueled by gas or electricity.

Free-standing ranges are purchased by most people. They can stand alone, or they can be

GUIDE TO FREEZING

FOOD	APPROXIMATE STORAGE TIME (in months)
Fruits	
Fruits (in syrup or sugar)	12
Fruits (unsweetened)	5 to 6
Vegetables	
Most vegetables	8 to 12
Mushrooms	6
Dairy Products, Eggs	
Margarine	12
Butter	6
Whipped cream	3
Milk	3
Ice cream and sherbet	1
Cheese (some)	2 to 6
Eggs (beaten with 2 mL [1/2 teaspoon] salt or sugar)	3
Meat	
Beef	6 to 12
Veal	6 to 9
Pork	3 to 4
Frankfurters	1
Smoked ham	1 to 2
Ground beef, veal or lamb	3 to 4
Ground pork	1 to 3
Poultry	
Whole chicken or turkey	12
Chicken pieces	9
Turkey pieces	6
Fish and shell fish	
Salmon, tuna, sardines	3
Cod, flounder, perch	6
Shrimp	12
Oysters, clams	3 to 4
Baked goods	
Bread and rolls	3
Pound cake	6
Fruit pies	4
Cookies	6 to 8
Prepared dishes	
Meat pies	3
Poultry casserole	6
Fish casserole	3
Pasta, rice casserole	1 to 3
Stews	3 to 4

4-5 This guide to freezing tells you how long various foods should keep in your freezer.

placed between two counters. Free-standing ranges have an oven below the cook-top. Some have an additional oven above the cook-top. This type of free-standing range is called a "double-oven" or "split-level" range. See 4-6.

Slide-in ranges have unfinished sides. Because this type of range fits snugly between two cabinets, its sides are hidden. The oven is located below the cook-top.

Built-in ranges have separate cook-tops and ovens, 4-7. The cook-top is built into a counter top. The oven is built into a wall or a specially designed cabinet.

Cooking with gas

In gas ranges, 4-8, heat is produced when gas mixes with oxygen in the air and begins to burn. The amount of heat that is produced depends upon the amount of gas that is used. As more gas mixes with oxygen, more heat is

HOTPOINT

4-7 In a built-in range, the cook-top is separated from the oven or ovens.

TAPPAN

4-6 This double-oven range has a microwave oven above the cook-top and a conventional gas oven below.

WHITE-WESTINGHOUSE

4-8 Most gas ranges have four surface burners. Some have six.

produced. As less gas is used, less heat is produced.

When you turn on the surface burners of a gas range, you will see a blue flame. The flame will be low or high, depending upon the temperature you have chosen. If the flame looks orange, the burner is not properly adjusted. Carbon will collect on the bottom of pans used with a poorly adjusted burner. An authorized repair person can adjust the burner for you.

Some gas ranges have one or more *pilot lights*. A pilot light is a tiny flame which ignites a gas burner when the control is turned on. In some gas ranges, pilot lights burn all the time. If one should accidentally go out, you will smell gas. In this case, you will need to relight the pilot with a match. Always light the match *before* turning on the gas. If the pilot light does not light immediately, turn off the gas and call a repair person.

Most new gas ranges do not have *continuously burning pilot lights*. Instead, they have an energy-saving feature called *electric ignition*. Electricity is needed to light the burners on these ranges.

The oven and broiler. Like the gas range, either a pilot light or an electric ignition is used to light the gas oven.

Before lighting the oven, open the oven door. (This will allow any fumes which may have built up to escape.) Then turn on the oven control. There will be a short delay before the burner is fully lighted. You will usually hear a "whooshing" noise when the gas ignites. After the gas has ignited, close the oven door and set the desired temperature. If the burner does not light and you begin to smell gas, turn the oven off. Air the oven and try again. (If your oven has a continuous burning pilot light, you may need to relight it.)

The broiler may be part of the gas oven. It may also be a separate unit located below the oven or on the side of the oven. The same control used to turn on the oven also turns on the broiler. A special broiler pan fits in the broiler compartment. It can be adjusted close or far away from the flame, so that foods of varying thicknesses can be broiled.

Cooking with electricity

When an electric range is turned on, electric current flows through coils of wire and produces heat. The coils of wire are called *heating elements*. The heating elements on most electric ranges are visible, 4-9. On some ranges, the heating elements are hidden below a smooth glass ceramic surface, 4-10.

The amount of heat given off by each heating element depends upon the temperature you select. Most electric ranges have several temperature settings.

Most electric ranges have two different sizes of heating elements. The smaller elements should be used with smaller pans. When a small pan is used on a large heating element, energy is wasted.

In a gas range, heat is produced as soon as the burner is lighted. The heat stops as soon as the gas is turned off. But in an electric range, the electricity must flow through the coils before heat is produced. Because there is a time delay, you need to be more patient when cooking with electricity. Food takes longer to get hot. And the food will continue to cook for a short time after the heat has been turned off. This is because the heating element cools slowly. Also, while cooking, when you turn the temperature control to a lower heat setting, the temperature will not change immediately.

The oven and broiler. The oven in an electric range is really an oven and broiler in one. If you look inside an electric oven, you will see two heating elements. One is on the top, and one is on the bottom. The top element becomes hot when the oven is used for broiling. The bottom element becomes hot when the oven is used for baking. (In some ovens, the top heating element heats slightly during baking to improve heat distribution.)

When broiling in an electric oven, the oven door should be left slightly open. This is done for several reasons. If the door is tightly closed, the temperature will build up. This may cause the thermostat to turn the broiling element off. Secondly, the open door will allow any moisture to escape. This means that the product being broiled will have the desired crispness. Thirdly, the open door helps reduce the risk of a fire.

Specially designed broiling pans are used in an electric oven. They help prevent melted fat from smoking. Foods of different thickness can be broiled by adjusting the oven racks.

Special features

Special features are available on both gas and electric ranges. These features can make using and caring for the range easier. But they add to the purchase price of the appliance. And some features increase operating costs.

Many ranges have built-in clocks and timers. Some timers will turn the oven on and off at preset times. Some ranges have special burners or heating elements which are controlled by thermostats. These surface units can be set to maintain a certain temperature just like an oven. Grills, griddles and rotisseries are available on some range models. They usually fit into place over a portion of the cook-top.

You may have seen ranges with *hoods* over them. (Refer to 4-10 again.) These hoods help ventilate the cooking area by removing heat and odors. Most hoods have filters which absorb grease and smoke. These filters need to be cleaned or replaced periodically.

Many consumers buy gas and electric ranges with automatic cleaning features. Two types of cleaning features are available: *self-cleaning* and *continuous cleaning*.

Self-cleaning ovens use very high temperatures (400 to 540°C or 750 to 1000°F) to burn away food spills. After the cleaning cycle has been used, you may need to wipe the oven with a damp cloth. This removes the ash-like residue which remains in the oven after cleaning. All self-cleaning ovens are well insulated. This is because of the high temperatures used in the cleaning cycle. This extra insulation aids in energy conservation whenever the oven is used.

Continuous cleaning ovens have specially coated walls. The coating causes the food spatters and spills to be oxidized or "burned away" over a period of time. The cleaning takes place whenever the oven is used. Since

4-9 The heating elements on electric ranges heat and cool slowly.

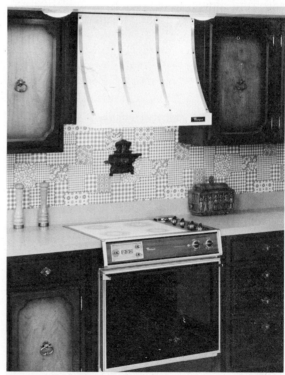

4-10 This electric range has a smooth cook-top. Sometimes a hood is installed above a range to remove heat and food odors.

very high temperatures are not needed, these ovens do not have extra insulation. Continuous cleaning ovens do not cost as much as self-cleaning ovens. But some people find them less effective.

Microwave and convection ovens are two other special features found in some ranges. You will learn more about these later in this chapter.

Using your range safely

Safety guidelines are very important when using a range. Before using your range for the first time, read the *manufacturer's use and care booklet*. It will describe your range's special features. It will also explain how the range can be safely operated. If you do not have a use and care booklet, you can obtain one by writing to the manufacturer. Be sure to include the model number of your range. You will find this number on the identification plate. This plate is usually located on the back of a large appliance.

When using a range, follow safety guidelines to prevent burns and fires. Always put pans on the surface units *before* turning on the gas or electricity. Use pot holders to grasp hot pans and baking utensils. Point all pan handles inward (away from the front of the range) to prevent accidental tipping. Also, wear tight-fitting clothes when working around the range. Ties, scarves and large, loose sleeves can be safety hazards. To prevent burns, always be sure to pull oven shelves out when placing foods in the oven.

If a fire should start anywhere on or in a range, turn off the heat and smother the flames. You can smother the flames by pouring salt or baking soda on them or by using a fire extinguisher. If the fire is in a pan, you can smother the flames by covering the pan. These methods cut off the oxygen supply which a fire needs to burn. DO NOT pour water onto a grease fire. Water causes hot fat to splatter. Hot fat can cause a serious burn.

Taking care of your range

Keep your range clean. A clean range not only looks nicer, it also works better.

If you let spills build up, they will bake onto the surface of the range. Baked-on spills are hard to remove. In most ranges, surface units can be removed. This makes it easy to clean beneath them. The grates and drip trays of a gas range can be washed in the sink. The heating elements of an electric range are self-cleaning. Do not wash them. The drip bowls below the heating elements can be washed in the sink.

Warm, soapy water will remove most spills on the surface of a range. If a spill is very stubborn, you can use a plastic scrubber and an all-purpose cleaner. Do not use abrasive cleansers because they can scratch the surface. Do not use cold water to remove spills from a hot range surface. Sudden temperature changes can cause the porcelain-enamel finish to crack. After washing, range parts and surfaces should be rinsed with clean water and dried.

The oven also needs to be cleaned. Each time the oven is used, spills should be removed as soon as the oven has cooled. Ovens without special cleaning features may need periodic cleaning with a special oven cleaner. Oven cleaners are products designed to dissolve burned-on food. Follow directions carefully when using these products. It is always a good idea to protect the floor around the oven with several layers of newspapers.

Microwave ovens

Microwave ovens, 4-11, are found in many homes, schools, restaurants, hospitals and company lunchrooms. Why are microwave ovens so popular? Microwave ovens can defrost, warm, cook and reheat food much faster than conventional cooking methods. One baked potato, for instance, cooks in about four minutes in a microwave oven. Baking a potato in a conventional oven takes 45 to 60 minutes, depending upon the temperature.

In conventional ovens, heat is directed to the outside of food. The food absorbs heat and cooks from the outside to the inside. This is why the edges of medium-rare slice of roast beef are more well-done than the center.

In a microwave oven, the cooking process is different. High frequency radio waves called *microwaves* are produced in a special tube. The microwaves are distributed throughout the inside of the oven. When microwaves enter the food, they cause the molecules in the food to rub against each other. The movement creates friction, and the friction creates heat. This heat cooks the food. The process is very fast. Depending upon the food being cooked, food may cook two to 10 times faster than by conventional methods.

Speed is only one advantage of microwave cooking. With microwave cooking, the oven does not become hot. Because microwaves are a *form* of energy which is not hot, a microwave oven stays cool. Dishes also stay cool when cooking times are short. But during long cooking periods, dishes do become hot. This is because the hot foods transfer heat to the cooking dish.

Microwave ovens are easy to clean. Because the inside of the oven does not become hot, food spills do not cook or burn onto the oven.

Microwave ovens help save energy when small amounts of food are cooked. Cooking time increases as the amount of food being cooked increases. Thus, it may be more energy-efficient to cook large amounts of food in a conventional oven.

In some cases, food cooked in a microwave oven are more nutritious. Many vegetables, for instance, retain more nutrients. This is because the cooking time is shorter, and little or no water is needed.

Using your microwave oven. Many different materials can be used as "cooking utensils" in a microwave oven, 4-12. You can use paper towels, paper plates, waxed paper, glass, plastic wrap and some plastic dishes. Microwaves pass through these materials to the food being cooked.

On the other hand, some common cooking untensils cannot be used. Metal pans, for instance, should not be used in most microwave ovens. This is because metal reflects microwaves. The microwaves will bounce off the pan instead of being transmitted to the food. Using metal utensils in some microwave ovens can damage the ovens permanently. (Small amounts of certain metals can be used in some models. But check the manufacturer's use and care booklet before placing any metal objects in your microwave oven.)

Most foods which can be cooked on or in gas and electric ranges can be cooked in a

JENN-AIR

4-11 Some microwave ovens have special browning units and temperature probes.

HITACHI

4-12 A variety of nonmetallic materials can be used in a microwave oven.

microwave oven. But some foods will give better results if certain methods are followed. The size and shape of pans, for instance, can affect how foods cook. Foods cooked in shallow, small, round pans tend to cook more evenly than foods cooked in deep, large, square pans. Foods such as roasts cook more evenly if they are turned once or twice during the roasting process. Some foods need to be removed from the oven before they look done. Because heat is retained, the food will continue to cook as it stands on the counter. Cakes, for example, will continue to cook. They can become very tough. The use and care booklet which comes with the microwave oven will give tips on cooking.

Special features. Microwave ovens are not all alike. Some have separate power settings for cooking, defrosting, reheating and warming foods. Newer models may have built-in computers which allow you to preset cooking times for foods you regularly cook in your microwave oven.

Some microwave ovens have special browning features. These are designed to give food the brown color it would get in a conventional oven. Some ovens have temperature probes. The probes "read" the temperature of the food as it is being cooked. When a preset temperature is reached, the oven can maintain that temperature or shut itself off.

Size and convenience are important features to consider. Some microwave ovens take up just a small amount of counter space. Some ovens are large enough to cook an entire meal. Double-oven ranges are available with one conventional oven and one microwave oven. Other ranges have one oven which can be used as a conventional oven, as a microwave oven or as both ovens at the same time.

Caring for your microwave oven. A microwave oven is easy to keep clean. Why? Because the inside of the oven stays cool during cooking, spills do not burn onto the oven walls. You can keep the inside of your microwave oven spotless by occasionally wiping the walls with a soapy cloth. Then rinse and dry with a soft cloth. The outside of the oven can be cleaned in the same way. (Ovens with browning elements are exceptions to these general guidelines. Browning elements create heat inside the ovens. Therefore, ovens with this feature may be harder to clean.)

The door seal on a microwave oven helps prevent any radiation leakage. It should be checked for food spills each time the oven is used. Any spills should be cleaned up immediately so the seal is not broken. If you notice any change in the way the door seal looks or works, call a repair person right away.

Microwave ovens should not be operated when they are empty. Turning on an empty oven can damage it. For this reason, it is a good idea to keep a small dish of water in the oven when it is not being used.

Convection ovens

Convection ovens use a *circulating-air system* to cook food, 4-13. Convection ovens are fairly new to home kitchens. But they have been used for a long time in commercial bakeries and restaurants.

Convection ovens have many features that make them popular. They cook faster than

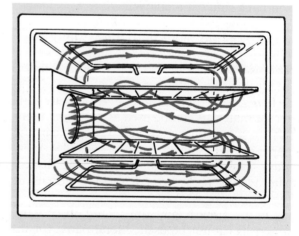

4-13 Because of the circulating-air system in a convection oven, food can be cooked at lower temperatures for shorter periods of time.

conventional ovens. They also use lower temperatures. Foods cook more evenly than either conventional or microwave ovens. Baked foods are often higher in volume and more evenly browned. The same cooking utensils used in conventional ovens can be used in convection ovens.

How does a convection oven work? A fan circulates hot air around the food. This circulating air heats food more directly and quickly than in a conventional oven which uses still air.

Convection ovens use less energy. Compared to conventional ovens, cooking temperatures are reduced as much as 25°C (as much as 75°F). Also, cooking times are decreased by one-fourth to one-half, depending upon the food. Most convection ovens come with booklets which give directions for converting recipes to convection cooking.

THE CLEANUP APPLIANCES

Dishwashers, food waste disposers and trash compactors all help with kitchen cleanup. *Dishwashers* wash eating and serving utensils. *Food waste disposers* dispose of soft food wastes. *Trash compactors* compact both food and nonfood wastes.

The dishwasher

Dishwashers come in two basic styles: built-in and portable. *Built-in dishwashers* fit between two cabinets, 4-14. They are permanently connected to a hot water line, a drain and an electrical circuit. Most built-in dishwashers are front-loading. *Portable dishwashers* can be stored anywhere. They are rolled to the sink for use, 4-15. The portable dishwasher must be plugged into a wall outlet. It is connected to the faucet by a water supply hose and a drain hose. Water enters and leaves the portable dishwasher through these hoses. Portable dishwashers can be front or top-loading. Some can be converted into built-ins.

Using your dishwasher. A dishwasher cleans by spraying a mixture of hot water and detergent over the dishes. The dishes are then

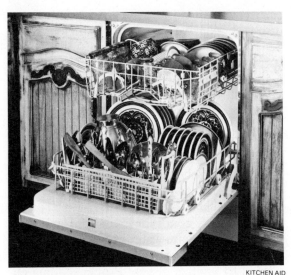

KITCHEN AID

4-14 A built-in dishwasher fits between two cabinets. Dishes are cleaned properly when the dishwasher is loaded correctly.

KITCHEN AID

4-15 Portable dishwashers are pushed to the sink for use.

rinsed with very hot water and dried. Some dishwashers have a special *air-dry feature*. This feature saves energy because the heater turns off during the drying period. The heated air already in the dishwasher dries the dishes.

A dishwasher gives the best results when four conditions are met.
1. The water temperature is between 60 and 70°C (140 and 160°F).
2. The water pressure is adequate.
3. The dishwasher is loaded properly.
4. A detergent, specially designed for dishwashers, is used.

Why are these conditions so important? Hot water and adequate water pressure are needed to clean dishes thoroughly. Hot water is also needed to sanitize dishes. Proper loading ensures that the detergent and hot water will reach all sides of each dish. The wrong detergent will not clean as well and may even damage the dishwasher.

Use a rubber scraper to remove food scraps from dishes before they go into the dishwasher. If you are not going to run the dishwasher right away, rinse the dishes. Food which has dried onto dishes is more difficult to remove.

Load the dishwasher so that the water and detergent solution will reach all sides of each dish. (Refer to 4-14 again.) Do not crowd dishes. Cups and bowls should be loaded so that the water will run off. (The manufacturer's use and care booklet will show you how to load your dishwasher.)

Fill the detergent container to the level recommended by the manufacturer of your dishwasher. Too little detergent will not clean dishes thoroughly. But too much detergent is wasteful and could damage the dishwasher.

Next, close and lock the dishwasher door. Then select the *cycle* (number and sequence of washes and rinses) which best suits the dishes you are washing.

Dishwashers have different cycle settings. The three most common are "normal," "pots and pans," and "fine china." The number of washes and rinses vary along with the amount of time. For instance, a "pots and pans" cycle often has a prerinse, two washes and three or four rinses. These are needed to clean the greasy soil from pots and pans.

When the final drying period ends, the dishwasher will automatically turn off. The dishes inside, however, will still be very hot. Most people wait until the dishes have cooled before unloading the dishwasher. Unloading cool dishes is safer because you are less likely to drop them.

Cleaning your dishwasher. Dishwashers are self-cleaning appliances. But occasionally the drain screen needs to be cleaned. This is done to remove the food particles which have collected in the screen. The drain screen is on the bottom of the dishwasher. It should be lifted out, emptied and rinsed. Follow the directions in the use and care booklet. Some dishwashers do not have this feature.

If you live in a region with very hard water, mineral deposits may form inside your dishwasher. These can be dissolved by using dishwasher cleaning products or white vinegar. Follow directions in the use and care booklet.

The outside of the dishwasher can be cleaned with a damp cloth. Abrasive cleansers should not be used because they can scratch the surface.

Food waste disposers

Food waste disposers make it easy to eliminate soft food waste. They are installed beneath the kitchen sink. Food scraps are put into the disposer opening. When a switch is turned on, the disposer grinds them into small pieces. Running water flushes the pieces down the drain.

Food waste disposers come in two styles: continuous feed and batch feed. In a *continuous feed disposer,* a switch is turned on. Then the food is put down the disposer opening in a continuous manner. In a *batch feed disposer,* a certain amount of food is put down the disposer opening. The lid is put into place, and the disposer is turned on. These three steps are repeated until all of the food scraps are gone.

Using your food waste disposer. Before using your food waste disposer, check for foreign objects in the sink. Sometimes, objects such as a spoon or fork may accidentally fall into the disposer.

Never use your fingers or a metal object to shove scraps into the disposer opening. A rubber spatula or wooden spoon should be used instead, 4-16. In some models, if the disposer should jam, it will automatically shut off. After the food particle has been dislodged, you will need to push the reset button, usually located at the base of the disposer. This will allow you to start the disposer again.

When using the disposer, turn on the *cold* water. (Cold water is needed to harden fat so it will grind more easily.) Then follow the manufacturer's operating instructions. When grinding is complete, turn off the disposer. Let the cold water run for a short time. The water will rinse the last food particles down the drain.

Caring for your food waste disposer. Certain items cannot be put down a food waste disposer. These include paper, plastic, metal, very large bones, and clam and oyster shells. Some manufacturers may also tell you not to put corn cobs and other very hard or fibrous foods down the disposer. The use and care booklet will tell you what foods you should and should not grind.

Foods such as the rinds of citrus fruits and melons, should be cut into smaller pieces before grinding.

Food waste disposers are self-cleaning. Never pour lye or chemical drain cleaners down the kitchen drain. If you do, you may damage the disposer.

Trash compactors

Like the food waste disposer, the *trash compactor* is a cleanup appliance, 4-17. A trash compactor can handle all of the food wastes a food waste disposer can handle. A trash compactor also can handle food wastes a disposer cannot handle as well as nonfood wastes such as cans and bottles.

Trash compactors compress a large amount of waste into a small bundle. They do this by applying great pressure to the waste. Most trash compactors reduce waste to one-fourth its original size.

MAYTAG CO.

4-16 A food waste disposer is installed in the kitchen sink. Use a rubber spatula or a wooden spoon when putting foods into the disposer.

WHIRLPOOL

4-17 A trash compactor crushes food wastes and nonfood items such as cans, cartons and boxes into compact bundles.

Using your trash compactor. Trash compactors have a container which is lined with a special bag. The compactor is opened, and the waste is placed in the bag. When the waste reaches a certain level, the compactor is turned on and the waste is compacted.

Caring for your trash compactor. Because each compactor works a little differently, be sure to follow the manufacturer's instructions. The correct type of bag should be used in the compactor. The bags should be removed as soon as they are full. Never place flammable products or products in aerosol cans in a trash compactor. These products can explode under pressure. Dispose of them separately.

THE PORTABLES

Small electrical appliances which can be moved from one place to another are called *portable appliances.* Examples include toasters, coffee makers, electric skillets and food processors. See 4-18. Some portable appliances, such as toasters, have been around for a long time. But others, such as electric woks, are rather new. New portable appliances appear on the market all the time.

Portable appliances are popular for many reasons. Some portable appliances make cooking easier. It is easier to grate cheese in a food processor than with a hand grater. Other portable appliances save energy. Baking two potatoes in a toaster-oven uses less energy than baking two potatoes in a conventional oven. Some portables increase cooking capacity. If all the surface units on a range are in use, a coffee maker makes it possible to brew coffee at the same time.

Some portable appliances are very specialized and only perform one task, such as a hot dog cooker or donut maker. Other portable appliances can perform more than one task. An electric skillet, for instance, can fry, roast, or simmer foods, 4-19. If the skillet has broiling element, it also will broil pork chops. Some mixers have blender and meat grinding attachments. And some electric can openers can be used to sharpen knives.

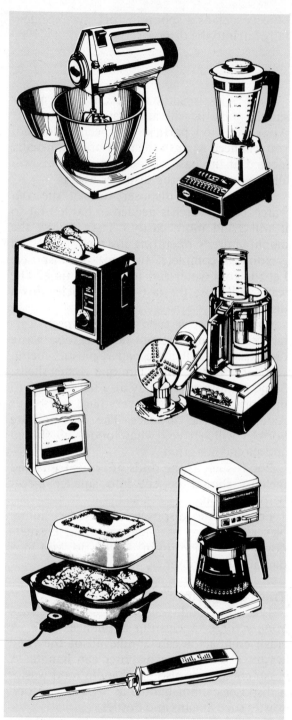

SUNBEAM

4-18 There are many electric portable appliances on the market. They can make cooking easier and save energy.

Two appliances can often perform the same task. You can crush crackers into fine crumbs in a blender or a food processor. And you can cook a stew in an electric skillet or in an electric crock pot.

Using your portable appliances

The use and care booklet which comes with each portable appliance will tell you how to use the appliance safely. Certain guidelines apply to nearly all portable appliances.

Some portable appliances require more electricity than others. This is especially true of appliances which heat up, such as toasters and coffee makers. For this reason, it is important not to connect too many appliances to one electrical circuit. If you do, you will either blow a fuse or trip the circuit breaker. Too many appliances connected to one outlet can also be a fire hazard.

Because portable appliances are electric, they must never be used around water. Water and electricity do not mix. Together, they usually result in shocks which could be severe or fatal.

Be sure the control is in the "off" position before you connect or disconnect a portable appliance. If the appliance has a detachable cord, attach the cord to the appliance before you plug the other end into the outlet. Disconnect an appliance by grasping the plug, not the cord.

Cleaning your portable appliances

Cleaning directions are included in the use and care booklet which comes with each appliance. Some appliances are *immersible* (can be put into water). These appliances have removable heat controls and electric parts which are protected. Immersible appliances are much easier to clean than appliances which cannot be immersed.

Appliances with chrome finishes or plastic housings can be cleaned with a soapy cloth, and rinsed and dried with a soft cloth. Most mixer and food processor bowls, as well as some blender containers, can be washed in a dishwasher. But it is a good idea to check with the manufacturer's use and care booklet first.

SHOPPING FOR AN APPLIANCE

You probably won't buy a major appliance for a while. But you may go shopping with your parents or other adults for a major appliance, 4-20. Or you may want to buy a portable appliance for yourself or as a gift for someone else. In any case, a few tips on buying appliances will come in handy.

SWIFT AND COMPANY

4-19 An electric skillet can be used to prepare a meal without heating your range.

TAPPAN

4-20 When shopping for an appliance, consider your need for the appliance, the space available for the appliance and your budget.

Before you enter the store, first consider three basic factors:

1. Your need for the appliance.
2. The amount of space you have to use and store the appliance.
3. Your budget.

You can choose from many different appliances that do many different jobs. Appliances come in all sizes, shapes and colors. You have to decide which appliances you need and which ones you don't need. To avoid buying an appliance you don't need, first find out what the appliance does. Then ask yourself if you have another appliance which does the same jobs as well. If so, you probably do not need the new appliance. Finally, ask yourself how often you would use the appliance. If you would use it just once or twice a year, you may not need it. If you would use the appliance several times a week, you could probably say that you do "need" it.

The second factor to consider is space. If you are shopping for a major appliance, measure the available floor space. Looking at large ranges would be a waste of time if you only have room for a small one. For some appliance, such as refrigerators, you may also need to measure the height of the space.

If you are shopping for a portable appliance, remember that they take up counter space. Too many appliances can greatly limit the amount of work space in a kitchen. Appliances are designed to save you time and energy. But to do so, they must be convenient to use. If you have to store an appliance in an awkward place, you will probably not use it very often. You will not want to spend the time and effort needed to get the appliance ready for use.

The third factor to consider when shopping for an appliance is your budget. Most appliances come in several price ranges. Therefore, it pays to comparison shop. Compare the quality and features of several brands and models before making a purchase.

Comparing appliances

Once you know you need an appliance, you have space for it and you can afford it, you are ready to shop. You might want to begin your "shopping trip" at the library. Magazines such as *Consumer Reports* describe the design features of many appliance brands and models. They usually give performance ratings for each model. Sometimes they outline safety features and give suggested retail prices. Once your research is complete, you are ready to look at appliances.

Because most appliances are costly, you expect them to last a reasonable length of time. You should expect an appliance to be easy to operate and clean, safe and energy-efficient. The appliance should also be protected by a warranty.

An appliance should be *durable*. Check the appliance carefully. Does it look and feel well-built? The finish on a range should be evenly applied with no thin spots which could wear through. A refrigerator should have sturdy shelves and shelf supports. A portable appliance should be well-balanced. Appliances which produce heat, such as toasters, should be made of materials which can withstand heat. The handles of all portable appliances should be firmly attached and should remain cool to the touch.

An appliance should be *safe to use*. Therefore, safety standards are important. If you are shopping for an electrical appliance, look for the *Underwriters Laboratories (UL)* seal. If you are shopping for a gas appliance, look for the blue star certificate given by the *American Gas Association (AGA)*. Both of these seals tell you the appliance meets safety standards, 4-21.

An appliance should be *easy to operate*. Look for controls which are located in convenient spots. The markings should be easy to read. Oven racks should slide in and out easily. Attachments, such as mixer beaters, should be easy to insert and remove.

An appliance should be *easy to keep clean*. Removable shelves and storage drawers make it easier to keep a refrigerator clean. Self-cleaning features on ranges save cleaning time. Portable appliances which are immersible are easier to clean than non-immersible ones. Nonstick finishes help with cleanup too.

An appliance should be *energy-efficient*. Some appliance models use more energy than others. *EnergyGuide labels* now appear on many major appliances, such as refrigerators, freezers and dishwashers. See 4-22. These labels are helpful in comparing different models. They can give you an idea of how much it will cost you to operate the appliance. Find out how much energy a certain model uses. An appliance with energy-saving features may have a bigger price tag. But it could save you money in the long run because it will cost less to use.

An appliance should have a warranty. A *warranty* is the seller's promise that a product will work as it should and be free from any defects. Most warranties have a time limit.

You will find two types of warranties: full warranties and limited warranties. A product with a *full warranty* will be repaired or replaced free of charge if it does not work properly. (The warrantor or seller will decide if the product should be repaired or replaced.)

You cannot be asked to do anything unreasonable to have the item repaired or replaced. A product with a *limited warranty* will be repaired or replaced, but you might be charged for the repairs. You might also have to bring or mail the appliance to the warrantor for repairs or take other steps to have it repaired.

Reading a warranty is important. Check to see that a warranty answers the following questions:

1. How and where can you have the warranty fulfilled?
2. Are both parts and labor covered?
3. How long is the warranty in effect?

If you have any questions about a warranty, write to the manufacturer.

4-21 *Look for the Underwriters Laboratories seal on electrical appliances. Look for the blue star certificate of the American Gas Association on gas appliances.*

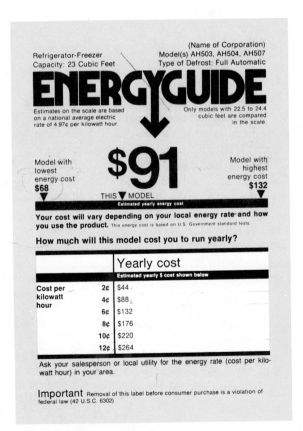

4-22 *An EnergyGuide label can help you compare energy costs of major appliances.*

to Define

AGA blue star certificate . . .
batch feed disposer . . .
built-in . . .
circulating air system . . .
condensation . . .
continuous cleaning oven . . .
continuous feed disposer . . .
convection oven . . .
cycle . . . defrost . . .
electric ignition . . .
EnergyGuide label . . .
full warranty . . .
heating element . . .
hoods . . .
limited warranty . . .
microwaves . . .
pilot light . . . portable . . .
self-cleaning oven . . .
thermostat . . . UL seal

to Discuss

1. Name the three basic styles of refrigerators.

2. Describe the special care a refrigerator requires each week. What additional care is needed periodically?

3. Discuss how food should be stored in a refrigerator in order to keep food fresh and safe to eat and to prevent undesirable odors.

4. Explain why a family might find a separate freezer desirable.

5. Name two advantages of chest freezers and two advantages of upright freezers.

6. Describe how heat is produced by a gas range. How is heat produced in an electric range?

7. Describe how food is cooked in a microwave oven.

8. Give three advantages of microwave cooking.

9. Explain why metal cooking utensils cannot be used in most microwave ovens. What types of materials can be used?

10. Describe how a portable dishwasher differs from a built-in dishwasher.

11. List four conditions which should be met in order for a dishwasher to give the best results.

12. Why should you turn on the cold water when using your food waste disposer?

13. Explain why portable appliances are so popular.

14. List six factors which should be considered before purchasing an appliance.

to Do

1. Demonstrate how to defrost a refrigerator.

2. Visit a store which sells refrigerators. Make a list of all the food storage containers and refrigerator organizers which are available.

3. Compare the purchase price and operating costs of manually defrosting, automatically defrosting and frost-free refrigerators. What do the energyguide labels on these appliances tell you?

4. Design a bulletin board which lists important safety tips to follow when using a range.

5. Demonstrate how to clean an oven.

6. Visit an appliance store. Make a list of all the special features available on gas and electric ranges. How do these features affect the purchase price of the appliance?

7. Poll your neighborhood to see how many families own microwave ovens and how they use them. Report your findings to the class in an oral presentation.

8. Prepare a display of cooking utensils specially designed for use in microwave ovens. Include the uses and cost of each utensil.

9. Demonstrate how to safely operate a food waste disposer.

10. Make an appliance record. Locate the serial number and model number of each appliance in your home. List them on a sheet of paper and store it with the use and care booklets.

11. Select a kitchen appliance that you might purchase for yourself or as a gift. Gather information about the appliance. Then visit stores to compare prices, features and warranties. Report your findings to the class.

12. Compare three different warranties for the same type of appliance (range, refrigerator, etc). What are the advantages and disadvantages of each warranty? Which warranty gives the consumer the most protection?

The cook's tools

What tools do you use for cooking? After reading this chapter, you will be able to recognize and name the tools which belong in a well-equipped kitchen. You will be able to describe the uses of each tool. You will also be able to analyze basic kitchen arrangements and suggest ideas for a well-organized kitchen.

All kinds of workers, including mechanics, secretaries and cooks, have special tools. These tools help them do their jobs well. You may be surprised to learn how many kinds of kitchen tools there are. Experienced cooks have many different kitchen tools. Why? Because the right tool makes any job easier and safer.

Most people do not start out with a fully equipped kitchen. They begin by buying very basic tools that are needed for general cooking. They add other, more specialized tools as their cooking skills develop.

When you start to equip your first kitchen, select utensils that will serve many purposes. For instance, an oven-proof bowl can be used for mixing, as a baking casserole and even as a serving dish.

Kitchen tools can be grouped according to how and when they are used. You will need some tools to help you prepare food before it is cooked. For example, you will need tools for cutting, peeling and grating. You will need other tools for measuring, cooking and baking. You may also want some special tools for special jobs. For instance, you can crush garlic with a knife, but a garlic press makes the job easier.

TOOLS FOR PREPARING FOOD

Many foods require some preparation before cooking. A recipe may call for shredded cheese, peeled potatoes or chopped onions. Using the proper tools will make these preparation steps easier.

It is very important to use preparation tools correctly. Sharp tools, such as knives, can cause painful cuts. These tools should always be handled carefully.

Tools used in preparing food for cooking are shown below.

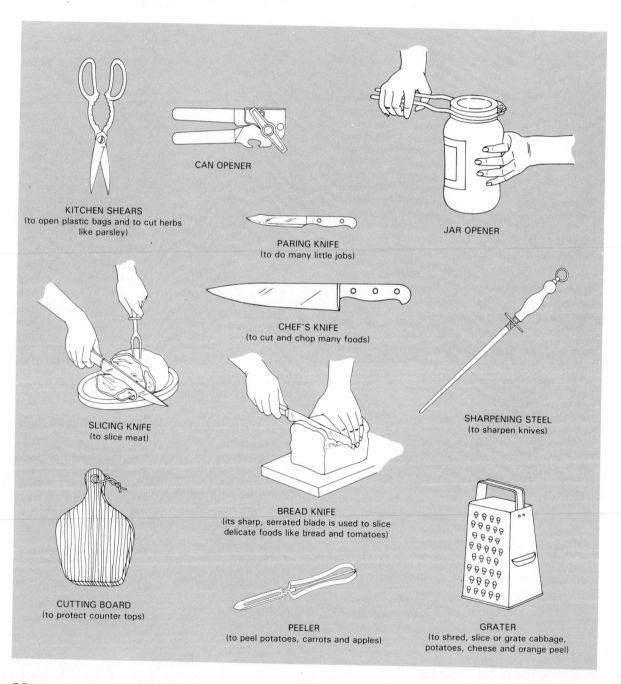

KITCHEN SHEARS
(to open plastic bags and to cut herbs like parsley)

CAN OPENER

JAR OPENER

PARING KNIFE
(to do many little jobs)

CHEF'S KNIFE
(to cut and chop many foods)

SLICING KNIFE
(to slice meat)

SHARPENING STEEL
(to sharpen knives)

BREAD KNIFE
(its sharp, serrated blade is used to slice delicate foods like bread and tomatoes)

CUTTING BOARD
(to protect counter tops)

PEELER
(to peel potatoes, carrots and apples)

GRATER
(to shred, slice or grate cabbage, potatoes, cheese and orange peel)

TOOLS FOR MEASURING

Every kitchen should have a set of standard measuring tools. These tools are used to measure liquid and dry ingredients. It is difficult to prepare a recipe accurately without them.

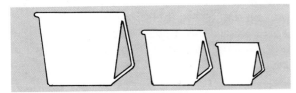

Liquid measures have handles and pouring lips. They are usually made of glass. Liquid measures are used to measure liquid ingredients such as milk and maple syrup. They are available in 250 mL (1 cup), 500 mL (2 cup) and 1 L (4 cup) sizes. When measuring liquids, set the measure on a flat surface and look at the liquid at eye level.

Dry measures are made of plastic or metal. They are used to measure dry ingredients such as flour and sugar. Dry measures are available in 50 mL (1/4 cup), 125 mL (1/2 cup) and 250 mL (1 cup) sizes. (A 1/3 cup conventional dry measure is also available.)

Small measures are made of plastic or metal. They are used to measure small amounts of liquid and dry ingredients. Small measures are available in 1 mL (1/4 teaspoon), 2 mL (1/2 teaspoon), 5 mL (1 teaspoon), 15 mL (1 tablespoon) and 25 mL (1/8 cup) sizes.

TOOLS FOR COOKING

Cooking will be easier if you store the following tools near the range where they are used most often.

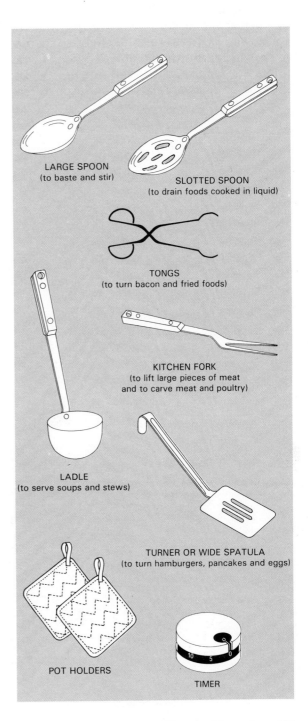

LARGE SPOON
(to baste and stir)

SLOTTED SPOON
(to drain foods cooked in liquid)

TONGS
(to turn bacon and fried foods)

KITCHEN FORK
(to lift large pieces of meat
and to carve meat and poultry)

LADLE
(to serve soups and stews)

TURNER OR WIDE SPATULA
(to turn hamburgers, pancakes and eggs)

POT HOLDERS

TIMER

Pots and pans

Pots and pans come in all shapes and sizes. The pots and pans you have in your kitchen will depend upon two things: the foods you cook most often and the amount of storage space you have.

When shopping for pots and pans, there is a wide variety from which to choose. Choose those which are sturdy and well-made. Look for secure handles and close-fitting lids. Make sure the bottoms are flat. It pays to invest in durable pans which conduct heat evenly. These pans can last a lifetime with proper care. Pots and pans made of cast iron, aluminum and stainless steel with aluminum or copper bottoms conduct heat evenly.

Some pots and pans are coated with special finishes to keep food from sticking. These pans need to be used and cleaned carefully to prevent damage to their nonstick surface.

Most well-equipped kitchens have the following pots and pans.

SKILLETS
(small and large with covers—to fry, pan-broil and braise foods)

SAUCEPANS
(small and large with covers—for a variety of cooking chores)

DUTCH OVEN
(for long, slow cooking of meats and stews)

LARGE POT
(6 L [6 quart] or larger—to cook soups and spaghetti and to blanch vegetables)

TEA KETTLE
(to boil water)

DOUBLE BOILER
(to cook foods such as chocolate and custard over gentle heat)

GRIDDLE
(to grill thin pieces of meat, cook pancakes and fry eggs)

ROASTING PAN AND RACK
(to roast meat or poultry in the oven)

BROILING PAN
(to broil foods)

94

TOOLS FOR BAKING

Baking requires some special tools. Some of these tools are used to make a variety of baked products. Mixing bowls are one example. Other tools are more specialized. A pastry blender, for instance, is generally used only when making pastry or biscuits.

The following tools are commonly used for baking.

MIXING BOWLS
(small, medium and large—for many different tasks)

WOODEN SPOONS
(various sizes and styles—to mix and stir)

PASTRY BRUSH
(to brush baked
products with
butter, milk or egg;
baste foods)

ROTARY BEATER
(to mix, beat and whip)

ROLLING PIN and PASTRY CLOTH
(to roll out cookie, pastry and biscuit dough)

SIFTER
(to combine dry ingredients)

PASTRY BLENDER
(to combine fat with flour when
making pastry and biscuits)

RUBBER SPATULAS
(to scrape sides of bowls and to fold
one ingredient into another)

Baking pans

Baking pans come in many shapes and sizes. Most baking pans are made of lightweight metal. But some are made of glass-ceramic or stoneware. Some have nonstick finishes.

You may want to have the following baking pans in your kitchen.

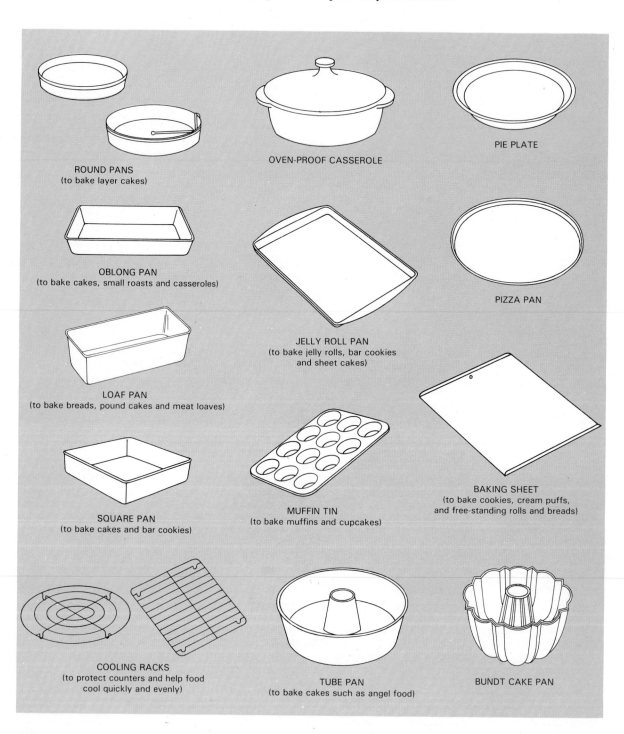

ROUND PANS
(to bake layer cakes)

OVEN-PROOF CASSEROLE

PIE PLATE

OBLONG PAN
(to bake cakes, small roasts and casseroles)

JELLY ROLL PAN
(to bake jelly rolls, bar cookies
and sheet cakes)

PIZZA PAN

LOAF PAN
(to bake breads, pound cakes and meat loaves)

SQUARE PAN
(to bake cakes and bar cookies)

MUFFIN TIN
(to bake muffins and cupcakes)

BAKING SHEET
(to bake cookies, cream puffs,
and free-standing rolls and breads)

COOLING RACKS
(to protect counters and help food
cool quickly and evenly)

TUBE PAN
(to bake cakes such as angel food)

BUNDT CAKE PAN

TOOLS FOR SPECIAL PURPOSES

As you gain experience in the kitchen, you may find that special tools can be useful. Although these tools are not essential in a basic kitchen, they do come in handy at times. The following are special purpose tools.

VEGETABLE SLICER

NUTCRACKER

APPLE CORER

MALLET
(to pound meat and
make it more tender)

FOOD GRINDER
(to grind foods, especially
meats, for various uses)

JUICER
(to squeeze juice
from citrus fruits)

GARLIC PRESS
(to crush whole
cloves of garlic)

STEAMER
(to hold vegetables above water in
a pan so they are cooked in steam)

MELON-BALL CUTTER
(to form ball-shaped pieces
of food, especially melons)

COOKIE CUTTERS

POTATO MASHER
(to mash cooked potatoes)

CUSTARD CUPS
(for custard and small
servings of other foods)

FRYING BASKET
(to hold foods as they
are deep-fat fried)

COLANDER
(to rinse fruits and vegetable
and to drain cooked foods)

RING MOLD
(for salads and desserts)

FUNNEL
(to pour food into
a small container)

STRAINER
(to separate solids from liquids
and to drain foods)

WHISK
(to whip cream and egg whites)

SKEWERS
(to hold foods in shish-kebab style
during grilling or broiling)

CARING FOR KITCHEN TOOLS

Kitchen tools will give many years of service if you care for them properly. Wood, plastic, glass and metal tools require special care.

Tools made of wood, such as cutting boards, should never be put in the dishwasher or soaked in water. Prolonged contact with water can cause wood to warp. Wooden tools should be wiped with a soapy cloth, rinsed with warm water and dried immediately.

Tools made from some types of plastic should not be washed in a dishwasher. If they are, they could melt from the high temperatures. Other plastics tend to absorb fat. As a result, they may be difficult to wash. Sometimes they become stained. Spaghetti sauce, for instance, can stain plastic storage bowls. On the other hand, some plastic tools are very durable and do not need special care. Always follow the care instructions given by the manufacturer.

Glass, porcelain and glass ceramic pans as well as pans with nonstick finishes should be cleaned with care. Do not use abrasive cleansers or steel wool. These cleaning products can scratch the finish.

Some substances can discolor aluminum tools. Hard water, eggs and baking soda can darken them. The dark stains in pots and pans can be removed by heating a vinegar and water solution in them. Because aluminum can dent and scratch fairly easily, be careful when using and washing aluminum tools.

Copper tools (and pans with copper bottoms) can be kept clean and shiny with a special copper cleaner or lemon juice.

Cast iron pans must be *seasoned* before they are used for the first time, 5-1. You can do this by heating a small amount of vegetable oil in it. Remove the excess oil with a paper towel, and the pan is ready to use. This treatment helps prevent rust and it helps keep foods from sticking. Cast iron utensils should never be washed in a dishwasher or soaked. They should be wiped with a damp cloth and thoroughly dried. (If cast iron is not thoroughly dried, it will rust.) Cast iron utensils may need to be re-seasoned occasionally.

ORGANIZING YOUR KITCHEN

A well-organized kitchen can save a cook time and energy. You probably can't change the basic shape of your kitchen to make it more efficient. But you can organize the space you have.

Kitchen design

The basic arrangement of a kitchen helps determine its efficiency. A kitchen's arrangement is based upon the placement of the refrigerator/freezer, sink and range. These three units form the points of an imaginary triangle. This triangle is called a *work triangle*. See 5-2. When you cook, you travel back and forth between the three points of the work triangle many times. If the distance between the points is fairly short, cooking takes less time and energy. Ideally, the total distance between the three points should be no more that 6 m (21 feet).

Study the work triangles in the six basic kitchen arrangements shown in 5-3. Most kitchens are variations of one of these basic arrangements.

EKCO HOUSEWARES CO.

5-1 To season a pan, lightly coat the inside with oil. Heat the pan slowly. Then turn off the heat and let the pan cool slowly. Wipe the surface with a paper towel.

Work centers

The work triangle points out the three most important kitchen work centers.

The refrigerator-freezer is the focal point of the *food storage center,* 5-4. In addition to the refrigerator-freezer, cabinets and counter space are also important parts of this center. Cabinets are needed to store foods such as canned goods, flour, sugar, cake mixes and cereal products. Counter space is needed when groceries are unpacked. Counter space in this center may also be used for mixing and baking.

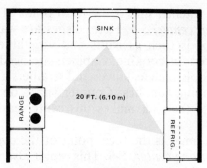

5-2 *The work triangle includes (1) the refrigerator area, (2) the sink area and (3) the range area.*

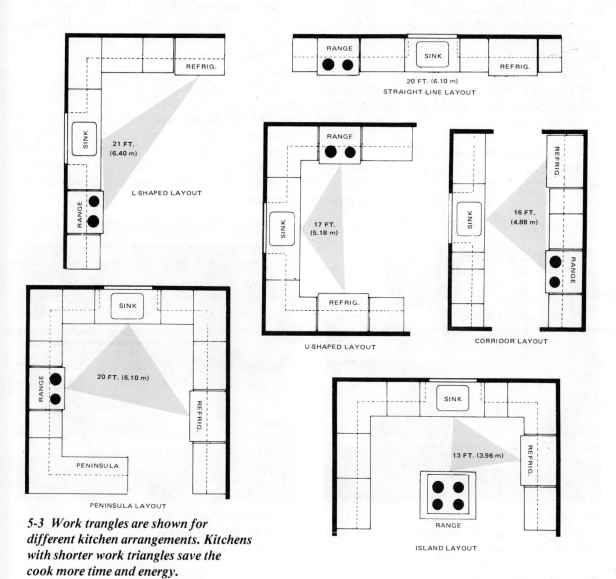

5-3 *Work trangles are shown for different kitchen arrangements. Kitchens with shorter work triangles save the cook more time and energy.*

The kitchen sink is the focal point of the *cleanup center,* 5-5. Here, dishes are washed, and foods such as fruits and vegetables are prepared for cooking. Cabinets are needed to store tools such as knives and strainers as well as cleaning supplies. Counter space on both sides of the sink makes this center easier to use.

The range is the focal point of the *cooking and serving center,* 5-6. This center also needs some cabinet space for storage. Food preparation equipment such as pots, pans and measuring tools should be stored here. Ideally, small appliances and serving dishes should also be stored in this area.

Some kitchens have enough space for additional work centers such as *mixing* and *planning centers.* The mixing center contains such tools as an electric mixer and baking pans. The planning center may contain a desk area and telephone. Here, cookbooks and recipes are often stored.

Storing utensils for easy access

Storage is very important in kitchen arrangement. Food preparation is most efficient when tools are stored where they are most often used. For instance, turners, ladles and skillets are used at the range. They should be stored within easy reach, as shown in 5-7. Cutting boards and knives might be located near the sink since many foods need to be washed before they are cut.

Some small kitchens have very limited storage space. In these kitchens, frequently-used tools can be hung on pegboard or from the ceiling. Tools can also be left on the counter in containers where they are easy to reach. Tools which are used less often and some canned goods may have to be stored elsewhere in the home.

Some kitchen cabinets are built for convenient storage, as shown in 5-8. In other cases, cabinet space can be made more usable by adding ready-made storage devices. See 5-9 and 5-10.

Does your kitchen need more storage space? If so, you can often find ideas by looking through home furnishings magazines and visiting local kitchen supply centers. Sometimes utility companies have demonstration kitchens or publications about kitchen arrangements. These are good sources of ideas too.

QUAKER MAID

5-4 *A counter next to the refrigerator-freezer makes it easy to sort foods before storing them.*

KIRSCH

5-5 *Counter space on both sides of the kitchen sink makes cleanup chores easier.*

GENERAL ELECTRIC

5-6 *This cooking and serving center is located near the dining area. A pass-through makes serving food quick and easy.*

5-7 *It may be possible to hang frequently-used tools near the range where they are handy.*

AMERICAN GAS ASSN.

5-8 *This cabinet has dividers which help separate cookie sheets and other large, thin items.*

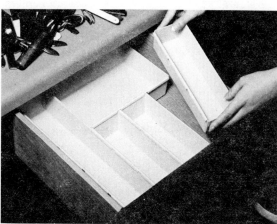

RUBBERMAID INC.

5-9 *A drawer insert organizes tools.*

RUBBERMAID INC.

5-10 *Pull-out shelves make it easier to reach items stored in the back of cabinets.*

to Define

cleanup center . . .
cooking center . . .
dry measures . . .
food storage center . . .
liquid measures . . .
mixing center . . .
planning center . . .
season . . . serving center . . .
small measures . . .
work triangle

to Discuss

1. When you start to equip your first kitchen, what types of tools should you select?
2. How do liquid and dry measures differ?
3. Which characteristics are most important to consider when selecting pots and pans?
4. Name at least five pieces of equipment you would need for baking.
5. List materials from which baking pans are usually made.
6. Why should tools made of wood never be put in the dishwasher or soaked in water?
7. What are the three main areas of the work triangle?
8. How can a small work triangle help the cook to be more efficient?
9. What tools would you want closest to the sink?
10. What tools would be used most often at the range?
11. Why is storage important in kitchen arrangement?

to Do

1. Make a list of all the tools in your home or school kitchen. Note where they are stored and how often they are used. Suggest ways to improve the organization of the kitchen.
2. Collect pictures of different kitchens. Analyze the work triangle and the various work centers in each. Which kitchens seem most efficient? Which have the best storage arrangements? Create a plan for your "ideal kitchen."
3. List factors to consider (material, cover design, cost, etc.) when selecting pots and pans. Visit the housewares department of a local store to compare the kinds of pots and pans available.
4. Suppose you were given $200 to furnish your first kitchen with the tools described in this chapter. How would you spend the money? Which tools would

you buy first? Which tools would you buy new? Which tools would you buy used? Which tools would you be unable to afford on this limited budget?
5. Create a display showing clever storage ideas.
6. Divide into two groups. Each group (using the same recipe) will make biscuits. Group one will prepare the recipe using measuring tools. Group two will prepare the recipe using no measuring tools. Compare and discuss the results.
7. Demonstrate how to season a pan.
8. Plan a meal. List all the tools you would need to prepare the meal. Can some tools be used for more than one task?
9. Demonstrate the various uses for a food grater.
10. Create a display of tools made from different materials (such as aluminum, copper, wood, glass, etc.). How does the material influence the care and appearance of the tools?
11. Invite a kitchen designer to class to discuss kitchen planning.

The kitchen cupboard

6

What would you expect to find inside a typical kitchen cupboard? After reading this chapter, you will be able to explain the importance of keeping a supply of staple foods. You will be able to list the staple foods needed in a typical kitchen and describe how to use and store them properly.

Years ago, almost every home had a *pantry*. The pantry was a small room lined with shelves. It was a storage place for kitchen supplies, especially food. In a typical pantry, you could find flour, sugar, coffee, tea, seasonings and fats such as lard. You could probably also find many foods that had been pickled and canned at home.

Today, few homes have a pantry. Supplies are now stored in rather small kitchen cabinets (or cupboards).

Why don't we need pantries anymore? One reason is that we shop more often. This allows us to buy smaller amounts of food. A second reason is that we cook fewer foods from scratch. As a result, we need fewer ingredients. A third reason is that we don't eat very many home-canned foods. Therefore, we don't have to store lots of jars of these foods. Finally, we use an appliance that didn't exist years ago—the freezer. We freeze many foods for future use.

Although our cupboards aren't as full as pantries were, we do need to keep some supplies on hand. There are no rules about what foods and other supplies to keep in your kitchen. However, the following paragraphs will give you some ideas. Beyond this basic knowledge, experience and common sense will be your best guides.

Staple foods are foods which are eaten or used regularly. Basic ingredients such as flour, sugar, fat and oils, spices, flavorings and vinegar are staple foods. They are used regularly to make many food products. Milk, fruit juices, coffee, tea, cocoa and beverage mixes are staple foods. Other foods you may keep on hand are meats, fruits, vegetables, cheese, eggs, bread, canned soup and basic mixes. *Condiments* can be considered staples too. Examples of condiments are catsup, mustard, relish, mayonnaise and salad dressings. Preparing a meal without some staple foods would be almost impossible.

You will need some foods in your kitchen to help you handle unexpected occasions such as surprise guests. If you have cheese and crackers, pretzels, chips and the ingredients for dips, you will be ready to serve snacks. You should also have the foods you would need to serve a simple meal on short notice. Canned soups can be a big help. They can be added to leftover meat and served over noodles, toast or biscuits. Cream soups can be used as a base for many casseroles. Cheese soup can be a quick cheese sauce for vegetables or main dishes. Canned fruits can be used to make attractive fruit salads, 6-1. Ice cream or fruit can be served for a quick dessert.

You should also be prepared for real emergencies. What would happen if your electricity were cut off during a storm? What could you eat for a day or two if you had no means of cooking? You could eat canned meats, canned fruits, peanut butter and crackers if these foods were in your cupboard. What foods could you eat if you became sick? Foods such as canned or dried broth, gelatin, tea and toast would come in handy then.

Your kitchen cupboard should also contain some materials for wrapping and storing foods. Plastic films are handy for wrapping or covering almost any food. Aluminum foil can be used in the same way. It is also useful for covering foods in the oven to keep them from drying out. Freezer paper is strong and specially coated for wrapping foods for freezing. Waxed paper and plastic bags can also be used for wrapping and storing foods.

This chapter will focus on various staple foods. It will suggest ways to use and store them. Some staples, such as fruits, vegetables and dairy products, will be described in other chapters.

STARCHES

Starches are used to thicken mixtures such as sauces, puddings and gravies. *Flour* and *cornstarch* are the starches used most often in cooking. At times you may find a recipe that calls for *tapioca* or another starch. Flour, of course, is also used in baking. There are several types of flour from which to choose.

Flour for baking

Most flour sold in the United States is made from wheat. *Bread flour* is made from hard varieties of wheat which have a fairly high protein content. This flour gives yeast breads a chewy texture. *Cake flour* is just the opposite. It is made from soft wheat. It gives cakes a fine, tender texture. Most people do not bake enough breads or cakes to make it worthwhile to keep these special flours on hand.

All-purpose flour is the most common flour sold. It is a blend of hard and soft wheats. As its name implies, all-purpose flour can be used for many purposes. *Self-rising flour* is like all-purpose flour, but it has salt and leavening added.

In some stores you may find other kinds of flours, such as whole wheat, rye, soy, rice, barley or buckwheat. Each of these flours is quite different from the others. Always use the kind of flour that a recipe specifies.

Using starches to thicken mixtures

Flour, cornstarch or tapioca can be used to thicken most gravies, puddings and sauces.

When used as a thickening agent, white flour makes a creamy, cloudy-looking mixture. Most people like the creamy look and texture of flour gravy, 6-2.

Cornstarch and tapioca produce almost transparent mixtures. (Tapioca forms a lumpy, but clear, mixture.) Because cornstarch and tapioca do not cloud the color of fruit, they are often used to thicken fruit mixtures. For instance, they are used in pie fillings and fruit glazes, 6-3. Cornstarch is also used in gravies and in many Chinese dishes.

Cornstarch has about twice the power to thicken as flour or tapioca. This is important to know if you want to make a substitution in a recipe. Suppose you didn't have cornstarch. You could use flour instead. You would have to use twice as much flour as the amount of cornstarch listed in the recipe.

When cooking with starches, lumps may form. There are three methods you can use to prevent lumps. Usually, a recipe will tell you which method to use.

1. Blend the starch with hot fat. Stir in the liquid slowly.
2. Stir the starch into a small amount of cold water. When mixed well, stir this into the other ingredients.
3. Mix the starch with other dry ingredients, such as sugar. Stir this mixture into the liquid.

Gravies, puddings and sauces made with starches should be cooked briefly after they thicken to improve the flavor. But be careful. If starch mixtures are heated too long, heated at too high a temperature or stirred too much,

EVAPORATED MILK ASSOC.

6-1 With a few cans of fruit, you can make a quick salad platter for unexpected guests.

REVERE COPPER AND BRASS, INC.

6-2 Gravies and sauces thickened with flour have a creamy appearance and texture.

the starch will begin to break down. The mixture will become thin.

Starches should be stored in tightly closed containers in a dry, cool place.

SUGARS

Sugar has many uses besides sweetening foods and beverages. It is a stabilizer, which means it can be used to help beaten egg whites and whipped cream keep their foamy shapes. In baking, it helps to tenderize the proteins of wheat and eggs. When sugar and fruit are combined, sugar will draw out juice from fruit, making a sweet syrup. When sugar is heated, it turns brown. This adds to the color of many foods, especially baked goods. Sugar adds flavor to many foods that don't taste sweet, such as soups and salad draessings. In strong concentrations (as in jams and jellies), sugar acts as a preservative.

Common table sugar is made from either sugar cane or sugar beets. *Granulated white sugar* consists of small, coarse crystals. *Superfine sugar* has smaller crystals. It is popular for beverages because it dissolves quickly. The finest sugar is *powdered* or *confectioner's sugar*. It is made by grinding granulated white sugar to a fine, soft powder. Powdered sugar dissolves very quickly. It is used in many icings. Sometimes baked products are "dusted" with a little powdered sugar. This is often done for decoration and a touch of extra sweetness, 6-4.

Brown sugar is not as refined as white sugar. Brown sugar contains some molasses left over from the refining process. The darker the color the brown sugar is, the stronger the flavor will be. Because brown sugar is moist, it must be measured differently than white sugar. The standard way to measure brown sugar is to pack it firmly into a dry measure.

Granulated brown sugar is available in some supermarkets. It handles and pours like granulated white sugar. *Liquid brown sugar* is also available. Don't substitute these products for regular brown sugar without checking the label directions.

All sugar should be stored in tightly covered containers in a cool, dry place. Brown sugar hardens if it dries out. This causes problems when measuring it. To soften the sugar enough to measure it, heat the hard lumps slightly in the oven. Or put an apple slice with the brown sugar in a tightly closed container overnight. This should restore some of the lost moisture.

SYRUPS

All *syrups* have one thing in common. They are rather thick, sticky liquids with some kind of sugar as the main ingredient. Many people use syrups on pancakes, waffles and French toast. Syrups are also used as ingredients in many recipes.

Maple syrup is made from the thin sap of sugar maple trees. Most of the water is evaporated to thicken the sap into a syrup. High-quality maple syrup is light and clear. *Maple-blended syrups* combine maple syrup with other sugar syrups. These are very popular, and they cost less than pure maple syrup, 6-5.

Honey is made by bees from the nectar of flowers. You may be able to buy honey with a piece of the honeycomb (where bees store honey in the hive). Usually, however, the honey is removed from the comb and sold separately. The color and flavor of honey vary according to the flower from which it is made.

Molasses is the brown syrup separated from raw sugar during manufacturing. Molasses varies from a light, sweet syrup with a mild flavor to a dark, rather bitter syrup. Light molasses is sometimes called "table molasses." This name refers to its use at the dining table—as a pancake syrup, for instance. Both light and dark molasses can be used in cooking. They add flavor and color to spice cakes, cookies, baked beans and certain candies.

Corn syrup is a mixture of water and sugars obtained from corn. Light corn syrup is clear and colorless. Dark corn syrup is made by mixing corn syrup with another type of syrup for extra color and flavor. Both light and dark corn syrups can be used as pancake

6-4 *Dusting a cake with powdered sugar is fast and makes the cake look attractive.*

REVERE COPPER AND BRASS, INC.

6-3 *Fruit sauces thickened with cornstarch are bright and clear.*

MARCELLO MARCOCCIA

6-5 *When shopping for maple syrup, check the labels. Imitation syrups may be labeled "maple-flavored syrup," "pancake syrup" or "breakfast syrup."*

syrup. Most often, they are used as ingredients in recipes.

You can store syrups at room temperature in tightly covered containers. A label may advise you to refrigerate a syrup once it has been opened. If crystals form, dissolve them by placing the bottle of syrup in a bowl or pan of hot water.

FATS AND OILS

Fats and oils come in many forms, as shown in 6-6. They have many uses. They are important ingredients in some foods. For instance, the texture and consistency of mayonnaise depends upon fats and oils. Fats and oils make pastry, cakes and other baked products tender. They add color, flavor and crispness to fried foods. They also help prevent foods from sticking to pans.

Butter and *margarine* are common fats. Both contain 80 percent fat. Butter is made from milk fat. Margarine is made from vegetable oils or a combination of vegetable oils and animal fats. The kinds of oil and fat used to make margarine are listed on the label. Butter and margarine can be substituted for each other in cooking.

Whipped butter and *whipped margarine* have air beaten into them. This increases the volume and makes them easy to spread. These whipped products contain less fat per volume. Therefore, they cannot be directly substituted for regular butter or margarine in recipes. *Diet* or *imitation margarine* is another product you cannot use as a substitute in a recipe. It has fewer kilojoules (Calories) than regular margarine, mainly because water replaces some of the fat.

All butter and margarine products should be wrapped or covered and stored in the refrigerator. For longer storage, well-wrapped butter or margarine can be frozen for a few months.

Shortening is the common term for "hydrogenated shortening." *Shortening* is a solid, white, 100 percent fat product. It is usually made from vegetable oils that have been hydrogenated to make them solid. It

may also contain animal fat. Shortening is used in baking and frying. When a recipe says to "grease the pan," it is a good fat to use. It is flavorless and does not burn easily.

Shortening should be stored in an airtight container away from heat and light. It can be stored at room temperature for a few months. For longer storage, it should be refrigerated.

Lard is a fat made from the fatty tissue of pork. Most lard sold today is used by professional bakeries. Some people buy it for home baking (especially for pie crusts) because it makes baked products very tender.

Some brands of lard can be stored on the shelf, but most need refrigeration. Check the label for storage directions.

Salad and *cooking oils* are made from one or more vegetable oils. These oils may come from peanuts, soybeans, cottonseeds, corn and other plant sources. The source of the oil is listed on the label. Except for olive oil, most salad and cooking oils have little or no taste. Olive oil has a unique flavor, and many people prefer it for making salad dressings. It is also widely used in Mediterranean cooking.

Oils should be stored in a cool part of the kitchen. For long term storage, they can be refrigerated. Refrigeration may make some oils look cloudy, but this will not affect their quality.

SEASONINGS AND FLAVORINGS

Seasonings and flavorings add exciting variety to foods. Just a tiny bit can turn a plain dish into a real taste sensation. The problem for most beginning cooks is knowing which seasoning to use and how much.

Spices come from the bark, root, fruit or bud of many kinds of plants. Usually, these plants grow in tropical climates. *Herbs* come from the leaves of certain plants which grow in many parts of the world. (You can even grow some of your own herbs, as pictured in 6-7.) *Blends* are popular combinations of spices and herbs. Examples are poultry seasoning, chili powder and seasoned salt.

Vegetable seasonings, such as onion and garlic, are available in powdered, salt and minced forms. *Seeds*, such as sesame, caraway and mustard seeds, are used to add flavor and texture to foods. MSG (monosodium glutamate) is a *flavor enhancer*. It has no flavor of its own, but it increases the natural flavor of many foods.

Extracts are the oils and flavor essences of certain foods, usually dissolved in alcohol. Common extracts are made from vanilla beans, almonds and oranges. You can buy pure extracts (the real thing) or imitation extracts. The rising prices of pure extracts have made imitation products more popular.

The variety of seasonings and flavorings may seem confusing at first. Start with just a few that are used most often. Your list of "basics" might include salt, pepper, parsley, garlic powder, cinnamon, nutmeg, seasoned salt, oregano, paprika and allspice. Become familiar with the effects these seasonings have on foods. Then gradually add others as you try interesting new recipes.

How to use seasonings

When you begin cooking with seasonings, use tiny amounts. You can add more later if you like, but it's hard to remove seasonings if you've added too much. Start with 1 mL (1/4 teaspoon) for every four servings if you are not following a recipe.

A few other tips on using seasonings may help you.

- Dried herbs are stronger than fresh ones. (This is because dried herbs are more concentrated.)
- Almost all fresh herbs bought in whole-leaf form need to be crushed, cut or "bruised" before you use them. This releases their flavors. You can do this with your fingers, a knife or scissors. Or you can press the leaves with a wooden spoon in a bowl.
- For uncooked dressings, such as French dressing, combine seasonings with other ingredients several hours in advance. Time is needed for the flavors to develop fully.
- For dishes cooked a long time, do just the opposite. Add the seasonings near the end of the cooking time. This prevents the flavors of the seasonings from "cooking out."

BERGWALL PRODUCTIONS, INC. FILMSTRIPS

6-6 Fats and oils are staples. They have many uses in food preparation.

EVAPORATED MILK ASSOC.

6-7 Many herbs are easy to grow in a garden or on a windowsill. Shown here are thyme, chervil and savory.

- When you use whole herbs and spices, such as bay leaves, sprigs of parsley, cloves or peppercorns, wrap them in a small piece of cheesecloth, 6-8. (A tea ball can be used in place of the cheesecloth. A tea ball is a small container full of holes made for holding loose tea leaves.) The cheesecloth makes it easy to remove the herbs and spices when cooking is finished. This helps you avoid biting into them later. The French use this method with herbs and call it a *bouquet garni*. This method is used often in soups and stews.

How to store seasonings

Seasonings tend to lose flavor easily. Herbs and spices should be kept as fresh as possible. They should smell rather strong when you open their containers.

Heat and dampness damage herbs and spices. The best way to store them is in tightly sealed containers away from the range and sink. Sunlight can also affect some seasonings.

Whole herbs and spices keep better than their ground forms, 6-9. Ground spices begin to lose their flavor after about six months. Dating your seasonings as you get them will help you keep track of their freshness.

VINEGAR

Vinegar is an acid liquid that adds a sour, tart flavor to most food. Vinegar is a basic ingredient in most salad dressings. It is used in many other foods, such as cakes, sometimes so subtly that you may not detect its flavor.

The color, flavor and odor of each type of vinegar depends upon the ingredients from which it is made. Vinegar can be made from fruits or grains. Common vinegars include cider vinegar, distilled white vinegar, wine vinegar and malt vinegar. Some vinegars are also flavored with herbs. The types of vinegar you keep on hand will depend on the taste you prefer and how you plan to use it. All vinegars have about the same level of acidity. For a milder flavor, you can dilute vinegar by adding water to it.

For best results, use the type of vinegar specified in a recipe. All vinegars can be stored at room temperature in tightly capped bottles.

COFFEE

Coffee is one of the most popular beverages in the United States, 6-10. People drink it to help them wake up in the morning. They take "coffee breaks" during the day. Coffee is served at most meals. It is almost always offered to guests. Coffee is something you'll always want to have on hand in your kitchen.

Coffee is made from the roasted beans of coffee plants. The flavor of coffee depends on the variety of the coffee plant and where it is grown (soil, altitude and climate). Most coffee sold in the United States is a blend of several varieties. Coffee flavor also depends on how the beans have been roasted. In Europe, a heavy roast is preferred. But in the United States, a mild to medium roast is more popular.

You can buy coffee in several forms: instant, instant freeze-dried and ground. Some people buy whole coffee beans and grind coffee themselves in a coffee mill.

Instant and *instant freeze-dried coffees* are popular because they are quick and easy to make, especially in small amounts. Instant coffee is made by drying brewed coffee. In making freeze-dried coffee, brewed coffee is frozen and then dried.

Most coffee sold in the United States is ground coffee. When you buy ground coffee, be sure to buy the grind best suited to your coffee maker. *Regular grind* is the coarsest grind. It should be used in percolators. *Drip grind* is a medium grind designed for drip coffee makers. *Fine grind* is used in vacuum coffee makers. *ADC grind* is a fine grind made especially for automatic drip coffee makers.

Whichever coffee-making method you use, read and follow the directions on the coffee maker and/or coffee package. For the best flavor, be sure the coffee maker is clean and the water is fresh and cold. Use the recommended amount of coffee. Do not brew the

6-8 A bouquet garni is made by wrapping spices and herbs in cheesecloth. They can then be removed easily when cooking is finished.

6-10 Coffee is often served with sweets for snacks and desserts.

6-9 Whole nutmeg will keep is flavor longer than ground nutmeg.

coffee too long or at too high a temperature. If you do, the coffee could taste bitter.

Caffeine, a substance that acts as a stimulant, is found in coffee. This is one reason why coffee is such a popular "pick-me-up." However, caffeine bothers some people. They become nervous and have trouble sleeping if they drink coffee at night. Fortunately caffeine can be removed from coffee. A variety of instant and ground coffees can be bought in *decaffeinated* form.

Espresso is a coffee that originated in Italy. It is brewed in a special coffee maker using dark roasted and finely ground coffee. Espresso is usually served in small cups because it is very strong. *Café au lait* is popular in many parts of Europe, especially France. It is a mixture of equal amounts of coffee and hot milk. *Iced coffee* is a popular summer beverage. It is made by pouring freshly made, strong coffee over crushed ice in a glass. There are also a number of *flavored coffees* available. These are usually instant coffees with flavorings such as mint, chocolate, or orange added to them.

Always store coffee in a tightly covered container in a cool place. Coffee loses some of its flavor at warm temperatures. Many experts recommend storing ground and instant coffee in the refrigerator or freezer.

TEA

Tea is made from the leaves of tea bushes, 6-11. Young tender leaves and unopened leaf buds make the best quality tea. Quality is also related to where the tea is grown (region, altitude, soil and climate).

The main categories of tea are *black* and *green*. Both black and green teas are made from the same kinds of leaves. The main difference is that leaves used to make black teas are fermented. During this process, some of the aroma is lost. But some of the more bitter flavor substances are lost too. Black tea has a yellow-brown color and tastes rich. Green tea has a green-yellow color and a bitter taste. *Oolong tea* is partly fermented. Oolong tea makes a tea that is a cross between black and green teas in aroma and flavor.

Most of the tea purchased in the United States is black tea. Sometimes you may notice words such as Orange Pekoe and Fannings on the label. These are not different flavors of tea. These words refer to the grade of a tea. (Grades are based on the size of the tea leaves used.) Broken Orange Pekoe is the best grade of black tea. The flavor of black teas varies. It can be delicate or strong in flavor. Most teas sold in the United States are blends of leaves from several varieties of tea bushes.

You can buy tea as loose tea leaves, in tea bags or in instant mixes. Many instant mixes have sugar and lemon added. A variety of spices and flavorings, such as cinnamon, mint or orange, may also be added to tea. See 6-12. Always prepare tea according to package directions. Use fresh cold water and the recommended amount of tea.

Many beverages called "teas" are made from plants other than tea bushes. *Herb teas* are made from the leaves of various herbs such as mint, basil, marjoram and sage. Teas can be made from some flowers. *Rose hip tea* is made from the small fruit that grows at the base of the rose blossom. *Sassafras tea* is made from the bark of the sassafras roots.

TEA COUNCIL U.S.A.

6-11 Tea is usually picked by hand in India.

Several other kinds of substances (such as nutshells) can also be brewed to make teas. Some people use teas for medical reasons, but beware of unusual health claims.

Teas should be stored in tightly closed containers in a cool, dry place.

CHOCOLATE PRODUCTS

Chocolate products are used in many foods and beverages, 6-13. Many forms of chocolate are available, and there are major differences between them. Be careful to use the type specified in your recipe.

Chocolate is made from roasted, ground cacao beans. The beans have a high content of fat called cocoa butter. When ground, they form a semi-liquid paste which hardens into a brown block called *bitter chocolate*.

Bitter chocolate is sometimes called *unsweetened chocolate* or *baking chocolate*. It is used only in cooking. It is usually sold in packages containing small squares. These squares of chocolate are usually melted before being added to other ingredients in recipes. See 6-14.

Semi-sweet chocolate and *sweet chocolate* have sugar added. These types of chocolate usually come in chips or bars.

Milk chocolate is used in some recipes. But it is best known as a candy, eaten just as it is. Sugar, milk and vanilla are added to chocolate to make this product.

Chocolate syrup is sweet chocolate in a liquid form. *Chocolate sauce* is thicker and richer than syrup. Both are popular as dessert toppings. Chocolate syrup is often used to flavor beverages.

Cocoa is a powder made from chocolate with some of the cocoa butter removed. Instant cocoa has cocoa, sugar, milk solids and flavorings added. It can be mixed with water, but milk makes a richer cup of cocoa.

Keep chocolate products in airtight containers or tightly wrapped packages. Store them in a cool, dry place. Cocoa keeps better

TEA COUNCIL U.S.A.

6-12 You can use spices and fruits to create your own flavored teas.

HERSHEY'S

6-13 Chocolate and chocolate products are used in a variety of baked goods and beverages.

than chocolate because it contains less fat. In hot weather, small white patches may appear on the outside of chocolate. These are only bits of cocoa butter. This may look unattractive, but the flavor is not affected.

ORGANIZING YOUR KITCHEN CUPBOARD

Stocking your kitchen can be expensive, especially when you are just beginning. Start slowly and build up your supplies gradually, as you need new items.

Avoid buying large amounts of things you will not use very often. When you are running low on something, add it to your next shopping list. That way, you won't get caught short in the middle of a recipe or meal preparation.

Keep staples by the counter area where you will be using them. Put items you use most often on lower shelves where you can reach them easily.

Remember, staples keep better if they are stored in a cool, dry area, 6-15. Generally, try to avoid using shelves right by the range or sink to store food. Also, before you buy decorative cannisters or storage containers, check them carefully to see if they are really suitable for storing food. They should protect food from air, moisture and insects.

SILVERSTONE® and TEFLON® —DUPONT'S NON-STICK FINISHES

6-14 Chocolate bars and squares are usually melted first when used as recipe ingredients.

6-15 Well-organized shelves make it easy to see what foods you have on hand. Foods which are properly stored keep their quality longer.

114

$_{to}Define$

all-purpose flour . . .
baking chocolate . . .
black tea . . . blends . . .
bouquet garni . . .
bread flour . . .
brown sugar . . . caffeine . . .
cake flour . . . cocoa . . .
condiments . . .
confectioner's sugar . . .
espresso . . . extracts . . .
flavor enhancer . . .
green tea . . . herbs . . .
instant freeze-dried coffee . . .
lard . . . margarine . . .
milk chocolate . . .
molasses . . . oolong tea . . .
self-rising flour . . .
semi-sweet chocolate . . .
shortening . . . spices . . .
staple foods . . . syrup

$_{to}Discuss$

1. Name some staple foods you are likely to find in a kitchen.
2. What kind of flour is best to keep on hand for general use?
3. Which has more power to thicken a sauce — flour or cornstarch?
4. How should you store regular brown sugar? Why?
5. What should you do if crystals begin to form in syrup?
6. Can you substitute butter and margarine for each other in recipes?
7. Which are stronger — fresh or dried herbs?
8. What two conditions are the most damaging to the flavor of spices and herbs? How should you store spices and herbs?

9. What might cause coffee to taste bitter?
10. What are the two main categories of teas? Which is the most common in the United States?
11. Why does cocoa keep better than chocolate?
12. Name four guidelines for organizing your kitchen cupboards.

$_{to}Do$

1. Make a list of the staple foods in your home or school kitchen. Put a check (✓) by the items you think are important to keep on hand. Did you find any unnecessary items? Were any necessary items missing?
2. Plan three menus you could prepare quickly if unexpected guests arrived at dinner time.
3. Find a pudding recipe. Divide the class into three groups. Prepare the recipe as directed, except that each group will use the same amount of three different thickening agents. Group 1 will use flour. Group 2 will use cornstarch. Group 3 will use tapioca. How do the puddings compare in thickness? Appearance?
4. Visit the grocery store and list the kinds of butters and margarines that are available. Note their sizes and prices. Which might you

choose for cooking? Which might you spread on toast or other breads? Give reasons for your choices.
5. Divide the seasonings and flavorings in your home or school kitchen into groups such as: herbs, spices, blends, seeds, vegetable seasonings, flavor enhancers and extracts. Take notes on the aroma, color and other characteristics of each. Then cover the labels. See if you can identify each seasoning or flavoring by the way it looks and smells.
6. Design a bulletin board that shows how to make coffee in at least three different types of coffee makers. Be sure to include information on what kind of grind should be used in each type of coffee maker.
7. Make coffee samples using (a) ground coffee; (b) instant coffee; (c) instant freeze-dried coffee; (d) decaffeinated instant coffee. Taste each type. Compare the flavor of each. Figure the cost per cup of each. Which would you buy? Why?
8. Make tea samples using tea leaves, tea bags and instant tea. Compare the flavor and cost of making each tea.

7

The cook's language

How are your favorite foods prepared? After reading this chapter, you will know how to follow basic recipes. You will be able to define words, symbols and abbreviations commonly used in recipes. You will also know how to measure accurately and how to make substitutions when certain ingredients are not available.

There are hundreds of terms used to describe special ways of preparing food. As a good cook, you will want to try interesting new recipes. But before you can cook with recipes, you must understand the special language cooks use.

THE LANGUAGE OF RECIPES

Recipes are like road maps. They give you directions. If you follow them properly, you will end up with good food. Recipes tell you what ingredients to use and how to prepare them. They also tell you how long to cook food. They may tell you what size pan to use and how many servings you can expect to get.

Following recipes

Recipes are written in many different ways. Sometimes they are written in paragraphs like this book. The paragraph format is fine for short recipes like whipped cream. But it is difficult to follow if the recipe has many steps.

The easiest and most common recipe format lists the ingredients and then lists the preparation steps. Ingredients are usually listed in order of use. Each step in preparation is described or explained. When the recipe is written so that each step begins on a new line, it is even easier to follow.

You should always read through the entire recipe before you start to cook. Check to see that you have all the ingredients and equipment you need. Make sure you understand exactly what you will need to do. If you are not sure what a term means, look it up. Your cookbook may have a section that explains terms and techniques. If not, use a dictionary.

Some recipes are written with standard symbols or abbreviations. They are the cook's shorthand. Magazines and cookbooks sometimes use this shorthand to save space. When you are copying a recipe, you may want to save time by using symbols or abbreviations. The most common ones are listed in 7-1.

MEASURING MAKES A DIFFERENCE

Most recipes list exact amounts of each ingredient you need to use. These exact amounts are called *measurements*. Measurements can be in grams, litres, pounds, ounces, cups, teaspoons, or tablespoons. It is important that you have the proper measuring tools for the recipe you are following. If your recipe lists metric measurements, you will need to use metric measures. If it lists conventional measurements, you will need to use conventional measuring cups and spoons.

Practice makes measuring faster. Liquid and dry ingredients are measured differently. See 7-2 for measuring tips.

Careful measurements are important when cooking most foods. Use the same amounts and follow the same preparation steps each time you prepare a recipe. You then should get the same good results. It is very important to measure accurately when you are baking. Recipes for batters and doughs have certain proportions of dry and liquid ingredients and

SYMBOLS AND ABBREVIATIONS USED IN RECIPES

mL	millilitre
L	litre
g	gram
kg	kilogram
tsp. or t.	teaspoon
tbsp. or T.	tablespoon
c. or C.	cup
pt.	pint
qt.	quart
oz.	ounce
lb. or #	pound

7-1 *Using symbols or abbreviations can save you time and space when you copy a recipe.*

MEASURING TIPS

Flour	Spoon sifted flour into a dry measure until it is overfilled. Level off the top of the measure with a metal spatula. Never pack flour into a measure.
Fat	Press fat into a dry measure so there are no air pockets. Level off the top of the measure with a metal spatula. Remove the fat with a rubber spatula. For best results, fat should be at room temperature. Butter and margarine in sticks can usually be measured using lines on the wrapper.
Granulated sugar	Spoon sugar into a dry measure until it is overfilled. Level off the top of the measure with a metal spatula.
Brown sugar	Firmly pack brown sugar into a dry measure. Level off the top of the measure with a metal spatula.
Powdered sugar	Spoon sifted powdered sugar into a dry measure until it is overfilled. Level off the top of the measure with a metal spatula.
Liquids	Place a liquid measure on a flat surface. Pour liquid into the measure until it reaches the desired line. View at eye level.

7-2 *When you prepare a recipe, each ingredient should be measured correctly.*

leavening agents. If you change these proportions, you may drastically change the product. See 7-3.

Sometimes exact measurements are not as critical. This is true with foods like soups, stews and casseroles, 7-4. Experienced cooks sometimes experiment with amounts of seasonings. You can often eliminate an ingredient. For instance, if someone in your family dislikes mushrooms, you can leave them out. But remember, the recipe will be slightly different. In general, it is best to follow recipes the way they are written. This is especially true if you are preparing the food for the first time.

When you want to make more or less

Sometimes you may want to double a recipe. You may be planning a large party. Or you may want to make more than you need and freeze part for future use. When you double a recipe, it's a good idea to write the doubled measurements on a piece of paper. Once you start working, you may forget that you are doubling the recipe. You may forget to double an important ingredient. A good safety precaution is to measure all the ingredients ahead of time. Then check your recipe a second time before you begin to cook.

To cut a recipe in half, you need to understand measurement equivalents. Suppose a recipe you wanted to cut in half called for a tablespoon of sugar. If you know that one tablespoon equals three teaspoons, then you will know how much sugar to add. One-half of three teaspoons (or one and one-half teaspoons) equals one-half tablespoon. Equivalents are also important when you have to work with odd measurements. Suppose you needed to divide one-third cup in half. There is no standard measuring tool for one-sixth cup. But if you know equivalents, you can figure out that one-sixth cup equals two tablespoons plus two teaspoons.

Measuring with the metric system is easy. It's less confusing because it has fewer units of measure. Using conventional measures, the same amount of milk could be called 16 tablespoons, 8 fluid ounces, 1 cup or 1/2 pint. In metrics, it would simply be called 250 mL. Common metric and conventional measures are listed in 7-5. Measuring will be easier if you remember the equivalent measures given in 7-6. Metric measures are not given in 7-6 because the metric system makes the use of equivalents unnecessary.

Substitutions you can make

Sometimes a recipe calls for an ingredient you do not have on hand. Many cookbooks have a special section which lists substitutes for ingredients. Common substitutions you can make are listed in 7-7. Remember, when you substitute certain ingredients for others, the end result may change slightly. For instance, margarine can be substituted for butter in cooking. But the taste of the product may be slightly different.

7-3 Accurate measurements are important in preparing foods such as cakes.

7-4 Measurements do not need
to be exact for most soups,
stews and casseroles.

COMMON METRIC AND CONVENTIONAL MEASURES

Metric	Conventional
1 mL	1/4 teaspoon
2 mL	1/2 teaspoon
5 mL	1 teaspoon
15 mL	1 tablespoon
25 mL	1/8 cup
50 mL	1/4 cup
125 mL	1/2 cup
250 mL	1 cup
500 mL	2 cups
1000 mL or 1L	1 quart
28 g	1 ounce
450 g	1 pound

7-5 The metric system can make
measuring easier.

BASIC EQUIVALENTS

Liquid and dry measures		Liquid measures		Dry measures	
3 teaspoons	= 1 tablespoon	2 tablespoons =	1 fluid ounce	16 ounces =	1 pound
4 tablespoons	= 1/4 cup	1/2 cup =	4 fluid ounces	8 quarts =	1 peck
5 tablespoons		1 cup =	8 fluid ounces = 1/2 pint	4 pecks =	1 bushel
plus 1 teaspoon	= 1/3 cup	2 cups =	1 pint		
8 tablespoons	= 1/2 cup	4 cups =	2 pints = 1 quart		
12 tablespoons	= 3/4 cup	4 quarts =	1 gallon		
16 tablespoons	= 1 cup				

7-6 Knowing these equivalents will make
measuring easier when you follow recipes.

SUBSTITUTIONS

If you don't have this:	You can substitute this:
15 mL (1 tablespoon) cornstarch	30 mL (2 tablespoons) flour
250 mL (1 cup) cake flour	225 mL (7/8 cup) all-purpose flour
250 mL (1 cup) honey	300 mL (1 1/4 cup) sugar plus 50 mL (1/4 cup) liquid used in recipe
30 gm (1 ounce) unsweetened chocolate	50 mL (3 tablespoons) unsweetened cocoa powder plus 15 mL (1 tablespoon) butter or margarine
250 mL (1 cup) heavy cream	175 mL (3/4 cup) milk plus 75 mL (1/3 cup) butter
250 mL (1 cup) milk	125 mL (1/2 cup) evaporated milk plus 125 mL (1/2 cup) water
250 mL (1 cup) sour milk or buttermilk	15 mL (1 tablespoon) vinegar or lemon juice plus milk to make 250 mL (1 cup). Let this mixture stand 5-10 minutes before using.

7-7 In some cases, you can make substitutions
for ingredients you don't have on hand.

PREPARING FOOD FOR COOKING

A recipe may call for food to be prepared in a special way before it is actually cooked.

Vegetables and meats are often *breaded* before frying. To do this, you dip the food in a liquid such as beaten egg or milk. Then you roll it in crumbs made from bread, crackers or some type of cereal.

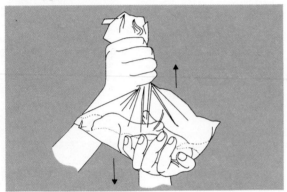

Food that is *dredged* is covered with a dry ingredient such as flour or sugar. A plastic bag makes dredging an easy task for small pieces of food.

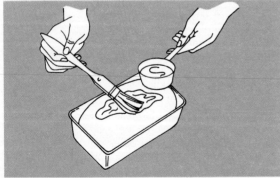

Sometimes you *brush* food with a liquid such as melted butter, orange juice or egg white. Use a pastry brush for this task.

Casseroles and other baking dishes are often *greased* before food is placed in them to prevent sticking. Use waxed paper or paper towel to spread a thin layer of shortening over the inside of the dish.

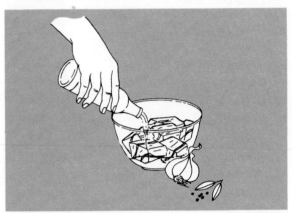

When food is *marinated,* it is usually placed in a seasoned liquid for several hours before cooking. The seasoned liquid is called a marinade. Marinades add flavor and increase tenderness of meats.

Many recipes call for dry ingredients to be *sifted* before they are measured. Sifting helps to separate particles of flour, powdered sugar and other dry ingredients. It also helps to combine the dry ingredients thoroughly in a recipe.

Pie crusts are sometimes *fluted* before baking. To flute pastry, press the dough with your fingers to form an edge which stands up. Pastry can also be "crimped" by pressing the edge with a fork.

Cutting food

There are many ways of cutting food. Sometimes you need to remove the outside layer of a food before you use it. And sometimes you need to cut food into various shapes and sizes.

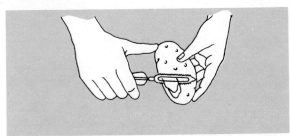

When you *pare* food, you cut away the skin with a knife or peeler. Foods that are pared include apples, potatoes and carrots. (You "peel" the outer skins of bananas and oranges.)

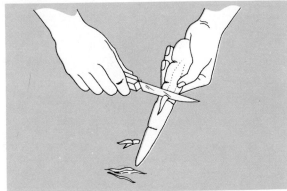

Sometimes you can *scrape* the outer skin away by rubbing it with the sharp edge of a knife. Carrots are an example of a food which can be scraped. When you scrape, you remove less of the nutritious peel than you would when you pare.

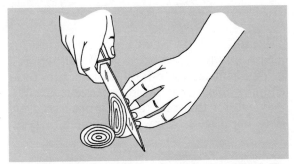

Some recipes call for food to be *sliced*. To slice, cut the food into flat pieces. The recipe may tell you if the slices should be thick or thin.

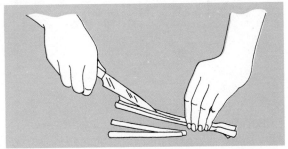

A recipe may call for food to be cut in strips. For food like ham or cheese, you would cut the food first into slices and then into long strips. For carrots and celery, you would cut the food into long, narrow pieces. When food is cut into long, thin strips, it is called *julienne*.

Food that is *cubed* or *diced* is cut into pieces the same size and shape. When you cube food, the pieces are 1 cm (1/2 inch) or larger. When you dice food, the pieces are smaller than 1 cm (1/2 inch).

Chop is a term found in many recipes. It means that the food is cut into small, uneven pieces. You can chop food with a knife, food chopper, blender or food processor. Recipes may call for the food to be chopped coarsely (into big pieces) or finely (into small pieces).

Food which is *shredded* is cut into very narrow strips. Lettuce and cabbage can be shredded with a knife. Most vegetables and cheese can be shredded with a grater.

Food which is *grated* is cut into very fine pieces. To grate food, place the food against the grater and rub it back and forth. A grater has different size grids or cutting edges. Lemon rind should be grated on the finest grid. Cheese will grate easier on a larger grid.

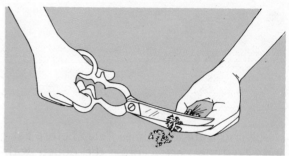

To *mince* refers to cutting food into very tiny pieces, even smaller than diced or finely chopped foods. Recipes often call for minced garlic or parsley. You can use a chef's knife to mince most foods. Parsley can be minced with a pair of kitchen shears.

To *mash* foods such as potatoes or squash, use a potato masher. This crushes the food until it has a smooth texture.

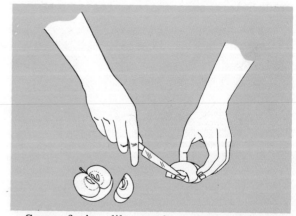

Some fruits, like apples, pears and pineapples, need to be *cored*. Remove the core of the fruit with a coring tool or paring knife.

Sometimes food such as fruit is cut into *wedges*. A wedge is thick on one side and thin on the other.

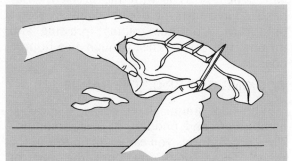

Your recipe may call for meat to be *trimmed* and *scored* before cooking. To trim meat, cut away some of the fat from around the edges. To score meat, make slashes through the outer edge of fat left on the meat. (Do not cut into the meat.) Scoring prevents the meat from curling as it cooks.

Mixing food

The following mixing terms are found in many recipes. They describe ways to put ingredients together.

Mixing is a general term for combining or blending ingredients.

To *stir,* move your spoon in a circle to mix the ingredients. Work your spoon around the outside of the bowl toward the center.

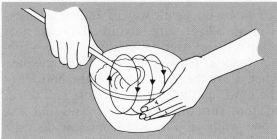

Beating uses a faster motion than stirring. To beat, use a brisk, up-and-over motion. This adds air to the mixture and makes the mixture smooth. You can use a spoon, whisk, rotary beater or electric mixer to beat.

Whipping uses the same up-and-over motion as beating. But whipping is done even faster. Whipping adds more air to the mixture. This makes the mixture lighter and larger in volume. You can use a wire whisk, rotary beater or electric mixer to whip.

Some recipes call for you to *cream* a fat, such as butter, and sugar. To do this, first soften the butter by pressing it with the back of a spoon. Then add the sugar, a little at a time. Beat the mixture until it is fluffy.

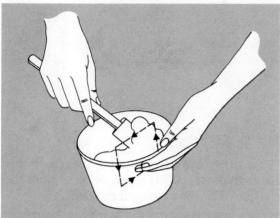

Folding is a gentle way of adding an ingredient to a light, airy mixture. To fold, pour the ingredient over the mixture. Using a rubber spatula, cut down through the mixture. Then move the spatula across the bottom of the bowl, up through the mixture and across the top. Turn the bowl often as you fold. Use slow, gentle motions so the mixture does not lose its lightness.

When you make pastry and biscuits, you may have to *cut in* shortening with a flour mixture. Cutting in means to cut solid shortening into small pieces. The pieces are completely covered with the flour mixture. You can use either a pastry blender, two knives or a fork to cut in.

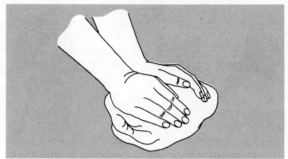

Kneading is a special technique used with doughs. To knead, first fold the dough in half. Then press it with the heels of your hands. Then turn the dough about a quarter of a turn. Continue folding, pressing and turning. It is best to knead dough on a floured board.

COOKING ON TOP OF THE RANGE

What do soup, green beans, pancakes, hamburgers and pudding have in common? They are all foods you can cook on top of the range. These foods don't look the same or taste the same. They aren't cooked the same either. Many different cooking methods are used to cook foods on top of the range.

To *boil* means to cook in liquid at a temperature high enough so that the liquid bubbles. The bubbles rise to the surface and break. Some recipes call for the liquid to be at a "rolling boil." This means that the temperature is high enough so that the bubbles form very fast throughout the liquid. A recipe may call for you to "boil down" or "reduce" the liquid. This means that you should take the cover off the pan and let some of the liquid evaporate.

To *simmer* means to cook in liquid at a temperature below boiling. Tiny bubbles form slowly on the bottom or sides of the pan. They break before they reach the surface.

Braising and *stewing* are two ways of simmering foods. Braised foods are cooked slowly in a small amount of liquid in a covered pot. Stewed foods are cut into small pieces, covered with liquid and simmered in a large pot. The pot may or may not be covered.

Delicate foods like fish and eggs can be *poached*. To poach, cook the food in hot or simmering liquid. There should be enough liquid in the pan so the food can float. Handle the food carefully so it keeps its shape.

Some foods, such as vegetables and fish, taste especially good when they are *steamed*. To steam food, place it on a rack or in a

basket. Then put the rack or basket in a deep pot with a small amount of water. The water should not touch the food or the rack. Cover the pot, and bring the water to a boil. The steam from the water cooks the food. Check once in a while during cooking to make sure enough water is left in the pot to create steam.

Some recipes call for milk to be *scalded*. To scald, heat milk to just below the boiling point. Tiny bubbles will form at the edge of the pan. Scalding can also mean to dip food into boiling water or to pour boiling water over foods such as peaches or tomatoes.

Food is often *browned* at the start of the cooking time. To do this, the food is cooked quickly at a high temperature until the surface becomes brown. You can brown food in a skillet using a small amount of fat. You can also brown food in an oven which has been preheated to a high temperature. Browning gives the food color and flavor. *Searing* is another word for browning. Browning can refer to any food. Searing refers only to meat.

Browning or searing is just a beginning step in cooking meat. Before the meat is served, it must be cooked further, usually by braising or stewing.

When you *pan broil,* you cook meat in an uncovered skillet. Extra fat is poured off as it builds up.

Pan frying or *sautéing* is also done in a skillet. But pan broiling and pan frying differ in two ways. One difference is that extra fat is removed during pan broiling. In pan frying, extra fat is added. In most cases, a small amount of fat is heated in a skillet. Then food is added to the hot fat. The other difference is that pan broiling refers only to meat. Pan frying refers to any food.

Food which is *deep-fat fried* is cooked in hot fat until it is brown. When you deep-fat fry, there should be enough fat for the food to float. The fat should be hot enough to cook the food quickly before the fat can soak into the food. Use a deep-fat thermometer to check the temperature of the fat before you add the food. If there is moisture on the surface of the food, use paper towels to pat the food dry before it is placed in the hot fat. Moisture can cause hot fat to splatter. This can cause a painful burn. Often food is dredged or breaded before it is deep-fat fried.

COOKING IN THE OVEN OR BROILER

When cooking in the oven or broiler, your recipe may tell you to *preheat.* Preheating means to turn on the controls in advance. This is done so that the oven or broiler reaches the proper temperature before you start to cook. You will usually need to preheat when you are preparing foods such as cakes and breads. In some cases, you can save energy by not preheating. It is usually unnecessary to preheat for foods such as meats and casseroles.

Sometimes recipes do not give the exact temperature you should use. They may tell you to cook the food in a slow, moderate or hot oven. The temperatures you should use when your recipe does not state one are shown below.

OVEN TEMPERATURES		
Very slow	120°C	250°F
Slow	150°C	300°F
Moderately slow	160°C	325°F
Moderate	180°C	350°F
Moderately hot	190°C	375°F
Hot	200°C	400°F
Very hot	230°C	450°F
Broiling	260°C	500°F

The most common terms used in oven cookery are baking and roasting.

Baking means to cook in an oven. Foods such as cookies, breads, pies, cakes and casseroles are baked.

Roasting also means to cook in an oven. But the term often refers to cooking meats or poultry in the oven. The meat or poultry may rest on the pan bottom or on a rack. A thermometer can be used to determine doneness.

Roasts and poultry can be *basted* with juices, seasoned broth or special sauce. Basting helps to keep food from drying out during cooking. To baste, spoon or brush liquid over the food several times while the food is cooking.

Food is *broiled* using the broiling unit. Food is placed on a broiling pan which is placed directly under the heat source (element or gas flame).

Sometimes a recipe may tell you to *dot* a pie or casserole with butter. To do this, cut the butter into small pieces. Place the pieces over the top of the pie or casserole before cooking.

to Define

bake . . . baste . . . beat . . .
boil . . . braise . . .
bread . . . broil . . .
brown . . . chop . . .
core . . . cream . . .
cube . . . cut in . . .
deep-fat fry . . . dice . . .
dredge . . . flute . . .
fold . . . grate . . .
grease . . . grind . . .
julienne . . . knead . . .
marinate . . . mash . . .
mince . . . mix . . .
pan broil . . . pan fry . . .
pare . . . poach . . .
roast . . . sauté . . .
scald . . . score . . .
scrape . . . sear . . .
shred . . . sift . . .
simmer . . . slice . . .
steam . . . stew . . . stir . . .
trim . . . whip

to Discuss

1. What is the most common recipe format?

2. Why should you always read a recipe before starting to cook?

3. Why are abbreviations often used in recipes?

4. Why are exact measurements necessary in baking?

5. Why should you always write down measurements when you are doubling or dividing a recipe?

6. What can you do if your recipe calls for 250 mL (1 cup) of buttermilk and you do not have it on hand?

7. What is the difference between boiling, rolling boil and simmering?

8. What do stewing, braising and poaching have in common?

9. What is the difference between pan broiling and sautéing?

10. When baking or roasting, do you need to preheat an oven for all foods? For which foods is it necessary to preheat? For which foods is it unnecessary to preheat?

to Do

1. Select a recipe that is written in paragraph form and re-write it using a list format.

2. Practice doubling and dividing recipes. Select three recipes. First double them and then divide them in half.

3. Select recipes for five of your favorite foods. What cooking techniques and terms mentioned in this chapter are included?

4. Test your oven by using an oven thermometer. Place the thermometer in the center of the oven and then set the oven at various temperatures. Allow time for the oven to reach the temperature on the dial. Then check to see that the oven has reached that temperature. If the oven is not heating properly, note the adjustments you will need to make.

5. Create a game which includes cooking terms and measuring techniques included in this chapter.

6. Look at different cookbooks—children's, general, speciality, foreign, gourmet. Note the difference in completeness of directions in the recipes. Which cookbooks are for more experienced cooks? Which cookbooks would be easier for the beginning cook to use?

The science of cooking

What do science and cooking have in common? After reading this chapter, you will be able to explain how following a recipe is much like doing a scientific experiment. By knowing some of the chemical and physical traits of foods, you will be able to describe what happens to food as it cooks and how ingredients in recipes affect each other.

Do you have a science lab in your home? You probably do, without knowing it. In many ways, your home kitchen is like a science lab. In the kitchen, chemicals are heated, cooled, mixed and dissolved. Scientific formulas — or recipes — tell you what materials you need and how to use them. One wrong step may turn the entire "experiment" into a failure.

Cooking raises a lot of interesting scientific questions. You can use your "kitchen laboratory" to answer them.

Sometimes cooking makes meat tender, and sometimes cooking makes meat tough. How can cooking do both?

Meat contains protein. When protein is heated, it *coagulates.* It turns from a loose, jelly-like material to a firm substance. You can see this happen by watching an egg cook, 8-1. (Eggs contain protein too.)

Both time and temperature affect coagulation. Long cooking times and hot temperatures make protein firmer and tougher. Therefore, over-cooking in dry heat makes meat tough. (Over-cooking also dries out some of the fat and moisture in meat. When this happens, meat loses some of its juices and flavor.)

The process of protein coagulation explains why cooking makes meat firm and sometimes tough. But how does cooking make meat tender?

Meat contains protein in muscle tissue. This protein becomes firm when it is cooked. Meat also contains protein in *connective tissue.* Connective tissue holds together, or "connects," the muscle cells in meat. There are two kinds of protein in connective tissues: *elastin* and *collagen.* Elastin doesn't change very much during cooking, but collagen does. Some of the collagen turns to gelatin when meat is cooked in moist heat. (Gelatin is very tender.) Therefore, cooking in moist heat helps make meat tender. Stewing and braising are moist heat cooking methods.

If you add an acid ingredient to meat, it will speed up the change from collagen to gelatin. This is why very tough cuts of meat are often marinated or cooked in a liquid containing an acid. Lemon juice, vinegar and tomato juice are common acid ingredients.

This information comes in handy when you're ready to cook. Suppose you plan to serve a rolled rib roast, T-bone steaks or pork rib chops for dinner. These are tender cuts of meat. They have little connective tissue. You would want to cook them: using a dry heat method such as roasting or pan broiling; for a fairly short time; and at a low to moderate temperature. This method of cooking will keep the meat tender and juicy. See 8-2.

You might want to serve a blade roast, round steak or lamb riblets another night. These are less tender cuts of meat. They have quite a bit of connective tissue. You would want to cook them: in moist heat such as braising; for a longer time; and at a fairly low temperature. You might want to add an acid ingredient such as tomato juice. This will soften the connective tissue and make the meat more tender. See 8-3.

What makes bread rise?

Several factors work together before and during baking to make bread and other baked goods rise. Ingredients which make baked goods rise are called *leavening agents.*

Yeast breads depend mostly on yeast to make them rise. *Yeast* is made up of many tiny, one-celled plants. When yeast is combined with water and sugar, it produces carbon dioxide gas, 8-4. This gas is trapped in the dough and forms many little bubbles. These bubbles give a light, airy texture to the dough.

When bread is put into the oven, the heat causes two changes. More carbon dioxide gas is produced more quickly. And the gas expands in volume. (All gases expand when they are heated.) These changes cause the bread dough to rise quickly for the first few minutes of baking. Before long, the temperature becomes so hot that it kills the yeast plants. Then no more carbon dioxide is produced.

Why don't the gas bubbles burst as they expand? They don't burst because they are trapped by the gluten structure in the dough. *Gluten* is a stretchy substance made from protein. See 8-5. It is formed when moistened flour is stirred or kneaded. Gluten strands can be stretched very long and thin without breaking. The stronger the gluten is, the more a bread will be able to rise.

Gluten does more than trap gas bubbles in the dough. Because gluten is made of protein, it coagulates (becomes firm) when it is heated. When bread bakes, the protein coagulates and sets around the expanded gas bubbles. This makes the bread hold its shape, even after it cools.

Many baked products do not use yeast to make them rise. There are other ways of making gas bubbles which expand to make baked goods light and airy. *Baking soda* is the leavening agent in many cakes and quick breads. When baking soda combines with an acid, the reaction produces carbon dioxide. Some common acid ingredients include cream of tartar, vinegar, sour milk, buttermilk, molasses and some fruit juices. Some of these ingredients also add flavor to the baked product.

Some recipes call for *baking powder* rather than baking soda. Baking powder is a combination of baking soda and an acid ingredient in dry form. When you add liquid, the baking soda and acid combine to form carbon dioxide. "Double acting" baking powder contains two kinds of acid. One reacts as soon as liquid is added. The other reacts when the product is heated during baking. This prevents all of the gas from forming too soon and escaping before the bubbles are trapped by gluten.

In some cases, ordinary *air* is used as a leavening agent. The dough or batter may be beaten to create air bubbles inside it. Or,

8-3 Braising will make this cut of meat more tender.

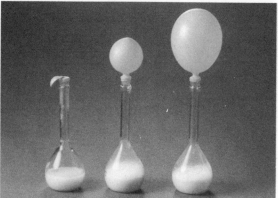

Left: Water that is too hot kills the yeast. No carbon dioxide is produced.

Center: When the water is too cool, the yeast grows slowly. Only a small amount of carbon dioxide is produced.

Right: When yeast is mixed with warm water, more carbon dioxide is produced.

8-4 Yeast grows best at a warm temperature.

8-1 As an egg cooks, the protein coagulates.

8-2 Roasting will keep this meat tender and juicy.

8-5 Gluten is a stretchy substance that forms the framework of bread.

The science of cooking   131

beaten egg whites may be folded in to add air bubbles to the mixture. This air expands when heated to make the product rise even more.

Another common leavening agent is *steam*. Water is present in all doughs and batters. For this reason, steam helps all baked goods rise to some extent, even when other leavening agents are used. Steam is the major leavening agent for popovers and cream puffs.

Why do cookies become crisp when they are baked, while cakes become soft and moist?

Even when most of the ingredients in two recipes are the same, the results may be very different. This is because of the proportions of the ingredients. Adding more or less of one ingredient can change the way another ingredient works, 8-6.

Flour is a basic ingredient in baked products. It is needed for gluten development. Gluten is formed when flour is mixed with liquid and then stirred, beaten or kneaded. The more a dough is handled, the more the gluten develops. Yeast breads need a strong gluten framework. Folding and kneading yeast bread dough develops the gluten as fully as possible. Delicate pie crusts and biscuits do not need a strong gluten framework. You have to be careful not to overdevelop the gluten in these doughs. You mix them as little and as quickly as possible.

Liquids are another basic ingredient in baked products. Liquids moisten flour and dissolve other ingredients. The proportion of flour and liquid determines the type of mixture you will have. Batters contain about equal amounts of flour and liquid. Batters can be poured. Cakes and waffles are made from batters. Doughs contain more flour than liquid. They cannot be poured. Most cookies and breads are made from doughs.

The amount of liquid in baked products affects gluten development. In a very dry mixture, the gluten does not develop fully. Pie doughs and many cookie doughs are fairly dry for this reason. On the other hand, in a batter, the large amount of liquid dilutes the gluten. This causes the gluten strands to slide

past each other instead of sticking together. This promotes tenderness in products such as cakes and crêpes. Gluten develops best in a thick, sticky mixture where the gluten strands can cling firmly together. This is the ideal mixture for bread dough.

Sugar does more than making some baked goods taste sweet. Sugar helps baked goods to turn brown in color. It also makes them tender. Sugar interferes with the development of gluten and weakens it. As more sugar is added to a recipe, the product becomes more tender. If a cake batter has too much sugar, the gluten structure may be so weak that the cake may fall.

Shortening and other fats, such as lard, vegetable oils and butter, are important in baked products. They add flavor and can make baked products more tender. Fats cause gluten strands to slip and slide across each other. They prevent the gluten from forming long strands needed for a firm network. Recipes for cookies and pie dough usually call for large amounts of shortening to make the products flaky or crumbly.

Leavening agents are used to make baked products larger in volume and softer in texture. Light, airy products such as cakes use more leavening than crumbly, compact products such as cookies.

The proportion of ingredients is what makes one baked product different than another. Each ingredient in a cookie recipe works with all the other ingredients. Together, they make the cookies crisp and tasty. Similar ingredients, used in different proportions, work together to make cakes soft and moist.

Why does food cook faster in a pressure cooker?

Food cooks faster in a *pressure cooker* because the temperatuare is actually hotter than in a pot of boiling water. To understand why, let's look at why water boils in the first place.

When water is heated, it turns into water vapor (steam). This happens easily at the surface of water, and we call it *evaporation*.

If the water gets hot enough, bubbles form. These bubbles are not made of air. They are made of water vapor. The bubbles of vapor form below the surface of the water. These bubbles then rise to the surface where they break and release their heat into the air. This is called *boiling*, 8-7.

Normally (at sea level), water will boil at 100°C (212°F). This is called the *boiling point*. At this temperature the pressure building up inside the bubbles becomes greater than the pressure of the air on top of the water.

The temperature of water will not go higher than the boiling point. Any extra heat is carried to the surface by the bubbles and released.

But what happens inside a pressure cooker? Here, the steam (and its heat) is trapped inside the cooker. See 8-8. Trapped steam creates extra pressure. This means that the air pressure

BERGWALL PRODUCTIONS, INC. FILMSTRIPS

8-7 Water is boiling when bubbles of steam rise to the surface and break.

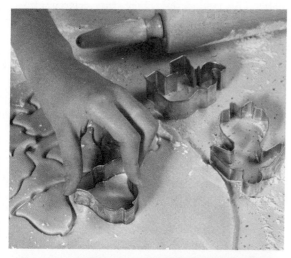

BERGWALL PRODUCTIONS, INC. FILMSTRIPS—SILVERSTONE® AND TEFLON®—DU PONT'S NON-STICK FINISHES

8-6 Cookie and cake recipes may call for many of the same ingredients. But the final products are very different.

NATIONAL PRESTO INDUSTRIES, INC.

8-8 A pressure cooker traps steam which creates pressure. This pressure makes food cook faster.

The science of cooking   **133**

on top of the water is greater than it would be in an open pot. Under this extra pressure, water does not boil at 100°C (212°F). The water must get hotter to make bubbles with more pressure inside them. For the water to boil, the pressure inside the bubbles has to become greater than the pressure that has built up on the surface of the water. The result is that both the water and the steam inside the cooker get hotter than 100°C (212°F). At this higher temperature, food cooks faster.

Cooking in the mountains is different than cooking at sea level. The higher the altitude, the lower the *atmospheric pressure* is. (Atmospheric pressure is the pressure of air.) Lower atmospheric pressure allows bubbles of water vapor to form more easily. This means that water will boil at a temperature lower than 100°C (212°F). Foods, therefore, need to be cooked for a longer time. Or, a pressure cooker may be used in mountain areas to increase the water temperature.

Now you can see that water boils at different temperatures, depending on the pressure on it. The hotter the temperature is, the faster a food cooks. Since water can become hotter in a pressure cooker than in a regular pot, it cooks food faster.

Why do lettuce salads become limp if you add the dressing too early?

Lettuce, and other leafy green salads become limp if you add the dressing too early because of a process called *osmosis,* 8-9. Osmosis is the passage of liquids through a membrane. When the liquid on one side of the membrane contains more dissolved materials than the liquid on the other side, osmosis occurs. The process continues until the liquids on both sides of the membrane are balanced.

In plants, osmosis occurs as liquids pass through cell walls. Normally, the liquid inside the plant contains more dissolved materials than the liquid outside the plant. This causes the cells to draw water inward. But sometimes the water outside the plant contains a large amount of dissolved materials, such as salt or sugar. When this happens, water is drawn out. This makes the plant soft and limp.

Now you can see why salad dressing makes lettuce and other greens limp. Most dressings are liquids which contain ingredients such as salt, sugar and spices. When dressing comes in contact with the greens, it draws water out of the plant cells by osmosis. This makes the greens lose their firm, crisp texture.

You can reverse this process and make water go back into some plants. For instance, if you have some limp celery, just put it in plain cold water. Now the liquid on the outside of the plant (plain water) has fewer dissolved materials than the liquid inside the plant cells. As a result, water is drawn into the cells. This makes the celery stalk crisp again.

Why do some salad dressings separate while others stay mixed?

Whether a salad dressing will separate or stay mixed depends on what kind of an *emulsion* it is, 8-10. An emulsion is a combination of two liquids that do not mix. Oil and water are examples of two such liquids. When you put them together in a bottle and shake it, you make an emulsion. Droplets of one liquid float around in the other liquid. In time, the two liquids will separate again. The heavier liquid (in this case, water) will sink to the bottom. The lighter liquid (the oil) will rise to the top. This type of emulsion is called a *temporary emulsion.*

Vinegar and oil dressings are temporary emulsions. Each time you want to use one of these dressings, you have to shake the bottle first to mix the liquids. Then you have to pour quickly before the liquids separate.

In some emulsions, the liquids do not separate. These are called *permanent emulsions.* To make any emulsion, you have to shake, beat or stir the liquids. This breaks one of the liquids into tiny droplets which float around in the other liquid. To make a permanent emulsion, you also have to add an *emulsifier.* This forms a film around each droplet and prevents the droplets from joining together again. Common emulsifiers include eggs, gelatin, starch paste and certain proteins.

Thousand Island dressing and mayonnaise

are permanent emulsions. They are ready to use when you open the bottle. You don't have to shake them first.

What makes gravy lumpy?

Gravy has three basic ingredients: starch, liquid and fat. The starch is usually flour. The liquid may be water, milk or broth. The fat usually comes from meat or poultry drippings.

The key to smooth gravy is separating the particles of starch before they come in contact with hot liquid. Once starch is combined with hot liquid, it swells and thickens. It turns from a dry powder to a sticky paste. This process is called the *gelatinization* of starch.

If gravy is not made carefully, gelatinized starch can form a sticky coating around lumps of dry starch. This prevents the liquid from reaching the starch inside the lump.

You can prevent these lumps from forming. To do this, you must separate the particles of starch. Then the liquid can reach all of the starch at the same time. All of the starch will gelatinize into a smooth, even mixture, 8-11.

MARCELLO MARCOCCIA

8-10 The salad dressing on the left is a temporary emulsion that has separated. The dressing on the right is a permanent emulsion.

CALIFORNIA ICEBERG LETTUCE COMMISSION

8-9 Salad dressings should be added to salads just before serving. Otherwise, the salad may become limp due to osmosis.

REVERE COPPER AND BRASS, INC.

8-11 Gravy will be smooth if starch particles are separated before they are combined with hot liquid.

There are two ways to separate particles of starch:

1. Mix the starch *thoroughly* with the fat before adding the liquid.
2. Mix the starch with *cold* liquid, stirring quickly and *thoroughly*. Then add the mixture to the hot fat.

At this point, continue to heat the gravy, stirring constantly. This completes the process of gelatinization.

If you want to make the gravy thicker, do not add more flour directly to the hot gravy. (This would create lumps.) Instead, mix the flour with a little more cold liquid. Then add the mixture to the hot gravy.

Whenever you cook with starch and hot liquid, you have to watch out for lumps. Always separate the particles of starch before you combine the starch with hot liquid.

Why do some vegetables change color during cooking?

The pigments that give vegetables their color are chemical compounds. Like other chemicals, they are affected by heat, acids and alkalies.

Chlorophyll is the green pigment in vegetables. Both heat and acid make chlorophyll turn from bright green to dull, olive-green. On the other hand, alkalies make chlorophyll turn even brighter green. Baking soda is an alkali. Some restaurants add a pinch of baking soda to green vegetables to make them look good. However, alkalies can make vegetables mushy. Even more important, alkalies can cause the loss of vitamins. Thus, adding baking soda to vegetables is *not* a good idea.

Bright green is the most difficult color to keep during cooking. See 8-12. To help preserve a bright green color in a vegetable, keep the cooking time short. Bring the water to a boil before you add the vegetable. Leave the lid off the pan for a minute or two. This allows some of the vegetable's natural acids to escape with the steam. Then cover the pan and cook just until tender. Covering the pan speeds cooking and reduces the loss of vitamins.

While acid dulls the green pigment, it preserves the red pigment found in vegetables. A little acid (vinegar or lemon juice) in the cooking water preserves the red color of red cabbage and beets. In an alkaline solution, red cabbage turns a purple or blue color. But if acid is added, the cabbage will turn red again.

Carotene gives an orange or yellow color to carrots, corn, pumpkin and squash. It is not affected much by cooking. (Carotene is used in the body to make vitamin A.)

White vegetables, such as onions, potatoes and cauliflower, may turn yellow in a very alkaline solution. An alkaline solution can be very hard water or water to which baking soda has been added. Adding a bit of acid (vinegar or cream of tartar) to the cooking water will restore the white color.

What makes microwave ovens different from conventional ovens?

In conventional cooking, heat comes from a source such as a kitchen range or a campfire. The heat is transferred from the source to the food. In microwave cooking, the heat is created inside the food itself, 8-13. This ability to heat food directly is the main advantage of microwave cooking. You don't have to waste time and energy heating cooking equipment. All the cooking time and all the oven's energy are used to cook the food.

In a conventional oven, the oven must be heated first in order to heat food. But in a microwave oven, the oven is not heated. Instead, a special device called a magnetron tube creates *microwaves*. These microwaves, in turn, create heat inside the food. They do this by causing water and fat molecules to vibrate. This rapid movement of the molecules causes friction which creates heat. (This same thing happens when you rub the palms of your hands together.) This heat is spread throughout the food.

Microwaves do not stop at the surface of foods. They go inside foods. For this reason, it is difficult to brown the surface of foods. Some manufacturers now provide special "browning platters." Browning platters absorb microwaves and become hot enough to sear and brown the surface of meats. Some microwave ovens have a heating element at the top that will brown foods.

The ability of microwaves to go inside foods makes it possible to cook many foods very quickly. Since the inside of the food heats sooner, cooking may be two to ten times faster by microwave. For instance, one potato may bake in 4 to 6 minutes by microwave. The same potato would need 45 minutes or more to bake in a conventional oven.

SILVERSTONE® AND TEFLON®–DU PONT'S NON-STICK FINISHES

8-12 Brussels sprouts will keep their bright green color if they are cooked properly.

SEARS, ROEBUCK AND CO.

8-13 A microwave oven cooks food with microwaves. Heat is created inside the food.

to Define

boiling . . . coagulate . . .
collagen . . . elastin . . .
emulsifier . . . emulsion . . .
gelatinization . . . gluten . . .
leavening agent . . .
microwaves . . . .osmosis . . .
pressure cooker

to Discuss

1. What happens to protein which is cooked too long or at too high a temperature?
2. What kind of protein in connective tissue changes when meat is cooked? What cooking methods help to tenderize less tender cuts of meat?
3. How does gluten help bread dough rise? How does gluten help baked bread keep its shape?
4. Name three leavening agents which produce carbon dioxide to make baked goods rise.
5. What do you need to do to yeast bread dough to help the gluten develop? Should you handle pie dough the same way?
6. Which recipe is likely to use more liquid—a cake recipe or a cookie recipe?
7. Do foods take a longer or shorter time to cook in a pressure cooker? In the mountains, does water boil at a temperature higher or lower than 100°C (212°F)?
8. Why does salad dressing make salad greens limp?
9. Name an example of a temporary emulsion, a permanent emulsion and an emulsifier.
10. Name the three basic ingredients in gravy. Explain two ways of combining these ingredients to prevent lumps from forming.
11. What can cause broccoli to turn a dull olive-green when it is cooked?
12. How can a microwave oven save energy?

to Do

1. Prepare a recipe for white bread. Divide the dough into thirds. Prepare one-third according to recipe directions. Prepare one-third without kneading. Prepare one-third without allowing the dough to rise. Bake each small loaf and compare the size and texture of the loaves. Discuss what happened to produce the differences.
2. Compare several cookie recipes with cake recipes. Prepare a cake and some cookies. Compare their textures. Why are the textures different?
3. Make two lettuce salads. Pour salad dressing on one of them and let it stand for 30 to 60 minutes. Then pour dressing on the second and compare the two salads. Which one is more crisp?
4. Show how the color of some vegetables is changed by acids and alkalies. Choose one (or more) of the following: fresh or frozen green beans, red cabbage, peeled white potatoes, and carrots. Cook one-third of the vegetable according to regular steaming directions. Cook one-third with 1 teaspoon of baking soda added to the water. Cook the last third with 1 tablespoon of vinegar in the water. Record your results.
5. Compare different ways of cooking. Cook four carrots by steaming them in a saucepan. Cook four carrots in a pressure cooker, according to the directions in the use and care manual. Cook four carrots in a microwave oven, according to the directions in a microwave cookbook. Compare cooking time, flavor, color and texture.

$\mathcal{S}$hopping for food

9

What should every shopper know? After reading this chapter you will be able to plan a shopping trip. You will know where to look for information about the food you buy. You will also be able to use shopping tips that help you get the most value for your food dollar.

$\mathcal{S}$hopping for food is not easy. The average supermarket stocks thousands of items on its shelves. Many new products are added every year. But most new products do not survive over one year. Is the food industry trying to confuse consumers? Or is it simply trying to meet consumer needs?

Consumer needs are constantly growing and changing. Today's consumers have less time to spend preparing food. Therefore, they buy foods that can be prepared quickly. They may buy canned soups, frozen waffles, and cake mixes. Many of these foods were not even available in the past, 9-1. As consumers' needs have grown, the food industry has grown too.

In today's market, uninformed consumers may become confused by all the choices and may make poor decisions. On the other hand, informed consumers take advantage of all the choices. They compare sizes, brands and grades. Informed consumers plan food shopping very carefully. They make wise decisions and get just what they want. This can save money, time and effort.

GETTING ORGANIZED FOR SHOPPING

Organization comes in handy for almost any job. Grocery shopping is no exception.

Organized shoppers save both time and money in the store. They know what foods they need to buy. Organized shoppers also save frustration at home. They rarely run out of foods they need as they are cooking. With practice, you can become an organized shopper too.

Making a shopping list

A good shopping list is the key to organized shopping. There are two basic approaches to making a shopping list.

A *specific shopping list* includes everything needed for a certain period of time, such as the next four days. A specific list makes shopping simple, but it depends on detailed menus being planned in advance.

A *general shopping list* is not as detailed. It lists general needs, such as meats for five meals; three fruits and vegetables; milk; and bread. This is a "buy now, plan later" type of list. The flexibility allows you to take advantage of unadvertised specials and choice fresh produce. Since there is much less planning, however, there is a greater chance that you will not get everything you need. Extra trips to the store cost time and energy.

Most shoppers are comfortable with a list that combines both approaches. The kind of list you use is a personal decision. The important thing is to have some kind of shopping plan. People who shop with no plan are likely to wind up with many things they don't really need, and without some things that are really necessary. They are also likely to spend more money on food.

You'll find it helpful to keep a pad of paper and a pencil handy in the kitchen. Jot down basic supplies as you see you're running low.

Before you leave for the store, organize your list according to the layout of the store. Once you've shopped in a certain store a few times, you will have an idea of where things are located. You can save yourself a lot of time and steps by taking a few minutes to organize your list.

It's usually best to concentrate your shopping in the store that advertises the best prices. Going to many stores takes more time and gas.

Deciding what to buy

Buying decisions are personal. They depend on your food preferences and cooking skills. They also depend on the equipment, money and time you have available. Wise shopping is not just a matter of spending as little as possible. It means getting the most value for the money you spend. There is no such thing as the "best buy" for everyone. The best buy for you is a decision based on your own needs and resources.

How much should you buy? Usually the larger package is more economical. But a larger package is not a good buy if you have to serve the product at every meal for the next week to use it up. Consider how much of the food you can store easily. Also, decide how much of the food you are likely to use before it spoils or becomes stale.

Learn how to figure the *cost per serving*. The cost per serving is how much each portion costs. A package of short ribs, for instance, may cost a little less than the same size package of round steak. But how many servings can you get from each package? The round steak has fewer bones and less fat. It will provide at least twice as many servings as the short ribs.

Try to economize on meat, fish and poultry if your food budget is limited. These are usually the most costly foods in a meal. To save money, watch for specials. At a good sale, you may be able to afford some cuts that are usually beyond your food budget. Plan to use leftovers in casseroles, sandwiches, soups and salads. Use dried beans and peas, eggs and peanut butter instead of meat now and then. These are less costly protein foods that will add variety to your meals.

Compare different forms of foods, such as fresh, frozen, dried and canned. Decide which is best for you by asking yourself the following questions:

- How much storage space do you have in the refrigerator, freezer and kitchen cabinets?
- How long do you want to keep the food?
- How do you plan to use the food?
- How do prices compare?

Buy fresh fruits and vegetables when they are *in season*. In season means at the time of harvest. If you can't remember when a food is in season, the fresh produce displays give plenty of clues. The selection will look good. You'll find the best quality at the lowest prices when foods are in season. See 9-2.

Evaluate the "convenience" of *convenience foods*. Convenience foods are faster and easier to prepare than foods made from scratch. Some of the work has already been done. Convenience foods come in many forms—from cake mixes to TV dinners. Generally, the more that has been done to

9-1 A typical shopping cart today is full of products unknown to consumers 50 years ago.

CEREAL INSTITUTE, INC.

9-2 When fresh fruits and vegetables are in season, the selection is better, and the prices are lower.

BERGWALL PRODUCTIONS, INC. FILMSTRIPS

make a food convenient, the more it will cost. Judge convenience foods before you buy them. Is a product simply a combination of ingredients that you could put together easily? Or is the built-in convenience really going to save you time and energy? Buying frozen fried chicken rather than preparing your own, may be worth the extra cost if you're in a hurry. But are peas in butter sauce worth the extra cost? How much time and effort does it take to add your own butter to frozen peas?

Be sure that sales are really sales. A special promotion is not always a sale. Do not be misled by eye-catching displays. Check the prices.

Clip money-saving coupons. Small savings add up quickly, 9-3. But use coupons only if you need the items. Check prices of other brands to make sure you're not paying more than necessary, even with the coupons.

Try *store brands* of foods. Store brands are promoted by a certain store or chain of stores. Store brands are usually less expensive than name brands. *Name brands* are nationally advertised products. The packaging of store brands may not be as pretty, but the quality of the food is often just as good. In fact, the same company may produce both brands.

You can find *generic brands* in many stores. Generic brands are "no brand" brands. The packages and labels are plain. Only the legally required information appears on them. Generic brands usually cost less than either store or name brands. See 9-4.

Reading before you shop

To be a good shopper, you need to be informed. Information helps you make good decisions. Useful information can come in the form of advertising, booklets, articles and buying guides.

The food industry spends huge sums of money on advertising every year. Advertisements try to influence your buying decisions.

Some ads appeal to your logic. They give you information about their products. They tell you why they think their products are better than other products. This information can be helpful as you compare products.

Other ads appeal to your emotions. They try to make you think that their products will make you more attractive or popular. Think about what an ad is really saying before you spend your money. Will you really be more popular if you use a certain brand of coffee or cake mix? Will drinking one kind of soft drink rather than another be more fun for you? Clear thinking will help you use ads wisely.

Food store ads in newspapers can be helpful, 9-5. Every week, stores advertise sale prices to attract customers. Compare the specials to decide where to do your shopping. Plan menus around advertised meat, poultry and fish specials. If you find a good sale and you have freezer space, buy extra food and freeze it for later use. Food store ads can be helpful, but read them carefully. The items they list may not all be on sale. Some items are only featured, with a reminder of the current price.

Ads by food companies encourage you to buy a certain product. These ads are not limited to special "sale" days. Sometimes they feature recipes or ideas on how to use the product. Clip out good ideas and save them for a time when you're looking for something new to try, 9-6.

CON EDISON

9-3 Each coupon may be worth only a few cents. But they add up quickly into a nice savings.

Ads are not the only source of information about food. The United States Department of Agriculture (USDA) and the Cooperative Extension Service are government agencies which provide information about food. They publish many food related booklets and answer individual questions. Other sources of useful information include food companies, food store chains, newspapers, magazines and books. For information about a certain product, write to the company that produces it. Use the address given on the product label.

WHERE TO SHOP

In most areas, there are many stores that sell food. Each type of store has advantages and disadvantages.

How do you decide where to shop? According to marketing studies, these are the main reasons people give for choosing a store:
- Generally low prices.
- Convenient location.
- Wide variety of items stocked.
- Friendly personnel.

Supermarkets

The idea behind *supermarkets* is to sell very large amounts of food at low prices. Low

9-5 *Newspaper ads can help you in planning meals and deciding where to shop.*

MARCELLO MARCOCCIA

MARCELLO MARCOCCIA

9-4 *These packages of spaghetti are examples of a name brand, a store brand and a generic brand.*

MARCELLO MARCOCCIA

9-6 *Clip out appealing food ideas shown in ads to give variety to your meal planning.*

prices are possible because of the large volume of products sold.

The trend in supermarkets has been toward larger stores that offer more products and services, 9-7. Some supermarkets offer delicatesses and bakery products. Many also sell health and beauty aids, magazines, greeting cards, school supplies and sewing notions. Experts believe this "super store" trend toward one-stop shopping will continue.

Neighborhood stores

Until supermarkets became widespread, people bought most of their food at small *neighborhood stores.* These stores usually have a friendly atmosphere and offer personal service. Today, many of these stores have disappeared. Supermarkets offer a wider range of choices and lower prices. This has hurt the small stores.

Some neighborhood stores still exist. They offer the convenience of being close by when an item is needed. Neighborhood stores often open earlier and close later than the local supermarkets. Customers also like the friendly, personal service they get. Some neighborhood stores will carry certain foods especially for their regular customers.

Specialty shops

Specialty shops include bakeries, cheese shops, fruit and vegetable stands, meat shops and health food stores. Few people buy all of their food at these stores. Usually, they stop at a specialty shop in addition to their regular trip to the supermarket.

Specialty shops usually offer products local supermarkets do not have. If you want a birthday cake or a fresh loaf of bread, a bakery is likely to have it. Small meat stores or butcher shops can be very helpful to customers. They may prepare special cuts of meat and wrap meat for the freezer. They also may provide helpful advice on how to prepare a certain cut of meat. Many butcher shops are known for selling high-quality meat.

Health food stores sell *organic foods.* (Organic foods are foods grown without commercial pesticides or fertilizers.) They also sell "health" foods (foods that are supposed to produce special health benefits) and a wide range of vitamins and other supplements. Some people shop in health food stores for unusual foods such as herbal teas and rose hip jelly. Some shop for foods they need to follow special diets. Others shop for products that claim to cure an illness or correct a condition.

Prices are often high in health food stores. Sometimes prices are more than twice as much as the prices for the same items in a supermarket. While some products and some stores are good, the industry has a great deal of fraud and quackery.

Food co-ops: group buying power

More and more consumers are forming *food cooperatives or co-ops.* Co-ops are a way of buying more food for the dollar. The type of organization and number of members vary greatly. The most common type is a group of 10 to 50 families. These families get together and make up a huge shopping list. They buy food in large amounts from wholesalers at a big discount. Then they divide the food among themselves. Some co-ops focus on only one group of foods, such as meats.

Other co-ops are large stores. These may have a thousand or more members. Members often must buy a membership in order to shop in such a store. In some cases, members must also work a few hours in the store.

The main advantage of a food co-op is lower prices. The main disadvantage is a limited selection. You cannot be sure that an item you want will be available. Another disadvantage is that there are few shopping conveniences. For instance, you may have to bring your own bags. This keeps the expenses of running the store low.

Other places to shop

Supermarkets, neighborhood stores, specialty shops and co-ops are the most common places to buy food. But they aren't the only places to buy food.

Quick-stop stores are located in many towns and cities. These stores offer a limited number of products. They usually charge higher prices than supermarkets. But they are conveniently located, and they stay open late. (Some are open 24 hours a day.)

Warehouse-supermarkets are new to many areas. Products are displayed in open cartons, stacked to form aisles. These stores have few customer conveniences but offer low prices.

Farmers' markets or *roadside stands* are good places to find fresh produce in season and fresh eggs at low prices.

Day-old stores are a specialized type of food store. They sell breads and other baked goods at reduced prices.

INSIDE THE STORE

You can learn a lot about food at the grocery store. The information is easy to find, once you know how and where to look.

Package dating

For years, the food industry has used coded dates on food packages. Dating the products helps employees stock the shelves. Items which have been in the store for the longest time are put toward the front of shelves. This is because the products in front are most likely to be picked up first by shoppers. The dates also determine which products should be removed because they are too old. Coded dates are helpful to food store employees. But consumers cannot use them.

Now, many products display *open dating* which consumers can read. See 9-8. Four different types of dates may be used.

A *pack date* tells you when the product was processed or packaged. This date may not be very helpful unless you know how quickly a certain food spoils.

A *pull* or *sell date* often reads "sell before . . . " This is the last date the product should be sold. This date allows some time for the consumer to store the food at home. Cold cuts, ice cream and milk are examples of foods with pull dates.

An *expiration date* often reads, "Use before . . . " After that date, the food should not be eaten or used. Baby formula and yeast are products that may carry expiration dates.

A *freshness date* is much like an expiration date. The difference is that the freshness date may allow for normal home storage. Bakery products often have freshness dates. These products may be sold at a reduced price for a short time after the freshness date. Or they may be stored at home for a short time after the freshness date.

Time is not the only factor that affects the quality and freshness of food. The way food is handled in the store and at home also affects food. Cool, dry storage helps food products keep their quality and freshness.

JEWEL FOOD STORES

9-7 Supermarkets offer a wide selection of products from which to choose.

9-8 Open dating tells you that this yogurt should remain fresh until at least April 28.

Unit pricing

It's not always easy to compare prices in a supermarket. Suppose you wanted to get a good buy on green beans. Would you buy a small package or a large package? Brand A or brand B? Fresh, frozen or canned?

Unit pricing can help you make wise decisions. Unit pricing tells you the price per unit. The unit may be a weight (such as a kilogram or a pound) or a number (such as a dozen). The unit is whatever seems to be the best way to measure the product. Unit prices are listed on shelf markers like the ones shown in 9-9.

Unit pricing can help you figure out which size can of peaches will give you the most for your money. Unit pricing will tell you that a 450 g (16 ounce) can selling for $.72 costs $.72 per 0.45 kilogram (pound). A 840 g (30 ounce) can selling for $.97 really costs $.52 per 0.45 kilogram (pound). If you buy the larger can, you will be getting more for your money. You can use this same method to compare different brands and different forms (fresh, frozen and canned) of foods.

Universal product code

More and more supermarkets are using computers to make their business more efficient. The *universal product code* (UPC) was developed for use with a computer system.

Most products sold in supermarkets now have an assigned UPC. It consists of a long number translated into a series of lines and bars, 9-10. Some stores have already installed the special checkout equipment needed. The checkout clerk simply passes the item over an electronic scanning machine connected to a computer. The computer stores all the price information and sends it back to the cash register. The tape lists the items you bought in addition to the prices you were charged, 9-11.

How does the UPC help shoppers? Checking out is much faster. It reduces the chance of errors by checkout clerks. The store can keep better records of its inventory to maintain supplies. Eventually, it will eliminate the need to mark the price on every box, can and bottle in the store. (Prices are stored in the computer and can be posted on the shelves for consumers to see.) By helping the store cut down its expenses, the UPC should help to hold down the cost of food.

9-9 To get the most for your money, compare the unit prices of products.

9-10 The universal product code is found on many food packages. Some stores use UPC to make checking out faster.

Labeling information

Most shoppers use labels simply to identify products. But labels have a lot of useful information. Some of it is required by federal law. Other information may be provided to help you use the product, such as cooking directions and recipe ideas. See 9-12.

Three pieces of information must appear on all food labels. They are:

1. The name of the product (such as peaches).
2. The net contents or net weight. (This includes the liquid in which canned foods are packed.)
3. The name and address of the manufacturer, packer or distributor.

Additional information may be required. For instance, certain products, such as canned fruits and vegetables, must state the style or form of the contents. Words such as sliced, whole, or packed in heavy syrup must appear.

On most labels, a list of ingredients, in descending order of amounts used, must appear. (The ingredient used in the largest amount is listed first.) Some foods are an exception to this rule. If the food meets a federal *standard of identity,* only the identifying name must appear on the label. Foods

```
GROCERY          .79
PRODUCE          .43
1/2 GAL MILK    1.03
LARGE EGGS       .57
GROCERY         1.39
JELLO PUDD       .32
FR SLOPPY JO     .39
HH SL STRAWB     .66
CAM MUSHROOM     .30
TV GUIDE         .40
PRODUCE          .86
GROCERY         1.64
MEAT            6.24
MEAT            2.45
DYNAMINTS SP     .25
DAN STR VGRT     .51
DECOOL WHIP      .69
W UNSWT STRA     .10
GROCERY          .31
MIRACLE WHIP     .81
HH TOM PASTE     .20
TAX DUE         1.00

TOTAL          21.34
CSH TENDER     21.34
CHG DUE          .00
```

9-11 Your UPC cash register tape will tell you what you purchased along with the prices you were charged.

9-12 This label includes information required by federal law plus cooking directions and a recipe idea.

with a standard of identity include mayonnaise, catsup and some other foods. These foods must contain the ingredients found in their official descriptions.

Nutrition information may or may not appear on labels. It must appear if a nutritional claim, such as "low-Calorie," is made for the product, either on the label or in advertising. Nutrition information must also appear if nutrients have been added to the food. If a company decides to put nutrition information on a label, it must include specific information in a certain format. See 9-13. This information includes:

1. The size of the serving for which the data is given.
2. The number of servings in the container.
3. The number of Calories in each serving
4. The amounts of carbohydrate, protein and fat per serving, measured in grams.
5. The percentage of the U.S. RDA for protein, vitamin A, vitamin C, thiamin, riboflavin, niacin, calcium and iron in the food as it comes from the package.

Other information *may* be added, such as the U.S. RDA percentages for any of 12 other nutrients. The amounts of cholesterol, sodium and different kinds of carbohydrates and fats may be given. You may also find nutrition information for the food as it is usually served. For instance, many cereal labels list the nutritional values of a bowl of the cereal eaten with milk, 9-14. A box of cake mix may provide nutrition information for a serving of the cake prepared according to package directions.

How to use nutrition labeling. The nutrition information on labels can help you learn more about food. It can help you make wise decisions about buying and eating food.

If you are watching your weight, for instance, you will be especially interested in kilojoules (Calories). But nutrition labeling can also tell you what nutrients you are getting with those kilojoules (Calories). For instance, compare labels for a cola and skim milk. With the milk, you are getting a lot more than just kilojoules (Calories).

Compare different foods for a particular nutrient. Suppose you are looking for a good source of vitamin A for tomorrow's dinner. Compare the labels of different vegetables to find one that is high in vitamin A.

Use nutrition labeling as you compare brands of the same food. Is a more expensive name brand of canned green beans better for you than a cheaper brand? Probably not. Does a fancy grade supply more nutrition? Probably not. Grades are based mostly on the appearance of foods, not on nutrition. Does the more costly can of "diet" plums have fewer kilojoules (Calories) than a can of ordinary plums? How does a "natural" cereal compare with pre-sweetened corn flakes? What is the difference between apple drink and apple juice? These are examples of questions that nutrition labeling can help you answer.

9-13 Nutrition labels are required to include specific information in a certain format.

THE PRICE YOU PAY FOR FOOD

When you buy food, the price includes many expenses. The price of a can of tomatoes, for instance, includes the cost of growing and harvesting them. It also includes the costs of canning, shipping, warehousing and selling the tomatoes to wholesalers. Wholesalers then sell the tomatoes to retailers who sell them to consumers. Advertising and other promotion expenses are also included. Each person involved adds to the the price charged to you, the consumer.

Processing and packaging techniques are increasing. Many foods cost more because of added convenience. Convenience foods are usually more expensive than foods you prepare from scratch.

Shopping habits that cost consumers money

The thoughtless behavior of some shoppers costs you and other consumers higher prices. Careless shopping habits include:

- Damaging fresh produce by squeezing, pinching or peeling, which results in produce having to be thrown out.
- Opening jars or other packages to smell or taste a product.
- Leaving "change-of-mind" items wherever it's convenient, rather than putting them back where they belong.
- Shoplifting or stealing items. (This is a criminal offense.)
- Leaving shopping carts in the middle of parking spaces where they are likely to be damaged.

Avoid these careless habits. Remember, anything that increases a store's cost of doing business ends up increasing the prices all consumers pay for products. Good shopping habits can cut costs for the grocer and for you, the consumer.

WHAT ARE FOOD ADDITIVES?

For thousands of years, people have added substances to foods to make them taste better, look more attractive and keep longer. These are called *food additives*. Food additives often used in the past and today are familiar ingredients such as sugar and salt. As you shop for food and read food labels, some additives may not seem so familiar. People are sometimes confused by the chemical name of

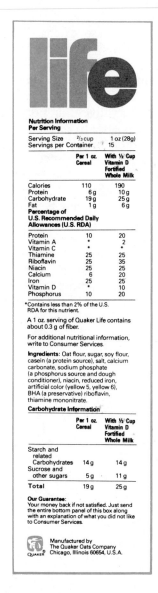

9-14 *This nutrition information label gives two sets of nutritional values. One is for the cereal alone, and one is for the cereal served with milk.*

some additives. They forget that foods themselves are a combination of chemical compounds. The Food and Drug Administration requires very extensive testing for food additives to insure their safety.

Food additives are used in foods for a variety of reasons. These are the major groups of food additives:

- *Preservatives:* These extend the life of a food. Most often, the specific job of a preservative is to prevent the growth of microorganisms (such as bacteria) that cause food to spoil. Antioxidants are a group of preservatives that prevent spoilage caused by exposure to oxygen in the air.
- *Nutritional additives:* Nutrients are sometimes added to food in specified amounts. When this is done, the food has been *enriched.* In other instances, vitamins, minerals, or protein may be added to make a food extra nutritious. This is called *fortification.* This is especially important when a certain nutrient is lacking in most diets. (Iodine added to salt to prevent goiter is a good example.)
- *Emulsifiers, stabilizers, thickeners:* These additives give foods a desired consistency.

In some cases, such as mayonnaise or chocolate candy, an emulsifier keeps the fat from separating. Stabilizers and thickeners give a smooth, even texture to foods such as ice cream.

- *Flavorings and colorings:* Flavorings include natural spices, herbs, and flavor extracts as well as synthetic ones. Synthetic flavorings are important because there simply would not be enough of many of the natural flavorings to meet the demands for them. Color, the most important visual aspect of food, adds a great deal to appetite appeal.
- Other additives: *Leavening agents, no-kilojoule (no-Calorie)* or *low-kilojoule (low-Calorie) sweeteners,* and *curing agents* (used in bacon, ham and other processed meats) are other types of food additives. Others include *anti-caking agents,* which keep powders and salts flowing freely, and *humectants,* which help to keep foods from drying out. *Clarifying agents* are used to prevent cloudiness from developing in a clear liquid. And *foaming agents* are used to control the amount of air in products such as whipped toppings.

to Define

convenience foods . . .
cost per serving . . .
expiration date . . .
food additives . . .
food co-ops . . .
generic brand . . .
in season . . .
name brand . . .
neighborhood stores . . .
open dating . . .
organic foods . . .
pack date . . . pull date . . .
speciality shops . . .
standard of identity . . .
store brand . . .
supermarkets . . .
unit price . . . UPC

to Discuss

1. Why is a shopping list important? Give at least two reasons.
2. Are large packages always a better buy than smaller ones? How can you determine the best buy as far as size is concerned?

3. Where can you get more information about food products?
4. List at least four reasons for choosing to shop in a certain store.
5. Why can supermarkets generally charge lower prices than small shops?
6. Name three examples of speciality shops. What advantage do they offer over a supermarket?
7. What information must appear on a product label?
8. If a bottle of salad dressing is labeled "low Calorie," must a nutrition label appear?
9. What information can you find on a nutrition label?

to Do

1. Make a bulletin board on how to use newspaper food ads to plan money-saving menus.
2. Develop a brief questionnaire on what influences people to shop where they do. Survey at least 10 neighbors or relatives. Summarize your results and report them to the class.
3. Compare the prices of milk, eggs and a loaf of bread in different types of stores in your community. What kind of store offered the best prices? Make a poster or bulletin board illustrating your findings.
4. Prepare a report on how food co-ops work. The librarian can help you find recent articles on the subject. If possible, interview someone who shops in a co-op.
5. Make a poster showing the kinds of information you can get by reading a food label.
6. Design a new label for a food product. Include features that would appeal to you as a consumer. (Remember to include the information that is required by law.)

Working with food

*Knowing how to buy, prepare and
store foods are all a part of
working with food.*

153

10

Dairy products

How should you buy and use dairy products? After reading this chapter, you will be able to describe different types of milk and other dairy products. You will know how to select and store all forms of dairy products. You also will be able to explain some of the techniques used when cooking with dairy products.

What do chocolate pudding, cheese fondue, yogurt and an ice cream sundae have in common? They are all made with milk or milk products.

Milk can come from many different animals, such as cows, goats, sheep and camels. In the United States, cows provide about 95 percent of the milk we use.

Milk is the best food source of calcium. It is also an excellent source of protein, riboflavin and phosphorus. Some milk contains vitamin A naturally. Other milks may be *fortified* with both vitamins A and D. (Fortified means that vitamins, minerals or other nutrients have been added to a food to improve its nutritional value.) Several other vitamins and minerals are found in milk in smaller, but important, amounts.

The term *dairy products* includes both milk and milk products. Milk products such as yogurt, sour cream, cheese and ice cream supply many of the same nutrients as milk. But some of these foods supply the nutrients in smaller amounts. See 10-1.

Dairy products are used in many ways, 10-2. Milk can be served either plain or flavored with syrups, powders or fruit. Milk is also the basis for many soups, sauces and desserts. Yogurt and cheese are eaten plain or used in cooking. Creams and sour cream are used in many recipes. Ice cream, by itself, is a good dessert. It can also be used with other foods to make frozen desserts and beverages.

FRESH MILKS

Milk comes in many different forms, 10-3. When buying fresh milk, you may choose from whole, low-fat and skim milks. Buttermilk and flavored milk beverages may also be available.

Fresh milks are perishable. This means they will spoil if they are not used within several days or if they are not kept refrigerated. Containers of fresh milk often show a freshness date. Properly stored, the milk should remain fresh until that date.

"Grade A" on the container means the milk is wholesome. It also means the milk has been *pasteurized*. Pasteurization is a heat treatment that kills bacteria. Usually, milk is also *homogenized*. This process breaks up the milk fat and disperses it evenly throughout the milk. Years ago, when you bought a bottle of milk, you would find a layer of cream floating on the top. Today this is prevented by homogenization.

Milk is classified by the amount of fat it contains. Whole milk has the most fat. Low-fat milk has less fat, and skim milk contains the least fat. When fat is removed from the milk, the kilojoule (Calorie) value is reduced. Skim milk, for instance, has almost half as many kilojoules (Calories) as whole milk.

10-2 *Dairy products can be combined to make a variety of nutritious treats.*

UNITED DAIRY INDUSTRY ASSOC.

UNITED DAIRY INDUSTRY ASSOC.

10-1 *Dairy products other than milk usually contain the same nutrients as milk, but in lesser amounts.*

UNITED DAIRY INDUSTRY ASSOC.

10-3 *Most stores sell many forms of milk.*

Cultured buttermilk is made from skim or low-fat milk. Lactic acid bacteria are added to the milk. The result is a thickened milk with an acid flavor.

Flavored milk beverages can be made from whole, low-fat or skim milk. Flavors such as strawberry, coffee or maple can be used. Chocolate is a popular flavor. When chocolate is added to whole milk, it is called chocolate milk. When chocolate is added to low-fat milk, it is called chocolate low-fat milk. When chocolate is added to skim milk, it is called chocolate drink. When cocoa is used instead of chocolate, the beverages are called "chocolate-flavored" milk, low-fat milk and drink.

OTHER FORMS OF MILK

Other forms of milk are processed for long-term storage. Processed milks include dry milk, canned evaporated milk and sweetened condensed milk.

Dry milk is usually sold as either dry whole milk or nonfat dry milk. *Dry whole milk* is made by removing water from whole milk. *Nonfat dry milk* is made by removing water and fat from whole milk. These products are usually mixed with water before they are used. They should be chilled several hours after mixing to allow the flavor to develop. Nonfat dry milk will keep for months. Dry whole milk does not keep as well. It tends to develop an off-flavor if it is not used soon after the package is opened.

Evaporated milk is whole milk with about half of the water removed. This product is sealed in cans and sterilized to preserve it. Evaporated milk is often used in cooking. It can also be mixed with an equal amount of water and used in place of whole milk. Evaporated skim milk is available in some stores.

Sweetened condensed milk is another type of canned milk. Basically, it is made by adding a large amount of sugar to evaporated milk. Sweetened condensed milk is a sweet, syrupy product which is often used in desserts. Never substitute sweetened condensed milk when your recipe calls for evaporated or whole milk.

BUTTER, CREAMS AND YOGURT

Butter is made by churning cream. Most butter has salt added to help preserve it. Unsalted butter is usually labeled "sweet" or "unsalted" butter. Coloring may also be added. Federal standards define grades for butter based on flavor, body and color.

Whipped butter is butter that has been whipped to make it easier to spread. Whipping also increases the volume of the butter. Thus, whipped butter can't be directly substituted for regular butter in a recipe.

Cream is classified by the amount of fat it contains. *Heavy whipping cream* contains the most fat. *Light cream* (often called coffee or table cream) contains less fat than whipping cream. *Half-and-half* contains the least fat. Half-and-half is a homogenized mixture of milk and cream.

Sour cream is a smooth, thick product made by adding lactic acid bacteria to light cream. This produces a pleasant, slightly sour flavor. Sour cream is often used for dips or as a topping for baked potatoes and fresh fruit.

Yogurt is made by adding special bacteria to whole, low-fat or skim milk. It is thick and smooth, with the same nutritional value as the milk from which it is made. Yogurt has become popular as a satisfying snack. Plain yogurt can be used in many ways. It can replace sour cream in many dips, sauces and salad dressings. Fruit and various flavorings may be added to yogurt, 10-4. Frozen yogurt is a tasty dessert.

FROZEN DESSERTS

Ice cream is made from milk, cream, sugar, stabilizers and various flavorings. *French ice cream* has egg yolk added. This gives the product extra richness. *Ice milk* is similar to ice cream, but it contains less fat.

Sherbet is made from sugar, milk solids, water, food acid (often from fruit) and flavorings. Sherbets contain about twice as much sugar as ice cream, but much less fat.

Ice cream, ice milk or sherbet can be the basis of many nutritious and appealing treats. See 10-5.

CHEESE

Cheese is made by separating the solids in milk (called *curds*) from the liquid (called *whey*). Variations in this basic process produce dozens of different cheeses. Several are shown in 10-6.

Each type of cheese has its own flavor, appearance and texture. These characteristics depend on how the cheese is made. Differences among cheeses may be the result of the kind of milk used and the way the curd is separated from the whey. Special bacteria or molds used to ripen cheese also create differences among cheeses. The length of time a cheese is cured (aged) affects cheese flavor too. The longer a cheese is cured, the sharper its flavor will be.

Cheese choices

Being familiar with different types of cheese can help you make wise cheese choices.

Cheeses are grouped according to how they are made. The three main types are natural, pasteurized, and coldpack. Flavor can vary greatly from one cheese to another. A basic understanding of the different types will be helpful as you choose new cheeses to try.

Natural cheeses. These cheeses are usually cured (aged) for a period of time to develop their flavor. Usually, the longer the curing time, the stronger the flavor becomes. Some natural cheeses are *ripened*. During ripening,

LEA AND PERRINS, INC.

10-4 Make a low-kilojoule (Calorie), nutritious dip by seasoning plain yogurt. Even your friends who aren't dieting will enjoy this snack.

UNITED DAIRY INDUSTRY ASSOC.

10-5 Ice cream floats, ice cream waffle sandwiches and sundaes on sticks are good sources of calcium.

a mold or bacteria is added to give the cheese a distinct flavor. Swiss cheese is an example of a cheese ripened by bacteria. Blue cheese is an example of a cheese ripened by mold. Cheeses may also be *unripened*. Cottage and cream cheese are examples of unripened cheeses.

Natural cheeses are often grouped according to the amount of moisture they contain. Those with the least moisture are "very hard" cheeses. They are generally used in grated form, such as Parmesan or Romano. "Hard" cheeses include Swiss and cheddar. "Semisoft" cheeses include mozzarella, Muenster, brick and blue. "Soft" cheeses have the most moisture. They include cottage, cream, ricotta and Neufchatel.

Pasteurized process cheese. This cheese is a blend of natural cheeses. The cheeses are shredded and mixed together. The mixture is then pasteurized or heated to keep the cheese from ripening any further. Emulsifying agents are added so that the cheeses will not separate. Process cheese melts easily when heated. It is often used in casseroles and grilled cheese sandwiches.

Pasteurized process cheese food is similar to pasteurized process cheese, but it contains more moisture and less fat. Since cheese food is more moist, its texture is softer, and it spreads more easily. Process cheese food is milder in flavor and melts more easily than process cheese. Spices, vegetables and meats may be added for flavor.

Pasteurized process cheese spread contains even more moisture and less fat than pasteurized process cheese food. Process cheese spread is often sold in jars.

Coldpack cheeses. These cheeses are similar to the process cheeses except that they are not heated. Coldpack cheeses are softer than natural cheeses and they spread more easily. Spices, wine or other flavorings may be added.

Coldpack cheese food is made the same way as coldpack cheese is made, but other ingredients are added. Coldpack cheese food is milder in flavor and more moist. It is also easier to spread.

Tips on choosing cheese

Food stores carry many types of cheese. You'll find a lot of useful information on the labels of cheeses that will help you make good buying decisions. Natural cheeses must be labeled with their specific names, such as "Swiss cheese," "cheddar cheese" or "Muenster cheese." Pasteurized process cheeses, coldpack cheeses, cheese foods and cheese spreads should be clearly labeled. The label should list the kinds of cheeses used in these products. Other ingredients that were added should also be listed.

When choosing cheese, ask yourself several questions. What kind of flavor do you want? Natural cheeses vary, depending on the way they are ripened and cured. Look for words such as "mild," "medium" or "mellow" if you want a mild flavor. "Aged" or "sharp" cheese has a stronger flavor. Pasteurized process cheeses are often milder than natural cheeses.

Which form of cheese should you buy—whole, sliced or grated? Your choice will depend on how much money you want to spend and how you plan to use the cheese. The cheapest way to buy cheese is in large, uncut pieces. For sandwiches, you may prefer to buy individually wrapped slices of cheese. They often cost more, but they are convenient to use. Shredded cheese is quick and easy to use in foods like sauces and pizza, but it's easy to shred cheese yourself. You'll have to decide if the convenience is worth the cost.

How can you get the most for your money? Check the unit price of each package. This will tell you how much the cheese costs per kilogram (pound). Domestic cheeses (made in this country) cost less than imported ones. A store brand often costs less than a brand name.

Swiss and cheddar cheeses may carry a USDA grade shield. This means the cheese meets certain quality standards.

NONDAIRY PRODUCTS

Many substitutes for dairy products are found in the dairy section of food stores. These are called nondairy products. You will also find some, such as whipped toppings, in

1—Swiss. 2—White Cheddar. 3—Colby (Longhorn). 4—Muenster. 5—Blue. 6—Gorgonzola. 7—Port du Salut. 8—Monterey Jack. 9—Caraway. 10—Colby (Midget). 11—Provolone. 12—Fontina. 13—Brick. 14—Limburger. 15—Brick. 16—Scamorze. 17—Camembert. 18—Brie. 19—Ricotta. 20—Gouda. 21—Cheddar. 22—Parmesan (grated). 23—Romano. 24—Parmesan. 25—Cheddar wedge. 26—Edam. 27—Bel Paese. 28—Cream. 29—Cottage.

10-6 Large varieties of cheeses are available. How many of these have you tried?

the frozen food section. Others, such as powdered coffee whiteners, can be found on various store shelves.

It's important to read the labels when you are looking at nondairy products, 10-7. Nondairy products appeal to people who have trouble digesting milk and to groups following religious dietary laws. But these products may confuse consumers who are looking for products with unsaturated fats or with fewer kilojoules (Calories). Many nondairy products are made from saturated vegetable fats, and may be just as fattening as dairy products. Nutrition labels will help you compare the contents and nutritional values of dairy and nondairy products.

HOW TO STORE DAIRY PRODUCTS

All fresh milk products and creams should be stored in covered containers in the refrigerator. Fresh milk products and creams are best when used within three to five days. Unopened canned milk can be stored on a shelf for a long time. Once it is opened, it should be treated as fresh milk. Simply cover the can and store it in the refrigerator. Dry milk can be stored on a shelf for six to eight months. Once it is mixed with water, it should be handled as fresh milk.

Butter should be covered or wrapped so that it does not pick up odor from other foods. It will keep a week or two in the refrigerator or for a few days in the butter compartment in the refrigerator. Butter can be kept frozen for several months.

Ice cream, ice milk and sherbet should be stored in the freezer in a tightly closed container. These foods will keep up to two months.

Cheese should be tightly wrapped or covered and stored in the refrigerator. Some, such as cottage cheese and cream cheese, should be used within a few days after you buy them. Most cheese will keep well for several weeks if properly stored. When you cut off pieces, cover the remaining cheese with an airtight wrap to keep the edges from drying out. Mold may form on the surface of cheese during storage. This is not harmful and can be cut off before the cheese is used.

Cheddar, Swiss, and many other cheeses can be frozen. Careful, air-tight wrapping will prevent cheese from drying out and losing flavor. Small, unopened packages can be frozen without rewrapping. Larger pieces should be cut into smaller chunks and tightly sealed in plastic wrap or aluminum foil. Process cheese products will keep in the freezer for up to four months. Other cheeses should be used within a month or two. Thaw frozen cheese in the refrigerator a day before using it. Use cheese fairly soon after it has been thawed.

MAKING WHIPPED TOPPINGS

Whipped cream is used in many dessert recipes. It is also used as a topping for pies and puddings.

The more fat cream has, the better it will whip and stay whipped. This is why heavy whipping cream is usually used.

Cream whips best when it is well-chilled. For best results, chill the mixing bowl and beaters, too. Don't whip the cream too long. If you do, it will turn into butter.

Evaporated milk and nonfat dry milk can also be whipped. Use evaporated milk as it comes from the can. Put it in the freezer until fine ice cyrstals form. Then whip the milk. Fold in a little lemon juice at the end of the whipping to increase the stability of the foam.

When using nonfat dry milk, mix equal amounts of the dry milk and cold water. Pour the milk into a mixing bowl, and chill it in the freezer until tiny ice crystals form around the edges. Whip the milk just before serving. Whipped milk tends to lose air as it stands. After whipping, add lemon juice to help it keep its shape.

You can flavor whipped toppings by folding in sugar and vanilla.

COOKING WITH MILK

Milk is a basic ingredient in a variety of recipes. See 10-8. When cooking with milk, three things can happen to cause failure. A skin can form, the milk can curdle, or the milk can stick to the pan and scorch. Each of these can be prevented if you take some special care.

How to prevent a skin from forming

When milk is heated, a layer of *skin* may form on the top. You may have noticed this when making hot chocolate. The skin is made up of milk solids which have separated and floated to the top. The easiest way to prevent skin from forming is to stir the milk while it is heating. But if you forget, and the skin does form, just remove it with a spoon. Don't stir it into the mixture. The skin will make the mixture lumpy.

How to prevent curdling

Sometimes when you are cooking with milk, you may find that the sauce or soup has *curdled*. Small, soft lumps, which look like tiny curds of cottage cheese, have separated out. Curdling is most likely to happen when you combine milk with an acid or salty food. It can happen when you use milk which is just about to turn sour. High temperatures can also cause curdling.

To prevent curdling, use fresh milk and cook at a low temperature. If you are adding acid foods to milk, either the milk or the acid should be thickened first. For instance, if you are making tomato soup, add tomato juice to thickened milk. The soup will be less likely to curdle.

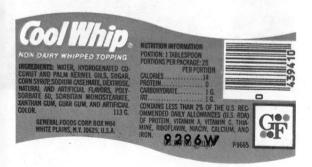

10-7 Read the labels of nondairy products before you buy them.

How to prevent sticking and scorching

Milk is very sensitive to heat. It will curdle when high heat is used. It can also *scorch* (burn) easily and ruin your entire dish. To prevent milk from sticking to the bottom of the pan and scorching, always use low heat. Stir the mixture constantly until cooking is finished. Choose a pan which spreads heat evenly. Many cooks prefer to cook milk-based foods in a double boiler to prevent scorching. See 10-9.

MILK COOKERY

White sauce — (White sauce is a basic combination of milk, fat, flour and salt. It is used as a base for many sauces, cream soups, souffle's, casseroles and gravies.)
1. Melt fat over low heat.
2. Remove pan from heat and quickly stir in flour and seasonings.
3. Slowly add cold milk, stirring constantly until sauce is smooth.
4. Cook over moderate heat, stirring gently just until the sauce begins to boil.
5. Cook for one minute longer to cook the starch.

Cream soups
1. Prepare vegetables and/or meat. These foods may be cooked and cut into small pieces or pure'ed. (You can pure'e foods by using a food processor or by pressing them through a sieve.)
2. Prepare a thin white sauce.
3. Add vegetables and seasonings to the white sauce.
4. Heat just to the boiling point, stirring constantly. (Do not boil.)

Puddings — (Serve alone or use to make fillings for other desserts.)
1. Mix starch with sugar. (This separates the starch granules and will prevent the mixture from becoming lumpy.)
2. Slowly stir in cold milk.
3. Cook in a double boiler.
4. Stir constantly until mixture thickens.

10-8 Cooking with milk is a skill used in making white sauce, cream soups and puddings.

How to scald milk

Some recipes call for milk to be scalded. Recipes for yeast bread are examples. *Scalding* destroys enzymes in the milk. To scald milk, heat it slowly until bubbles form around the edges. Never boil milk. It can scorch or curdle. If a skin forms, remove it before you use the scalded milk. Evaporated milk and reconstituted dry milk (dry milk to which water has been added) do not require scalding.

COOKING WITH CHEESE

Cheese is a versatile food. It can be eaten plain, with fruit or crackers. It can also be used in salads, sandwiches, and a variety of main dishes. *Cheese fondue* is a popular main dish. It is a melted cheese sauce into which pieces of bread, fruits, or vegetables are dipped, 10-10. Cheese can be added to the sauces of many casseroles and vegetable dishes. Chart 10-11 lists ways some popular cheeses are used.

When cooking with cheese, remember that cheese will get stringy and tough if it is overcooked. Cheese has a low melting point. It takes only a few moments under a broiler to cook an open-faced cheese sandwich. If you leave it under the broiler too long, the cheese will burn.

When cheese is used in cooking, it is usually cut into pieces. The smaller the pieces are, the faster the cheese will melt. Generally, recipes call for cheese to be sliced, cubed or grated.

To cube cheese, cut it into thick slices and then cut the slices into strips. Finally, cut the strips into cubes. Slicing soft cheese like American or mozzarella can be difficult because the cheese tends to stick to the knife. To prevent sticking, coat the knife with flour or cornstarch or rinse the knife under very hot water.

To grate cheese, use a grater, blender or food processor. Most cheese is easier to grate when it is cold.

When adding grated cheese to a sauce, wait until the last few minutes of cooking. Remember, cheese will become tough if it is overcooked. When cheese is used as a topping for a casserole, it should be added during the last part of the cooking time. This prevents it from getting too brown and becoming tough and stringy.

Sometimes cheese is sprinkled over food which is broiled. This style is called *au gratin*. (Potatoes are often served au gratin.) When you are preparing a food au gratin, put it under the broiler for only a few moments, until the cheese melts and is bubbly.

BETTY CROCKER FOOD AND NUTRITION CENTER

10-9 Using a double boiler can prevent milk-based foods from scorching.

10-10 Cheese fondue originated in Switzerland. It is a popular dish for entertaining in the United States.

GUIDE FOR USING COMMON CHEESES

Cheeses	Toppings	Sauces	Casseroles	Breads	Cakes and pies	Salads	Sandwiches
Cheddar	✔	✔	✔	✔		✔	✔
American	✔	✔	✔	✔		✔	✔
Swiss	✔	✔	✔			✔	✔
Mozzarella	✔		✔				✔
Romano	✔	✔		✔			
Parmesan	✔	✔		✔		✔	
Provolone	✔		✔			✔	✔
Monterey Jack	✔	✔	✔			✔	✔
Brick	✔	✔	✔	✔		✔	✔
Muenster	✔		✔				✔
Edam		✔				✔	✔
Gouda		✔				✔	✔
Blue						✔	
Ricotta			✔		✔		
Cottage			✔		✔	✔	
Cream					✔		✔

10-11 Cheese can be used in a variety of ways.

You can make tasty, nutritious drinks with milk. Shown here are: chocolate milk, tangy fruit refresher, spicy coconut creamer, tomato twister, carrot curler and strawberry sipper.

toDefine

au gratin . . . butter . . .
coldpack cheese . . .
cultured buttermilk . . .
curdled . . . dry milk . . .
evaporated milk . . .
flavored milk beverages . . .
fortified . . .
half-and-half . . .
heavy whipping cream . . .
homogenized milk . . .
ice cream . . . ice milk . . .
low-fat milk . . .
natural cheese . . .
pasteurized . . .
pasteurized process cheese . . .
process cheese food . . .
process cheese spread . . .
scalding . . . scorch . . .
sherbet . . . skim milk . . .
skin . . . sour cream . . .
sweetened condensed milk . . .
whole milk . . . yogurt

toDiscuss

1. Besides drinking it, name three ways to include milk in your diet.
2. What is the purpose of homogenizing milk?
3. How do whole milk and skim milk differ in fat content? Which has fewer kilojoules (Calories)?
4. Why should dry milk be chilled several hours after mixing it with water?
5. Can you substitute evaporated milk and sweetened condensed milk for each other in recipes?
6. How is yogurt made?

7. Which cheese is likely to have the stronger flavor — one labeled "mellow" or one labeled "aged"?
8. What type of fat is often used in nondairy products?
9. How should fresh milk products be stored?
10. How should you store cheese?
11. For best results, when you make whipped cream, should you start with cream that is cold or at room temperature?
12. Name three things that could cause failure when cooking with milk. How can you prevent these from happening?
13. What happens to cheese if it is overcooked?

toDo

1. Visit a local supermarket. Make a list of different forms and types of cheese available, including package sizes and prices. Which are the best buys?
2. Buy small containers of plain yogurt and sour cream. Mix each with dry onion soup, to make a dip. Taste each. Evaluate them for taste, price, nutritional value and kilojoules (Calories).

3. Visit a supermarket and compare the prices of different brands of chocolate ice cream in various sizes. Which sizes and brands are the best buys?
4. Calculate the cost per unit (litre or gallon) of fresh whole milk, nonfat dry milk, and evaporated milk. Which would you buy to drink? Which would you buy for cooking and baking? Explain your answers.
5. Set up a cheese tasting display. Buy at least six different types of cheese and cut them into small pieces for sampling. Write down a brief description of each cheese as you sample it, including the color, texture, and flavor. List at least three ways each cheese might be used.
6. Bring in samples of imitation dairy products. Read the ingredient listing on each product. Taste each product and compare the flavor and texture with the dairy product it imitates. Compare the costs. Compare the kilojoule (Calorie) values, if possible. Does the imitation product offer you any advantages?
7. Compare ice cream and ice milk. How do they compare in color, texture, flavor and kilojoules (Calories)?

11

Meat and other protein sources

What do meat, poultry, fish and eggs have in common? After reading this chapter, you will know that they are excellent protein sources. You will also know that certain plants supply protein. You will be able to explain how to purchase and store these foods. You will also be able to use basic cooking skills to prepare protein foods.

Meat, poultry, fish and eggs are excellent sources of high quality protein. Many plant foods are also important protein sources. All through life, protein is needed to build and repair cells and to control other body functions. Foods that supply protein also provide many vitamins and minerals.

Sources of protein are the most expensive part of your food budget. You can save money and eat a more interesting variety of foods by including many different protein sources in your food planning. This chapter will cover the basic information on buying, storing and preparing sources of protein.

MEAT

Meat is the flesh of animals. Meats commonly found in stores include beef, veal, pork and lamb.

The term *beef* refers to meat from mature cattle. *Veal* is a mildly flavored meat that comes from very young cattle, usually less than three months old. *Pork* is meat from hogs. *Lamb* comes from sheep less than one year old.

Meat is made up of three major parts. Two of these parts—muscle and connective tissue—contain protein. The third major part of meat is fat. Fat surrounds different cuts of meat. For instance, you'll find fat along the sides of T-bone steaks. Some fat is also found with the muscle fibers. These small streaks of fat are called *marbling*. Marbling in meat usually means that the meat will be more tender and juicy, 11-1.

Variety meats are the edible organs of animals. The most common variety meats are liver, heart, brains, kidneys, sweetbreads and tongue. These meats often cost less than regular cuts of meat. Because many nutrients are stored in some organs, most variety meats are very nutritious. Liver, for example, is a rich source of iron. Variety meats can be prepared in a number of interesting and tasty ways, 11-2.

Processed meats are simply meats that have been processed to permit longer storage. Processing may involve curing, smoking, drying, canning, freezing or freeze-drying.

Curing, smoking and drying are used most often for meat products such as hams, bacon and sausages. Canning may be used for almost any meat or meat product. Canned products are very convenient and easy to store, although a few need to be refrigerated. Check the can for storage directions.

Frozen products include many simple cuts of meat, plus a large variety of heat-and-serve entrees, from pot pies to roasts.

Freeze-dried meats are dried at freezing temperatures. Lightweight and easy to keep, they are popular among campers.

What makes meat tender?

The *connective tissue* of the animal makes meat tough. Connective tissue is what holds the muscle cells in meat together. This tissue gets thicker and more developed as muscles are used and as the animal ages.

Tenderness is related to the grade, kind and

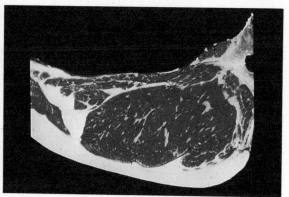

11-1 Marbling is the small streaks of fat among the muscle fibers of meat. It helps to make the meat juicy and tender.

11-2 Variety meats are rich in nutrients and can be served in many different ways. Shown here are tongue and liver.

cut of meat. All cuts of lamb and pork tend to be tender. Tenderness varies among beef cuts. The various sections of beef are shown in 11-3. The most tender beef cuts come from the rib and loin sections of the animal. This is because the muscles in this area are used least. Steaks and roasts cut from rib and loin sections are usually very tender and more expensive. Less tender cuts come from areas of the animal where the muscles are used most often. These cuts usually cost less.

Less tender meats are just as nutritious as tender cuts. There are ways to make less tender cuts of meat more tender. One way to tenderize meat is to cut through the connective tissue. You can grind the meat or pound it with a spiked meat mallet. Another way to break up the connective tissue is to slash the meat with a sharp knife.

Another way to tenderize meat is to *marinate* it in a liquid containing an acid. Acid ingredients such as lemon juice, vinegar and tomato juice soften some connective tissue.

Commercial meat tenderizers may be used. They contain enzymes that break down the protein in connective tissue. The enzymes do not become active until the meat is heated during cooking. Enzymes only work in certain temperature ranges. When the temperature gets too hot or too cool, they do not work. (This is why meat tenderizers do not affect the proteins in your body.) Always follow the package directions when you use commercial meat tenderizers. If the tenderizer is not used properly, the meat may become grainy and mushy.

One of the best ways to tenderize meat is to cook it slowly in a liquid. The slow, moist cooking softens much of the tough connective tissue. This makes the meat tender. Moist heat cooking methods will be discussed later in this chapter.

Buying meat

Because meat probably takes up a great deal of your food budget, you will want to shop carefully. At first, shopping for meat may seem a little confusing to you. Success in buying meat will depend on your knowledge of what you are buying. You need to know how to identify meat cuts and know what meat grades and inspection seals mean. Meat labels can be an important guide for you when buying meat. They not only tell you what kind of meat you are buying, but how much the meat costs.

When shopping for meat, consider how you plan to cook the meat and how many people you plan to serve. You can often save money at meat sales. Look for meats with little waste in fat and bone. These are good meat buys. You can get more servings per person with boneless, lean meat than with meat with lots of fat and bone.

How to identify meat cuts. The meat industry has developed a meat labeling program that is used by most stores. This labeling system makes it easy to identify cuts of meat.

Look at the meat label in 11-4. Listed first is the kind of meat such as beef or lamb. Next is the name of the wholesale cut. This tells you from what part of the animal the cut came, such as rib, loin or chuck. The standard name for the retail cut is then given, such as blade roast, ground beef or center loin. Use these labels as a guide when buying meats.

What do meat grades mean? Meat *grades* are a guide to quality. Quality is determined by the age of the animal, marbling and the appearance of the meat in terms of color, firmness and texture. Usually, younger animals are more tender. High quality meat is well marbled. (It has flecks of fat in the lean meat.) Firm meat with a fine texture is another sign of quality.

What do grades mean to you as a shopper? They help you know what to expect in terms of tenderness and juiciness. Lower grades are leaner. Because they contain less fat, they are less tender and juicy. They are also less expensive than the top grades. Grades are *not* related to nutritional value.

Why is meat inspected? Meat is *inspected* for wholesomeness. This is a check to make sure the animals are free from disease and the meat is safe to eat. Inspectors also check the processing plant for cleanliness.

How much does meat cost? Meat labels give

important price information. Both the weight and the cost per unit of weight appear on the label. These two figures are multiplied together to determine the price of the meat in the package.

When you buy meat, estimate the *cost per serving*. How many servings will the meat provide? Divide the number of servings into the cost. The result will be the cost per serving.

Low-priced meat that has a lot of bone and fat may have a high cost per serving. On the other hand, lean cuts that are more expensive are sometimes good buys in terms of cost per serving.

Which package of meat should you buy? Your choice depends on your budget, your taste preferences and how you plan to use the meat. For instance, ground beef prices are generally related to the fat content of the meat. The ground beef with the least fat usually costs the most. A package labeled "ground chuck" or "lean ground beef" has less fat than one labeled "ground beef." You may decide to buy leaner ground beef if you are making hamburgers. For a meat loaf or spaghetti sauce, you may prefer the less expensive ground beef with more fat.

How much meat should you buy? The amount of meat you need to buy depends on the cut and how many people you plan to serve. Meat with no bones and little fat will provide more servings than the same amount of meat with lots of waste. As an example, compare equal amounts of canned, boneless ham and spareribs. The ham would provide many more servings per unit of weight.

You may decide to buy extra meat and to use the leftovers in later meals. Leftover meat loaf, for instance, can be used for sandwiches

11-4 A meat label tells you the kind of meat, the wholesale cut and the common name for the cut.

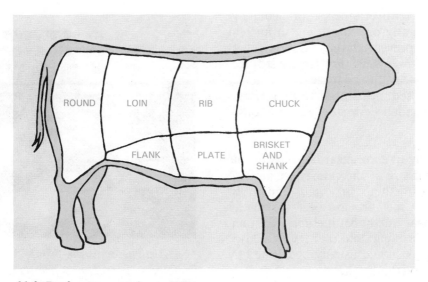

11-3 Beef cuts come from different sections of the animal.

the next day. You might use leftover roast as the basis for a hearty stew. There are many ways to use leftover meats. Look for ideas in magazines and cookbooks.

How to store meat

Fresh meat spoils quickly if it is not stored properly. Store meat in the coldest part of the refrigerator or in the meat compartment. Prepackaged fresh meat can be refrigerated in its original package. If you purchase meat that is wrapped in butcher paper, rewrap it in plastic wrap or aluminum foil.

Generally, you should not store fresh meat in the refrigerator for more than two days. For longer storage, you can freeze meat. Prepackaged meat can be stored in the freezer without rewrapping for one to two weeks. For longer than a week or two, rewrap the meat tightly. You can wrap the meat in freezer paper, aluminum foil or plastic wrap. Or you can put the meat in airtight containers designed for freezer use. See 11-5.

To thaw frozen meat, take it out of the freezer a day in advance and put it in the refrigerator. Most microwave ovens have defrost cycles that thaw foods quickly. Large roasts can be cooked without thawing first, but the cooking will take longer. This uses more energy.

Refrigerate leftover meats immediately. Cover them tightly or store them in airtight containers to prevent drying. Use leftovers within two or three days. For longer storage, most leftover meats can be frozen.

Some processed meats need to be refrigerated. Check the label for storage directions.

How to cook meat

The best way to cook meat depends on the tenderness and size of the cut. There are two main cooking methods: *dry heat* and *moist heat*. Dry heat methods are best for tender cuts. Dry heat methods include roasting, broiling, panbroiling and panfrying, 11-6. Less tender cuts should usually be cooked by a moist heat method. The slow, moist heat helps to tenderize these cuts. Moist heat methods include braising and cooking in

liquid, 11-7. Dry heat and moist heat methods for cooking meat are described in 11-8.

Meat shrinks as it cooks. It loses juices and becomes smaller in size. By carefully following directions for cooking meats, you can cut down on the amount of shrinkage. The meat will also be moist and flavorful.

Temperature is an important factor in cooking meat. High temperatures cause more juices to be lost. Therefore, shrinkage is greater. Meat thermometers are the best way to check the doneness of larger pieces of meat. The tip of the thermometer should be centered in the cut. It should not touch a bone or rest in fat. (This will make the temperature reading inaccurate.)

POULTRY

Suppose you were asked to list some typical American foods. Southern fried chicken and Thanksgiving turkey would probably be among the first foods on your list. Chicken and turkey are *poultry*. Other kinds of poultry include duck, goose and game birds.

All types of poultry are excellent sources of protein. Depending on the cooking method, poultry is generally lower in kilojoules (Calories) than other meats. Because of its

11-5 Airtight, moisture-proof containers or wrappings protect meats from drying out in the freezer.

SILVERSTONE® AND TEFLON®—DUPONT'S NON-STICK FINISHES

11-6 Tender cuts of meat are prepared using dry heat methods. This meat is being panbroiled.

SILVERSTONE® AND TELFON®—DUPONT'S NON-STICK FINISHES

11-7 Less tender meats are prepared using moist heat methods. Stews are a delicious way to use less tender cuts.

MEAT COOKERY

DRY HEAT METHODS

Roasting — (For large, tender cuts of meat.)
1. Season, if desired.
2. Place meat, fat side up, on rack in shallow roasting pan.
3. Insert meat thermometer into thickest part of meat. Do not let the thermometer bulb touch bone or rest in fat.
4. Do not add water. Do not cover.
5. Roast in oven at 150 to 180°C (300 to 350°F).
6. Roast to recommended degree of doneness:
   Beef — 60 to 75°C (140 to 170°F)
   Veal — 75 to 80°C (170 to 180°F)
   Lamb— 60 to 75°C (140 to 170°F)
   Pork — 80 to 85°C (180 to 185°F)
7. Let meat rest for 15 to 20 minutes after you take it from the oven. This will make it easier to carve.

Broiling — (For tender steaks, chops and patties.)
1. Trim and slash fat around the edges of steaks or chops to prevent curling.
2. Set the oven regulator for broiling. Preheat broiler, if desired. (An outdoor grill can be used instead of an oven.)
3. Place meat on rack of broiler pan 8 to 13 cm (3 to 5 inches) from the heat.
4. Broil until meat is brown on one side.
5. Season, if desired.
6. Turn meat and cook until done.

Panbroiling — (For tender cuts less than 2.5 cm [1 inch] thick.)
1. Place meat in heavy skillet.
2. Do not add fat or water. Do not cover.
3. Cook at a medium temperature and turn the meat often for even cooking.
4. Pour fat from pan as it accumulates.
5. Season, if desired.

Panfrying — (For thin pieces of tender meats or less tender meats which have been tenderized.)
1. Add a small amount of oil or fat to the pan for lean meats or pieces that have been coated with flour or crumbs. (Do not add fat if the meat already contains quite a bit of fat.)
2. Brown meat on both sides.
3. Season, if desired.
4. Do not cover.
5. Cook at medium temperature until done. Turn meat occasionally.

MOIST HEAT METHODS

Braising — (For less tender cuts of meat.)
1. Brown meat on all sides in heavy skillet or pot.
2. Season, if desired.
3. Add a small amount of liquid (water, vegetable juices or soup).
4. Cover tightly.
5. Cook at low temperature until tender.

Cooking in Liquid — (For large cuts of less tender meat or for meats to be used in stews.)
1. Brown meat on all sides for extra flavor and color, if desired.
2. Season, if desired.
3. Cover meat entirely with water or other liquid (such as vegetable juice).
4. Cover and simmer (cook below boiling point) until tender.
5. If you plan to add vegetables, wait until the last part of the cooking time.

11-8 You can prepare meat in a variety of ways depending upon the tenderness and size of the cut.

mild flavor and tenderness, poultry can be prepared in many different ways, 11-9.

Chicken

Chicken comes in many different sizes and forms. The kind of chicken you buy will depend on how you are going to cook it. The number of people you plan to serve should also be considered.

Rock Cornish game hens. The smallest chickens you can buy are Rock Cornish game hens. Usually, an entire bird is one serving, but a large bird may serve two people. Game hens are often stuffed and roasted, but they can also be split in half and broiled.

Broiler-fryers. The most common form of chicken found in stores is the broiler-fryer. Broilers-fryers can be stuffed and roasted whole. Cut up, they can also be broiled, fried or used in stews and casseroles. Broiler-fryers are sold whole, cut in halves or quarters, or in packages of special pieces. Chicken parts that are packaged according to cut (such as legs, thighs and breasts) are usually cut from broiler-fryers.

Roasting chickens and capons. Young birds which are larger than broiler-fryers are called roasting chickens or capons. Roasting chickens are female, and capons are males. Capons have a greater amount of white meat than roasting chickens. Roasting chickens and capons are usually stuffed and roasted. They usually cost more per kilogram (pound) than broiler-fryers. But roasting chickens and capons have more meat in relation to the bone.

Stewing hens. Mature chickens are called stewing hens. Meat from older birds often has more flavor but is tougher. This is why stewing hens are so good for stews. They add lots of flavor, and the moist heat cooking method makes the meat more tender.

Turkey

For many Americans, turkey is associated with fall and winter holidays. But turkey is available in most stores year-round. Generally, turkey is frozen, except at holiday time when stores may feature fresh turkey. Whole frozen turkeys are sometimes specially treated with cooking fat and are labeled "self-basting." Whole turkeys come in many sizes.

Turkey roasts are either all light meat or a combination of light and dark meat. They can be either baked in the oven or barbecued on a spit. Some stores carry other turkey products like turkey steak, ground turkey and turkey hot dogs, 11-10. Turkey cutlets are made from the white meat and taste similar to veal cutlets.

Other forms of poultry

Other forms of poultry include duck, goose, guinea hen, squab (young pigeon), pheasant and quail. Sometimes you will be able to find these at food stores. These forms of poultry are usually stuffed and roasted and served on special occasions. You can expect to pay more for unusual forms of poultry than you would for chicken or turkey.

Buying poultry

When you buy poultry, select clean birds which are not discolored or bruised. Breasts, thighs and legs should be plump.

Figure the cost per serving to decide which poultry is the best buy. When you purchase poultry, look for the large, plump birds. That way you'll be getting more meat in relation to bone and a better buy.

You can usually save money by buying whole chickens and cutting them up yourself. When chicken is on sale, buy several and create your own packages of parts. Wings, thighs and legs make great fried chicken. Breasts can be used in many different ways, such as in salads and casseroles. Backs, necks and giblets can be combined with vegetables and water to make chicken soup. Remember, when you buy chicken already packed according to parts, you usually pay more for the convenience.

Generally, you pay more per kilogram (pound) for small birds than for large ones. And you will have to pay extra for turkeys that are self-basting.

Some stores carry turkey parts. You may be able to buy turkey legs, wings and breasts separately. These allow you to include turkey in family meals without having to purchase an entire bird. Parts may cost a little extra per kilogram (pound), but you will have less waste.

Inspection and grades. Poultry is inspected for wholesomeness by the U.S. Department of Agriculture. It then may be graded for quality. High quality birds are meaty and attractive in appearance.

How to store poultry

Fresh poultry should be wrapped loosely and stored in the coldest part of the refrigerator. It should be used within two days after purchase. Leftover poultry should also

11-10 Turkey can be processed to taste like several different meats. Turkey hot dogs are an example.

11-9 Whole chicken can be roasted uncovered in the oven or braised in a covered pot.

be refrigerated. Always remove any stuffing and store it in a separate container. See 11-11.

You can freeze fresh and leftover poultry for later use. Fresh poultry should be rinsed off and patted dry. It should then be wrapped in moisture-proof freezer wrap. Leftover poultry should be stored in airtight containers or wrapped tightly in freezer wrap. Frozen poultry will keep several months if stored at −18°C (0°F).

The best way to thaw frozen poultry is to place it in the refrigerator overnight. Large turkeys may take one to three days to thaw. You can thaw poultry more quickly by placing the wrapped poultry in cold water. Depending on the size of the bird, it should thaw in two to six hours.

Never allow thawed poultry to stand at room temperature. It can spoil easily. Do not thaw commercially frozen stuffed poultry. This should be cooked according to package directions.

How to cook poultry

Most poultry can be cooked using either dry or moist heat cooking methods. Dry heat methods include frying, broiling and roasting. Moist heat methods include braising and stew-ing. See 11-12.

Sometimes you may notice that meat near the bones in poultry may darken after cooking. This is from the pigment of the bone marrow. The quality and taste of the meat is not changed by this darkening.

Many people like to stuff whole birds before roasting them. If you are going to stuff poultry, do so just before you cook it. If you stuff it ahead of time, the warm stuffing provides just the right conditions for bacteria to grow. This can cause food poisoning. Prepare stuffing in advance and store it in the refrigerator until you're ready to cook the bird.

It is safer and easier to cook the stuffing separately. Simply put the stuffing in a greased casserole dish. Place it in the oven during the last part of the cooking time.

FISH AND SHELLFISH

Whether you catch them yourself or buy them fresh, frozen or canned, fish and shellfish are delicious. All forms of fish and shellfish are excellent sources of protein. They also contain important minerals, including iron and phosphorous. Fish and shellfish that live in salt water are rich in iodine.

TUPPERWARE® HOME PARTIES

11-11 Leftover poultry and stuffing should be stored separately. Never refrigerate leftover stuffing in the bird itself.

POULTRY COOKERY

DRY HEAT METHODS

Frying

1. Cut poultry into serving pieces.
2. Rinse pieces and pat them dry.
3. If desired, coat pieces to make them crispy when cooked. (A coating can be a dry ingredient such as seasoned flour, bread crumbs or cornmeal. A batter can also be used.)
4. Heat a small amount of oil or fat in skillet.
5. Place pieces in a single layer in the hot fat.
6. Brown pieces evenly, turning occasionally.
7. Reduce heat. Cover and cook until tender.
8. Drain on paper towels to absorb excess fat.

Deep-fat frying — (Same as frying, Steps 1-3.)

4. Preheat enough fat to cover pieces.
5. Place pieces in fryer.
6. Brown pieces evenly in fat.
7. Cook until tender.
8. Drain on paper towels to absorb excess fat.

Ovenfrying — (Same as frying. Steps 1-3.)

4. Place pieces in a single layer in a shallow baking dish, skin side down.
5. Bake at 190 °C (375 °F) for about an hour.

Broiling

1. Cut into halves, quarters or pieces.
2. Place on broiling pan, skin side down.
3. Brush each piece with melted butter or a sauce to prevent drying.
4. Place pieces about 23 cm (9 inches) from heat source. If barbecuing, place pieces about 8 to 15 cm (3 to 6 inches) from hot coals.
5. Turn every 15 minutes until brown and tender.

Roasting

1. If desired, prepare stuffing.
2. Rinse bird and pat it dry.
3. If desired, fill neck opening lightly with stuffing. Then fasten the skin to the back with a skewer. Turn the bird over and fill the main body cavity. Don't overpack the stuffing. It will expand during cooking as it absorbs the juices. Use skewers and string to hold the opening together.
4. Fold the wings across the back so that the tips of the wings touch.
5. Tie the legs and tail together with string.
6. Put the bird, breast side up, on the roasting rack in a shallow roasting pan.
7. Brush top with fat.
8. Place tip of meat thermometer in the thickest part of the thigh or breast. (If you do not have a meat thermometer, you can use a cookbook table to estimate cooking time.)
9. Place in 160 °C (325 °F) oven.
10. Poultry is cooked when the internal temperature is 85 °C (185 °F). (If you do not have a meat thermometer, poultry is cooked when the leg joint moves easily in its socket.)
11. After poultry is removed from the oven, allow it to stand 10 to 20 minutes. This makes carving easier.

Baking

1. Cut poultry into halves, quarters or pieces.
2. Rinse pieces. Place them in a shallow baking dish or roasting pan.
3. Baste occasionally with a sauce, if desired.
4. Bake at 180 °C (350 °F) for about one hour.

MOIST HEAT METHODS

Braising — (Fricassee is a word often used in poultry cookery. It means to braise.)

1. Cut into pieces. Rinse and pat dry.
2. Brown pieces in a small amount of fat.
3. Add a small amount of liquid. Cover pan.
4. Cook in oven at 160 °C (325 °F) or simmer on range-top.
5. Cook until tender.

Stewing

1. Cut poultry in half, quarters or pieces.
2. Rinse pieces. Place in deep pan.
3. Add enough water to cover poultry. Add seasonings.
4. Bring to a boil. Then reduce heat.
5. Cover pan and simmer until tender.
6. Simmer until poultry is tender.

11-12 Poultry can be prepared in a variety of ways.

Fish

Fish include both saltwater and freshwater fish. They have scales, gills, a backbone and fins. There are many varieties of fish. At the store, you may find fresh fish sold in different ways. *Whole* or *round fish* are fish as they come from the water. *Dressed fish* has all the waste except bones removed. *Fillets* are lengthwise slices cut away from the backbone. *Steaks* are cross-sectional slices of large dressed fish.

Processed fish is also available. When fish is processed, it is smoked, salted, marinated or canned. See 11-13. Frozen fish is available in many forms—from whole fish to bite-size portions. Sometimes frozen fish is sold with a breaded coating or in a sauce.

Shellfish

Shellfish can be divided into two groups — mollusks and crustaceans, 11-14. *Mollusks* have hard outside shells which are either in one piece or hinged. Oysters, clams, scallops, mussels, snails and conchs are mollusks. *Crustaceans* have legs and crust-like shells with joints. Crustaceans include lobsters, crabs, crayfish and shrimp.

How to buy fish and shellfish

Most fresh fish are available on a seasonal basis, depending on where you live. Check local stores to see what kinds they have. If fresh fish are not available, many popular kinds are available frozen.

When choosing whole fresh fish, look to see that the eyes are bright, clear and full. The gills should have a reddish-pink color. The scales should lie tightly against the skin and have a bright sheen. The flesh should be firm and not separating from the bones. Fish and shellfish should not have a strong or bad odor. Frozen fish should have no discoloration or brownish tinge.

In coastal regions, fresh shellfish is usually available, depending on the season of the year. In other regions, it may be available, but it is usually quite costly. Shellfish is also frozen. You can often find frozen shrimp, lobster tails, oysters and crabmeat in local stores. Shrimp, lobster, crabmeat, oysters and clams are also canned.

Inspection and grading. Inspection and grading of fish and shellfish are voluntary. The top grades are given to fish and shellfish which have a uniform size, good flavor, and few blemishes or defects.

How to store fish and shellfish

Fresh fish and shellfish are very *perishable.* (Perishable means that they spoil quickly.) Therefore, proper storage is important. Wrap fish and shellfish in moisture-proof paper and store them in the coldest part of the refrigerator. See 11-15. Use fish and shellfish within one or two days after purchase or catch.

For longer storage, fish and shellfish should be frozen. They can be kept in the freezer for four to six months. Fish and shellfish should be wrapped tightly in moisture-proof paper.

Cooked fish products should be refrigerated

CANNED SALMON INSTITUTE

11-13 Many salads, sandwiches, snacks and casseroles can be made from convenient canned fish.

in a covered container for no longer than three or four days. they can be kept in the freezer for two to three months.

To thaw fish or shellfish for cooking, place the package in the refrigerator. Allow about 24 hours for thawing. For quicker thawing, place it under cold running water for about an hour. Do not thaw fish products at room temperature or in warm water. Thawed fish products should not be refrozen. Try to schedule thawing so that you will be cooking fish or shellfish soon after it has thawed. Thawed fish products should not be kept for longer than one day before cooking. Breaded fish products are not thawed. They are cooked from the frozen state.

TUPPERWARE® HOME PARTIES

11-15 Fish spoils easily, so it is important to store it properly.

GENERAL ELECTRIC, "COOKING WITH A FOOD PROCESSOR"

11-14 Shrimp and clams — two kinds of shellfish — are used to make this hearty stew.

How to cook fish and shellfish

There are many different ways to prepare fish and shellfish. Fish and shellfish can be cooked by most of the methods used to cook meats. Popular methods of preparation are described in 11-16.

The most important thing to remember is that fish cooks quickly. When it is over-cooked, it becomes tough and dry, and may develop an unpleasant flavor. Color is one guide to doneness. The flesh of fish and shellfish becomes a more solid color (usually white) when it is done. Shrimp may have more of a pinkish color. Lobster and crab shells turn red. The shells of mussels and clams open when they are cooked.

For fish, texture is an important guide to doneness. You can tell when fish is cooked by testing it with a fork. Press a fork against the thickest part of the cooked fish. If it starts to flake apart, it is done. (Cheesecloth is sometimes tied around fish to help it keep its shape. This is because the muscle fibers of fish separate easily during cooking.)

EGGS

You have probably eaten eggs in many forms, from plain fried eggs, to soufflés, to custards. Eggs are found in many meals, from main dishes to desserts.

Eggs are an important source of protein in meals. They are an inexpensive protein food, usually costing much less per serving than meat.

Buying eggs

Eggs are usually sold by the dozen. The price you pay depends on the *grade* and *size* of the eggs. The grade and size are usually printed on the egg carton. Egg grades are determined by the quality of the egg and the appearance of the shell. Grades of eggs usually found in stores are Grade AA, Grade A and Grade B. Grade AA eggs have very thick egg whites and well-centered yolks. Grade AA and Grade A eggs are good for frying and poaching because of their good appearance. Grade B eggs can be used for general cooking.

FISH COOKERY

DRY HEAT METHODS

Baking
1. Place in a greased baking dish.
2. Season to taste or as recipe directs.
3. Bake at 180°C (350°F) until done.
4. If desired, baste with a sauce or melted butter to prevent dryness.

Broiling — (Pieces of fish about 2.5 cm (1 inch) thick are good for broiling.)
1. Place on greased broiler pan. Brush with melted fat or a sauce to prevent drying.
2. Place pan 5 to 10 cm (2 to 4 inches) from the heat source.
3. Dressed fish or fish steaks will probably need to be turned over halfway through cooking.

Barbecuing
1. Grease the grill well to prevent sticking.
2. Cook about 10 cm (4 inches) from hot coals.
3. If desired, baste with a sauce or marinade.
4. Thick pieces will need to be turned once.

Frying
1. Dip pieces in a liquid (such as beaten egg, milk or French dressing), or in a batter and then in crumbs, seasoned flour or cornmeal.
2. Heat fat to about 190°C (375°F).
3. For panfrying, the fat should be about 0.3 cm (1/8 inch) deep in a skillet. (For deep-fat frying, use enough oil to completely cover the pieces.)
4. Cook until golden brown.

Ovenfrying
1. Dip and coat pieces as for regular fried fish.
2. Place in a well-greased baking pan.
3. If desired, baste with a sauce or marinade.
4. Thick pieces will need to be turned once.

MOIST HEAT METHODS

Poaching
1. If desired, wrap fish in cheesecloth.
2. Use enough liquid (water, milk or broth) to just cover the fish.
3. Simmer until fish is cooked.

Steaming
1. Wrap fish in cheesecloth. Shellfish should remain in shell.
2. Place on a well-greased rack over boiling water.
3. The steam will cook the fish or shellfish.

11-16 Both dry and moist heat methods can be used to prepare fish.

All eggs are alike in nutritional content.

Eggs come in sizes from peewee to jumbo. The U.S. Department of Agriculture has set standards for egg sizes based on the weight of a dozen eggs. Most recipes are developed for large eggs.

When buying eggs, you may notice that some eggs are brown and others are white. Shell color is determined by the breed of hen which laid the egg. Shell color does not affect the grade, nutritive value or flavor of eggs.

How to store eggs

Eggs can be stored in the refrigerator for one to two weeks. The egg carton is a perfect storage container. It keeps eggs covered and in position with the large end up. See 11-17. This position holds the yolk in its proper place and maintains the quality of the egg.

When a recipe calls for egg whites only, you can store the yolks for later use. To do this, cover the yolks with cold water and refrigerate them in an airtight container. Use the yolks within one or two days.

Eggs can be frozen if they are removed from the shell. They cannot be frozen in the shell. This is because they expand when they are frozen and would break the shell. Eggs are sometimes separated before freezing. The whites can be frozen plain. The yolks should

have a small amount of salt or sugar added to them before freezing. This prevents them from becoming lumpy. Eggs should be used promptly after they have thawed.

How to cook eggs

Eggs can be served in many ways, 11-18. They can be eaten at any meal.

When you cook eggs, use gentle heat to keep them tender. If you use high heat or

11-18 Variety is easy when you cook with eggs. Shown here (clockwise from top) are: eggs goldenrod, a soufflé, a plain omelet, eggs Benedict, a quiche and a puffy omelet.

11-17 Egg cartons are excellent containers for storing fresh eggs in the refrigerator.

overcook eggs, they become tough. They may even develop an off-taste.

Eggs may be prepared in five basic ways: cooked in the shell, fried, scrambled, poached and baked. These methods are described in chart 11-19.

Eggs are also useful in general cooking. Many recipes call for them. Sometimes eggs are used to thicken custards, puddings and sauces. Soufflés and popovers depend on eggs for leavening. Meat loaf recipes call for eggs to help bind ingredients together. Many fried foods are dipped first in beaten eggs and then in crumbs before they are fried. Sometimes beaten egg is brushed on top of breads and cookies. This gives the baked products a shiny appearance and a flavorful crust. Eggs also make attractive garnishes for salads and platters of food.

When a recipe calls for eggs to thicken a dish, do not add the eggs to a hot food. If you do, the eggs may curdle. This is because the protein in eggs coagulates quickly when heated. To prevent curdling, add a small amount of the hot mixture to the beaten eggs. Be sure to stir the eggs while you are adding the hot mixture. Then add the egg mixture to the food you are thickening.

Beating egg whites is a special cooking skill. It isn't hard, but it can be tricky. The first step is to let the eggs warm to room temperature. Beaten egg whites reach their best volume at this temperature. Next, you must separate the egg white from the egg yolk. Make sure no egg yolk becomes mixed with the egg white. The egg yolk contains fat. Even the smallest speck of fat from the yolk or the bowl will keep the egg whites from becoming light and fluffy. Use *three* bowls for separating eggs—one for yolks, one for whites and one for the egg you are separating. That way, you won't ruin other whites if a yolk breaks as you are separating it from a white.

Egg whites can be beaten to three stages. The first stage is the *foamy stage*. At this stage, the egg whites are still liquid. They still look transparent. Bubbles and foam have formed on the surface.

If you continue to beat the egg whites, they will reach the *soft peak stage*. The egg whites will be white, shiny and at their full volume. When you raise the beater, the foamy egg whites will rise in peaks. The peaks will bend at the tips.

With continued beating, the egg whites will reach the *stiff peak stage*. They will still be white, shiny and at their full volume. When you raise the beater, the foamy peaks of egg whites will stand up straight. Beating past the stiff peak stage makes the egg whites lose volume and become dry.

PLANTS WHICH PROVIDE PROTEIN

Certain plants are good sources of protein. *Legumes* (dried beans, split peas and lentils), seeds, nuts and grains are plant foods which provide protein, 11-20. For this reason, they are discussed in this chapter along with other protein foods.

Plant proteins differ from all the essential amino acids in the amounts you need to build and maintain body tissues. (Amino acids were discussed in Chapter 2.) Different plants contain different amino acids. It is possible to combine them in dishes so that all the amino acids are present. For instance, one combination is rice and beans. When beans are added to a rice dish, all the essential amino acids are present.

You can also combine plant proteins lacking certain amino acids with animal proteins. Animal proteins are found in milk, eggs, cheese, meat and fish. By doing this, your body will be able to use the plant protein more fully. This is because the animal protein contains the missing amino acids. An example of such a combination would be ham and beans or a cheese sandwich.

Dried beans, peas and lentils

Dried beans, peas and lentils are food bargains. They are usually low in cost and high in nutrition.

Grades have been set for these legumes, but grading is not required. If a package is not marked with a grade, try to buy legumes which are sold in a see-through package.

EGG COOKERY

COOKING METHODS

Cooking eggs in the shell—cold water method

1. Place eggs in pan and cover them with enough water to come at least 2.5 cm (1 inch) above eggs.
2. Cook over high heat until water boils.
3. Immediately cover the pan and remove it from the heat.
4. For soft-cooked eggs, let eggs stand in water for 1 to 3 minutes.
   For hard-cooked eggs, let eggs stand in water for 15 minutes.
5. Remove the eggs from the hot water and cool immediately in cold water. (This prevents further cooking and makes it easier to remove the shell. It also helps to prevent a dark surface on the yolk of hard-cooked eggs.)

Cooking eggs in the shell—hot water method

1. Place cold eggs in a dish of lukewarm water to prevent cracked shells.
2. Bring water in a pan to a boil, using enough water to come 2.5 cm (1 inch) above eggs.
3. Transfer eggs from lukewarm water to boiling water with a spoon.
4. For soft-cooked eggs, immediately cover the pan and remove it from heat. Let eggs stand for 6 to 8 minutes.
   For hard-cooked eggs, reduce heat to keep water simmering (below boiling) and hold for 20 minutes.
5. Cool eggs immediately in cold water. (This prevents further cooking and makes it easier to remove the shell. It also helps to prevent a dark surface on the yolk of hard-cooked eggs.)

Fried eggs

1. Heat butter or other fat in a skillet.
2. Crack the eggs into the pan, being careful not to break the yolks.
3. Slip the egg into skillet and reduce heat.
4. Cook slowly until the egg is cooked to desired doneness.
5. For eggs "sunny-side-up," you may want to cover the skillet to cook the top of the egg with steam, or spoon the hot fat over the egg so the top cooks.
6. To make eggs "over easy," turn eggs over and cook them for several seconds.

Scrambled eggs

1. Beat eggs with a fork in a small bowl until they are a uniform yellow color.
2. Add 15 mL (one tablespoon) of liquid (milk or water), if desired. The liquid makes the scrambled eggs fluffier and softer.
3. Heat butter or other fat in a skillet.
4. Pour in the beaten eggs and cook slowly.
5. When eggs begin to set on the sides, gently push them to the center of the pan. This will allow the liquid egg to flow to the sides and cook. Repeat this several times, but don't stir the eggs.
6. Meat, cheese and cooked vegetables can be added when the eggs first begin to thicken.
7. When the eggs are thickened, but still moist, they are ready to serve.

Plain omelet — (A variation of scrambled eggs)
(Same as scrambled eggs, Steps 1-4.)

5. When eggs start to thicken, cover the pan. This will allow steam to cook the top of the omelet.
6. If desired, add meat, cheese or vegetables.
7. Fold omelet in half and turn it onto a plate.

Poached eggs

1. Fill pan or deep skillet with enough water to cover eggs.
2. Bring water to a boil and then reduce heat to a simmer. (Bubbles will collect on the bottom of the pan and a few will rise to the surface and break.)
3. Break the eggs into a small dish or cup. Slip them carefully into the hot water.
4. Cook the eggs three to five minutes.
5. Carefully remove eggs with a slotted spoon.
6. Pat them dry with a paper towel and serve.

Baked eggs

1. Preheat oven to 160 °C (325 °F).
2. Grease a baking dish.
3. If desired, place vegetables or meat in the bottom of the dish.
4. Crack eggs and slip them into the dish or on top of the food.
5. Bake about 15-20 minutes or until the eggs are cooked.

11-19 Eggs can be prepared in many different ways.

Look for uniform shape and size and bright color. There should be no foreign matter, such as tiny stones or bits of straw. Store dried foods in tightly covered containers in a cool, dry place. They will keep for many months.

There are many different varieties of dried beans. Among the most popular are lima beans, kidney beans, pinto beans and navy beans. Garbanzo beans (also known as chick peas) and black-eyed beans (also called black-eyed peas) are also popular. In recipes, you can often substitute one type of bean for another of the same size.

Soybeans. Because so many products can be made from soybeans, they deserve special attention. Soybeans contain even more protein than other legumes. This makes them a very important protein source. The soybean plays an important role in oriental cooking. Bean curd (tofu) is made from soybeans and is often cooked with vegetables. Soybeans are also fermented to make soy sauce which is used in many oriental dishes.

In recent years, scientists have found ways of using soybeans to make protein foods that resemble meat. There are soy protein products that look and taste like bacon, sausage, ham and chicken. These foods are called *meat analogues.* See 11-21. Soy protein is also used to make *meat extenders.* These are products which can be added to ground beef or processed meat to make it go further. You may find more and more soy protein products on the market in the future.

How to cook dried beans, peas and lentils

The first step in the preparation of dried beans, peas and lentils is a careful inspection. Remove any small sticks, pebbles, seeds, and discolored pieces. Next, rinse the legumes in cool water to remove dust and dirt.

Most legumes need to be soaked before cooking. This helps to reduce the cooking time. Split peas and lentils may be cooked without soaking. But they tend to keep their shape better if they are soaked for about 30 minutes before they are cooked.

Beans must be soaked before they are cooked. Place them in a large pot and cover them with water. Use about 750 mL (3 cups) of water to 250 mL (1 cup) of beans. Bring the water to a boil. Boiling prevents souring and helps to tenderize the skins. Continue boiling for two minutes. Then remove the pot from the heat. Cover the pot and let the beans soak for at least one hour or as long as overnight.

Beans can be cooked in the water in which they were soaked. Generally, they must be cooked for about two hours to tenderize

11-20 *A variety of legumes offer good nutritional value at low cost.*

them. They will usually swell to more than double their original size during soaking and cooking.

Some legumes, such as soybeans, kidney beans and navy beans, may be pressure cooked. Fill the pressure cooker no more than one-third full of food and water (to allow for expansion). Cook from three to 10 minutes. Some legumes should not be pressure cooked. These include black-eyed beans, lentils and split peas.

Other plant foods

Seeds and nuts are also good sources of protein. They are often used as ingredients in salads, breads and casseroles to add flavor, texture and nutrition. You can make a nutritious snack by combining seeds and nuts with oatmeal, raisins and other dried fruits, 11-22. Peanuts, which most people regard as nuts, are really legumes. Peanuts are used in cooking and are eaten salted and roasted. Peanuts are widely enjoyed snacks. Peanut butter sandwiches are popular with people of all ages.

QUAKER OATS

11-22 Granola is a nutritious snack. It contains seeds and nuts, which are good sources of protein.

MILES, MORNINGSIDE FARMS

11-21 Meat analogues are made by processing soybeans to look and taste like regular meat products.

to Define

beef . . . broiler-fryer . . .
capon . . .
connective tissue . . .
crustaceans . . .
dressed fish . . .
dry heat cooking methods . . .
fish fillets . . . fish steaks . . .
foamy stage . . . grades . . .
inspection . . . lamb . . .
legumes . . . marbling . . .
meat analogues . . .
meat extenders . . .
moist heat cooking methods . . .
mollusks . . . perishable . . .
pork . . . poultry . . .
processed fish . . .
processed meats . . .
roasting chickens . . .
Rock Cornish game hens . . .
soft peak stage . . .
soybeans . . .
stewing hens . . .
stiff peak stage . . .
variety meats . . .
veal . . .whole fish

to Discuss

1. What do meat, poultry, fish, shellfish, eggs and some plants have in common?
2. Name three examples of variety meats.
3. List at least three methods of processing meat to allow longer storage.
4. List at least three methods of tenderizing meat.
5. Why is a moist heat method a good way to cook less tender cuts of meat?
6. How do grading and inspection differ?
7. How long can you safely store fresh meats in the refrigerator? What should you do with meat that you don't want to use until next week?
8. List four dry heat cooking methods.
9. Describe how to place a meat thermometer in a roast.
10. Generally, which costs more per unit of weight—a whole chicken or one that has been cut into pieces?
11. Why should poultry never be stuffed until you're ready to cook it?
12. Name four examples of shellfish.
13. How can you tell if a fish fillet is done?
14. Are brown eggs more nutritious than white eggs?
15. How should eggs be stored?
16. What happens if you use a high temperature when cooking eggs?
17. Name three examples of legumes.
18. Are plant proteins nutritionally equal to proteins you get from animal sources?
19. Why are soybeans important?

to Do

1. Compare the cost per serving of five different protein sources you use often in your home. Report your findings to the class.
2. Make a poster of a meat label. Explain to the class how to read it.
3. Design a bulletin board or poster that shows the basic methods (braising, cooking in liquid, broiling, frying, etc.) of cooking meat, poultry and fish. Homemakers' magazines will be a good source of pictures, or you can draw your own.
4. Compare the costs of various forms of chicken at a local grocery store. Find the cost per unit of weight for whole broiler-fryers and packages of chicken pieces. Which form of chicken is more expensive? Which has more waste?
5. Compare fresh and frozen fish. Prepare both fish using the same cooking method, such as broiling. Is there much difference in taste? Compare the prices. Which would you buy? Why?
6. Demonstrate to the class how to separate egg whites from egg yolks. Beat the egg whites to the foamy stage, then to the soft peak stage, and then to the stiff peak stage.
7. Find a recipe for a main dish soup or casserole using legumes. Prepare it and calculate the cost per serving. How does the cost compare with serving other main dish protein sources?

12

Fruits and vegetables

Why should you eat fruits and vegetables? After reading this chapter, you will be able to explain why fruits and vegetables are important in your diet. You will be able to describe how to buy and store canned, frozen and dried fruits and vegetables. You will be able to properly prepare fruits and vegetables. You will also be able to explain various ways fruits and vegetables can be preserved.

Food stores carry a wide variety of fruits and vegetables. You may be able to select anything from apples and kiwifruit to sweet potatoes and zucchini.

Years ago, consumers had to rely on the *produce* (fresh fruits and vegetables) that was grown locally. This has changed because of modern transportation and storage techniques. Today, we can enjoy fresh fruits and vegetables from across the country all year long. Some produce is even imported from foreign countries.

In addition to fresh produce, canned, frozen and dried products are also available. Because canned, frozen and dried foods are processed immediately after harvest, their quality is usually good.

WHY ARE FRUITS AND VEGETABLES IMPORTANT?

Fruits and vegetables are important in a balanced diet. We depend on fruits and vegetables to supply many vitamins and minerals. This food group includes especially good sources of vitamins A and C. Dark green and deep yellow fruits and vegetables such as spinach, apricots and carrots are outstanding sources of vitamin A. You should try to include one good source of vitamin A in your diet at least every other day. Citrus fruits such as oranges are the most famous source of vitamin C. Other fruits and vegetables such as strawberries and broccoli are fine sources too. You need to eat a good source of vitamin C every day.

Fruits and vegetables also add fiber to your diet. While you cannot digest fiber, it is important in helping your body get rid of waste. Most fruits and vegetables contain a lot of water. Most contain little, if any, fat. As a result, they are usually low in kilojoules (Calories).

Meals without fruits and vegetables can be dull. Fruits and vegetables add bright color and variety in texture and flavor to meals. When planning meals, choose fruits and vegetables that will enhance the other foods you are serving. If a meal needs some color, add pickled beets, pineapple slices or cherry tomatoes. Suppose you plan to serve a soft textured main dish such as an omelet or a stuffed crêpe. You could add interest and variety by serving a crisp, tangy salad made with orange sections, lettuce and celery.

Types of fruits

Most stores carry a variety of fruits throughout the year. There are six basic types of fruit: berries, citrus fruits, drupes, melons, pomes and tropical fruits.

Berries. Berries are seasonal fruits. Fresh berries, 12-1, are not always available. You can often find canned or frozen berries in your food store.

When fresh berries are available, choose ones that are ripe. The berries should look plump, juicy and bright in color. Avoid soft and moldy berries. If the container has wet or stained spots on the side or bottom, some of the berries have probably spoiled.

Fresh berries are very perishable. They should be used soon after purchase or picking. Cranberries are an exception. They will keep several months in the refrigerator. Some berries freeze well. These include blueberries, strawberries and raspberries.

Citrus fruits. Citrus fruits are available year-round because they store well, 12-2. They are grown in warm climates. Oranges are the most popular kind of citrus fruit.

BLUEBERRIES   BURPEE   STRAWBERRIES

12-1 Fresh berries add color to salads. They can also be used to make desserts and jams.

There are many varieties of oranges. Some are known for their juiciness, such as the Valencia orange. Others, such as Naval oranges, are best for eating whole or for sectioning.

Grapefruits are also popular citrus fruits. There are pink and white grapefruits. Some varieties are seedless. It is hard to tell just by looking, which grapefruits are seedless, pink or white. Read the signs in the store to make sure that you know what you are buying.

Other common citrus fruits include lemons and limes. At certain times of the year, special varieties of citrus fruits such as tangerines and tangelos are available.

Select citrus fruits which are firm and free of soft spots. The fruit should feel heavy. This is a sign of juiciness. Some citrus fruits have a brownish cast to their skin. This sometimes happens to fruits with thin skins and is not a sign of poor quality. Oranges are often artifically colored to make them appear bright orange. Oranges with greenish skins are just as ripe and nutritious as oranges with a bright orange color.

Citrus fruits, except for tangerines, should be stored in the refrigerator uncovered. Tangerines should be placed in a plastic bag and stored in the refrigerator.

Drupes. Drupes include fruits with a single seed or pit, 12-3. Peaches, nectarines, apricots, cherries and plums are drupes.

When choosing drupes, look for plump, juicy fruits. Avoid buying very soft fruits which may be too ripe. Also avoid fruits that are very hard. They may not ripen properly at home.

When ripe, drupes should be stored uncovered in the refrigerator. Plan to use ripe drupes within three to five days.

Most drupes are available in canned form. Some drupes are also available frozen.

CHERRIES

PEACHES   BURPEE

CITRUS FRUITS   SUNKIST GROWERS, INC.

12-2 Citrus fruits are available year-round in most stores. They are excellent sources of vitamin C.

12-3 Drupes such as cherries and peaches make refreshing snacks. Drupes should be plump and juicy.

Melons. Melons are seasonal fruits, 12-4. The most popular summer melons are cantaloupe, honeydew and watermelon. You may also find Persian and Crenshaw melons in the summer months. Winter melons include casaba and Spanish melons.

When choosing fresh melons, look for those that are firm and ripe. Avoid melons with bruises or soft spots. Most melons have a slightly sweet smell when they are ripe.

Melons will ripen at room temperature. They should then be stored in the refrigerator and used promptly. Honeydew and cantaloupe freeze well if they are cut into slices or chunks. Melon balls can be purchased frozen.

Pomes. Apples and pears are pomes, 12-5. These fruits have a core. The core is usually removed before the fruit is eaten. Pomes also have a smooth skin that can be eaten.

There are many varieties of apples. Some are better for eating, while others are better for cooking. Apples which are good for eating fresh are Delicious, McIntosh, Staymen, Jonathan and Winesap. Tart apples which hold their shape when cooked are best for pies

and other baked goods. Firm varieties such as Rome Beauty, Northern Spy and York Imperial are good choices.

The most popular variety of pear is the Bartlett pear. It is good both for eating fresh and cooking.

Select apples which are hard and have no soft spots. Pears taste best when their flesh is slightly soft to the touch. If pears are hard, they will usually ripen if left at room temperature for a few days. Apples and ripe pears should be refrigerated or stored in a cool, dry place. Apples and pears are often canned.

Tropical fruits. Tropical fruits are fruits which grow only in warm climates, 12-6. Some may be available in your local store, depending on the time of year.

Pineapples and bananas are two popular tropical fruits. Fresh pineapples have a golden or orange cast and a sweet smell when they are fully ripe. Pineapples should be used as soon as they are ripe. Store pineapples in the refrigerator.

Bananas should be firm and free from soft spots and bruises. They are ripe when their

WATERMELON

BURPEE

CANTALOUPE

12-4 Melons come in many shapes and sizes. Look for firm, ripe melons.

188

golden skin becomes speckled with brown spots. Bananas ripen at room temperature. They do not store well, so they should be used once they are ripe.

Other tropical fruits you may want to try are kiwifruit, mangoes, pomegranates, papayas, persimmons, avocados and figs. Plantains, a relative of the banana, are often served in place of starchy vegetables.

Types of vegetables

You can always find a number of different vegetables from which to choose when you go shopping. Depending on the season, you may buy them fresh. Or you may decide to purchase frozen, canned or dried vegetables. Have you ever stopped to think about what you are eating when you bite into a vegetable? Vegetables can be grouped according to the part of the plant from which they come. The eight basic groups are: bulbs, roots, tubers, stems, leaves, fruits, flowers and seeds.

Bulbs. The most common bulbs are onions and garlic. Both are used to add flavor to a variety of dishes. Sometimes they are used raw in salads and sandwiches.

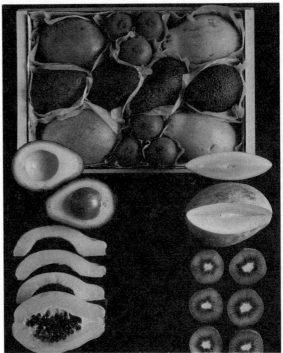

TROPICAL FRUITS   BLUE ANCHOR, INC.

12-6 Tropical fruits are a refreshing treat. Shown here are: (cut fruits, clockwise from top left) avocado, mango, kiwifruit and papaya.

APPLES   BURPEE

12-5 Apples and pears are pomes. They have cores which should be removed.

PEARS

Many varieties of onions are available. White and yellow onions are used in cooking. Larger Bermuda onions and Spanish onions have a slightly sweeter flavor. They are preferred for salads and sandwiches.

Less common bulbs include leeks, chives and shallots. All of these are milder in flavor than onions and garlic. They are used in recipes where a more delicate taste is desired. See 12-7.

All bulbs, except chives, have a thin outer layer of skin which must be peeled away before they are used. Chives should be washed before being used. The green stalk is usually finely chopped. Chives add color and flavor to soups, salads and dips.

When choosing bulbs, check to see that they are firm and dry. Chives should look crisp and not wilted.

Bulbs should be stored in a cool, dry place or in the refrigerator. Chives should always be refrigerated. Keep a few onions in the refrigerator for daily use. Cold onions do not make your eyes tear as quickly as onions kept at room temperature.

Roots. Carrots, turnips, beets, rutabagas and radishes are common root vegetables, 12-8. Most root vegetables are cooked before they are eaten. Some roots, such as carrots and radishes, can be served raw in salads or for snacks.

When choosing root vegetables, look for evenly shaped vegetables that are not overly mature. They should be firm to the touch, not soft. Store root vegetables in a cool, dry place or in the vegetable crisper of the refrigerator. They will keep for several weeks or more.

Tubers. Tubers are like bulb and root vegetables in that they grow underground. Unlike root vegetables, which grow from seeds, tubers can be grown by planting a piece of the tuber that contains a "bud" or "eye." Potatoes are the most popular tuber eaten in the United States, 12-9. Jerusalem artichokes are less common tubers with a unique flavor.

Tubers are classified as starchy vegetables. They contain more carbohydrates than most other vegetables. There are many ways to cook and serve potatoes. They can be baked, boiled, or fried. They can be served whole,

ONIONS

BURPEE

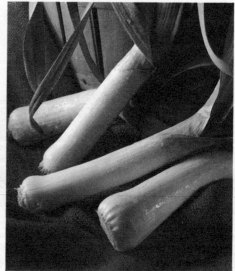

LEEKS

12-7 Onions and leeks are bulbs. They are often used to add flavor to dishes.

mashed, or cut into pieces. Potatoes are also used in stews, soups, casseroles and salads.

Select tubers which are well-shaped, firm and free from blemishes and decay. Avoid tubers which are shriveled or sprouted. Tubers should be stored in a cool, dry place. They will keep for several weeks or more.

Stems. Celery and asparagus are stem vegetables. Celery is often eaten raw, either plain or with a dip. It is a great snack food for dieters since it is low in kilojoules (Calories). Celery is also used to add flavor and texture to soups and stews. See 12-10.

Fresh asparagus is sold in the spring. Asparagus is also available in canned and frozen forms. Cooked asparagus can be served plain or with a sauce. It is also served cold in salads.

When choosing stem vegetables, check for crispness. Stalks should be firm and straight. Asparagus should have tightly closed tips. Slim stalks come from younger plants and are likely to be more tender.

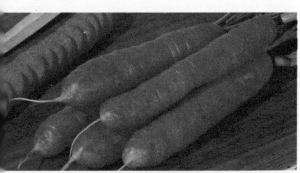

CARROTS

TUBERS   THE POTATO BOARD

12-9 The potato is a tuber. Select tubers which are well-shaped, firm and free from blemishes and decay.

BEETS   BURPEE

12-8 Carrots and beets are examples of root vegetables. Look for firm, evenly shaped vegetables.

CELERY   BURPEE

12-10 Celery is a stem vegetable. It is often used in salads, soups and stews.

Stem vegetables should be stored in the refrigerator in airtight containers or in the crisper. They tend to wilt and lose quality if left uncovered. After celery has been cut, it should be stored in a small amount of ice water to keep it crisp.

Leaves. When you think of a tossed salad, you usually think of leafy vegetables. Lettuce, cabbage, spinach, escarole and endive are used raw in salads. See 12-11. Other nutritious leaves include chard, kale, turnip greens and Brussels sprouts. Some leafy vegetables are cooked. Because of their delicate texture, they taste best when they are cooked quickly and served with seasonings or a sauce.

When choosing leafy vegetables, look for crisp, closely bunched leaves. Avoid bruised or wilted greens. Store leafy greens in airtight containers or in the crisper in the refrigerator. Plan to use them quickly since they are perishable.

Vegetable-fruits. Many vegetables are classified as fruits because they are formed from the flower of the plant. Popular vegetable-fruits include cucumbers, tomatoes, peppers, okra, eggplant, squash and pumpkin, 12-12. Most vegetable-fruits have edible skins. Win-

ter squash and pumpkin are exceptions. However, many people prefer to remove skins before eating.

There are many ways to serve vegetable-fruits. Cucumbers, tomatoes, peppers and summer squash are popular raw ingredients in salads. They can also be braised, stewed and used in casseroles. Eggplant, winter squash and pumpkin can be cooked, mashed and served with seasonings. Sometimes vegetable-fruits are stuffed and baked. Tomatoes, peppers, eggplant and summer squash all can be prepared this way.

Select vegetable-fruits that are firm and unblemished. Bright color is a guide to ripeness. Most vegetable-fruits are stored in the refrigerator. They should be used as soon as possible. Vegetable fruits with hard skins, (winter squash, pumpkin) can be stored in a cool, dry place.

Flowers. Certain vegetables are eaten during the flowering stage, 12-13. An artichoke is really a flower that has not fully bloomed. Broccoli is a popular vegetable flower consisting of flowerlets on an edible stem. You can probably tell from its name that cauliflower is also a vegetable flower.

LETTUCE   BURPEE

12-11 Leafy vegetables are often used in salads. Some may be cooked. Look for leafy vegetables which are crisp.

CABBAGE

PEPPERS

ARTICHOKES

EGGPLANT

BROCCOLI

PUMPKIN   BURPEE

*12-12 Some vegetables are called
vegetable-fruits because they come
from the flowers of plants.*

CAULIFLOWER   BURPEE

*12-13 Vegetable flowers should be
evenly colored.*

Vegetable flowers are usually cooked and served plain or with sauces. Artichokes are usually cooked and served with a dipping sauce. Sometimes they are stuffed and baked. The center heart of the artichoke is flavorful. Cooked artichoke hearts are often added to salads and casseroles.

When choosing vegetable flowers, check them for even coloring. Discoloring such as yellow buds on broccoli suggests that the vegetable is overly mature. Refrigerate vegetable flowers in airtight containers or in the crisper to preserve their quality.

Seeds. Beans, peas and corn are examples of vegetables which are classified as seeds, 12-14. They can be purchased fresh during some months. They are also available canned and frozen. Vegetable seeds can be used in many ways. They can be cooked and served plain or used in soups, stews and casseroles.

Fresh green beans, peas and sweet corn have a delicate flavor. They taste best when they are freshly picked. The longer they are stored, the more the flavor changes. When buying, try to select those which are young and of even size. Large beans, peas and kernels of corn are overly mature and will not have the best flavor. You can store vegetable seeds in the refrigerator in airtight containers. Use them as soon as possible.

HOW TO BUY FRUITS AND VEGETABLES

Since you can buy fruits and vegetables in many forms, your choices will depend on these factors:
- Your food budget.
- The time you have available for food preparation of fruits and vegetables.
- The storage space you have available.
- The way you plan to use the food. (For instance, fresh produce is used for most salads.)

Fresh fruits and vegetables

Produce is usually highest in quality and lowest in price when it is being harvested. This is when produce is *in season.* Fruits and vegetables that are grown locally are usually very good buys when they are in season. When produce has to be transported, the price goes up.

Your senses of sight, touch and smell are tools that can help you select the best produce. When choosing fresh fruits and vegetables, look for bright color, 12-15. Avoid buying produce that is bruised, wilted or discolored. These are signs that the produce has not been properly stored or that it is past its prime. Gently touch firmer produce such as cucumbers, apples, pears, tomatoes and peaches. Cucumbers and apples should feel firm and solid. Ripe pears, tomatoes and peaches should give slightly. Often your sense of smell can help you select a ripe melon or pineapple.

Stores often prepackage produce. Sometimes this can be a disadvantage. The package may contain some produce which is starting to spoil. Or perhaps you don't need the full amount. For instance, maybe you need only four oranges, but the package contains eight. Ask to have the package opened so that you can buy just what you need and want.

Canned fruits and vegetables

Most food stores carry a good selection of canned fruits and vegetables. When fresh produce is very expensive you may find that canned versions are cheaper.

Canned fruits and vegetables are convenience foods. They are fully cooked and may be served directly from the can. Often they are cut into halves, slices or cubes. This can save you time. Usually canned vegetables are heated briefly before serving. Unopened cans may be stored at room temperature for a year or more.

All canned fruits and vegetables are packed in some type of liquid. Often, this is water or natural juice. Fruits may be canned in sugar syrup. (Sugar helps fruit keep its shape.) The syrup may be light or heavy, depending on how much sugar is used. A few vegetables, like peppers, may be packed in oil.

Frozen fruits and vegetables

Frozen fruits and vegetables are more like

PEAS
BURPEE

GREEN BEANS

CORN

*12-14 Seeds include peas, beans and corn.
These vegetables have the best flavor
when served soon after they have been picked.*

fresh produce in flavor, color and texture than canned products. Frozen foods can cost more than canned foods because they cost more to ship and store. Many people find frozen foods are a fine substitute for fresh produce when it is out of season.

Frozen fruits are often used in baked goods and for dessert toppings. You can also eat them plain. Serve them before they are completely thawed. Most people prefer the texture of the fruit when it still contains a few small ice crystals.

Many frozen vegetables are packaged plain. Others are packaged with sauces or as combination dishes like "stir-fry vegetables." Frozen vegetables are ready to cook. They have been cleaned, trimmed, peeled and cut into pieces for you. Some even come in boilable pouches or in containers ready for the oven. These forms can add to the purchase price.

When buying frozen fruits and vegetables, inspect the packages carefully to see that they are solid. Soft packages are a sign that the temperature of the display chest is too warm.

TUPPERWARE® HOME PARTIES

*12-15 When buying fruits and
vegetables, select those which look
bright and fresh.*

The quality of the food may be affected. Don't buy a stained package. Staining is a sign that the food has thawed and has been refrozen. Frozen food must be stored at a constant temperature of $-18°C$ ($0°F$) or lower to insure safety and top quality.

Dried fruits and vegetables

Dried fruits and vegetables are easy to store and can be used in many ways. Dried fruits such as raisins, prunes, apricots and figs make good snacks. They can be added to cookies, breads and cakes. Or they can be cooked in a light sugar syrup. Dried vegetables help save time, energy and money. Legumes such as peas, beans and lentils are economical sources of protein. Dried potato products save time and energy.

Store dried foods in tightly covered containers at room temperature. They will last for a long time. Dried foods are lightweight and pack well for camping trips.

STORING FRUITS AND VEGETABLES

Most fresh fruits and vegetables should be stored in the refrigerator and used as soon as possible. The longer produce remains unused, the more the flavor and texture will change. Most refrigerators have special storage compartments called *crispers*. These compartments help to prevent drying. You can also store produce on refrigerator shelves using covered containers or plastic bags, 12-16.

Unripened fruit should be stored at room temperature until it ripens. Not all fruits ripen at room temperature. Strawberries, for instance, ripen only on the vine. They will not continue to ripen after they are picked.

Most fruits with edible skins should be washed and dried before storing. Berries and cherries should not, because water helps to increase mold growth. Wash them just before serving. If mold appears, throw them away. Don't wash vegetables until you are ready to use them. If they are very dirty, they can be rinsed before storing.

Plan to use berries and leafy vegetables as soon as possible. They tend to spoil quickly, even when properly stored. Firmer fruits and vegetables, such as apples, cucumbers and winter squash, will retain their quality longer. Certain fruits and vegetables can be stored in a cool, dark, dry place such as the cellar. White potatoes, onions, winter squash, turnips and unripened apples are examples of foods which can be stored in the cellar for several months.

Unopened canned fruits and vegetables can be stored on the shelf. After they've been opened, they should be kept in the refrigerator. Dried fruits and vegetables should be stored in airtight containers on the shelf. Frozen food should be stored in the freezer at $-18°C$ ($0°F$). At that temperature, frozen fruits and vegetables will last several months.

USING FRUITS IN MEALS

Fruits add interest to meals. They are often served as appetizers. Fruits are also used in salads and as garnishes. See 12-17. Many interesting desserts can be made with fresh, frozen or canned fruit. For instance, fruit can be served plain or topped with milk or cream. Sliced fruit can be served over ice cream or cake. Fruit can also be used to make gelatin desserts, puddings, cakes and pies.

Serving fresh fruits

The easiest way to serve fresh fruits is to wash them and place them in a bowl or basket. Whole fresh fruits served with cheese make a great dessert.

Fruits can be cut up and used many ways. Melons are often served in wedges or slices. Fruits such as cantaloupe and pineapple can be cut in half and filled with sherbet, cottage cheese or salad. Prepared this way, they can be used as a main dish. Another fruit which can be halved and filled is the avocado. It is often filled with a meat or fish salad.

Most fruits make great snacks. Usually they are eaten whole, but they can be cut or crushed for fruit salads and sauces. Once fruit has been cut, it should be stored in the refrigerator until serving time.

Fresh citrus fruits can be served many ways.

You can divide them into sections or cut them into wedges or slices. Grapefruit is often cut in half and then sectioned.

Fruits with thin skins, such as apples, pears and peaches, do not require peeling. But sometimes you may want to serve them without their skins. Apples and pears can be peeled with a paring knife or vegetable peeler. Peaches will peel better if they are *blanched* first. To blanch peaches, dip them into boiling water for a few seconds. Drain them and peel away the skins.

When serving fresh fruit in pieces, be sure to remove the cores, pits and seeds in advance.

Fruit salads. Fresh, frozen and canned fruits can be used to make tasty salads, 12-18. To make a fruit salad, combine two or more fruits. You can use your imagination to combine whatever fruits you happen to have on hand.

Low acid fruits such as apples, bananas, peaches, pears and avocados will turn brown when exposed to air. If you are using these fruits, be sure to add them at the last minute. Or coat them with lemon juice after you have cut them and before you add them to the salad. (The lemon juice will help prevent discoloring.)

Fruits are sometimes added to tossed

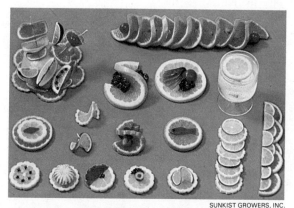
SUNKIST GROWERS, INC.

12-17 Use citrus fruits to make a variety of colorful garnishes.

RUBBERMAID

12-16 Store fresh produce in the crisper of the refrigerator or in covered containers.

CALIFORNIA ICEBERG LETTUCE COMMISION

12-18 You can create a delicious fruit salad by combining different fruits. Other ingredients such as lettuce and cottage cheese might also be used.

salads. Orange slices and grapefruit sections add a unique flavor to tossed greens.

Molded salads can be made with fruit and flavored gelatin. The fruit should be added after the gelatin has started to set. That way, the pieces of fruit will stay in place throughout the gelatin and will not float to the top. Store molded salads in the refrigerator until mealtime. Unmold the salad just before you serve it. On hot days, place the salad over a platter of crushed ice to keep the gelatin from melting.

Fruit juices. Fruit juices are refreshing during meals and for snacks. You can make them from fresh fruit, but canned or frozen forms usually cost less. When buying fruit beverages, read the labels very carefully. Many *fruit drinks* contain added sugar and water. These drinks often cost as much or more than the pure fruit juices. Some are fortified with additional vitamins. By law, the actual juice content of fruit beverages must be specified. "Drinks" and "ades" do not have to contain as much fruit as "juices." Some have no fruit juice in them.

Cooking with fruit

Most fruits can be cooked. See 12-19. For instance, apples can be baked with sugar and spices. Grapefruit can be broiled. Fruits like apricots, peaches and pears can be simmered gently in water or syrup.

The way a fruit is cooked will determine whether it will be soft or firm. Fruit that is cooked in syrup will hold its shape better. For instance, this method is used when cooking pears. Pears cooked in water will become soft and break apart. If sugar is added, the pears will hold their shape. When applesauce is made, the sugar is added after the apples have cooked. This gives the applesauce a softer, smoother texture. When cooking fruit, always cook it quickly but gently in as little water as possible. This will help to retain nutrients.

When fruit is added to baked goods, it provides interest and flavor. The next time you make muffins or pancakes, try adding your favorite fruit. You might use berries, sliced apples or bananas. Try combining fruits when baking. How about cherry and peach pie? Or apple and raisin cookies?

Cooked fruits make attractive garnishes. Pineapple slices add color to baked ham. Preserved crab apples or peach halves look nice on poultry platters. Use cherries to add bright color to desserts.

USING VEGETABLES IN MEALS

Part of the "art" of cooking is selecting the right vegetable. Vegetables are versatile. They can be served raw or cooked in many different ways. Raw vegetables can be served with dips and sauces. Most salads are made with raw vegetables. You can cook vegetables by steaming, boiling, frying, baking, broiling or deep-fat frying. Vegetables can be creamed, scalloped or added to casseroles, soups and stews.

Cleaning fresh vegetables

Most fresh vegetables should be washed just before they are used. If they are quite dirty, they can be cleaned before they are stored. If this is the case, dry them before you put them in the refrigerator. Too much moisture can cause the vegetables to spoil.

Before cooking, rinse fresh vegetables to remove garden dirt and chemical sprays. Root vegetables may need extra scrubbing to remove clinging dirt.

Leafy vegetables should be rinsed in cold water to remove dirt and sand. You may need to trim head lettuce before washing. Discard damaged leaves and remove the core. Fill a large bowl with cool water and swish the leaves around. Keep changing the water until no dirt remains in the bottom of the bowl. Use a colander to drain the leaves. If you are washing leafy vegetables for salad, blot them dry with a clean towel or paper towel. Then place them in a covered container in the refrigerator.

Most vegetables need some peeling or trimming before being used. Use a paring knife to remove stems, tops, cores, leaves or blemishes. You may want to peel vegetables like potatoes, eggplant, carrots and tomatoes before cooking. Tomatoes can be peeled easily by blanching them (dipping them in boiling water) for 10 seconds before peeling. Other vegetables should be peeled using a vegetable peeler or paring knife. After the vegetables have been washed, trimmed and peeled, they can be cut into slices, strips, chunks or cubes. Cut vegetables into pieces just before cooking or serving to preserve nutrients.

Serving raw vegetables

Serving vegetables raw is the most nutritious way of serving them. Raw vegetables are popular snacks for dieters. Many vegetables such as carrots and celery can be served raw. Cauliflower, summer squash, rutabaga, mushrooms, freshly picked peas and asparagus are delicious raw too. You can make appetizers by arranging raw vegetables on a platter and serving them with your favorite dip.

Vegetable salads. Salads are pleasant additions to meals, 12-20. They provide variety in both flavor and texture. Lettuce is a basic ingredient in many salads. Other greens can be used besides lettuce. Spinach, Chinese cabbage and escarole are popular salad greens. Salads often contain other raw vegetables such as tomatoes, onions, carrots or peppers. You can also add cooked vegetables such as beans, beets, peas, asparagus or artichoke hearts to a salad.

When a salad is served as a main course, it should contain a protein food such as meat, seafood, cheese or eggs. Chef's salad is a popular main dish salad. It has leafy greens, strips of meat (such as ham and turkey), cheese and hard-cooked eggs.

Fruits are sometimes used in vegetable salads. Try adding orange or grapefruit slices to a green salad. Avocados, pears, pineapple slices and peaches also add texture and give variety and color.

CALIFORNIA ICEBERG LETTUCE COMMISSION

12-20 A fresh, crisp salad is nutritious and can add color and texture to a meal.

SUNKIST GROWERS, INC.

12-19 Fruits should be cooked quickly and gently. They can be served in many different ways.

Molded salads often contain fresh or canned vegetables. Molded salads must be made in advance so that the gelatin can set. You can use flavored gelatin such as orange, lemon or lime for molded salads. You can also use unflavored gelatin and combine it with broth or juice.

Cold *marinated* vegetables can be used as salads. Vegetables are marinated by letting them stand in a seasoned acid liquid. This adds flavor to the vegetables. Often vegetables are marinated in salad dressing. You can create your own marinade by combining oil, an acid such as vinegar or lemon juice, and seasonings. Oregano and basil give an Italian touch to your marinade, while soy sauce and ginger give it an Oriental flavor. Vegetables should marinate several hours before serving in order to acquire the best flavor.

Many different types of salad dressings may be used on salads. You may prefer to purchase ready-made salad dressings, or you may want to make your own. Oil and vinegar are the basic ingredients used to make Italian and French salad dressings. Mayonnaise is a basic ingredient in creamy dressings such as Russian, Thousand Island and creamy cheese dressings. You can substitute cooked salad dressings in recipes calling for mayonnaise. Mayonnaise is made with oil, acid and egg yolks. Cooked salad dressings are made with flour, eggs and usually some acid. Sour cream and yogurt have also become popular bases for salad dressings. Wait until the last minute to add any type of dressing to a tossed salad. This will keep the greens from wilting and will preserve the crisp texture of the salad.

Cooking vegetables

Cooked vegetables taste best when they retain their color, flavor, texture and nutritional value. See 12-21. Overcooking vegetables affects all of these characteristics.

The basic guides for cooking vegetables are:
- Use as little water as possible. Vegetable flavors and nutrients can be lost in water during cooking.
- Depending on the recipe, try to cook vegetables in large pieces. This prevents loss of flavors and nutrients.
- Keep cooking time short. Cook vegetables just until they are fork-tender (firm, but tender). Overcooking can affect color, flavor and texture. It can also destroy certain nutrients.
- In general, use moderate heat. High heat destroys many vitamins.

Sometimes the cooking method may have to be adjusted to suit the vegetable you are preparing. The color and flavor of a vegetable will affect how you cook it.

Green vegetables such as broccoli and green beans can change from a bright green to a dull olive color. Heat and acid cause this to happen. You can prevent this color change by cooking green vegetables quickly. Use a small amount of rapidly boiling water. Add the vegetables and cook until they are fork tender. Leave the pan lid off for the first few minutes of cooking. Then cover until the vegetables are done. Serve immediately. If left in the covered pan, the vegetables will continue to cook and turn olive green.

The yellow or orange color in vegetables such as corn and carrots is not destroyed by heat. However, the color can escape into the cooking water if the vegetable is overcooked. Cook yellow and orange vegetables in a small amount of water for a short time with the pan covered.

White vegetables such as potatoes and cauliflower may turn from white to yellow or gray during cooking. White vegetables which are not strongly flavored should be cooked in a moderate amount of water in a covered pan.

Red vegetables such as red cabbage may turn purple or blue during cooking. You can prevent this change by adding a small amount of acid (vinegar or cream of tartar) to the cooking water. Red vegetables are usually cooked with a small amount of water in a covered pan.

Mild flavored vegetables such as peas and corn should be cooked in a small amount of water. The pot should be covered to help keep the flavors from escaping with the steam. These vegetables should be cooked quickly.

Strong flavored vegetables such as cabbage, turnips and cauliflower should be cooked quickly for a different reason. The longer these vegetables cook, the stronger their flavor becomes. To prevent a strong flavor, these vegetables should be cooked quickly in a large amount of water in an uncovered pan. The large amount of water helps to dilute the strong flavor. Keeping the lid off helps some of the flavor to evaporate which makes the flavor of the vegetable milder.

Very strong flavored vegetables such as onions should also be cooked in a large amount of water in an uncovered pan. But they should be cooked for a longer period of time. The strong flavor will then be released in the steam.

There are many ways of cooking vegetables so that they are both nutritious and tasty. Vegetables can be boiled or steamed. They can also be baked. Baking takes a longer time than boiling and steaming. Suppose you are

12-21 *When vegetables are cooked properly, they are both tasty and nutritious.*

using the oven to cook a roast. You can save energy by planning to bake vegetables such as carrots and potatoes at the same time. Broiling, braising, stir-frying and deep-fat frying are other methods of cooking vegetables. These methods are described in 12-22.

PRESERVING FRUITS AND VEGETABLES

If you have a garden or fruit trees, you may have extra fruits and vegetables at harvesttime. Or perhaps you can purchase fresh produce in quantity at a farm market. What can

BASIC VEGETABLE COOKERY

Boiling

1. Using a saucepan with a tight fitting lid, bring a small amount of liquid to a boil.
2. Place vegetables in the pan.
3. Boil vegetables just until they are fork-tender (tender, but firm).
4. Serve with butter, sauces or seasonings.

Steaming

1. Place a small amount of water in a deep pan with a tight fitting lid.
2. Bring the water to a boil.
3. Place a rack in the pan so the vegetables do not touch the water.
4. Place the vegetables on the rack.
5. Cover the pan.
6. Steam the vegetables until they are fork-tender.
7. Serve with butter, sauces or seasonings.

Baking

1. Place vegetables in a casserole dish.
2. Add seasonings and a small amount of liquid.
3. Cover and bake in a moderate oven until the vegetables are tender. The exact amount of time depends on the vegetable and the size of the pieces. (Vegetables can also be baked in the same pan along with meat. Usually, the vegetables are added during the last hour of cooking.)

Broiling

1. Preheat the broiler and adjust the broiler rack so that the vegetables are 5 to 7 cm (2 to 3 inches) from the heat source.
2. You may want to season the vegetables before broiling.
3. Check vegetables often to see that they don't burn.

Braising

1. Cut vegetables into slices or pieces.
2. Melt a small amount of fat in a skillet.
3. Add the vegetables along with a small amount of water or other liquid.
4. Cover the pan and cook the vegetables over low heat.
5. Stir often to prevent the food from sticking to the pan.
6. Cook until the vegetables are just tender.

Stir-Frying

1. Cut vegetables into small slices or pieces.
2. Put a small amount of fat in a skillet or wok and heat it to a high temperature.
3. Add the vegetables and cook over high heat, stirring to prevent vegetables from burning.
4. Cook 3 to 5 minutes or until fork-tender.

Deep-fat Frying

1. After washing vegetables, carefully dry them. This will prevent splattering. (Before deep-fat frying potatoes, rinse them in cold water to remove the surface starch and then dry them.)
2. In a deep pan, heat fat to 190°C (375°F).
3. Dip vegetables in a batter, if desired.
4. Carefully lower vegetables into the fat using a basket or slotted spoon. (Do not cook too many at one time.)
5. Fry vegetables with a batter coating until they are golden in color. Fry vegetables without a coating until they are tender but firm.
6. Remove the food using a basket or a slotted spoon.
7. Place vegetables on paper towels to drain the excess fat.

12-22 Vegetables can be cooked using a variety of methods.

you do with all this food? You can preserve it. *Food preservation* is done to keep food from spoiling for a fairly long time. Fruits and vegetables can be preserved by canning, freezing or drying.

Canning

Canning is a good way to preserve fruits and vegetables. Canning techniques are also used to make jams, jellies and pickles. See 12-23. Before you start to can, you should read about canning procedures in detail. USDA pamphlets available from county extension offices can provide basic, up-to-date information. Manufacturers of canning equipment also publish pamphlets on canning methods. Your local library will have books that explain canning techniques.

Use fully ripe, top quality fruits and vegetables for canning. For the best flavor, can them as soon as possible after harvesting. Wash them thoroughly to remove dirt and chemical sprays. Rinse them several times. Refer to your canning booklet for directions in preparation.

Canned food must be processed so that it will be safe to eat. First, fill clean canning jars, leaving space at the top of each jar. This is called *head space*. Head space is needed so that the food can expand as it is processed.

To process food, heat the filled jars for a specific amount of time. Your canning booklet will give you exact processing times. Heat cooks the food, and it also kills micro-organisms which cause food to spoil. Use a kitchen timer to be sure you have processed the food for the correct amount of time.

After the food has been processed it will have to cool. As hot jars cool, a vacuum is formed which seals them. When the jars are cool, label each one with the date. Store canned food in a cool, dry place. It will keep for up to a year. If the jars are exposed to heat, light or dampness, the food may discolor and spoil.

Always check canned food for signs of spoilage. If you see mold growing around the lid or in the food, discard the entire jar. If the food has gas bubbles, a bad odor, a slimy or spongy texture, or the liquid is cloudy, throw the food away. Never taste canned food to see if it is all right. Canned fruits can be served right from the jar. Canned vegetables should be thoroughly heated before serving.

12-23 Many of your favorite fruits and vegetables may be canned.

KERR

Canning takes time and special equipment. You must follow instructions carefully. If you take short-cuts or are careless, food may become contaminated, and food poisoning could occur.

Freezing

Frozen fruits and vegetables keep more of their color, flavor and texture than canned or dried fruits and vegetables. For best results use fruits and vegetables of good quality, 12-24. Directions for freezing most fruits and vegetables can be obtained from your county extension office. Follow the directions carefully.

Most fruits freeze well. Usually they are packed in sugar or syrup before freezing. (Syrup is made with water and sugar.) Fruits packed in sugar or syrup usually have a better texture than fruits that are frozen dry. Always leave some head space when you are filling freezing containers with fruit and sugar or syrup. This allows for expansion as the mixture freezes. A few fruits, such as berries and cherries, are frozen dry. They are placed on a cookie sheet, frozen and then packed into containers.

Most vegetables can be frozen. They will lose some of their crispness in the freezing process. Vegetables such as celery or leafy greens should not be frozen if they are to be used uncooked. They become limp after freezing and lose their texture.

Vegetables should be blanched before they are frozen. Blanching helps to prevent spoilage. Vegetables are blanched by placing them in boiling water or steam for a short time. They are then plunged into cold water so that they won't overcook. When packing vegetables, leave some head space.

Fruits and vegetables should be packed in airtight containers before freezing. This prevents freezer burn (food drying out on the surface).

All frozen foods should be labeled with the contents and the freezing date. Most fruits and vegetables can be frozen for eight to 12 months.

TUPPERWARE® HOME PARTIES

12-24 Take care in selecting produce for freezing. Choose fruits and vegetables of good quality.

Drying

Drying is probably the oldest method of preserving food, 12-25. Some foods that dry especially well are apples, bananas, pears, onions, peas and zucchini.

In the drying process warm air circulates around the food and draws out moisture. This helps to prevent spoilage. In warm, dry climates, foods can be dried outdoors in the sun. Foods can also be dried in dehydrators. *Dehydrators* are appliances that provide a controlled drying atmosphere.

You can dry fruits and vegetables in the oven. Convection ovens are especially well suited for this because the air circulates around the food. The oven temperature should be kept between 60°C and 70°C (140°F and 160°F). Stir or turn the food occasionally for even drying.

Some fruits and vegetables are treated before drying to help preserve flavor, color and texture. They may be dipped in an acid (lemon juice or vinegar). This helps them to retain their color. This is a good treatment for fruits such as apples, bananas and peaches. Another way to treat food before drying is to blanch it. Blanching softens the food, so it takes less time to dry. Many vegetables are blanched before drying.

Certain foods like onions, peppers and mushrooms require no pretreatment. Once they are cut up, they are ready to be dried.

DEL MONTE KITCHENS

12-25 Dried apples and apricots make great snacks. They can also be used in baked goods.

to Define

berries . . . blanching . . .
bulbs . . . citrus fruits . . .
crispers . . . dehydrators . .
drupes . . . flowers . . .
food preservation . . .
freezer burn . . .
fruit drink . . .
fruit juice . . .
head space . . . in season . . .
leaves . . . marinated . . .
melons . . . pomes . . .
produce . . . roots . . .
seeds . . . stems . . .
tubers . . . vegetable-fruits

to Discuss

1. What important nutrients are found in fruits and vegetables?
2. List the basic types of fruits and give at least one example of each.
3. List the basic types of vegetables and give at least one example of each.
4. When fresh produce is costly or not available, what other forms of fruits and vegetables can you buy?
5. Where should most fresh fruits and vegetables be stored?
6. List at least four ways of including fruits in meals.
7. What will prevent low acid fruits from browning?
8. Why is fruit sometimes cooked in syrup?
9. Why should fruits and vegetables be cut up just before cooking or serving?
10. What general guidelines should you follow to preserve flavor and nutrients when cooking vegetables?
11. List three methods of preserving fruits and vegetables.
12. Where can you obtain information on proper canning methods?
13. What are signs of spoilage in canned foods?
14. Why should vegetables be blanched before freezing?
15. What are three ways to dry foods?

to Do

1. Make a poster or chart showing the various types of fruits and vegetables.
2. Develop a lesson to teach preschool children the importance of eating fruits and vegetables.
3. Survey 20 people to discover their attitudes and eating patterns regarding fruits and vegetables. Which fruits and vegetables do they eat most often? Least often? Report your findings to the class.
4. Visit a store. Make a list of fresh fruits and vegetables you have never tasted. Select one and prepare it in class. Research its food value.
5. Keep a record of the fruits and vegetables you eat in a week. Which ones are high in vitamins A and C? Do you eat a variety of fruits and vegetables?
6. Demonstrate how fruits and vegetables can be used as garnishes.
7. Create a display which compares the cost of various forms of a given fruit or vegetable. For instance, compare various forms of peaches—fresh, frozen, canned, halves, slices, in light syrup, in heavy syrup.
8. Conduct an experiment using freezer wraps to see which ones do the best job of preventing freezer burn. Wrap equal amounts of a fruit or vegetable in various wraps—foil, plastic, waxed paper, sandwich bags and freezer paper. After two weeks, examine them and compare them in the frozen state, thawed and after cooking. Which wraps did the best job?

13

Grain products

What role do grain products play in your diet? After reading this chapter, you will be able to describe a wide variety of grain products. You will know how to shop for grain products and how to store them at home. You will be able to prepare many grain products, including breads, breakfast cereals, pasta and rice.

*C*ornflakes, oatmeal, bread, pasta and popcorn all have something in common. They all are made from grains, 13-1. Grains are the main food source for most of the world's population. In the United States, farmers produce large amounts of grain. Some of the grain is exported to other countries. Grains most often used for food are wheat, rice, corn and oats.

We rely on grain products to supply certain nutrients, mainly carbohydrates, iron, the B-vitamins and some protein. As grains are processed and refined, many important vitamins and minerals are lost. Some grain products are *enriched* to make up for the lost nutrients. Specific amounts of iron, thiamin, riboflavin and niacin that were lost during processing are added. If the label says *fortified,* various nutrients have been added beyond the amounts found in the original grain.

Some dieters think that cutting out grain products will help them lose weight faster. Actually, most of these foods are not especially high in kilojoules (Calories). More important, bread, pasta, rice and other foods in this group supply key nutrients that are a vital part of a balanced diet.

GRAINS — THE INSIDE STORY

When you hear the word *cereal,* you probably think of a breakfast food. Actually a "cereal" is any grain that is used for food, 13-2. The parts we eat are the seeds, called *kernels.* Many different products can be made from kernels.

The basic structure of all kernels is the same. Each kernel is a complete seed. There are three main parts to every kernel: the germ, endosperm and bran. See 13-3.

The *germ* is the part that would produce a new plant if the kernel were allowed to sprout and grow. Most of the fat and much of the protein and vitamins are found in this part of the kernel.

The *endosperm* is the largest part of the kernel. It consists mainly of starch along with some protein.

The outer part of the kernel is made of several thin layers of fiber called *bran.* Although humans cannot digest bran, it is very important in helping the intestines pass along wastes. The bran layers contain important vitamins and minerals.

Wheat

Wheat is the grain most often used for food in the United States. The Midwest is known for its vast wheat fields. Flours, breakfast cereals, pasta and many snack foods are made from wheat.

Bulgur is made by steaming the whole wheat kernel and then drying it. Some of the outside bran is removed, and what is left is cracked. Bulgur is used as a hot cereal, as a side dish and in casseroles and puddings.

Wheat germ is a nutritious product made from the germ of the kernel. It is usually toasted to bring out its nutlike flavor. Some people like wheat germ as a breakfast cereal or as a topping for many dishes.

Bran products are popular because they are good sources of fiber. Most often, bran products are eaten as breakfast cereals. Bran is sometimes used as an ingredient in quick breads. It can also be used as a substitute for bread crumbs in dishes like meat loaf.

Corn

A wide variety of products are made from corn. Breakfast cereals, snack foods, breads and cornmeal are made from corn. Corn syrups and corn oil (used as a cooking oil and also as an ingredient in many margarines) are also made from corn. Cornstarch is a popular thickening agent. Sweet corn is often served as a vegetable.

Popcorn is a popular snack. Popcorn is a type of corn with kernels which have a hard, waterproof covering. When the kernels are heated, the moisture inside them turns into steam and explodes the kernels.

Hominy is made by removing the germ and the hard, outer hull from mature kernels. It can be cooked and served as a side dish. But hominy is most popular when it is crushed and sold in a granulated form called *grits.* Grits are a popular breakfast cereal and side dish in the South.

Cornmeal is made by grinding kernels into a fine meal. It may be white or yellow depending on the kind of corn that was used to make it. Cornmeal is used in many baked products, as a hot cereal and as a coating for fried foods.

TUPPERWARE® HOME PARTIES

13-1 Grains are the bases of many versatile food products.

Oats

The oats we eat are in the form of *oatmeal*. Oatmeal is used in breakfast cereals and in cooking and baking. To make regular oatmeal, the tough hulls that cover the kernels are removed. The kernels are then called groats. The groats are rolled to form flakes of oatmeal.

Quick oatmeal differs from regular oatmeal only in the size of the flakes. Groats used for quick oatmeal are cut into tiny pieces, steamed, and then rolled into thin, small flakes. The smaller flakes cook more quickly.

Instant oatmeal is made in the same way. The groats are cut into even smaller pieces and are steamed slightly longer. Instant oatmeal can be prepared quickly by simply stirring in some boiling water.

Granola is a crunchy, oats-based mixture. It is popular as a breakfast cereal, snack food and topping for many dishes. In addition to oats, granola usually contains wheat germ, honey, raisins, vanilla, oil and sunflower seeds. Granola may also include other ingredients such as nuts, brown sugar, coconut and dry milk solids. Many people like to make their own granola.

Rice

Rice is the staple food for over half of the world's population. In areas where it grows well, rice produces the highest yield of any cereal grain.

Mention rice, and many people think of Oriental dinners. While rice is the mainstay of most Asian diets, it is an international food. In the United States, rice is used in soups, salads, desserts, main dishes and side dishes, 13-4. Some people like it with milk or cream as a hot breakfast. Rice can also be

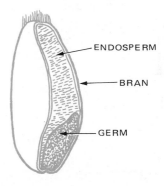

13-3 *All grain kernels have three main parts: the germ, endosperm and bran.*

13-2 *(Shown clockwise) Rice, oats, wheat and corn are the grains most often used for food in the United States.*

13-4 *Rice can be combined with other foods to make many interesting dishes. Here it is combined with bacon and chives.*

made into flour, wine and other products. Different types of rice will be described later in this chapter.

Other grains

Barley and rye are not as common as wheat, corn, oats and rice. But they are grains which are used for food in the United States.

Barley is more common in Europe than in the United States. It is used to make *malt*. Malt is used in making malted milk drinks and many fermented beverages, candies and bakery items. *Pearl barley* is the *polished grain*. (The bran has been removed.) Pearl barley is used to thicken soups.

Rye is another grain that is more common in Europe that in the United States. Most rye is used to make rye flour for breads and crackers.

Buckwheat is not a true grain. Buckwheat is the seed of a herb-like plant. Buckwheat is mainly used to make buckwheat pancake flour.

BUYING GRAIN PRODUCTS

Store shelves are stocked with a wide variety of grain products. As a group, grain products are economical foods. When buying them, consider the amount of money you have to spend. Also consider the amount of time you have to prepare the product. For instance, an instant rice product may take less time to prepare. But instant rice usually costs more than regular rice.

Nutrition is another factor to consider when shopping for grain products. Select products labeled "whole grain" or "enriched" for good nutritional value.

Flour

Flour can be made from a variety of grains. The grain used most often to make flour is wheat. Different types of wheat are used to make different types of flour.

There are three main types of wheat: soft, hard and durum (a very hard wheat). A major difference between soft and hard wheats is the protein content. The protein content deter-

mines the quality of *gluten* a flour will produce. Gluten is a sticky protein substance produced when water mixes with flour. Harder wheats produce stronger networks of gluten strands.

Durum wheat produces such strong gluten that it is not elastic enough for baking. It is used to make pasta products.

Hard wheat is used to make bread flour. Bread flour is used mainly by commercial bakers.

Soft wheat is used to make cake flour. Cake flour produces weaker gluten. It is used in products such as pastries, cakes and cookies.

Most people buy and use only one flour— *all-purpose flour*. All-purpose flour is made from a mixture of soft and hard wheats. As its name implies, it is generally good for all cooking and baking purposes.

Besides white flour, many stores stock whole wheat flour which is made from the whole grain. You may also find barley and rye flours. Barley flour does not produce gluten, and rye flour produces weak gluten. Since gluten is needed for bread to rise and have a light texture, loaves of barley and rye bread are heavy. To improve the texture of these breads, wheat flour is usually mixed with the barley or rye flour.

Bread

Bread is one of the oldest and most common foods. Some ancient types of breads are still eaten today. One example is *chapati,* a flat, unleavened wheat bread of India. Another example is *matzo,* the traditional bread of the Jewish Passover. The kinds of breads eaten in a certain region used to depend on the grains which were grown there.

Do you like bread with a light, fluffy texture? Or do you prefer a coarser texture, like that of homemade bread? Do you like it sliced thick or thin or not sliced at all? Do you like plain breads or breads with extra ingredients like nuts or fruit? When buying bread you have many choices. See 13-5.

If saving money is important to you, check the unit prices. Compare the price per kilogram (pound) for each loaf or package.

Hot dog and hamburger buns usually cost more per kilogram (pound) than a loaf of regular bread. For real savings, look for "day-old" specials. Sometimes commercial bakeries have small stores where you can buy day-old bread at low prices.

Breakfast cereals

As you walk down the cereal aisle of any grocery store, you will find a great variety of breakfast cereals. Cold or ready-to-eat cereals seem to come in all flavors, shapes and textures. Hot cereals have a wide range of flavors and textures too.

The cost of breakfast cereal depends on several factors. The package size, ease of preparation and ingredients are factors to consider when buying breakfast cereals.

Large packages of cereal are usually better buys than small ones. But check the unit prices to be sure. Buying single serving packages is one of the most costly ways to buy breakfast cereals. However, you may prefer these if you like a different cereal every day.

Most breakfast cereals could be considered convenience foods, since they are quick and easy to prepare. Ready-to-eat cereals are easiest to serve, 13-6. Hot cereals do require some preparation time, 13-7. Instant hot

13-6 A ready-to-eat cereal can be part of a nutritious breakfast.

13-5 Many kinds of bread are available. For good nutrition, buy enriched or whole grain bread products.

13-7 Hot cereals are hearty breakfast foods.

cereals can be made right in your bowl simply by stirring hot water into them. Quick-cooking cereals are prepared in a saucepan and take a few minutes longer. Regular-cooking cereals take the longest time to prepare. But the more convenient a food is to prepare, the more it usually costs.

Nuts and dried fruits are often added to cereals. In most cases, these extra ingredients add to the cost. You may wish to purchase plain breakfast cereals and add your own extra ingredients.

Breakfast cereals are not just for breakfast. They can be used as crunchy toppings for desserts and crispy coatings for foods to be fried or baked. They can also be substituted for croutons in a salad or eaten as snacks.

Pasta

The word *pasta* covers the whole family of products made from durum wheat flour. Two common types of pasta are macaroni and noodles. *Macaroni* includes a wide range of hollow or tube-shaped pasta. *Noodles* are flat ribbons of pasta. Noodles are made with eggs, so they have a little more protein than other types of pasta.

Pasta comes in many shapes, including rings, bows, stars, tubes, shells, ribbons, strings and squares. These may be made in a number of different sizes. They may also be straight, rippled, curled, grooved, bent or twisted. See 13-8.

The many shapes and sizes of pasta can be used in many ways. This economical food is often used in main dishes, side dishes, salads and soups. It is even used in some snacks and desserts.

Most pasta products are enriched with thiamin, niacin, riboflavin and iron. Some are also fortified with extra protein. Look for this information on package labels.

Rice

Most grocery stores carry a variety of rice products, 13-9. The most popular is white rice. *White rice* has been milled to remove the outer hull, the bran and the germ. Only the white starchy endosperm is left. During mill-

ing, many of the vitamins and minerals are lost. When buying white rice, be sure to look for the word enriched on the label.

You can buy white rice in short, medium or long grains. The short and medium grains usually cost less. But they are more likely to cling together when they are cooked.

Parboiled rice is put through a special steam and pressure treatment before being milled. This treatment helps to preserve the nutrients in the rice. It also changes the cooking characteristics of the rice. Parboiled rice requires longer cooking than regular white rice.

Instant rice has been precooked. It needs only a few minutes of cooking at home because it has already been cooked, rinsed and dried. Instant rice costs more than regular white rice.

Brown rice is whole grain rice. Neither the bran nor the germ has been removed.

Wild rice is the seed of a grass that grows wild in shallow lakes and marshes. It has a dark brown color and a nutlike flavor. Wild rice is expensive. You can often buy it mixed with long grain white rice, which isn't quite as costly.

Rice is a convenient food to cook and serve. Rice is also a common ingredient in many convenience foods. You can find Chinese fried rice, for instance, in cans or frozen cartons, ready to heat and serve. Many versions of seasoned or flavored rice are available in packages, cans or frozen cartons. The convenience may or may not be worth the extra cost. Compare as you shop. You may find, for instance, that frozen rice with mushrooms costs twice as much as regular rice and fresh mushrooms. You may or may not want to pay for the added seasonings and convenience of the frozen product. You will have to judge your resources of time, energy, skills and money.

STORING GRAIN PRODUCTS

Grain products, in general, should be stored in tightly closed containers in a cool, dry place. This will prevent loss of nutrients and will keep the products fresh longer. Some grain products, such as whole wheat flour, wheat germ and brown rice, keep best in the refrigerator. This prevents the fat in the germ part of kernels from developing a rancid flavor.

Grain products will keep better in airtight containers than in their original packaging. Cooking directions and recipes on the packages can be cut out and fastened to the containers.

When stored properly, breakfast cereals will keep two to three months. Pasta and rice will keep up to a year. Covered containers of cooked rice and pasta will keep in the refrigerator for several days. If you wish to store these products longer, they can be frozen for about six months.

Rolls and breads with hard crusts (such as French or Italian bread) should be used as soon as possible. They can be stored in their paper wrappers for a day at room temperature. But they quickly begin to dry out. For longer storage, put them in airtight bags or wrapping. That way, they will keep on the shelf for a few days. They will keep in the refrigerator for a week and in the freezer for

over a month. To freshen the bread, wrap it in foil and put it in a hot oven for a few minutes. (For extra moisture, you can cover the bread with lettuce leaves before wrapping it in the foil.)

Breads with soft crusts usually come from the store in plastic wrapping. You can store most breads in this wrapping at room temperature for up to a week. Summer heat and humidity may produce mold. (Throw out moldy bread.) You may try keeping the bread in the refrigerator. Refrigeration, however, will make bread taste stale sooner. For long storage, freeze bread in airtight wrapping.

COOKING WITH GRAIN PRODUCTS

Grain products are used in a variety of baked goods. Some of the most popular baked goods are quick breads and yeast breads. As you read recipes for these baked goods, you will see the words *batter* and *dough*. These words describe the consistency or thickness of flour mixtures. Doughs are much thicker than

13-8 Many different types of pasta can be found in the supermarket.

TUPPERWARE® HOME PARTIES

13-9 There are many different types of rice. You can buy rice plain or combined with other ingredients. Grain products keep well in containers which can be tightly sealed.

TUPPERWARE® HOME PARTIES

batters. The proportion of liquid to dry ingredients makes the difference. Products like pancakes and muffins are made from batters. Products like yeast breads and biscuits are made from doughs.

Other cereal products such as breakfast cereals, pasta and rice require special preparation methods. When prepared correctly, these products should not be lumpy or sticky. Cooking directions on the packages are usually reliable guides in preparing hot cereals, pasta and rice.

Quick breads

One difference between quick breads and yeast breads is the leavening agents used to make them. *Quick breads* are made with baking soda, baking powder, steam, air or a combination of these leavening agents. These leavening agents work fast which is why these products are called "quick." *Yeast breads* use yeast as the leavening agent.

Quick breads include such products as muffins, biscuits, pancakes and waffles. Most fruit or nut breads (such as banana bread) and sweet breads (such as coffee cakes) are also quick breads.

Muffins. Muffins look much like cupcakes with rough, rounded tops, 13-10. The basic muffin batter is made from milk, eggs, fat (oil or shortening), flour, baking powder, salt and sugar. Many other ingredients may be added for variety, such as fruits, jam, cheese, bacon, nuts or even peanut butter.

Muffins are made using the *muffin method.* See 13-11. All of the dry ingredients are combined in one bowl. The moist liquid ingredients are mixed in another bowl. To combine the two mixtures, make a "well" in the dry mixture and pour the liquid mixture into it. Mix all ingredients together quickly. The muffin batter is mixed enough when all of the ingredients are moistened. It will look lumpy, and you may think it is not mixed enough. But if you stir the batter until it is smooth, you will overmix it. Overmixing makes the muffins tough. Overmixing can also cause "tunnels" or holes to form in the muffins as they are baked.

The pan in which you bake muffins should be greased, or you may use paper liners. Fill each cup about two-thirds full, and bake the muffins immediately.

Biscuits. Biscuits are made from a dough. You may roll out the dough and cut it to make smooth, round biscuits. Or, by adding a little more liquid, you can simply drop the dough in small mounds on a baking sheet.

Plain biscuit dough is made with flour, baking powder, salt, shortening, and milk or water. The *biscuit method* of mixing ingredients is very different from the muffin method. To make biscuit dough, first combine all the dry ingredients. Then cut in the shortening as shown in 13-12. Continue until the mixture looks like small peas. Add the milk or water, and stir with a fork just until the mixture begins to look like a rough dough.

Put the dough on a flat surface that is lightly covered with flour. Knead the dough quickly and lightly several times. Kneading makes

13-10 Serve fresh baked muffins hot from the oven.

the dough smoother and will improve the texture of the biscuits. Too much kneading, however, will make the biscuits tough.

Roll out the dough to a thickness of about one cm (one-half inch) for soft, high biscuits. (If you want crusty, thinner biscuits, roll the dough thinner.) Then cut the dough. You can use a floured biscuit cutter or glass. Or, you can simply use a knife to cut the dough into squares, diamonds or triangles. Transfer the biscuits to an ungreased baking sheet. If you want the sides of the biscuits to be soft, put them close together. If you want the sides to be crusty, leave space between them. Biscuits take a short time to bake and should be served hot, 13-13.

There are many other things you can do with biscuit dough besides making biscuits. You can wrap a hot dog in a rectangle of thinly rolled dough and bake it. You can make a crust to put on the top of a casserole. For a cobbler dessert, drop pieces of the dough on the top of a hot fruit mixture and bake. Look through magazines and cookbooks for other ideas.

Pancakes and waffles. Basic pancakes and waffles are made with the same ingredients, but waffles tend to contain more fat and eggs. Waffle batter contains more fat to keep it from sticking to the waffle baker. The extra eggs in waffles make them lighter and crisper than pancakes. Both pancakes and waffles are

13-12 *A pastry blender is used to cut shortening into dry ingredients for biscuits. You can also use two table knives using a cross-cutting motion.*

13-13 *Freshly baked biscuits served with jelly are delicious. Biscuits should be light, flaky and golden brown.*

A—Make a well in the center of the dry ingredients. Then pour in the liquid ingredients.

B—Mix batter quickly. The mixture will look lumpy. Do not overmix.

C—Gently drop batter into greased muffin cups.

13-11 *Muffins take little time to prepare.*

mixed by the muffin method. (The dry ingredients are combined; a well is made; and the liquid ingredients are added.) Some waffle recipes call for separating eggs. The yolks are added with the liquid ingredients. Then the whites are beaten and gently folded into the batter.

Pancakes may be cooked in a skillet, but a griddle is easier to use because it has no sides. Lightly grease or oil the cooking surface, or use a griddle with a nonstick finish. The griddle should be hot before you start cooking. Pour the batter onto the hot griddle. The pancakes are ready to turn when the surfaces lose their shiny look and are covered with little bubbles. See 13-14. Brown the other side of the pancakes, and serve them hot.

Crêpes are a French pancake variation. The batter is much thinner, and often it contains no baking powder. You can eat crêpes at any meal. For breakfast, you might have crêpes with syrup or a fruit or cheese filling. For a main dish, you could use a meat, poultry, fish or cheese filling. Crêpes served with fruit, nuts, powdered sugar or whipped cream make a good dessert.

You need a waffle baker to make waffles, 13-15. Electric waffle bakers have a light to tell you when the grids are hot enough to pour in the batter. This light later tells you when the waffle is cooked. Waffles may be served with syrup, jam, fruit or whipped cream. Waffle and ice cream sandwiches make a nutritious snack or dessert.

Yeast breads

The yeast breads category includes all plain breads made with yeast. It also includes a variety of dinner rolls and specialty breads. Dinner rolls are made by shaping small amounts of yeast dough. Specialty breads are often made from yeast dough with some extra ingredients such as jam, nuts, fruits or spices.

Basic ingredients. A basic yeast bread contains yeast, sugar, flour, liquid, shortening and salt. Each of these ingredients has a special job to do.

Yeast is a tiny plant. When yeast and a small amount of sugar are dissolved in water,

it produces carbon dioxide gas. This gas causes the bread dough to stretch and rise. Always make sure the yeast you are using is fresh before you start. The package should have a date on it. (After that date the yeast may not be as active as it should be.)

Sugar is needed for the yeast to grow. Sugar is also needed for good texture in the bread and for browning the crust. However, be

EKCO HOUSEWARES CO.

13-14 Pancakes are ready to turn when the uncooked side is dotted with little bubbles that are starting to break.

SILVERSTONE® AND TELFON® DUPONT'S NON-STICK FINISHES

13-15 Waffles and crêpes are delicious for any meal and make great desserts.

216

careful not to use too much sugar as this could slow down yeast activity.

Flour provides structure in breads. You may notice that yeast bread recipes usually do not give exact flour measurements. The moisture in the air and the way you handle the dough can affect the amount of flour needed. Start with a small amount of flour and add more as you need it. Generally, the dough loses its stickiness when it has enough flour.

The liquid used in making bread moistens the flour and dissolves the yeast. Liquids should be warm to lukewarm. Cool temperatures slow yeast activity, and hot temperatures can kill the yeast.

Shortening helps to keep the bread from drying out and getting stale quickly. Shortening also increases the tenderness of the bread.

Salt helps to control the action of the yeast. It also adds flavor to the bread.

All of these ingredients work together to give bread good volume, good texture and good flavor.

Mixing, shaping and baking. There are many ways of mixing and shaping yeast breads. Steps in the traditional method are shown in 13-16. Following this method, mix the warm liquid, sugar and yeast together.

A—Mix the ingredients and beat until smooth. Add flour until the dough forms a soft ball.

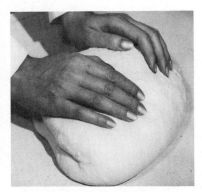

B—Knead the dough until it forms a smooth ball. To knead, fold the dough toward you; push it away with the heels of your hands; turn it one-quarter turn; and repeat.

C—Grease a bowl and rub the dough lightly against the bowl. Let the dough rise in a warm place.

D—The dough should double in size. Test it by sticking two fingers in it. If it has risen enough, the impression will stay.

E—Punch down the dough after it has risen, and allow it to rise again.

F—Shape dough into loaves pinching the ends together and folding them under.

13-16 Follow these steps in making yeast breads.

Grain products   **217**

Add about one half of the flour. Beat the mixture until smooth. Next, blend the shortening and salt into the mixture. Add the remaining flour until the dough forms a soft ball.

The next step is to put the dough onto a lightly floured surface. Your work surface should be kept lightly floured. This helps to prevent sticking, which can tear the dough. Cover the dough with a towel. Let it rest for five to 10 minutes.

After resting, the dough is ready to be kneaded. *Kneading* is a fold-push-turn action. Using your fingers, fold half of the dough toward you. Then using the heels of your hands, push the dough away from you. Then give the dough a one-quarter turn. Repeat these three steps until the dough forms a smooth ball. (All kneading is done by hand unless you have a food processor or a heavy-duty mixer with a dough hook. See 13-17.)

Grease a bowl thoroughly. Rub the dough lightly against the bowl so that it is covered with a light film of oil. This prevents drying. Put the bowl in a warm place, about 27 to 29°C (80 to 85°F), away from cool drafts. If the room is too cool, fill a large bowl with hot water, and cover it with a wire cooling rack. Then put the bowl of dough on the rack. Cover the bowl of dough with a clean kitchen towel. Replace the hot water in the lower bowl when it cools.

The dough should double in size. You can test it by sticking two fingers into it. If it has risen enough, the impression will stay. When the dough has risen enough, punch it down to release some of the gas. The dough is often allowed to rise again before it is shaped into rolls or loaves. After the dough is shaped, it should rise and double in size again before baking.

Yeast dough can be used to make all kinds of rolls, buns and coffee cakes. You can shape it into dinner rolls such as crescent rolls and cloverleaf rolls. Breakfast rolls and coffee cakes are often made from a sweeter dough.

Loaves may be shaped in different ways. One way is especially good for getting rid of large gas bubbles in the dough. First, gently roll out the dough to form a rectangle. Then carefully roll up the dough. Seal the lengthwise seam by pinching the dough. Seal the ends and fold them under.

To bake a loaf of bread, place the loaf in a pan with the seam on the bottom. Put the pan in a warm place and let the dough rise until it doubles in size. Follow the temperature and time directions in your recipe.

The bread is done if you hear a hollow sound when you tap the crust. To cool the loaf, take it out of the pan right away. Place it on a wire rack. You may want to brush the loaf with butter right after baking.

Convenience products

Baking breads from scratch is not hard, but there are a number of products on the market that save time and energy.

Brown-and-serve breads. These are the easiest of all to use. All they need is a few minutes in the oven for browning. These can be stored in their original wrapping in the refrigerator for about a week. They can be stored in the freezer for a couple of months.

Mixes. When you buy a mix, you are paying for the convenience of having some ingredients already measured and combined. But you still have to add one or more ingredients before baking. Some mixes save you more time and energy than others. Some save you only the time of measuring flour, salt and baking powder. And you are charged quite a bit for this service. Evaluate the cost and true convenience of mixes before you buy them.

Frozen dough. Frozen dough must be kept frozen until you're ready to use it. If it is a yeast dough, you will have to allow time for the dough to rise before baking. Check the label for information on how to thaw and prepare the dough for baking.

Refrigerated doughs. These doughs are available for several kinds of rolls and breads. The plain doughs can be used in many ways. For instance, pieces of biscuit dough can be flattened by hand and used as the bases for tiny pizzas. The dough can also be reshaped into bread sticks and rolled in sesame seeds. Other ideas are shown in 13-18.

Each can of refrigerated dough is stamped

with an expiration date. This date assures the quality of the product. Refrigerated doughs must be stored in the refrigerator. They should not be frozen. Once you open the can, bake all of the dough. It will not keep.

Crumbs and croutons

Although several kinds of crumbs and croutons are available in most stores, they are very easy to make yourself. They are also much less expensive when homemade. Making your own crumbs and croutons is a good way to use up stale or leftover breads and rolls.

Crumbs can be made from bread, crackers, ready-to-eat cereals and even crisp cookies. For dry bread crumbs, start with very dry or toasted bread. Break the bread into pieces.

Put the pieces in a blender at high speed for a few seconds. You can also use the blender to make cracker, cereal and cookie crumbs. Or you can put pieces of crackers, cereal or cookies in a plastic bag or between sheets of waxed paper. Then crush them with a rolling pin.

13-18 Use your imagination; refrigerated biscuit dough can be rolled, filled, cut and shaped in many different ways.

SUNBEAM

13-17 A mixer with a dough hook can be used to knead yeast doughs.

Recipes often call for crumbs to "stretch" the meat content in a dish or to make a crunchy topping, 13-19. *Breading* foods (coating them with crumbs) is a delicious way to add flavor and crispness to meats, fish and vegetables. Usually, a beaten egg or milk is used to make the crumbs stick to the surface of the food. Although most breaded foods are fried, many can be broiled or baked.

Croutons are small, crunchy bread cubes. They are used in soups, salads and casseroles. To make croutons, cut slices of bread into cubes. Brown the cubes in a skillet with a little butter or oil. (Experiment with herbs, garlic, onion or other seasonings for extra flavor.) Drain the croutons on paper towels. Another way to make croutons is to butter both sides of bread slices before cutting the slices into cubes. Then put the cubes on a baking sheet in a hot oven for a few minutes. Turn or shake the cubes a few times to make sure they brown evenly.

Cereals

Cooked cereals should be smooth and creamy, 13-20. As cereals are cooked, the starch granules absorb the water (or other liquid). This causes the granules to expand or swell. To prevent lumps, you need to make sure that all the granules swell evenly. Otherwise, the granules may stick together in clumps that are dry and uncooked inside.

The basic cooking method is to stir the dry cereal slowly into rapidly boiling water. The stirring and the bubbles in the boiling water help keep the granules separate until they have begun to swell. When all the cereal has been added and the mixture starts to boil again, turn the heat down to low. Cook for the length of time specified on the package. At the end of the cooking time, all the water should be absorbed. The cooked cereal should be smooth but not pasty.

The amount of water used and the cooking time vary for different cereals. Always check package directions, and measure accurately.

Instant cereals are easy to prepare. You just add boiling water. This kind of cereal is popular among people who want a hearty, but quick and easy, breakfast. For variety, you can buy instant cereals with extra ingredients such as raisins, dates, brown sugar or honey.

Pasta

The key to cooking pasta is to use lots of water and to know when it has cooked just enough. See 13-21.

Use a large, deep pot so you can use plenty of water. This will allow the pasta to cook evenly and move around freely without clumping. Heat the water to a rapid boil. Add salt according to package directions. Then add the pasta. The bubbles in rapidly boiling water help to keep the pieces apart. Stir gently once or twice during cooking. (A small amount of cooking oil added to the water helps to prevent the water from boiling over.)

The cooking time for pasta depends on the size and shape of the pieces. Package directions are good guides, but the "bite" test is the only sure way to check doneness. Simply take a sample out of the pot, cool it quickly under cold running water and bite into it. The pasta should be cooked through (no hard, white

KELLOGG CO.

13-19 A crumb topping adds a crunchy texture to a cooked fruit dessert.

220

center) but still firm and chewy.

When the pasta is cooked, pour off the water. A colander or large strainer is handy for draining the pasta. You may want to quickly rinse the pasta under warm running water to remove any loose starch. You may also want to stir in a little butter to keep the pasta from sticking together.

Rice

Cooked rice should be tender and fluffy, 13-22. The most important things to remember when cooking rice are to measure accurately and to watch the cooking time carefully. Different types of rice need different amounts of water. Rice absorbs water and expands as it cooks. Always check the package for specific cooking directions.

Generally, the first step in cooking rice is to combine the rice, water (or other liquid) and salt. Use a pot with a tight-fitting lid. (Some package directions also call for a small amount of butter. This helps keep the grains separate.) Bring the mixture to a boil. Stir the mixture, and cover the pot. Lower the heat, and simmer for the recommended time. When the rice is cooked, fluff it gently with a fork and serve.

13-21 Many main dishes are made with pasta. Shown here is macaroni with sausage eggplant sauce.

QUAKER OATS

13-20 When prepared correctly, cooked cereals are smooth and creamy. They are delicious topped with nuts, brown sugar or fruit.

RICE COUNCIL

13-22 The variety of dishes made with rice is endless.

to Define

all-purpose flour . .
batter . . .
biscuit method . . .
bran . . . cereal . . .
dough . . . endosperm . . .
enriched . . . fortified . . .
germ . . . gluten . . .
kernel . . . kneading . . .
muffin method . . .
pasta . . .quick breads . . .
yeast breads

to Discuss

1. Name four or more food products made from grains.
2. What are the three parts of a kernel? Which part is fiber? Which part is mostly starch? Which part contains most of the fat and much of the protein and vitamins?
3. List at least four products that can be made from corn.
4. What type of flour would you use for most cooking and baking purposes?
5. How can you save money when buying breads?
6. Which form of breakfast cereal is usually a better buy, large packages or single serving packages?
7. In general, how should grain products be stored?
8. Name four types of quick breads.
9. What happens if you mix muffin batter too much?
10. How do you knead yeast dough?
11. How can you make your own bread crumbs?
12. How can you prevent lumps in hot cereal?
13. Why is it important to use a lot of boiling water to cook pasta?
14. How can you tell when pasta is done?
15. What are two important keys to successful rice cooking?

to Do

1. Compare different types of rice. Purchase several rice products. Prepare each product according to package directions. Calculate the cost per serving of each product. Compare the texture, color and flavor of the products. Evaluate the convenience of preparing the products. Which ones would you choose for family meals? Why?
2. List all the forms (not brands) of pasta sold in a local store. Record the cost per serving of each form. Which is the most economical? The most expensive? Buy a package of a form of pasta you haven't eaten before, and prepare a dish using it.
3. Compare the cost and nutritional content of one serving of five different ready-to-eat cereals without milk. Make a chart illustrating your findings, and post it in your classroom. Did your findings change your ideas about your favorite cereals?
4. Homemade granola is easy to make and is a delicious snack or breakfast food. Find a recipe for granola. Prepare it and share samples with other class members.
5. Make homemade croutons using three slices of bread. Add garlic, salt or other seasonings if you wish. Compare the cost and taste of your homemade croutons with packaged croutons. Report your findings to the class.
6. Design a bulletin board that shows the variety of foods made from grains. Use pictures from magazines and food packages or draw your own.
7. Demonstrate the importance of following recipe directions carefully. For example, what happens if bread dough isn't kneaded? Divide into two groups. Group I will prepare the bread according to recipe directions, leaving out the kneading step. Group II will prepare the bread as the recipe directs so that you will have a good basis for comparing the results. Which loaf is larger? Which bread is lighter in texture?

14

Baking basics

What are the basics of baking? After reading this chapter, you will be able to explain the functions of basic baking ingredients. You will also be able to perform basic baking skills in the preparation of cookies, cakes and pies.

*B*aking at home used to be a necessity. Today, many people bake for fun. Baking allows you to be creative and to enjoy freshly baked cookies, pies and cakes, 14-1.

Cookbooks and magazines are good sources of recipes for baked goods. But before you begin to bake, you need to know the basics of baking.

BASIC BAKING INGREDIENTS

Most ingredients used in baking are basic kitchen supplies such as flour, milk, sugar, salt, eggs, baking powder and shortening. Some recipes call for extra ingredients such as fruit, nuts or chocolate.

It is important to follow recipes carefully when you bake. In many kinds of cooking, you can add or subtract ingredients to suit your tastes. If you like garlic and onions, for instance, you can safely add a little more to a stew or casserole. But in baking, you must measure carefully and use the exact ingredients specified. Carelessness can lead to baking failures.

Recipes for baked products are like scientific formulas. Each ingredient has one or more jobs. Some ingredients affect the flavor. Others affect the texture or tenderness. Some make a product rise. Some help it to brown during baking. Understanding how the ingredients react in baking will help you as you develop baking skills.

Flour

Flour gives baked products structure and shape. As you learned in Chapter 13, different types of flour have special uses. For most baking, all-purpose flour will produce good results. But suppose you are making a cake, and your recipe calls for cake flour. Then it is important to use cake flour instead of all-purpose flour.

Liquid

The liquid used in baked products moistens dry ingredients like flour and dissolves some ingredients such as sugar. Liquids can also be leavening agents. This happens when they are turned to steam during baking.

The liquid used in baking can be milk, fruit juice or water. Milk and fruit juice add nutrients and flavor to baked products. Milk also aids in browning.

Different amounts of liquid are used for different types of baked goods. For instance, a cake recipe usually calls for more liquid than a cookie recipe. Too little liquid is likely to result in a dry, coarse texture. Too much liquid may produce a soggy or soft texture.

Sugar

Sugar adds a sweet flavor to baked products. But it has other important jobs, too. It helps baked products to brown during baking. Sugar also helps to tenderize gluten, making sweet baked goods generally tender.

Eggs

Eggs add color and flavor to baked products. Eggs help products rise because they contain moisture that turns to steam during baking. Beaten eggs also add structure to baked products by trapping air bubbles in the dough or batter.

Fat

Fats have an important role in blending the seasonings and flavors of other ingredients. Fats also help make products tender. In cakes, the creaming of fat and sugar mixes in air. This air is held in the batter by the fat. This adds to the volume of the cake. Butter, margarine, shortening, lard and cooking oil are the main fats used in baking.

Leavening agents

Leavening agents are used to make doughs and batters rise when they are baked. This makes baked goods light and soft in texture. Air and steam are the main leavening agents in a few foods such as angel food cakes. The most common leavening agent used in baked goods is carbon dioxide gas. This gas can be produced by three different agents: baking

BETTY CROCKER FOOD AND NUTRITION CENTER

14-1 Baked goods are fun to make and eat.

soda, baking powder and yeast.

Baking soda and baking powder produce carbon dioxide more quickly than yeast. They are used in many baked goods such as cakes and cookies.

Baking soda is a chemical compound that produces carbon dioxide when combined with an acid. Recipes which call for baking soda also call for some kind of acid ingredient. Common acid ingredients are sour milk, fruit juice and cream of tartar.

Baking powder is a mixture of baking soda and a dry acid powder. There are two types of baking powder: single-acting and double-acting. *Single-acting baking powder* begins to produce carbon dioxide as soon as it is mixed with liquid. *Double-acting baking powder* reacts twice. It begins to react when moistened, and it reacts again when the batter or dough is heated. Be sure to store baking powder in a dry place. If it begins to cake or harden, replace it. This is a sign that it has lost its leavening power.

Yeast is also a leavening agent. It is used in a variety of breads. (Yeast was discussed in Chapter 13.)

COOKIES

Cookies are as much fun to make as they are to eat, 14-2. Cookies usually contain flour, sugar, liquid, fat, salt, eggs and leavening. You can find many recipes for nutritious cookies. Raisins, nuts and oatmeal add nutrients to cookies. Look for other nutritious ingredients such as pumpkin, wheat germ and peanut butter.

There aren't any special tricks to making most cookies. Mixing cookie batter and doughs usually starts with creaming the sugar and fat together. Next, the eggs, liquid and flavorings are mixed in. Then the dry ingredients are added. Special ingredients such as nuts, chocolate chips, raisins or oatmeal are usually stirred in last.

Try to make all your cookies about the

14-2 These freshly baked oatmeal cookies are delicious and nutritious.

EVAPORATED MILK ASSOCIATION

same size and shape so they will bake evenly. You have to watch the baking time closely because most cookies bake in only a few minutes. They will burn if you aren't careful. Most cookies should be transferred to cooling racks immediately after baking.

Types of cookies

There are six main types of cookies. These are: drop, bar, molded, rolled, pressed and refrigerator.

Drop cookies are probably the easiest cookies to make. They are made from a stiff batter that is dropped from a spoon onto a baking sheet. See 14-3. Check the recipe to see whether or not the sheet should be greased. Cookies that contain quite a bit of fat usually do not need a greased baking sheet. Chocolate chip cookies and oatmeal cookies are popular drop cookies.

Bar cookies look like some cakes. They are made from a stiff batter spread in a well greased pan. See 14-4. After they are baked, let them cool slightly. Cut and serve the cookies right from the pan. Brownies are a favorite bar cookie.

Molded cookies are made from a dough that you can shape by hand. The dough is placed on the baking sheet in small balls. Some molded cookies are flattened before they are baked. See 14-5. Peanut butter cookies, for instance, may be flattened with a fork. Some are flattened with the bottom of a glass dipped in sugar. Some cookies can be filled. This is done by pressing a finger into the middle of each ball of dough to make a little pocket. The pocket is then filled with jam, jelly or other filling.

Rolled cookies are made from a stiff dough. The dough is rolled into a thin layer and cut with cookie cutters or with a knife and cardboard patterns. The dough is easier to roll if it is chilled thoroughly. With a creamy filling or frosting, you can sandwich rolled cookies together. Rolled cookies (such as sugar cookies) are fun to decorate with frosting or sugar sprinkles. You can also use a "paint" made from food coloring and a liquid. Use your imagination in decorating rolled cookies. See 14-6.

Pressed cookies are formed by forcing the dough through a cookie press. See 14-7. Spritz cookies are made this way. You often see pressed cookies at holiday gatherings, teas and receptions. Because they are small, they are easy to handle and eat at a party.

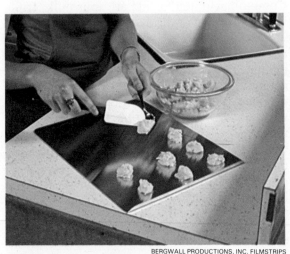

14-3 Drop cookies are made by dropping small portions of a stiff batter onto a baking sheet.

14-4 Brownies are bar cookies. They are made from a stiff batter spread in a greased baking pan.

BETTY CROCKER FOOD AND NUTRITION CENTER

14-5 Molded cookies are often flattened before they are baked. Create interesting designs by using your imagination and common kitchen items.

Refrigerator cookies are made from a stiff dough that must be refrigerated several hours before it is cut into cookies. The dough is molded into a roll and wrapped in plastic wrap or foil, 14-8. After it is well chilled, it is cut crosswise with a sharp knife into thin slices and baked. You can keep the dough in the refrigerator for several days and bake the cookies as you need them. Pinwheel cookies are refrigerator cookies.

BETTY CROCKER FOOD AND NUTRITION CENTER

14-7 Pressed cookies are made by forcing a stiff dough through a cookie press.

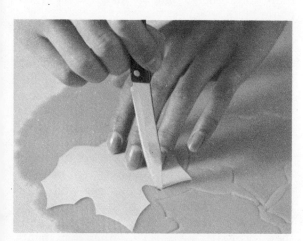

BETTY CROCKER FOOD AND NUTRITION CENTER

14-8 Refrigerator cookies are made from a stiff dough which must be wrapped tightly and stored in the refrigerator. Once cookies are baked, they can be stored in the freezer in airtight containers or wraps.

BETTY CROCKER FOOD AND NUTRITION CENTER

14-6 Rolled cookies are cut from a stiff dough that has been rolled into a thin layer. Here, leaves are cut from a cardboard pattern and painted with food coloring.

Storing and freezing cookies

Once cookies are thoroughly cooled, they can be stacked and stored in a container with a tight cover. If cookies become slightly stale or limp, you can usually freshen them. You can do this by putting them in a hot oven for a few minutes. Since this tends to dry them out, they should be eaten right away.

You can freeze cookie dough or baked cookies. Freeze the dough in a freezer container, or wrap it tightly in freezer wrap. Baked cookies can be frozen in plastic bags or foil. If the cookies are fragile, you should use a freezer container. Do not unwrap frozen cookies until they have thawed. This helps to prevent limpness.

CAKES

Cakes are a traditional part of many celebrations such as weddings and birthdays. They are often used as symbols of friendship. In many areas, people welcome a new neighbor with a cake. Dinners for company often end with cake for dessert.

Cakes can be made in many sizes and shapes, from cupcakes to large wedding cakes. They can be plain or very fancy, depending on the occasion and your creativity. Cakes can be filled and frosted. You may even want to create special designs such as animal figures for a child's party.

Types of cakes

There are two basic types of cakes: shortened cakes and foam cakes. See 14-9. *Shortened cakes* include some kind of fat, such as butter, margarine or shortening. *Foam cakes,* such as angel food, are made without fat. *Chiffon cakes* are a mixture of these two main types. They are made with fat, but they depend on beaten egg whites to produce the light, foamy texture of foam cakes. Foam and chiffon cakes are usually baked in tube pans.

Cake mixing methods

The method used to mix a cake depends on the type of cake being made. Shortened cakes are usually made using either the conventional method or the one-bowl method. Foam cakes and chiffon cakes are made using the foam cake method. To get the best results, always follow the recipe directions exactly. They are based on the specific ingredients and proportions used in the recipe.

The *conventional method* has several steps. The fat and sugar are first creamed together until the mixture is very light and fluffy. Then the eggs are beaten in. The flour, salt and baking powder or soda are mixed in a separate bowl. This dry mixture is added to the creamed mixture alternately with the liquid, a little at a time. This method is more involved than the others, but it makes very fine-textured, light cakes.

The *one-bowl method* is very popular because it is easy and uses only one bowl. The dry ingredients are combined in a large mixing bowl. The fat, flavorings and part of the liquid are added. This mixture is then beaten vigorously for about two minutes. Finally, the rest of the liquid and the eggs are added. Again, the batter is beaten vigorously.

The *foam cake method* is used for angel food, sponge and chiffon cakes. All of these depend on the air beaten into egg whites for leavening. For an angel food cake, the egg whites are beaten with some of the sugar until they form stiff peaks. The other ingredients are mixed separately and then gently folded

BETTY CROCKER FOOD AND NUTRITION CENTER

14-9 The two basic types of cake are shortened cakes and foam cakes.

into the beaten egg whites. For sponge cakes and chiffon cakes, the dry ingredients are beaten into the egg yolks. The whites are beaten until stiff. The egg yolk mixture is then gently folded into the egg whites a little at a time.

Baking the cake

Your recipe should tell you what size pan to use. Be sure to use the right size pan. If your pan is too small, the cake is likely to overflow, 14-10. If it is too large, the cake will look pale and flat. If you aren't sure how large your pans are, measure them across the bottom. The size of the pan helps determine how long the cake will need to bake. Cupcakes, for instance, bake faster than large, rectangular cakes.

For shortened cakes, grease and flour the pans lightly but thoroughly. You can use a paper towel to coat the pans with a thin layer of shortening. Then sprinkle a little flour into the pans. Shake and turn the pans until their entire inside surfaces are lightly dusted with flour. You do not have to grease and flour the pans for cupcakes if you use paper liners instead. Fill the pans or paper liners about two-thirds full of batter. Spread the batter evenly in the pans with a rubber spatula, if necessary.

For a foam cake, do not grease the pan. Gently pour the batter into the pan, 14-11. It will nearly fill the pan because of all the air in the batter. With a rubber spatula, gently push the batter against the tube and sides of the pan. Cut through the batter with a few smooth, even strokes. This will help to prevent large air bubbles.

When you bake a layer cake, place the pans in the oven so that they are not touching each other. The cake pans should not be too close to the sides of the oven. Space around the pans allows the air to circulate for even baking. See 14-12.

There are several ways to tell when a cake is done. The baking time given in the recipe is a good guide. There are a few other signs of doneness for which you can check. The cake should spring back when gently touched in the center. Or a wooden toothpick inserted in the

BERGWALL PRODUCTIONS, INC. FILMSTRIPS

14-10 If you use a cake pan that is too small or if you fill the pan too full, the cake may overflow.

BERGWALL PRODUCTIONS, INC. FILMSTRIPS

14-11 Do not grease the pan when making a foam cake. Pour the batter evenly into a tube pan.

EKCO HOUSEWARES CO.

14-12 When you bake a layer cake, arrange the pans so that hot air can circulate around the pans.

center should come out clean. Shortened cakes also tend to come away from the sides of the pan when they are done.

All cakes should be cooled before being removed from their pans. See 14-13. Layer cakes should be placed on wire cooling racks for about 10 minutes. This makes it easier to remove the cake from the pan. Remove the cake from the pan by running the tip of a metal spatula around the sides of the cake. Place the cooling rack over the pan and gently flip the pan and cooling rack over. The cake should come out of the pan easily. The cake should be allowed to cool thoroughly before it is frosted.

A tube cake is cooled by turning the pan upside down over a funnel or bottle. This helps prevent the cake from shrinking or falling as it cools. When the cake is cool, loosen the cake from the sides of the pan. You can do this with a metal spatula or knife, using a sawing motion. Turn the pan upside down and tap the sides with the knife handle. The cake should then slip out.

Frosting the cake

You can be creative with frosting. It can make your cakes look and taste special.

Buttercream frosting is very popular and easy to make. This creamy frosting is made with confectioner's sugar, butter, milk and flavoring, such as vanilla extract. There are many variations of this basic recipe. A fruit juice, for instance, is sometimes used in place of milk.

Boiled frosting is light and fluffy. It is made by boiling a sweet, syrupy mixture, cooling it and folding it into stiffly beaten egg whites.

Royal frosting is used to make the fancy decorations such as flowers that you see on professionally decorated cakes. With some practice and the proper tools, you can learn to make these beautiful decorations yourself.

You don't have to be an artist to make a frosted cake look good, 14-14. Just follow these basic steps:

1. Be sure the cake is completely cool before frosting. A warm cake can make the frosting soft and runny.

2. Brush aside all the loose crumbs.
3. Frost the top of the bottom layer, and put the layers together.
4. Frost the sides of the cake.
5. Frost the top of the cake.

Cakes don't have to be frosted. You can, for instance, serve cake with a fruit topping or with pudding. You can also sprinkle the top with confectioner's sugar or with a sweet crumb mixture. Many people like ice cream or whipped cream on cake. Cake is also delicious served plain.

Storing cakes

A freshly baked cake will keep its freshness longer if it is covered tightly to keep air out. Cake that is not covered can dry out and taste stale.

Cakes can be frozen with or without frosting. (But don't freeze frosting that contains egg whites.) Cakes in airtight containers or wrapping will keep well in the freezer from four to six months.

PIES

Baking pies is an American tradition. Fruit pies, cream pies and meat pies all begin with golden brown pastry. The secret of making tender, flaky pastry is really no secret at all. It's a matter of knowing how to prepare and handle the dough properly.

How to make a basic pastry

A basic pastry is made from flour, salt, water and fat. The fat may be shortening, lard, butter or oil. If you use a solid fat, start by breaking the fat into pieces in the flour and salt mixture. This technique is called *cutting in*. A pastry blender is a special tool designed for cutting in. But a fork or two knives will also do the job. Continue cutting in until the mixture looks like tiny peas or coarse cornmeal. See 14-15. If you use oil instead of a solid fat, simply mix the oil into the dry mixture with a fork.

The next step is to add water. Ice water helps to keep the dough cool, which makes it easy to handle. Sprinkle the water over the shortening and flour mixture a spoonful at a time and stir lightly with a fork. When the mixture is moist enough to hold together, gently form it into a ball. If your recipe is for a double-crust pie, divide the dough in half and handle each half separately. Pastry should be handled gently and as little as possible. Too much handling can make the pastry tough.

The dough can be rolled out on a floured bread board or pastry cloth. It can also be rolled out between two sheets of waxed paper. Whatever surface you choose, begin rolling from the center and work toward the outside edges. Try to keep the dough in the shape of a circle. Work as quickly as you can. Too much handling will make the dough tough.

When you finish rolling the dough, it should be thin and even. It should be large enough to fit your pie pan, with about 5 cm (2 inches) extra all around.

The next step is to transfer the dough to the pie pan. Handle the dough carefully to avoid tearing it. Fold the dough gently in half. Then fold it again into quarters. Pick the dough up and gently unfold it in the pan, being careful not to stretch it. Carefully fit the pastry to the pan. Trim off the uneven pieces of dough

EKCO HOUSEWARES CO.

14-14 When you frost a cake, put a "collar" of waxed paper around the bottom of the cake to keep the plate clean.

EKCO HOUSEWARES CO.

14-13 Cool layer cakes on wire racks. Cool a foam cake by turning the pan upside down over a funnel, bottle or bowl.

SILVERSTONE® AND TEFLON® DUPONT'S NON-STICK FINISHES

14-15 To make flaky pastry, fat is cut into flour until the mixture looks like tiny peas or coarse cornmeal.

around the pan, leaving about 2.5 cm (1 inch) hanging over the edge.

An easy way to decorate the edge is to fold the extra pastry under, making a high pastry rim. With a fork, you can press grooves into the rim. Or you can *flute* the edge by pinching and shaping and dough as shown in 14-16. When the edge is finished, the pie shell is ready to be filled or baked. You may want to cover the edge of the pastry with foil for part of the baking time to prevent over-browning.

Baked pie shell. Some recipes, such as those for cream pies, call for baked pie shells. Before you bake an empty pie shell, prick the bottom and sides of the pastry with a fork. This prevents *blistering* (the formation of little pockets of air that make the crust bumpy and uneven). Do not prick the pastry if the pie shell will be filled before it is baked.

Double crust pies. A double crust pie has a layer of pastry covering the top of the pie. A double crust is often used for fruit pies and potpies. You roll out the top crust in the same way you roll out the bottom crust. Before you place the top crust over the filling, however, make slits in the dough or cut out designs to allow steam to escape during baking.

Gently fold the dough into quarters and transfer it carefully to the pie. Unfold it over the pie. Trim the edge to a 2.5 cm (1 inch) overhang. Fold the edge of the top pastry under the edge of the bottom pastry. Then pinch them together to seal the edges. Make a decorative edging if you wish.

Crumb crusts

Crumb crusts are not pastry. They are made from crumbs held loosely together with a fat such as melted butter. Graham crackers, breakfast cereals or cookies can be crushed to provide crumbs. A blender or a food processor makes crumbs quickly. The crumb mixture is pressed into the pie pan with a spoon. It may or may not be baked. Baking gives the crust a firmer, crunchier texture.

Pie fillings

You can use a wide variety of foods to fill pie shells. Many types of fruit can be used. Puddings, custards and gelatin mixtures (sometimes whipped into a soft, foamy chiffon) are other popular fillings. Nuts are sometimes added to give a crunchy texture to a soft filling.

Pies are not only served as dessert. They can be used for main dishes too. For instance, if you fill a pie shell with a beaten egg mixture, you have a *quiche*. If you fill a pie shell with a thick stew of gravy, vegetables and meat, you have a *potpie*.

Pie toppings

Although many pies do not require toppings, some cooks like to add them for decoration. Many kinds of toppings, such as lattices, can be made from dough. See 14-17.

Pies are sometimes topped with a *meringue*. A meringue is a sweet, foamy mixture of beaten egg whites and sugar, 14-18. Sweet crumb mixtures are sometimes sprinkled over pie fillings. Whipped cream is a popular topping for cream pies.

14-16 Fluting the edge is a simple but attractive way to finish a pie shell.

Freezing pies and pie shells

If you enjoy making and eating pies, you may want to make extra pastry to freeze for later use. Once you have all the ingredients and equipment together, it's not much trouble to make extra pastry. You can freeze the dough in a ball. Or you can freeze it after it has been rolled out and put into a pie pan—baked or unbaked. In any case, the pastry should be wrapped in airtight wrapping. A ball of dough or a baked pie shell should be thawed before you use it. An unbaked crust can go into the oven without thawing.

Fruit pies—baked or unbaked—freeze well. If you freeze them unbaked, you can bake them later without thawing. A frozen fruit pie may take 15 or more extra minutes to bake. The filling should be bubbly when it's done. You may need to cover the top with foil during the extra baking time to prevent over-browning. Baked fruit pies should be thawed at room temperature for about 30 minutes and then warmed in the oven.

Chiffon pies also freeze well. After a few hours of thawing at room temperature (or overnight in the refrigerator), they are ready to eat.

Potpies can be frozen in the same way as fruit pies. Other types of pies, such as cream pies or meringue pies, do not freeze well.

EKCO HOUSEWARES CO.

14-17 Lattices are attractive ways to decorate fruit pies. Cut strips of pastry and weave them over and under each other. Seal the ends of the strips to the pie shells.

BETTY CROCKER FOOD AND NUTRITION CENTER

14-18 Meringue toppings are pretty and delicious.

*to*Define

baking powder . . .
baking soda . . .
blistering . . .
boiled frosting . . .
buttercream frosting . . .
chiffon cake . . .
crumb crust . . .
cutting in . . .
flute . . . foam cake . . .
leavening agent . . .
meringue . . . potpies . . .
quiche . . . royal frosting . . .
shortened cakes

*to*Discuss

1. Name at least six basic ingredients used in baking.
2. Why is sugar important in baking?
3. How do baking soda and baking powder differ?
4. Name the six general types of cookies.
5. How should cookies be stored?
6. Explain the general differences between shortened, foam and chiffon cakes.
7. What is the main leavening agent in angel food, sponge and chiffon cakes?
8. How should layer cakes be placed in the oven?
9. Describe two ways to tell when a cake is done.
10. What ingredients are used in a basic buttercream frosting?
11. What kind of frosting is used to make fancy cake decorations such as roses?
12. Why should a cake be completely cool before you frost it?
13. Why should you use ice water in preparing pastry dough?
14. How should pastry be handled? How will too much handling affect pastry?
15. Why should you prick holes in an empty pie shell before baking?
16. How are crumb crusts made?
17. Name at least four foods that can be used as pie fillings.
18. What kinds of pies freeze well? Which pies should not be frozen?

*to*Do

1. Demonstrate the importance of correct measuring of ingredients in baking. Make two cakes. For cake "A," follow the recipe carefully using measuring equipment. For cake "B," follow the same recipe using no measuring equipment. Compare your results.
2. Prepare dough for dropped cookies. Place dough on the baking sheet in different amounts for three cookies: Cookie"A" — as the recipe suggests. Cookie "B" — twice the amount suggested in the recipe, Cookie "C" — half the amount suggested in the recipe. Bake the cookies as directed in the recipe. Describe your results.
3. Collect five or more recipes for cookies that offer good nutritional values. (Look for nutritious ingredients such as oatmeal, whole grain flour, nuts, fruits, peanut butter, etc.) Prepare one of the recipes to share with your class.
4. Invite a baker or a caterer to class to demonstrate how to decorate cakes and other party foods.
5. Demonstrate to your class the basic steps in frosting a cake.
6. Collect pictures of pies, and make a bulletin board that illustrates different ways to decorate the edges and tops of pies.
7. Prepare pie shells for two pies. Prepare both pie shells according to the recipe. However, when mixing and rolling the dough handle it as little as possible for pie shell "A" and handle the dough for pie shell "B" a lot. Bake both pie shells. Which pastry is most flaky? Which is tough?

Homemade cookies are always nice gifts to give and receive.

Managing mealtime

Management skills can help you to plan and serve attractive meals and refreshments. Knowing proper eating etiquette can help you to feel at ease in social situations.

15

Eating takes planning

What's the secret to preparing and serving great meals? After reading this chapter, you will be able to plan meals. You will be able to evaluate menus for nutrition, variety, economy and time and energy consumption. You will also be able to prepare meals using a meal preparation plan.

Good meals don't just happen. Somebody has to plan them. Who planned the meal you ate last night? Your parent? Your brother or sister? Your friend? Whoever it was, he or she probably dealt with many of the following questions.

What should I serve? Will the meal be nutritious? Are there any special dietary needs, such as weight control, to consider? Will the meal look attractive? Will the textures and flavors of the various foods go together? How much will the meal cost? How will I cook the foods? How much time will I need to prepare the meal? Do I have all the equipment I will need?

Perhaps you haven't given much thought to such questions. But when you plan meals for yourself or your family and friends, these are questions you will have to answer. Planning nutritious and tasty meals is a skill which you can develop with practice. The more you know about food preparation, the easier it will be for you to plan meals which:

• Are nutritious.
• Provide variety in color, texture and flavor.
• Are within your budget.
• Can be prepared in the time you have available, using the various equipment you have in your kitchen.

THINKING ABOUT MEAL PLANNING

Sometimes when you sit down to plan meals, you will have trouble coming up with good ideas. You may want to do something special, and yet have no idea of what to do. Or maybe you are bored with the same old thing, and you want to try something new.

Cookbooks can be a great help when you are looking for ideas. Other sources of ideas are newspapers and magazines. They often include recipes for foods that are in season. See 15-1. Most people who enjoy cooking collect their favorite recipes in a notebook or file box. You can file your recipes according to food type, such as "meats," "salads" and "desserts." This way, you can quickly find something new and different, or an old favorite.

Basic meal patterns

Meal patterns are basic designs for meals. A common meal pattern for lunch would be soup, a sandwich and fruit. *Menus,* on the other hand, outline the specific foods to be served at a meal. Tomato soup, a grilled cheese sandwich and a peach make up a menu based on this common meal pattern.

Many people follow the same basic eating patterns day after day. One family, for instance, has fruit juice, cereal with milk, and either coffee or hot chocolate every morning for breakfast. Lunch is usually soup, a sandwich and a piece of fruit or some cookies, 15-2. For dinner, they have meat and potatoes or a casserole, along with salad, milk and

TUPPERWARE® HOME PARTIES

15-1 You can find many good ideas in cookbooks, newspapers and magazines to help you plan meals.

15-2 This meal — soup, a sandwich and fruit — is an example of a typical lunch meal pattern.

BETTY CROCKER FOOD AND NUTRITION CENTER

dessert. This does not mean that the members of this family do not eat other foods. But most of their meals are variations of these patterns which have been developed over the years.

People with established eating patterns may find it hard to change their habits, 15-3. On the other hand, they may enjoy some variation. For instance, if members of your family enjoy meat and potatoes, they might also like meat with rice or noodles. Using cookbooks and other recipe sources, you can plan an almost endless variety of menus based on established eating patterns.

Meal planning on paper

Planning is easiest if you begin by sitting down with a pencil and paper. Actually write out menus for each meal you will serve during the next week. This will save you time when you do your grocery shopping.

Protein foods are generally the most expensive items in a food budget. A good way to start planning is to decide which protein foods you will serve. Start by checking the newspaper for sales of meat, fish and poultry.

Plan for variety in protein foods. Your week's menus might include three meat meals, one poultry meal and a fish dinner. A vegetarian meal and a casserole that uses leftovers can make up the rest of the week's menus. After deciding on the protein foods, you can go on to plan the other foods in the meal. Your decisions will depend on the food preferences of the people you will be serving as well as on nutrition.

A smart planner organizes meals in such a way that leftovers are really "planned-overs." Think about how leftovers can be used in other meals later in the week. For instance, if baked ham is served on Sunday, a ham omelet might be served on Monday. And ham salad sandwiches could be made for lunch several days during the week. By planning the use of the ham in advance, you will know how large a ham to purchase. Also, leftover vegetables can be used in soups and salads. You can even plan ahead to use the liquids from cooked vegetables in soups.

After planning your menus, prepare a shopping list of the items you need to buy. Divide the list of items into groups according to the layout of the store where you shop. The list should include the exact ingredients you need for the meals as well as staples like flour and sugar.

Before you go shopping, be sure you know the amounts of foods you will need in order to serve reasonable portions. If you don't know how much to buy, check a cookbook. Sometimes packages will state serving size and the number of servings in the package. As you gain experience, you will learn to estimate the amount of food you need.

Try to allow for some flexibility in your menus. Then you can take advantage of bargains you find when you go to the store. Instead of planning to serve green beans, for example, plan to serve a green vegetable. That way you can select whatever green vegetable is the freshest and least expensive.

NUTRITION COMES FIRST

You can quickly judge a meal for nutrition if you keep the Basic Four Food Groups in mind. (The Basic Four Food Groups are: milk, meats, fruits and vegetables, and breads and cereals. If you want to review them, refer back to Chapter 3.) Check your menus to see if they include foods from all four food groups. If they do, chances are fairly good that the meals will meet basic nutritional needs. But variety is important. Each day you should eat different foods from each group since the nutritive values of foods vary.

Sometimes a menu may not include a separate item from each food group. For instance, creamed tuna on toast could represent all four groups, depending on the recipe. The cream sauce contains milk. The tuna is high in protein and represents the meat group. The toast accounts for the bread and cereal group. And if the dish included a vegetable such as peas, that one dish would represent all four food groups. Main dishes that contain foods from several groups are sometimes called *one-dish meals,* 15-4. When you judge a menu for nutritional content, study the recipes to see which food groups are represented.

Careful planning can help people meet their nutritional needs, even if they don't like certain foods. Suppose your sister doesn't like to drink milk. She needs the nutrients in milk products, so her meals should be planned to include milk in other forms. She may have cereal with milk for breakfast. Her lunch could include a cheese sandwich, cottage cheese salad or creamed soup. And she might enjoy yogurt or ice cream for snacks and desserts. If her meals and snacks are planned well, she can meet her nutritional needs without drinking plain milk.

Meeting special dietary needs

Some people have special dietary needs which must be considered when planning

15-3 People with traditional eating patterns may not want a peanut butter and jelly sandwich for breakfast. But people with more flexible eating patterns might enjoy this unusual and nutritious breakfast.

15-4 These one-dish meals contain foods from all or several of the Basic Four Food Groups.

Eating takes planning　　**241**

meals. People with special dietary needs include those who want to lose weight and those who have food allergies or diabetes. Convalescents, pregnant women and children also have special dietary needs.

Probably the largest group with special needs are people who want to lose weight. One easy way to help dieters is to serve smaller portions, especially of foods which are high in kilojoules (Calories). For instance, serve half portions of fried foods instead of full portions. And of course, dieters should avoid second helpings.

When planning meals for persons who want to lose weight, focus on foods that are low in kilojoules (Calories). Do not serve fatty meats such as pork roast, bacon and sausage. Broil or poach food instead of cooking with butter or oil. Large servings of starchy foods such as pasta and rice should be avoided, along with rich desserts. Instead, serve lowfat milk; lean meats, poultry and fish; lots of fruits and vegetables; and plain breads and cereals.

Meals for dieters should include foods from all four food groups, including breads and cereals. Even the dieter needs four servings from this group in order to be well nourished. However, dieters should *not* have *more* than four servings. They should cut down on butter, margarine and mayonnaise which add kilojoules (Calories).

Perhaps you know people with food allergies or diabetes. You may be aware that they must follow special diets. People with *food allergies* cannot eat certain foods. If they do, they may become ill. Persons with *diabetes* must limit the amount of carbohydrates they eat. Their bodies cannot tolerate large amounts of sugar or starch. If diabetics ignore this and eat anything they want, the result could be a coma or even death. Most diabetics follow diets which have been carefully planned to limit the amount of sugar and starch they eat. These diets must be followed for life. Preparing meals for persons with food allergies or diabetes requires special planning. Be sure to find out what foods they can and cannot eat.

Persons recovering from surgery or illness sometimes require special diets, too. A speedy recovery can be aided by proper nutrition. Doctors often recommend special diets for convalescents. The meal planner needs to know exactly what is and is not allowed in these special diets.

Pregnant women must give special attention to the foods they eat. Studies have shown that a poor diet during pregnancy can severely affect the health of the baby. Doctors can recommend good diets for pregnant women.

Children also have special dietary needs. Milk is the basic food for babies. As babies grow older, strained foods are introduced along with special cereals. When babies start developing teeth, crackers, toast and well cooked vegetables can be added to their diets.

Preschoolers can be picky eaters, but they usually respond to foods that are fun to eat. They like "finger foods" such as strips of raw vegetables and slices of fruit. They also like foods which have interesting shapes and colors. Sandwiches with "child appeal" can be made with cookie cutters, as shown in 15-5. Pancakes with "faces" are fun for children to eat, too. Use raisins for the eyes and a banana slice or orange section for the mouth.

Young children are not always willing to accept new foods. Introduce new foods one at a time, and make sure the portion is not too big. A spoonful is a good start. If they like the food, give them more. It may take several weeks or even months for children to acquire new tastes. In any case, it's not a good idea to force feed children. When they are ready, they will accept the foods. And they will look forward to trying other new tastes as they grow older.

PLANNING ATTRACTIVE MEALS

When you are planning a meal, try to imagine how the foods will look together on a plate. Will they be colorful? Will they have a variety of shapes? Will the textures vary from soft to crunchy? Will the flavors taste good together? A well planned meal has a variety of colors, textures and flavors so that it is interesting to the senses.

Look at the meals in 15-6. Notice how dull and colorless they appear. Imagine the textures. Most of the foods are rather soft and mushy. Finally, try to imagine the flavors together. The meals seem rather bland. None of the foods provides a really zippy taste for contrast.

Now compare the meals in 15-6 with those in 15-7. Which meals would you rather eat? Notice how color adds interest and appeal to these meals. Notice how different textures and flavors are combined. Meals which include a variety of colors, textures and flavors are more interesting and enjoyable.

KEEPING FOOD COSTS DOWN

Most people have a limited amount of money to spend on food. A meal planned without thinking about cost can really surprise you at the checkout counter. The cost of a meal depends on the foods you choose and the amount of preparation already done for you. The energy used to prepare the meal will also cost money.

Choosing economical foods

One way to control food costs is to select less expensive items. Since protein foods are usually the most expensive part of meals, they will affect your budget most. Therefore, it's a good idea to choose the protein foods first. Meats are usually more expensive than dairy or vegetable proteins. You can stretch your food dollar by planning to use other protein sources. For instance, plan a dinner featuring macaroni and cheese or a bean casserole.

Sometimes you can substitute one protein

SWISS MISS PUDDINGS

*15-5 Children enjoy foods which
have interesting shapes.*

15-6 *These meals look boring because they lack variety in color, texture and flavor.*

15-7 *These meals look interesting. They have variety in color, texture and flavor.*

food for another and save money with little effect on your menu. For instance, suppose you wanted to serve veal cutlets. You could use chicken breasts or turkey cutlets instead of veal. The appearance and flavor would be very similar, but the cost would be less.

Quality and quantity. By buying the exact quality and quantity of food you need, you can often save money. For instance, you don't need top quality tomatoes for a soup. Canned chopped tomatoes will taste just as good in the soup as canned whole tomatoes which cost more. Ground chuck can be used for meat loaf instead of more costly ground sirloin. Dry milk can be substituted for fresh milk in many recipes without changing the final product. These are examples of *quality control.*

Another way to control food costs is to limit the size of the portions. This is called *quantity control.* You can use quantity control when you make hamburgers. Suppose you bought 450 g (1 pound) of ground beef. You could make two giant hamburgers, three generous ones or four average ones. By making the same amount of meat serve four people instead of two, you can save money. Another way to use quantity control is to check the number of pieces in a package of meat. If you need four servings of pork chops, don't buy a package with six chops. You'll have two extra portions. And while most people enjoy seconds, they really don't need them. Chinese people use this same concept. They combine a lot of rice and vegetables with small amounts of meat or fish to create delicious meals. You can do the same. For instance, use a lot of vegetables and a small amount of meat to make a tasty stew.

Sometimes you can combine quality and quantity control. Add a meat extender like bread crumbs or oatmeal to ground chuck when making meat loaf or hamburgers. You would be starting with a less costly meat (quality control). And you would be making it serve more people (quantity control).

Convenience costs

You may want to consider how *convenience products* would fit into your food budget.

Convenience products are food products in forms where some or all of the preparation has been done for you. See 15-8. Convenience food products usually cost more money than foods made from scratch. But if you don't enjoy cooking or if you don't have much time, you may want to use convenience products.

There are five basic types of convenience food products. *Ready-to-eat foods* such as cookies, cold cuts, breakfast cereals and canned fruits require no cooking. *Precooked foods* require heating before serving. These include canned vegetables, soups and certain frozen foods that are fully cooked. *Frozen foods* may need defrosting before serving. An example of this would be a frozen cake. Other frozen foods may require cooking, not just

15-8 A wide variety of convenience foods are available. Some require additional preparation while others are completely prepared.

heating. These include potpies, vegetables and casseroles. *Partially cooked foods* such as brown-and-serve rolls need some further cooking beyond heating before they are served. *Partially prepared foods* such as mixes, stuffings and sauces have had part of the work done in advance. You will have to combine partially prepared foods with water or other ingredients before cooking them. Remember that when you purchase convenience food products, you usually pay extra for the convenience.

Energy costs

Remember to think about energy costs when you plan menus. Imagine a meal including barbecued ribs, baked potatoes and corn on the cob. The total cost of that meal would depend on how the foods were prepared. If you used a grill, the oven and cook-top, you would have to pay for three energy sources. But if you cooked everything on a grill, you might spend less for energy.

If you think about controlling energy costs, you may come up with some good ideas. For instance, you can prepare an entire meal in the oven. Or you can steam several vegetables together at the same time in one pot.

Certain appliances can help save energy too. For instance, microwave ovens cook many foods in less time than conventional ovens. They are especially speedy when you are cooking a meal for just one or two people. A countertop broiler-oven costs less to use than a conventional oven, but it holds less food. When cooking foods that do not require much space, such as a potpie or a sandwich, use the broiler-oven instead, 15-9. You will find that many of your favorite foods take less time to cook in a pressure cooker, 15-10. Your local utility company can provide you with many suggestions on how to save energy.

PLANNING PREPARATION TIME

Some foods take a long time to prepare. Others can be ready to eat in a few minutes. A meat loaf may take an hour or more to cook,

plus five to 10 minutes to mix the ingredients. A hamburger will cook much more quickly.

Before deciding on a menu, ask yourself how much time you have. If you have just an hour until you must leave for a meeting, time will limit your menu choices. You may have to rely on convenience food products in order to leave on time, 15-11. On the other hand, if you have all afternoon to cook, you have more options.

Consider the time factors involved in preparing the following menu:

Broiled chicken
Buttered green beans
Steamed rice
Hearts of lettuce with Russian dressing
Cheesecake

If your time schedule is very tight, you could take several preparation shortcuts. You could buy chicken pieces rather than a whole chicken that you would have to cut up yourself. Using canned or frozen green beans would save you the time of snapping fresh ones. You could cook instant rice instead of regular rice and use bottled salad dressing instead of homemade. If you bought the cheesecake at a bakery, all you would have to do is serve it.

Remember that you pay a price for convenience. Instant rice costs much more than regular rice. You may not care for the taste of canned green beans as a substitute for fresh ones. Ready-to-serve cheesecake may not be as delicate as your homemade favorite, and it may cost more per serving. Convenience foods often cost more because you must pay for the extra labor someone else has put into them.

CHECKING EQUIPMENT NEEDS

Before you get too carried away with planning meals, be sure to check your equipment. If you forget this step, you may not be able to prepare all the items on your menus.

Equipment is seldom a problem when you use familiar recipes in a familiar kitchen. You know which pan to use for the pork chops and which one to use for the carrots. But equipment can be a problem when you want to use a new recipe. You may not have the loose-bottomed tart pan that is mentioned in a French tart recipe you want to try. In that case, you would have to get a tart pan, find a substitute pan or make a different dessert.

People who are setting up a kitchen of their own for the first time sometimes have equipment problems. They get all the ingredients for something together. And then they find that they don't have a rolling pin or the right size casserole dish. Perhaps you have heard a story like this one about Joe.

Joe had just moved into his first apartment. He was eager to show it off, so he invited some friends for dinner. Joe planned to serve a spaghetti and meatball dinner since it would be easy to make and fairly inexpensive. He bought all the ingredients and made a great sauce. He even had most of the work for the salad done before his guests arrived. But later, when he went to boil the water for the spaghetti, he realized his mistake. He didn't have a pot large enough to hold the spaghetti. Fortunately, a neighbor across the hall had a large pot Joe could borrow.

Other first-time hosts and hostesses often discover that they don't have enough forks, salad plates or serving dishes. With good planning, these embarrassing moments can be avoided.

Very large and special meals sometimes create special equipment needs. Think about a traditional Thanksgiving dinner for 20 people. Such a dinner would involve the preparation of many different dishes. Appliances

NATIONAL PRESTO INDUSTRIES, INC.

15-10 This electric pressure cooker saves energy by cooking foods in less time.

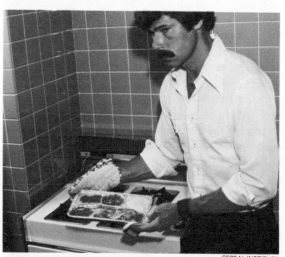

CEREAL INSTITUTE

15-11 When you are in a hurry, frozen dinners are convenience foods that can save you time.

BERGWALL PRODUCTIONS, INC. FILMSTRIPS

15-9 A small broiler oven uses less energy than the oven in your range.

such as slow cookers, electric skillets and coffeemakers would come in handy. They would free the cook-top and oven for use in cooking other dishes. With the right equipment, special meals can be managed, even in a small kitchen.

MANAGING MEALTIME

So far, a lot of careful planning has gone into your meal. You've planned what you are going to serve. You know that your meal will be nutritious and that it will look and taste good. You've purchased food according to your budget and decided how much time you can spend preparing the meal. Now you're ready to begin cooking. This involves still more planning. All the details of actually getting the meal on the table must be carefully worked out. Begin by studying your recipes carefully to make sure you understand every step.

Timing is the key to successful meal management. And it starts with organization. As you begin, you need to consider how and when each item on the menu should be prepared. You should think about how each food will be served. If your menu calls for foods which require several hours of cooking time, make sure you start early enough. Ask yourself these questions:

- When should I start each dish?
- How much time should I allow for preparation, cooking and serving?
- What food and utensils will I have to set up in advance so that I can work easily and efficiently?

The answers to these questions will help you to develop a preparation plan.

Develop a preparation plan

Inexperienced cooks may have trouble developing a *preparation plan*. A preparation plan assures that each food is cooked and ready to serve on time. With experience, you will learn to estimate preparation and cooking times. But in the beginning, it's a good idea to plot your plan on paper. This way you won't end up having to prepare everything at once,

15-12. Start by writing down the menu. Then review the recipes to make sure you have everything you need. You might even wish to make separate lists of the ingredients and utensils you will need.

By reading recipes carefully, you will get an idea of the order of preparation steps. Your recipe will state the cooking time and temperature. But you will need to estimate how long the pre-preparation will take. If you are making something for the first time, you will need to allow extra time.

Check the recipe to see if certain ingredients need to be cooked in advance. Make sure you allow time for that as well. For instance, when making lasagne, you will need to allow time to prepare a tomato sauce. (However, you may have decided to use a prepared sauce instead.) If your preparation plan doesn't allow time for making the sauce, the meal will have to be served late.

By thinking about preparation times and tasks which can be done in advance, you can save time and effort. Suppose your menu includes meat loaf, baked potatoes, broccoli, a salad, brownies and a beverage. Analyze the meal. List the foods in the order in which they will be prepared. Since the brownies require a different oven temperature than the meat loaf, they should be scheduled for the oven first. This allows time for the brownies to cool before serving. The potatoes can be put into the oven with the meat loaf. The broccoli and salad greens are washed at the same time, and the salad greens are placed in the refrigerator to crisp. Next the table is set. Finally, the broccoli is cooked. While the broccoli cooks, the salad is put together, and the beverage is poured.

Kitchen time savers

There are several ways to cut down on the time you spend preparing food. To reduce the total time you must spend in the kitchen, you can *dovetail* steps. This means that while one task is in progress, you can be working on something else. For instance, while onions are browning over low heat, you can wash vegetables or do some other quick job.

248

Everything ready and waiting. Save time by having everything ready before you start. This means you should take out all the ingredients and all the utensils you will need in advance. If the ingredients need to be washed or cut up, do that before you start cooking. You don't want to find that some important ingredient is missing when you have a dish almost prepared. Nor do you want to have to stop in the middle of cooking to cut up an ingredient. This could cause you to forget an important step. Hunting for a piece of equipment during cooking can cause problems too. For instance, when the pasta you are cooking is done, you shouldn't have to waste time looking for a colander. The pasta will be overcooked by the time you drain off the water. It's much better to have the colander out on the counter, ready to be used. An organized kitchen makes food preparation easier.

Advance preparation. One way of saving time when preparing meals is to do some advance preparation. You can make a casserole ahead of time and refrigerate it. It is then all ready to pop in the oven. Another example of advance preparation would be preparing salad greens. They can be washed and stored in plastic bags in the refrigerator until it is time to add the dressing. Salad greens will keep for a day or two stored this way.

The use of convenience foods can be considered another form of advance preparation. These foods range from canned soups and vegetables to frozen pizzas and waffles. Most convenience products have some of the work done for you. This helps to save you time getting the meal ready. Some convenience foods are versatile. They can be used several different ways. For instance, canned soup can become a sauce for rice or pasta.

You can also save time and money by making your own convenience foods. Many casseroles, soups and stews can be made ahead of time and frozen. Desserts such as cakes and cookies also freeze well. Try making meat patties and freezing them, 15-13. First, form the meat. Separate each patty with a layer of plastic. Wrap well and freeze. When you are ready to cook, thaw what you need.

Bread products, cookies, cakes and fruit pies can be made in advance and frozen. Other homemade convenience products include stews, casseroles, soups and certain sauces. When you prepare foods like these, make more than you need for one meal and freeze the rest. You can use these foods later when you have less time to cook. Most frozen convenience foods can be thawed in the refrigerator overnight. If they are still frozen when you start cooking them, allow extra cooking time.

TUPPERWARE® HOME PARTIES

15-12 Estimate preparation and cooking times. A meal requiring everything to be prepared at once can cause problems.

15-13 Make your own convenience foods. Frozen ground meat patties are convenient to have on hand.

Timesaving equipment. Another way to cut down on preparation time is by using special equipment. If you have a blender or food processor, you can save time slicing and chopping many foods, 15-14. A microwave oven cuts cooking time for most foods, and it defrosts foods quickly, 15-15. When making batters and doughs, using an electric mixer is faster than mixing by hand.

Learn to use your hand tools efficiently. Cutting is easier and goes faster when you know how to use a knife properly. Peeling apples and potatoes with a vegetable peeler is faster than doing it with a paring knife. You'd be surprised at the number of tasks which can be done with a pair of kitchen shears. You can mince parsley, cut apart poultry and even open jars. Good use of the right tools makes kitchen work easier.

BERGWALL PRODUCTIONS, INC. FILMSTRIPS

15-15 A microwave oven not only saves you cooking time. It also defrosts foods quickly.

BERGWALL PRODUCTIONS, INC. FILMSTRIPS

15-14 A food processor saves you time in the kitchen by performing tasks like slicing and chopping foods quickly.

toDefine

convenience products . . .
diabetes . . . dovetail . . .
food allergies . . .
meal patterns . . .
meat extender . . . menu . . .
one-dish meals . . .
preparation plan . . .
quality control . . .
quantity control . . .

toDiscuss

1. List at least three sources you can use for ideas when planning meals.

2. Why should you allow for some flexibility in menus?

3. How can you determine whether or not a meal is nutritionally balanced?

4. List three guidelines for planning meals for people who want to lose weight.

5. How should new foods be introduced to children?

6. What makes a meal interesting to the senses?

7. List at least three ways you can keep food costs down.

8. What are the advantages of buying convenience products? What are the disadvantages of buying convenience products?

9. Why do many convenience products cost more than regular products?

10. Why should you develop a preparation plan?

11. Why should you review a recipe before you start to cook?

12. Name at least two timesaving appliances.

toDo

1. Set up a recipe file with recipes for your favorite foods. Consult this file when planning meals.

2. Select a protein food (such as ham, turkey or roast beef) and develop five ideas for "planned-overs."

3. Plan a day's menus for a person trying to lose weight. Be sure the menus are nutritionally balanced.

4. Visit a preschool and talk with children about their favorite foods. Make a list of the foods which most children seem to like best.

5. Develop ideas for making food interesting and easy to eat for preschoolers.

6. Compile a list of ten convenience food products used often in your home. Select three products and compute the costs of making them from scratch. What are the differences in costs?

7. Invite an extension home economist or a consumer specialist from a utility company to come to your class. Be prepared to ask questions about ways to conserve energy in the kitchen. Then prepare a meal that utilizes the ideas that the speaker presented.

8. Plan a dinner menu that does not require the use of any gas or electricity for preparation of the meal.

9. Read magazines and newspapers to find ways to keep food costs down. Plan at least three menus using the ideas you have found. For each menu, note the source of the idea you have used.

16

A clean and safe kitchen

How can you keep your kitchen clean, safe and neat? After reading this chapter, you will know the basics of cleanup. You will be able to clean your kitchen with a minimum amount of time and effort. You will be able to prevent common kitchen accidents, and you will know how to deal with them if they happen. You will also be able to explain how to keep food safe through proper handling.

A kitchen that is clean, neat and safe makes kitchen work more enjoyable. In that kind of environment, you can work more efficiently. You can also avoid accidents and keep food safe to eat.

CLEANUP THE EASY WAY

Cleanup is the least popular part of cooking. Yet most cooking involves some type of cleanup. The first rule of easy cleanup is to do it as you go along. Wipe up spills as soon as they happen. Put ingredients back in the cupboard or refrigerator when you are done with them.

You can get a head start on washing dishes too. When you start cooking, fill a dishpan with warm, sudsy water. The warmer the water is, the better your soap or detergent can work for you. Dishes are easy to clean in warm, sudsy water if the food hasn't had a chance to dry and harden. As you finish using a spoon, pan or other utensil, slip it into the dishpan. Swish it around or wipe it with a cloth and rinse it.

Later, when you are ready to begin the real job of cleanup, you may want to wear rubber gloves. Hot water, dish detergent and other cleaning supplies tend to dry the skin.

Washing dishes

Families seem to have their own routines for washing dishes. A dishwasher obviously makes the job easier to do. Just be sure to follow the manufacturer's directions. Whether or not your family has a dishwasher, some dishes have to be washed by hand. If and when you are asked to help with this chore, the following information may help you.

Always wash just a few dishes at a time. If you overload the dishpan, there is a good chance that something might break. Begin by washing the glasses. Then wash the flatware, plates, miscellaneous items, and pots and pans. If the dishwater becomes grimy or cool, throw it out and start over with fresh water.

Some people like to rinse the dishes with hot water as they wash them. Those who are energy-conscious, wash all the dishes first and then rinse them all at once. People differ on drying methods too. Some let all the dishes air dry. Others prefer to dry flatware and glasses with a towel to prevent water spotting. Still other people dry all the dishes with a towel. Any method is fine, but if a towel is used, it must be clean. A dirty towel can be a good breeding ground for bacteria to grow and multiply.

Certain kinds of dishes require special attention. Don't plunge ice-cold glasses into hot water, or you may end up with a dishpan full of broken glass. Also, don't stack glasses, or they may break or chip. (If you forget, and stacked glasses are stuck together, place the bottom one in warm water. Then run cool water on the top one, and they will come apart.)

Always be careful when you are cleaning knives, 16-1. Wash each one separately. Never let them soak in a dishpan. It is too easy to reach in and grab the blade instead of the handle. This could cause a nasty cut.

Wooden utensils also require special care. Wood should never soak in water. Water raises the grain and ruins the finish of wood. To clean wooden utensils, wipe them with a damp dishcloth or sponge and rinse them quickly. Dry wooden utensils immediately,

before the water has a chance to damage the finish.

Check small electric appliances to see if they are immersible (can be put into water). Many are not. To clean an appliance, first wipe it out with a dishcloth or paper towel. Then fill with warm, sudsy water. For stubborn food stains, you may need to plug in the appliance and heat the water. (Be sure the plug and heating element are completely dry before you plug in the appliance.) When the appliance is clean, pour out the sudsy water, rinse with warm water and dry.

Cleaning methods vary for removing different kinds of foods from dishes. If a dish is greasy, try to wipe most of the grease off before putting the dish in the dishpan. Use a little extra detergent to help cut through the grease when you wash lots of greasy dishes. Never pour oil or grease down the kitchen sink. This could clog the drain.

Dishes which have held protein foods like eggs, milk and cheese should be rinsed first with cold water. Hot water can "cook" these foods onto the surfaces of dishes.

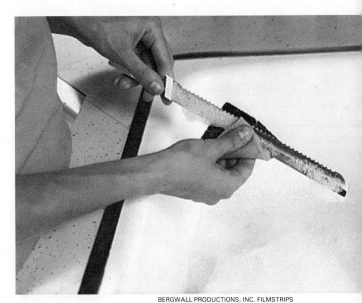

16-1 Special care should be taken when cleaning knives. Never let knives soak in a dishpan.

Once starchy foods have had a chance to harden, they can be difficult to remove, 16-2. For instance, a bowl that contains some hardened cookie batter will need to be soaked before it is washed. Flour can be difficult to remove from dishes, especially if you use hot water. The hot water causes the starch in the flour to become sticky. For this reason, always wipe off excess flour with a damp (not wet) cloth. If you are cleaning a flour sifter, never put it in a dishpan to soak. You'll have a sticky sifter that is almost impossible to clean. Instead, shake off most of the flour. Then wipe the sifter with a damp cloth. Let it dry thoroughly before using.

Removing stubborn foods and stains

Sometimes you need more than just warm sudsy water and a dishcloth to clean cookware. Different surfaces require different cleaning methods. When the manufacturer includes cleaning instructions with a utensil, be sure to follow them.

Porcelain enamel cookware should be protected from sudden temperature changes. Never allow these utensils to boil dry. To remove burned-on foods, soak the cookware with a solution of either detergent or baking soda and water. You may use a gentle scouring powder as long as you scrub with a light touch.

Heat-resistant glass cookware for cook-top and oven cooking should be handled and cleaned like porcelain enamel cookware. It's best to soak these utensils clean. Harsh abrasives will scratch them.

High heat can discolor stainless steel. Use moderate or low heat. Take care not to let pans boil dry. To remove burned-on food, heat a solution of 30 mL (2 tablespoons) baking soda and 1 L (1 quart) water in the dirty pan. When the solution boils, turn off the heat and allow the pan to soak. Avoid vigorous scrubbing which can cause scratches.

Aluminum cookware can be cleaned best with a soap-filled pad. Soaking with a strong detergent solution may discolor it. Alkaline foods and hard water may also cause aluminum to turn dark. Cooking an acid food in the pan will turn it bright again.

When you use cookware with a non-stick coating, use low to medium temperatures. Metal spatulas may be used with care, but it is much better to use wooden, plastic and rubber utensils. Remove stubborn foods with a plastic mesh pad. Never use steel wool or coarse scouring pads.

The final touches

The final phase of cleanup includes cleaning out the sink and wiping off counters and the range. Food particles that remain on these surfaces could become a breeding ground for bacteria. The food particles may also attract insects and rodents.

Wipe a porcelain sink with a sudsy cloth after each use. Clean stains with a mild cleanser. For stubborn stains, fill the bowl with hot water and add 30 to 45 mL (2 to 3 tablespoons of liquid chlorine bleach. Let this stand 15 minutes. Then drain the sink and rinse thoroughly with clear water.

After using a stainless steel sink, wipe it clean and rinse it. Towel dry the sink to help eliminate water spots. Use an all-purpose cleaner or metal polish for thorough cleaning.

Counter tops of laminated plastic (such as Formica) can be wiped clean with a soapy cloth. For more thorough cleaning, use kitchen wax or an all-purpose cleaner. These counter tops are durable, but they can be scratched. Therefore, don't use them as cutting surfaces, and don't clean them with abrasive cleansers or steel wool. Remove stubborn stains with a cloth or sponge moistened with a mild solution of chlorine bleach. Then rinse thoroughly with clear water.

The cooking surface of the range needs to be cleaned after each use. A warm, soapy cloth or sponge will do the job well, 16-3. Wipe away spills and spattered grease when the cooking surface has cooled or when it is still slightly warm. Be careful not to touch a hot burner or heating element. Towel dry any stainless steel or chrome parts to help eliminate water spots.

If food has boiled over, clean the burner,

drip pan and drip tray as soon as the unit has cooled. Use hot water and detergent. Do not wipe or wash the heating elements on an electric range. When they are turned on high, spills will burn off.

Taking out the garbage is also a part of a good daily cleaning routine. If garbage is allowed to pile up, it could cause unpleasant odors and attract insects and rodents into the kitchen.

PREVENTING ACCIDENTS

Most kitchen accidents happen when cooks are in a hurry, when they are careless or when they misuse their equipment. As you work in the kitchen, keep safety in mind. Develop safe work habits to reduce your chances of having an accident.

Keep your kitchen in good order. Store things where you can reach them so you don't have to do a balancing act whenever you need something. Put things away as you use them. By keeping your counters free from clutter, you can work more efficiently and safely.

Preventing cuts

Most cuts result from the careless use of knives, so be *careful* when you handle knives. Never pick up a knife by the blade. Always hold the handle and keep the blade pointing away from your body. As you cut food, use a cutting board to protect the counter, and keep your fingers away from the blade. See 16-4.

Knives should be stored in a special rack or holder. They should be kept sharp since dull knives do not cut well.

Kitchen knives should never be used for anything but cutting food. Do not try to open cans with a knife; use a can opener instead.

The sharp, jagged edges of can lids are another common cause of cuts. Handle them with care. Place them in the bottom of the empty cans and discard them in the garbage promptly.

Preventing spills and breakage

Spills occur for several different reasons. The most common reason is some sort of

TUPPERWARE® HOME PARTIES

16-2 Soak pans before the food left inside them has a chance to harden. This will make them easier to clean later.

16-3 One of the final steps in cleaning is wiping off the range.

BERGWALL PRODUCTIONS, INC. FILMSTRIPS

16-4 Proper use of knives will help prevent cuts. Handle a knife with care and keep your fingers away from the blade.

problem as you transfer food from one container to another. To prevent these spills, use utensils designed for this job, such as ladles, funnels and utensils with a pouring lip. And don't fill a container all the way to the top.

Spilling a hot liquid can cause a burn as well as a mess. Take the time to get a pot holder before you lift a container of hot liquid. Then you can hold on to the container with a firm, steady grip without burning yourself.

If you do spill something, wipe it up immediately. Food spills can cook onto a hot range, making them difficult to remove. Foods like mustard, tea and grape juice can stain counter tops. A spill on the floor can be dangerous since it can cause you to slip or fall. It can also create an extra mess if it is tracked throughout the house.

You may accidently drop something in the kitchen. If you break or even crack a glass container of food, be sure to throw away the food. Glass splinters, if swallowed, can cause internal bleeding. As you clean up the spill, be careful not to cut yourself. Handle large pieces of broken glass carefully. Use a damp paper towel to pick up tiny splinters.

Preventing burns

It's easy to burn yourself while working at the range if you aren't careful. Never reach over a hot burner or a pan of simmering liquid. Turn pan handles to the side so pans can't accidently be bumped or knocked off the range. See 16-5. When uncovering a pan, make sure you lift the lid away from your body. This will prevent the steam from rising toward your face.

Use pot holders when you are handling hot utensils, 16-6. Never pick them up with a damp dish towel. The moisture could carry the heat from the utensil to your hand and burn you.

When frying food, make sure the food is dry before you put it in hot fat. Moisture in the food can cause the fat to splatter, and fat splatters can cause painful burns. If a grease fire occurs in the frying pan or broiler, turn off the heat source immediately. Smother the flames by covering them with a lid or sprinkling them with a lot of salt or baking soda. See 16-7. A fire extinguisher can also be used.

Never fill a pan so full that it will boil over. If a pan boils over on a gas range, it may also put out the flame. The gas fumes could collect and cause a gas explosion. If the flame is out, first turn off the gas. Ventilate the room before relighting the burner.

Preventing electric shock

There are several steps you can take to prevent electric shock. Always unplug an appliance by holding the plug. See 16-8. Never pull on the cord. Make sure appliance cords are not worn or damaged. Be careful *not* to overload the circuit with too many appliances as shown in 16-9. The safest way is to operate one appliance on each outlet.

Water and electricity don't mix. Never operate switches or appliance controls with wet hands. Keep water away from electric appliances and their cords. Before you wash an electric appliance, check to see whether or not it can be submerged in water.

Never put a metal utensil such as a fork into a toaster while the heating element is on. If food is stuck in the toaster, first unplug the toaster and then remove the food, 16-10.

First aid in the kitchen

The most common kitchen injuries are cuts and burns. When you cut yourself, it is important to control the bleeding and prevent infection. If the cut is small, wash it with soap and water. Then apply a mild *antiseptic* which will help prevent infection. Cover the cut with a bandage, and keep the wound dry while it heals.

Deep cuts are more serious and generally should be treated by a doctor. If the cut is deep, press a clean cloth firmly over the area. Apply pressure to stop the bleeding. Keep the cut area elevated to help lessen the flow of blood. If the bleeding doesn't stop after several minutes, consult a doctor.

If you have been punctured with a sharp object like a knife or ice pick, be sure to consult a doctor. Puncture wounds don't bleed much, and they may not seem serious.

16-5 Prevent burns by placing pans on the range so that handles cannot be accidently bumped.

BERGWALL PRODUCTIONS, INC. FILMSTRIPS

16-6 Always use pot holders when handling hot utensils. When uncovering a pan, lift the lid away from your body.

BERGWALL PRODUCTIONS, INC. FILMSTRIPS

16-7 Keep a fire extinguisher, salt or baking soda near the range. They can be used to put out a fire.

16-8 The correct way to unplug an appliance is by holding the plug.

CONSOLIDATED EDISON, INC.

16-9 This overloaded circuit is dangerous. DO NOT overload a circuit with too many appliances. Check to see that appliance cords are not worn or damaged.

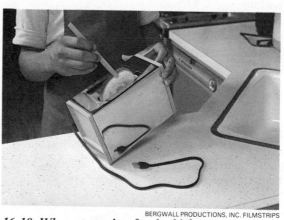

BERGWALL PRODUCTIONS, INC. FILMSTRIPS

16-10 When removing food which is stuck in a toaster, always unplug the toaster first.

However, they are easily infected, and if they are not treated properly, they can cause serious problems.

A burn is a painful experience. In treating burns, the basic rule is to keep the burned area away from direct contact with air. (This also helps prevent infection.) Never use butter on a burn since it can irritate the skin. To relieve the pain, run cold water over the burn. Or you can apply ice wrapped in a clean cloth to the burned area. Keep the burned area cold until it no longer hurts. Cold water or ice cools the burn and can sometimes help to prevent blisters from forming. Small burned areas can also be treated with burn ointment.

If a large area of your body is burned, cover it with a clean, dry cloth. Consult a doctor immediately. Never apply ointments to a severely burned area. They can cause infections and may be difficult to remove when the doctor treats the burn.

KEEPING FOOD SAFE TO EAT

It is important for you to learn how to handle food so that it does not spoil or become contaminated. Most foods are *perishable* which means that they will spoil if they are not stored properly. Some foods also contain bacteria that may cause illness. Ways to keep food safe are listed in 16-11.

There are two keys to storing food so that it will not spoil. One key is temperature, and the other is time. When perishable food is kept at temperatures where bacteria can multiply, food spoilage can occur. Room temperature is an ideal temperature for bacteria growth. The longer food is kept at room temperature, the greater chances are for food to become spoiled. So it is important to store perishable food in the refrigerator as soon as possible. Avoid leaving food at room temperature for more than an hour. See 16-12. Store leftover foods immediately after meals.

Food poisoning

Food poisoning can occur for various reasons. The food itself may be poisonous such as certain wild mushrooms. Or the food may contain harmful chemicals which can make you sick. These harmful chemicals may include mercury in fish or pesticides left on foods. A tiny worm called *Trichinella spiralis* is sometimes found in pork. It can cause the serious illness *trichinosis* unless it is destroyed by thorough cooking.

Food poisoning can also be caused by various bacteria. In some cases, the bacteria themselves cause you to feel ill. In other cases, the bacteria in food create *toxins* which are like poisons. When you eat the food, the toxin also enters your digestive tract and causes illness. Personal cleanliness is also important in preventing food poisoning, 16-13.

Bacteria which cause food poisoning

There are four common kinds of bacteria which cause food poisoning. They are: Staphylococcus aureus (Staph), Salmonella, Clostridium perfringens and Clostridium botulinum.

Staphylococcus aureus or "Staph" bacteria can be found on the bodies of healthy people — in their throat or nose and on their skin. Personal cleanliness is important in preventing Staph poisoning. Hands should be washed before preparing food. Avoid coughing and sneezing around food. Also, avoid handling food if you have an open sore.

Staph bacteria grow best at temperatures above 5°C (40°F) and under 60°C (140°F). As they grow, they produce a toxin. If foods like custards and ham, chicken, potato and egg salads are left at moderate temperatures, Staph poisoning could occur.

Fortunately, Staph food poisoning is not too serious. Its symptoms include nausea, vomiting, diarrhea and cramps. Symptoms usually begin eight to 20 hours after the food has been eaten and last for a day or two.

Salmonella bacteria are another common cause of food poisoning. They are found in the intestines of human beings and animals. Salmonella bacteria are also found in meat, poultry, eggs and dairy products. Salmonella may be spread to other foods by the hands or by contaminated utensils or work surfaces.

The longer food is left at room temperature,

the more the bacteria can grow. Salmonella bacteria are easily destroyed by heat. Therefore, foods that may have become contaminated should be thoroughly cooked and served while still hot.

The symptoms of Salmonella poisoning are more severe than those of Staph food poisoning. Symptoms include a severe headache, nausea, vomiting, diarrhea and fever. Symptoms usually begin four to eight hours after eating the food and last about three days.

Clostridium perfringens bacteria can also cause illness. Like Salmonella bacteria, they are found in meats, poultry and other high protein foods. This type of food poisoning occurs most often at banquets and in cafeterias and restaurants. Large amounts of food are prepared and then allowed to stand at room temperature for a long time. Foods that are neither very hot nor very cold encourage the growth of bacteria.

WAYS TO KEEP FOOD SAFE

1. When you are on a general shopping trip, buy food last. Refrigerate perishable food as soon as you get home.
2. Never handle food unless you have thoroughly washed your hands with soap and water. If you have to use the toilet or blow your nose, make sure you wash your hands before you handle food.
3. Don't let food stand at room temperature for long periods of time. Put leftovers in the refrigerator as soon as you've finished eating. Heat leftovers thoroughly before serving them.
4. If food is hot, keep it above 60 °C (140 °F), not just warm.
5. Keep foods cold by putting them in the refrigerator at a temperature below 5 °C (40 °F).
6. To cool hot food quickly, place the container in cold water.
7. Thaw frozen foods in the refrigerator, or under cold running water.
8. Keep working surfaces in the kitchen spotlessly clean. If you cut meat or poultry on a cutting board, wash the cutting board before putting other food on it.
9. When you stuff poultry, stuff it just before putting it in the oven and remove stuffing immediately after cooking. Store poultry and stuffing in separate containers.
10. If a food doesn't look or smell right, don't eat it.

16-11 Careful handling will help keep food safe to eat.

16-12 Do not leave food at room temperature. Immediately after meals, store leftovers properly and dispose of food scraps.

16-13 Always wash your hands thoroughly before handling food. Hands can carry bacteria that cause food poisoning.

A clean and safe kitchen 259

Symptoms of perfringens poisoning include diarrhea, nausea and stomach pain. Symptoms appear four to 22 hours after eating the contaminated food and last about a day.

The most deadly type of food poisoning is caused by bacteria called *Clostridium botulinum*. This food poisoning is called *botulism*. The bacteria produce a toxin which is so strong that a very tiny amount can be deadly. Botulism is often found in canned foods which have not been properly processed. You can guard against this food poisoning by never eating canned food which is in a leaking or bulging can. This includes both home-canned and commercially-canned foods. Other signs of botulism include an off-color, unusual odor or suspicious appearance. The saying, "When in doubt, throw it out," is an important rule to follow when using any canned food.

Botulism has symptoms quite different from other types of food poisoning. The poison attacks the nervous system. Symptoms include double vision and difficulty in speaking, swallowing and breathing. Over half the cases of botulism result in death. Symptoms can occur anytime from 12 to 36 hours after eating the food. If you ever think that you may have botulism, contact a doctor as soon as possible.

*to*Define

antiseptic . . . botulism . . . Clostridium botulinum . . . Clostridium perfringens . . . perishable . . . Salmonella . . . Staph . . . Staphylococcus aureus . . . toxin . . . Trichinella spiralis . . . trichinosis

*to*Discuss

1. How can you make cleanup easier?
2. Why should a towel used for drying dishes be clean?
3. Why shouldn't you allow knives to soak in a dishpan?
4. How can you clean greasy dishes?
5. Why should you use cold water to rinse egg, milk and cheese from dishes and utensils?
6. What can you do to remove stains from a porcelain sink?
7. Why do most kitchen accidents happen?
8. When uncovering a hot pan, why should you lift the lid away from your body?
9. What is the basic rule to follow when treating burns?
10. What temperature is a comfortable temperature for bacteria growth?
11. List four kinds of bacteria which cause food poisoning.
12. How can you prevent Staph food poisoning?
13. In which foods do Salmonella bactaeria grow best?
14. Where does Clostridium perfringens food poisoning occur most often?
15. What is the most deadly type of food poisoning caused by bacteria? How can you guard against this type of food poisoning?

*to*Do

1. Design a bulletin board showing basic rules for cleanup discussed in this chapter.
2. Invite a firefighter to demonstrate how to prevent and extinguish common kitchen fires and how to apply first aid to burns.
3. Develop a lesson to teach children about safety in the kitchen.
4. Invite an official from the Public Health Department to discuss food sanitation practices.
5. Select one type of food poisoning and prepare a report on it for class.

17

The art of serving food

How can serving food be an
art? After reading this chapter,
you will be able to create
attractive table settings. You
will know how to select and
coordinate table linens,
dinnerware, flatware and
glassware. You will be able to
set and clear the table
correctly. You will be able to
demonstrate the basic types of
table service and styles. You
will also be able to prepare and
serve foods outdoors.

A good meal deserves a pleasant setting. While we resort to "eat and run" meals at times, most people prefer to dine at an attractively set table.

You don't have to spend a lot of time or effort to create a pleasant atmosphere for meals. The important thing is that the table linens, tableware and food look good together. Adding a centerpiece is a special touch that most people enjoy. Arranging items carefully on the table helps too. This shows that you care, and it suggests to diners that you also took care in preparing the meal.

TABLE LINENS

The term *table linens* includes tablecloths, place mats and napkins. They are called table "linens" because the finest tablecloths and napkins have traditionally been made from linen fabrics. Today, table linens are made not only from linen, but also from cotton, polyester, plastic, paper and other materials. See 17-1.

One of the functions of table linens is to protect furniture from food spills and scratches. For extra protection from spills and hot dishes, some people use a table pad beneath a tablecloth. These table pads are also called "silence cloths" since they muffle the sound of dishes being placed on the table.

Another function of table linens is to add color and atmosphere to mealtime, 17-2. Pretty table linens can make your dishes and the foods you are serving look their best.

Attractive table linens do not have to cost a lot of money. A colorful sheet can be used to make an attractive tablecloth or set of place mats and napkins. Since place mats and napkins are rather small, they can be made from fabric remnants.

When you select table linens, consider the color and style of your dining area and dinnerware. A fine lace tablecloth would look nice in a formal dining room, but out of place in a kitchen nook. Also consider the care that the table linens will need. Most people want table linens which are durable, washable, stain-resistant and wrinkle-resistant. Plastic-coated tablecloths and place mats are popular for informal family dining because they are easy to wipe clean.

SETTING THE TABLE

Once you have chosen the table linens, you are ready to set the table. Your menu will determine what utensils are needed. In most cases, you will need to set a *cover* for each person. A cover is an individual place setting. It includes the dinnerware, flatware, glassware and linens needed by one person. See 17-3. Ideally, your table should be large enough to allow 75 cm (30 inches) for each cover so that people aren't crowded. However, this is not always possible.

Dinnerware

The term *dinnerware* includes plates, cups, saucers and bowls. Several materials are used to make dinnerware. *Fine china* is the most expensive form of dinnerware. It is used mainly for formal dining. Fine china is shiny and strong. It resists scratches and chipping. *Stoneware* is less formal than fine china. It is durable, but heavy. *Earthenware* costs less than either fine china or stoneware. But it is less durable, and it chips easily. *Ironstone* is a type of earthenware. It has been refined to make it stronger. *Glass ceramic* material is

used to make dinnerware which is lightweight and stronger than earthenware, stoneware and ironstone. It resists breaking, chipping and cracking. *Plastic* dinnerware is popular for everyday use. Most plastic dinnerware is made from *melamine*. Families with young children often use this type because it is lightweight and seldom breaks.

You can also find dinnerware made of glass, stainless steel, silver plate, sterling silver and wood. Usually, these materials are used to make special pieces such as dessert plates and underliners for appetizer courses. Metal plates are popular for steak platters. Wooden bowls are often used for salads.

Some types of dinnerware require special care. The manufacturer will usually provide care instructions with the dinnerware. If you have a dishwasher, be sure to check to see that your dinnerware is dishwasher safe. Some plastics and special decorations on dinnerware may be damaged in the dishwasher.

Dinnerware is sold in place settings, in sets of several place settings or as open stock. A *place setting* is a complete table service for one person. A typical place setting may include a dinner plate, cup and saucer, salad

17-1 Place mats are often used for casual meals. Interesting place mats can be made from a variety of materials.

plate and soup bowl. *Open stock* means that you can purchase individual items. This is convenient when replacing broken dinnerware. When selecting a dinnerware pattern, check to see if it is an open stock pattern.

After choosing your dinnerware, you will want to show it off by setting the table properly. Your table setting will depend upon the food being served. For most family meals, the dinner plate is usually placed on the table first. This helps to space the covers. The bread and butter plate is placed slightly to the left of the dinner plate, above the fork or forks. Salad plates or bowls are placed to the left of the forks. Cups and saucers are placed to the right of the spoon or spoons. Some people serve hot beverages at the end of the meal with dessert. In that case, cups and saucers may be placed on the table when dessert is served.

Flatware

Flatware is a term used to refer to knives, forks and spoons. Three metals are commonly used for flatware. They are sterling silver, silver plate and stainless steel. *Sterling silver* is the most expensive flatware. Sterling silver contains at least 92.5 percent silver. Because silver is a naturally soft metal, copper is added to make it harder. *Silver plate* is much less expensive than sterling silver because a base metal is covered with a thin coating of silver. The base metal in silver plated flatware is usually nickel, copper or brass. Silver plate may have more than one coating of silver. You may see advertising for silver which is *triple-plated*. That means that there are three coats of silver over the base metal. The cost of silver plate will depend on the amount of silver used. The more times it is plated, the more it will cost. The finest silver plate is reinforced with extra silver where there is the greatest chance of the silver wearing off.

One disadvantage of silver and silver plate is *tarnish*. Tarnish is caused by exposure to air and certain foods. Tarnish turns silver from bright and shiny to dark and dull. Silver must be polished regularly to remove tarnish. You can help prevent tarnish by storing silver in tarnish-proof bags.

Stainless steel is a popular alternative to silver flatware. It can range in price from very

LENOX

17-2 Table linens can help create a pleasant atmosphere for dining.

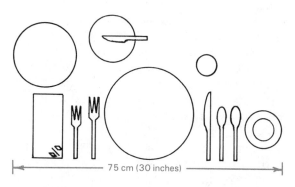

75 cm (30 inches)

17-3 A cover includes the dinnerware, flatware, glassware and linens which will be needed by one person.

inexpensive to quite expensive. The cost depends on the quality of the stainless steel and the manufacturing process used.

Flatware can be bought from open stock, however, most flatware is sold in place settings. A place setting usually includes a teaspoon, soupspoon, knife, dinner fork and salad fork. You can also purchase *service sets* for six, eight or 12 people. Service sets include place settings and serving pieces such as serving spoons and forks.

When placing flatware on the table, remember this basic rule: Forks are placed to the left of the plate, and knives and spoons are placed to the right. There are two exceptions to the basic table setting rule. Forks for eating seafood are placed on the right side, outside the spoons. This is done because this fork is used only in the right hand. Butter knives are placed horizontally across the bread and butter plate. Utensils are lined up in order of their use, with those being used first on the outside. They should be placed with the handles in a straight line 2.5 cm (one inch) from the edge of the table. Forks and spoons are placed with tines and bowls up. Knives should be placed with the cutting edge facing the plate.

Your menu will determine which pieces of flatware should be on the table. A breakfast of cold cereal with fruit, milk and toast would not require a fork. You would need a cereal (or soup) spoon and a knife for buttering the toast.

Glassware

Glassware includes glasses of many shapes and styles. The price of glassware ranges from inexpensive to expensive. It depends on how the glass is made. Fine lead crystal and hand blown glass are more expensive than ordinary pressed glass. Since glassware is fragile, and you may need to replace it, you should select it carefully. You will want to choose an open stock pattern.

Another factor to consider when selecting glassware is to select a type which will go with your table coverings, dinnerware and flatware. For instance, a lace tablecloth, fine china, sterling silver and fine lead crystal go together. However, fine lead crystal may look out of place with a plastic place mat, stoneware and stainless steel. Table linens, dinnerware, flatware and glassware should look like they belong together, 17-4.

In a formal or informal setting, water glasses are placed just above the knife on the right of the plate. Other glasses (such as for milk or iced tea) are placed on the right of the water glass.

Napkins

Napkins should be folded and placed to the left of the forks. If the covers are crowded or if you are setting an elaborate table, place the napkin on the dinner plate. If the dinner plate is not being set as part of the cover, you can put the napkin in its place. Napkins can also be rolled, fanned or pleated to stand upright.

Condiments and serving utensils

Place salt and pepper shakers in the center or at the ends of the table. This way they will be within easy reach of everyone at the table. Often several sets are placed on the table. Cream, sugar, catsup, steak sauce, relishes and pickles are condiments. They can be placed on the table in advance.

Serving utensils should be set on the table next to the serving dishes. If the food is very hot, use a hot pad under the dish to protect the table. Hot pads can be made from ceramic tiles, straw mats, wood and thick fabric pads.

Setting a tray

Sometime you may prepare a meal for someone confined to bed. Or you may want to eat a meal while watching television. This would require setting up a tray with a single cover. You may also want to include salt, pepper and other condiments on your tray. The tray should be set carefully and attractively. A carefully set tray makes it easier to carry food safely without spilling. An attractively set tray helps make eating alone more pleasant. The tray also makes it easy to clear dirty dishes after the meal has been eaten.

DRESSING UP MEALS

A meal is more appealing when it is "dressed up." You can dress up meals by adding a centerpiece to the table or garnishes to food. These decorations may be simple or elaborate. You may use a simple centerpiece such as candles or an elaborate floral arrangement. A garnish can be as simple as a sprig of parsley or as elaborate as radish roses. The important consideration is how a centerpiece or garnish will enhance the meal.

Centerpieces

You can add interest to any table setting by dressing it up with a *centerpiece*. When you plan your centerpiece, think about how it will coordinate with the table linens, tableware and food.

Flowers are often used as a centerpiece for the dinner table. If you have fresh flowers growing in your garden, you may wish to create an arrangement for the table.

There are many ways to add a decorative touch to everyday meals without fresh flowers. It's fun to create your own permanent centerpieces using dried flowers. Attractive arrangements can also be made with fabric or paper flowers. An arrangement of fresh fruit and vegetables can be simple or elaborate. It can also become a part of the meal. See 17-5.

SUNKIST GROWERS, INC.

17-5 A centerpiece and candles add a decorative touch to a meal.

17-4 Together, this dinnerware, flatware and glassware make a contemporary place setting.

Whatever you select as a centerpiece, it should not be so large that it crowds the table. Height is also important. Centerpieces should not be so high that they interfere with conversation across the table.

Candles add atmosphere and elegance to evening meals. They should be arranged on the table so that diners won't have to look directly into the flames.

Garnishes

Another way of dressing up the table is to dress up the food. See 17-6. *Garnishes* can add color and variety to food and help to make it look more appetizing. Chefs often rely on garnishes such as parsley, lemon wedges and tomato slices to add color and interest to foods. Any dish can be garnished with foods commonly found in the kitchen. A lemon or orange can be cut into wedges or slices and used to decorate a platter. You can make little baskets from lemons, oranges and tomatoes which can be filled with sauce, relish or salad.

Radishes, carrots and celery can be cut into interesting designs and arranged along with the food. Some people garnish food with preserved apple rings, peach halves and cherries.

When you garnish food, remember that you should select garnishes which complement the food in terms of flavor and color. For instance, lemon is often used as a garnish for fish because it complements the flavor of fish. A poor example of a garnish would be parsley with broccoli. The green parsley garnish would blend in with the green of the broccoli. A garnish of parsley would look great with most meat dishes. Broccoli could be garnished with a slice of lemon.

THE SKILL OF CARVING

If your meal includes a roast, turkey or ham, it will need to be carved before serving. You can do this in advance in the kitchen, or you can do this at the table. Attractively prepared meat can add to the dining atmosphere. If you know how to carve, you should plan to carve the meat at the table for all to see.

Roasts, turkey and ham should stand at room temperature for about 15 minutes before being carved. This allows the meat to cool slightly which makes carving much easier. The basic tools needed for carving are a very sharp knife and a fork to hold the meat securely on the platter. Slice enough meat to serve all the people at the table. Additional portions may be sliced when it is time for second helpings. Slicing the meat as it is needed helps keep the meat hot and prevents it from drying out.

Meats with bones create the greatest carving problems. It helps to learn the location of the bones so that you can make neat slices. Carving is not a difficult task, but it does take practice, 17-7. If you have had no carving experience, practice in the kitchen until you have confidence to carve at the table. Once you have done it several times, you will be able to carve in front of others.

KEEPING FOOD HOT AND COLD

Food is most enjoyable when it is served at the proper temperature. One way to help keep food hot is to preheat the dishes. They can be heated in a warm (but not hot) oven for a few minutes. (Use the very lowest setting.) Some dishwashers have a special warming cycle just for this purpose. You can also rinse dishes in warm water just before using them.

SUNKIST GROWERS, INC.

17-6 These soups look more interesting when dressed up with a garnish.

Chafing dishes, food warmers with candles and warming trays can be used to keep food hot at the table. Some portable appliances can be used at the table to keep food warm. Food can be cooked and served from portable appliances such as an electric skillet. See 17-8.

Dishes that are to be used for serving cold foods should be chilled in the refrigerator or freezer in advance. Some beverages taste best in a chilled glass. Chill glasses by placing them in a container of ice. Or you can put the glasses in the refrigerator or freezer. Beverages such as iced tea should be prepared ahead of time and chilled in the refrigerator.

SERVING MEALS

At home, most people serve food informally. In *family service,* the serving dishes of food are passed clockwise around the table. This casual type of service allows people to help themselves. See 17-9.

Another way of serving food is *English service.* In this service, the host serves the food at the table. The filled plates are passed clockwise around the table.

The most formal types of table service are *Russian service* and *continental service.* Normally, they are not used unless waiters or waitresses are available. These are the types of service found in most restaurants. With Russian service, the waiter or waitress brings a platter of food to you and serves you from the platter. Sometimes the waiter or waitress may hold the platter so that you can help yourself. Continental service is more common. With this type of service, a waiter or waitress brings you a plate of food.

If there are several courses in the meal, you may find it convenient to use *compromise service.* Appetizers, soups and desserts are dished out in the kitchen and brought to the table by a family member. This is similar to continental service. The main course is served English style by the host.

EVAPORATED MILK ASSOCIATION

17-8 One way to keep food hot is to serve it from the pan in which it was cooked.

CUTCO

17-7 Carving requires skill. A sharp carving knife and a sturdy fork make the job easier.

TUPPERWARE® HOME PARTIES

17-9 At home, food is often served using family service.

CLEARING THE TABLE

When the meal is finished, someone must clear the table. Serving dishes should be removed first, followed by the condiments. Finally, individual covers are removed. The guests' plates are removed before the host's.

To remove an individual cover, stand to the person's left and remove the dinner plate with your left hand. Transfer this plate to your right hand. Next, remove the salad plate and place it on top of the dinner plate. Then remove the bread and butter plate and flatware that will not be used later. This way you can remove one full cover at a time.

It is considered impolite to stack dirty dishes at the table in front of guests. However, this is often a common practice for family meals.

BUFFET SERVICE

On special occasions such as a party, tea or reception, you may wish to serve food using *buffet service*, 17-10. Buffets can be formal or informal. Buffet service is an easy way to serve food when there is a large group of people or when space is limited.

If you plan to serve food using buffet service, you must set up the table in advance. Dinner plates are placed on the buffet table so that guests can serve themselves. When people will not be seated at a table, set the buffet with all the utensils that will be needed. Flatware can be wrapped in a napkin for easy pickup, or it can be arranged attractively on the buffet table.

When setting up a buffet table, keep in mind how people will travel around it. Place dinner plates at the starting point, and flatware and napkins at the end of the line. Foods for a buffet should be easy to serve and carry. Try to avoid foods that spill such as soups. Slice meat in advance. You may even want to butter the rolls in advance. Guests should be able to serve themselves foods with one hand since they will be holding their plates with the other.

If you are having a large crowd, you may want to set the table with two serving lines. This way, guests won't have to wait a long time in line. It's also a good idea to serve appetizers and desserts as separate courses.

You may serve appetizers or hors d'oeuvres in the living room. While guests are serving themselves the main course, the appetizer dishes can be removed. After the main course, the buffet table can be cleared and set up for dessert and after-dinner beverages.

MEALS TO GO

Meals to go may include anything from a lunch carried to school to a picnic in the park. These meals require some special planning, 17-11. For instance, the menu should include foods which can be wrapped easily or packed in non-breakable containers.

Foods which spoil easily, such as meat, poultry, fish, eggs and dairy products, should be packed carefully. Pack them to keep cold foods cold and hot foods hot. You can do this by carrying your lunch or picnic in an insulated lunchbox or container.

You can keep your lunch or picnic foods cold by packing them with an ice pack. Make an ice pack by filling any leakproof plastic container with water and freezing it. Most insulated containers will keep food cold for

EVAPORATED MILK ASSOCIATION

17-10 This buffet table is arranged attractively.

268

several hours or more. Dry ice can also be used but it requires special handling.

Foods can be kept hot by wrapping the containers in several layers of newspaper. A wide mouth vacuum bottle is great for soups or beverages. It will keep hot or cold foods at the proper temperature.

Foods for meals to go are often finger foods such as sandwiches and fruit. However, if foods such as soups and salads are included, bring along the utensils needed to serve and eat them, 17-12. Paper or plastic plates, cups, knives, forks and spoons are ideal for meals to go. It's a good idea to bring along paper napkins or premoistened towelets too.

17-12 A picnic requires careful planning at home.

RUBBERMAID

17-11 When planning a picnic menu, choose foods which pack easily and are easy to keep safe from spoilage.

Barbecues

A picnic can become a *barbecue* if you cook foods outdoors. See 17-13. You may barbecue in the woods at a campsite or in your own backyard. A grill is usually used when barbecuing. Some grills use electricity or gas as fuel. Other grills use charcoal briquettes for fuel.

When barbecuing, it is important to take certain safety precautions. Protect yourself from flames by not wearing loose clothing. If you have long hair, it should be tied back. A long-handled turner is good to use when barbecuing as it allows you to stand farther from the grill. Make sure the grill is located away from shrubs, wood and buildings. Always grill foods outdoors. Keep a container of water or sand handy in case the fire spreads. Never use gasoline or alcohol to start a fire. Use a commercial starter when using wood or charcoal. Once the fire has started, never add more fire starter.

If you are cooking on a charcoal grill, you should start the fire about 45 minutes before you will begin cooking. Other grills, such as

17-13 Foods cooked on the grill add special appeal to a meal.

gas and electric grills are started by simply turning the control on. The first step is to prepare the grill for cooking. (You may want to line the bottom with aluminum foil. This will save cleanup time and the foil will reflect the heat to the food.) Next, place the charcoal briquettes in a pyramid at the bottom of the grill. The number of briquettes you will use will depend on what you are cooking and the size of your grill. If you use a commercial fire starter, read the label and follow directions. After lighting the charcoal wait 45 minutes or until the charcoal is light gray in color. When this happens spread the coals and knock off the gray ash. This will insure even heating. Now you are ready to barbecue.

Use imagination when planning a barbecue. Many foods can be barbecued. Meats take on extra flavor when cooked over an open fire, 17-14. You can also cook appetizers, vegetables and desserts on the grill. Foods containing a lot of moisture should be wrapped in foil and placed on the grill. This will prevent them from drying out.

17-14 Barbecuing is easy and fun. Serving and eating barbecued foods is fun too.

Serving food attractively is an art.

to Define

barbecue . . .
buffet service . . .
centerpiece . . .
compromise service . . .
continental service . . .
cover . . . dinnerware . . .
earthenware . . .
English service . . .
family service . . .
flatware . . . fine china . . .
garnishes . . . glass ceramic . . .
glassware . . . ironstone . . .
melamine . . . open stock . . .
place setting . . .
Russian service . . .
service sets . . .
silver plate . . .
stainless steel . . .
sterling silver . . .
stoneware . . . table linens . . .
tarnish . . . triple-plated

to Discuss

1. What functions do table linens serve?

2. What special two points should you keep in mind when buying table linens?

3. Which type of dinnerware is often used at formal dinners?

4. Why must you polish silver?

5. What is a basic rule to remember when placing flatware on the table?

6. Where should water glasses be placed on the table?

7. When selecting a centerpiece, what should you consider?

8. Why should roasts and poultry stand at room temperature for about 15 minutes before being carved?

9. List three ways of keeping foods warm at the table.

10. When clearing the table, how should an individual cover be removed?

11. What kinds of foods are best to serve at a buffet?

12. How can you pack foods for a picnic so they will not spoil?

13. List at least four safety precautions you should take when barbecuing.

to Do

1. Visit department stores to comparison shop for dinnerware, glassware and flatware. Which would you select for everyday use? Special occasions? All-purpose use?

2. Create a display of homemade table linens and centerpieces. Show the actual cost of each item.

3. Put together an "idea" book showing pictures of tablesettings, dinnerware, glassware, flatware and centerpieces that reflect your family's life-style and preferences.

4. Experiment with the effect a centerpiece has on family meals. If your family does not ordinarily use a centerpiece, plan different centerpieces for several meals for one week. Record any comments people make. Does the centerpiece seem to make mealtime more pleasant? Do the same experiment using garnishes for one week.

5. Select a specific fruit or vegetable and experiment to discover how many different garnishes you can make using that one item.

6. Design a table arrangement for a special occasion such as a birthday party, anniversary or holiday. Based on a specific menu, plan for the dinnerware, flatware, glassware, table coverings and centerpiece that will be needed.

7. Plan a menu for a buffet for 25 people. Draw a diagram showing how you would set up the table to serve guests easily.

8. Practice setting the table and using the various types of dinner service described in this chapter.

9. Design a bulletin board outlining basic safety rules you should follow when barbecuing.

18

Eating etiquette

Why should you know rules of etiquette? After reading this chapter, you will be able to explain why knowing etiquette can make you comfortable in social situations. You will know basic mealtime manners and the proper way to eat some foods. You will also know what to do when dining at a restaurant.

People tend to associate the term etiquette with rigid rules of conduct for special occasions. But etiquette is also a part of everyday life. *Etiquette* may be defined as social rules and customs held by a group of people. Rules of etiquette may vary in different societies.

Good manners are a part of etiquette. Why should you bother to learn good manners? Probably the best reason is that good manners help you fit into social situations more comfortably. Inviting guests to your home for dinner and going out to a restaurant are more pleasant experiences when you know proper eating etiquette. Good manners are based on consideration of other people. Knowing what to do in a social situation can make you and the people around you feel more at ease. It's not much fun to be with someone who is self-conscious or who makes a scene. It's more pleasant to be with someone who is confident, polite and well-mannered.

MEALTIME MANNERS

Consideration for others is the key to good manners. "Please" and "thank you" are used often during a meal by a well-mannered person. There are some simple rules which considerate people practice during mealtime.

Understanding mealtime etiquette by following good manners can help you feel comfortable and enjoy the meal. It also helps to make you a more pleasant person to be around.

Sitting down to a meal

When it is time to eat, wait until everyone has gathered around the table before you sit down. Your host will usually tell you where to sit.

Don't start to eat until everyone has been served. The host will begin to eat first. Sometimes he or she may encourage guests to begin eating so the food won't get cold. In this case, you may eat when you receive your food. Always chew food with your lips closed. It is unpleasant sitting at the table with someone who "chomps" loudly on food.

Sit up straight at the table. Don't lean on the table or over your plate when you are eating.

You are expected to remain at the table until the meal is finished. But sometimes you may have to leave early for something special such as a meeting, rehearsal or game. In these cases, always ask to be excused before others have finished.

Mealtime conversation

Conversation at mealtime should be pleasant. Avoid heated discussions or arguments which may interfere with digestion. Save these topics for another time and enjoy the good food instead.

Someone may ask you a question just as you've placed food in your mouth. It is not polite to talk with your mouth full. Take the time you need to chew and swallow the food before answering. People are willing to wait.

Give others a chance to talk. Do not monopolize the conversation. By practicing good conversation techniques at home and with friends, you will be more comfortable among strangers.

Serving yourself

In family service, serving dishes are passed around the table. When you serve yourself, take only the amount of food you know you will eat. Don't take a large portion for yourself unless you are sure there is plenty to go around the table. Never remove food from a serving dish with your own flatware. If the serving dish is difficult to handle, offer to hold it for the person on your right. See 18-1. Ask the person on your left to hold it for you.

When the food is too hot to eat

If food is too hot to eat, you may have to wait for it to cool slightly. Do not blow on food. Just be patient. Take tiny bites or sips so you won't burn your mouth. Eat other foods which aren't as hot. Before long, the food will be cool enough to eat.

If you don't like the food being served

You may be served an unfamiliar food or a food you don't like. It is considered bad manners to refuse a food unless you are allergic to it. Don't make a big fuss. It only makes the host uncomfortable. Ask for a small portion. If you find you like the food, you can always ask for more later. By trying new foods, you may find foods you really like.

At the end of the meal

When you have finished eating, don't push your plate away. Leave it in place until the table is cleared. Used flatware should never be placed on the table. After you have finished eating, the knife and fork should be left on the plate. A spoon used to stir coffee or tea is left on the saucer. The butter knife is left on the bread and butter plate. Salad forks and dessert spoons are also left on the plate or bowl.

After you have been excused, leave your napkin, unfolded, on the right side of the plate. Don't wad it up into a ball, even if it is a paper napkin.

Accidents can happen

Table accidents can be embarrassing, but they happen to everyone. If you accidentally spill something, your host should act quickly to take over. If food accidentally slips from your plate onto the table, quietly remove it without drawing attention to yourself. If you drop a piece of flatware on the floor, pick it up and ask the host for another. If you drop food on the floor, you have a responsibility to see that it is picked up immediately. Food spills could stain the floor or carpet or cause someone to slip and fall. Explain what has happened to the host and he or she should help you.

Sometimes food may spill into your lap. A napkin will protect your clothing. Dry or solid food that has spilled can be placed on the side of your plate. Moist food such as gravy should be scooped from the napkin with a spoon. A spill on clothing can be blotted with a napkin.

If you must cough or sneeze at the table, use your napkin to cover your mouth. This prevents germs from spreading to others at the table or to the food set before you.

When you're not sure what to do

The host sets an example for eating politely. Suppose you are served a food you don't know how to eat politely. Or suppose there is a utensil you don't know how to use politely. Watch the person at the head of the table. The host will be a model for you, and you should be correct in imitating him or her.

FOODS WHICH REQUIRE SPECIAL TECHNIQUES

Eating some foods may present special problems. Some people have trouble eating soup. It's not difficult to eat soup properly if you practice the correct way all the time. Dip the spoon into the bowl and move it away from yourself. Hold it so that you can sip the soup from the side. To avoid spills, don't overfill the spoon. Do not blow on soup to cool it. Instead, take small spoonfuls so the soup will cool as you bring it to your mouth. Do not sip soup directly from a bowl. Soup may be sipped only when it is served in a cup with a handle.

When you have finished the soup, place the spoon on the plate which is under the cup or bowl. If a flat soup plate is used, you may leave the spoon in the middle of the plate.

Spaghetti is another tricky food. A soupspoon can be used to help in winding the spaghetti onto the fork. Hold the spoon in your left hand. Take a small amount of spaghetti onto a fork and place the tines against the bowl of the soupspoon. Wind the spaghetti into a ball, 18-2. If a spoon is not provided,

18-1 When a serving dish is difficult to handle, hold it for the person on your right. This makes serving easier.

18-2 When eating spaghetti, take a small amount onto a fork and place the tines against the bowl of a soupspoon. Then wind the spaghetti into a ball.

cut the spaghetti into short pieces and eat it with your fork.

Most vegetables are eaten with a fork. However, some vegetables served in a side dish may be eaten with a spoon. These include stewed tomatoes, baby peas and creamed vegetables.

A baked potato may present a problem when served whole. First, the potato must be opened. Use your fork and fingers to do this. Then add butter or sour cream to the opening. Eat the potato with your fork. Do not scoop the potato out onto your plate. If you like potato skins, you may cut them with your knife and eat them.

You may be served salad which contains large pieces of lettuce or other greens. Cut them into bite-size pieces before you eat them. Generally, you can do this with a fork, but sometimes you may need to use a knife.

You may get pits or bones in your mouth when eating olives or fish. Don't swallow them, but don't spit them out either. Making as little fuss as possible, remove them from your mouth with your spoon or fingers. Place them on the side of your plate or on your bread and butter plate.

Often you will need to cut meat before eating it. It is considered impolite to cut up the entire serving of meat at one time. Hold the knife in one hand and your fork in your other hand, 18-3. Cut a few pieces of meat, then lay the knife on your plate and eat the meat with your fork. Cut more meat after you have finished eating these pieces.

Finger foods

Certain foods may be eaten with your fingers. These are called *finger foods*. See 18-4. Raw vegetable sticks, olives, pickles and potato chips are eaten with the fingers. Foods such as sandwiches, candy and nuts are finger foods, too.

Bread and rolls are also finger foods. Sliced bread should be broken into quarters. Each quarter may be buttered before eating, 18-5. Muffins, biscuits and rolls are usually cut or broken in half. If they are served warm, they are usually buttered immediately. Otherwise,

butter should be spread on each piece when you are ready to eat it.

A whole lobster may present a problem to some people. First it must be broken apart with the hands. Large chunks of lobster meat should be cut into smaller, bite-size pieces and

18-3 When cutting meat, cut a few pieces at a time.

18-4 Foods eaten at picnics and barbecues, such as lobster, chicken and corn on the cob, are finger foods.

eaten with a fork. Usually a cocktail fork is used. Chunks of lobster are often dipped in a butter sauce.

Sometimes chicken is a finger food. At picnics and barbecues, chicken is usually served in small pieces and eaten with the fingers, 18-6. If a half chicken is served at an informal meal, it should first be cut into smaller pieces (leg, wing, etc.), 18-7. Then each piece may be picked up and eaten. Anytime you aren't sure how to eat the chicken that is served, do what the host does. On more formal occasions, chicken may be served with the bones removed. This should be eaten with a fork.

Fresh fruits such as oranges, apples and pears are usually finger foods. However, they should not be eaten whole at the table. They should be cut into quarters or smaller sections before eating. Usually they are served with a fruit knife so they can be cut up.

The first time most people are served a whole artichoke, they wonder what to do with it. An artichoke is basically a finger food. Leaves are removed, one at a time, from the outside. Then they are dipped in a sauce. Eat the soft edible portion of the leaf by placing it in your mouth and running the leaf between your upper teeth and your tongue. Afterwards, put the remaining part of the leaf neatly on your plate. Part of the inside of the arti-

choke is like a thistle and should not be eaten. Cut this away with your knife. The remaining bottom part inside the artichoke is called the "heart." Cut the heart into bite-size pieces and eat it with a fork.

DINING IN A RESTAURANT

If you practice table etiquette at home, there is no need to worry when you go to a

18-6 Chicken is often eaten with the fingers at informal meals such as picnics and barbecues.

18-5 Break sliced bread into quarters before buttering and eating.

18-7 When a large piece of chicken is served, cut it into smaller pieces.

restaurant. At some restaurants, customers are served on a first-come, first served basis. But other restaurants require that you make a reservation. A *reservation* holds a table for you. To make a reservation, you should call the restaurant ahead of time. Tell how many people will be in your party and when you plan to arrive.

Some restaurants have special rules. For instance, formal restaurants may have a dress code. A *dress code* specifies what customers should wear. A restaurant may, for example, require men to wear a tie and jacket.

When dining in a restaurant, be considerate of others. Loud talking and noises can disturb others. Also, in consideration of nonsmokers, some restaurants have no-smoking areas for people who do not smoke. Smokers should not smoke in these areas.

When you enter a restaurant, you are usually greeted by a maître d'. The *maître d'* is the head of the dining room staff. The maître d' will show you to your table, help to seat you and give you menus.

Ordering from the menu

When eating out, don't forget about nutrition. Keep the Basic Four Food Groups in mind. Try to select foods from each of the four food groups. 18-8. When placing your order, give it clearly to the waiter or waitress. After you have placed the order, try not to change your mind. Once in a while, a waiter or waitress may make a mistake with your order. Quietly ask him or her to correct it.

If you are a guest, your host may suggest something for you to order. Assume that this is a clue to the amount of money he or she is prepared to spend. If you are not sure of his or her budget, ask for a suggestion.

Sometimes friends agree, in advance, to go "Dutch" (each person pays for his or her own meal). When you place your order, ask for separate checks. This will avoid confusion when the bill comes.

You may want to discuss the various items on the menu before ordering. Sometimes you may see terms on a menu with which you are not familiar. Some terms you might see on a

menu are listed in 18-9. If you aren't sure what an item is, ask the waiter or waitress to describe it for you.

Menus can be organized in different ways. If the menu is an *a la carte menu,* each item on the menu is priced separately. This means that you will be charged for any items you order. See 18-10. Another type of menu is the *dinner menu.* A dinner menu lists the price after the *entrée* (main course). But the price usually includes a choice of appetizers, salads and desserts. You will be charged that price even if you don't order everything included. See 18-11.

Paying the bill

Usually the waiter or waitress will bring the check at the end of the meal. When you have finished and are ready to leave, you can ask for your check if you haven't received it. Once the check arrives, look it over to make sure you have been properly charged for your meal. Take time to check the arithmetic. A busy person can make mistakes. Don't hesitate to ask about items on the check which you don't understand.

Unless the bill states "please pay cashier," pay the waiter or waitress at the table. Usually the check is presented on a small plate or tray. Put the money on the tray after reviewing the

18-8 Select foods from the menu with good nutrition in mind. Don't be afraid to try new foods.

check. The waiter or waitress will return with your change. Leave the tip on the tray or table when you leave.

A *tip* is left to express thanks for good service. Waiters and waitresses depend on tips for part of their income. Normally, you should tip them 15 to 20 percent of the total bill (not including the tax). However, if the service is very good you may wish to tip more. If the service is poor, the tip may be reduced.

To figure a 15 percent tip, first figure 10 percent by moving the decimal point one place to the left. Half of that amount is then added to get 15 percent. For instance, suppose you bill was $15.00. You would figure 10 percent of $15.00, which is $1.50. Half of that amount is $.75. So, 15 percent would be $1.50 + $.75 or $2.25. If the tip is 20 percent of a $15.00 bill, double the 10 percent amount. This would be $1.50 × 2 or $3.00.

DINER'S VOCABULARY

A LA MODE *(ä'lə·mōd')* — usually refers to pie served with ice cream.

ANTIPASTO *(än'tē·päs'tō)* — the Italian word for assorted appetizers.

AU JUS *(ō·zhoo')* — a French word meaning served in natural juice. Usually refers to roast beef.

BISQUE *(bisk)* — a rich cream soup, usually made with lobster or shrimp. Can also be made with pureed vegetables.

CREPE *(krep)* — a thin pancake. When filled with creamed meat or poultry is served as an appetizer or entrée. Dessert crepes are usually filled with fruit.

DU JOUR *(doo zhur)* — a French word which is used to indicate the special dishes being served on a particular day.

EN BROCHETTE *(än brō·shet')* — the French term for food cooked on a skewer.

ESCARGOT *(es'kär·go')* — the French word for snails. Snails are usually served as an appetizer. They are broiled in a garlic and butter sauce.

ESPRESSO *(es·pres'ō)* — an after dinner coffee, made from special beans and prepared in a special pot.

FILET MIGNON *(fi·lä min·yon')* — a small tender steak which comes from the beef tenderloin.

GAZPACHO *(gäz·pä'chō)* — a cold soup orignating in Spain. Made from tomato juice and served with chopped raw vegetables.

HOLLANDAISE *(hol'ən·dāz')* — a rich sauce made with egg yolks, butter and seasonings. Often served with vegetables and fish.

MACEDOINE *(mas'i·dwan')* — a mixture of fresh fruits. Also can refer to a mixed vegetable dish.

MAISON *(mä·zôn')* — the French word for "house". Items with "maison" usually refer to special dishes of the restaurant.

MARINARA *(mär'ē·när'ə)* — refers to food served with a spicy Italian tomato sauce.

MOUSSE *(moos)* — a rich dessert made with whipped cream and beaten eggs. Can also refer to meat or fish which has been ground fine and molded.

PARFAIT *(pär·fā')* — ice cream served in tall, stemmed glasses with fruit or sauce.

PARMEGIANA *(pär'ma·jän'ə)* — food made or seasoned with Parmesan cheese.

PATÉ *(pa·tä')* — the French word for "paste;" usually made with ground meats which are seasoned, baked and then served cold as an appetizer.

PILAF *(pē·läf')* — rice cooked in broth and seasonings.

SCAMPI *(skam'pē)* — a variety of shrimp which is broiled or sauted in butter usually with garlic.

TERIYAKI *(ter·ē·yä'kē)* — refers to a Japanese cooking style in which food is marinated in a soy sauce mixture and then grilled or broiled.

VINAIGRETTE *(vin'a·gret')* — an oil and vinegar sauce which is served with salads and cold vegetables.

18-9 At a restaurant, you may see these terms on a menu. Knowing what they are and how to pronounce them correctly can make ordering easier.

Hors d'Oeuvres

Avocat Farci (Avocado Stuffed with Crab)
Terrine de Canard (Paté of Duckling)
Cocktail de Crevettes (Shrimp Cocktail)
Escargots Bourguignonne (Snails in Garlic Butter)
Huîtres Cheminée (Baked Stuffed Oysters)
Palourdes Farcies (Baked Clams Alfredo)

Soupes

Soupe à l'Oignon (Onion Soup Gratinée)
Bisque de Homard (Lobster Bisque)
Vichyssoise (Cold Potato and Leek Soup)
Soupe du Jour (Chef's Soup of the Day)

Salades

Salade Caesar
Salade d'Epinard (Spinach Salad, Paprica Dressing)
Salade Vinaigrette
(Mixed Green Salad, Classic French Dressing)

Poissons

Sole Amandine (Dover Sole with Almonds, Sauted)
Turbot Poché (Poached Turbot, Sauce Hollandaise or Choron)
Homard à l'Americaine (Lobster in Brandy Sauce)
Cuisses de Grenouilles Beurre et Ail
(Frog Legs, Sauted, Butter-Garlic Sauce)

Volaille

Coq au Vin A L'Ancienne (Chicken in Red Wine)
Canard à l'Orange Flambé
(Roast Duck in Orange Sauce Flamed in Brandy)
Pigeonneau Farci
(Cornish Hen Stuffed with Fois Gras and Wild Rice)

Veau

Veau Marsala (Veal Scaloppine, Marsala Sauce)
Veau Florentine (Veal with Spinach in Cream Sauce, Glazed)
Veau Francaise Gloria (Veal with Garlic, Butter, Capers)

Viande

Boeuf Wellington
(Tenderloin in Pastry Crust, Sauce Périgueux)
Steak au Poivre (French Pepper Steak,
Madagascar Sauce, Flamed in Brandy)
Côtes d'Agneau (Broiled Lamb Chops)
Entrecôte Grillée (Broiled Sirloin Steak)
Tournedos Rossini (Beef Tenderloin served with Foie Gras)
Tournedos Béarnaise (Filet Mignon with Béarnaise Sauce)

Légumes

Asparagus Spears (Hollandaise Sauce)
Broccoli (Hollandaise Sauce or Butter)
Brussel Sprouts (Sauté)
Cauliflower (Gratiné)

LA CHEMINEE

18-10 This is a sample of selections from an a la carte menu.

FROM OUR BROILER

We cut and trim our own meats.

NEW YORK CUT BONELESS STRIP STEAK
    Regular Cut — 12 ounces
    The Pub Cut — 16 ounces

TOP BUTT STEAK **— one of the most flavorful**

FILET MIGNON AND MUSHROOMS **— most tender**
    Regular Cut — 8 ounces
    The Pub Cut — 10 ounces

BEEF STEAK EN BROCHETTE
    Chunks of Choice Steak, skewered with Fresh Vegetables, Char-Broiled

BLUE CHEESE STEAKS

**The above Dinners include Relish Tray, Choice of Potato,
Choice of Soup or Salad, Rolls & Butter.**

SEAFOOD

FRENCH FRIED JUMBO SHRIMP
    **Succulent and Tender with Cocktail
    or Tartar Sauce**

FRENCH FRIED COD FILETS
    **Succulent Filets of North Atlantic Ocean Cod
    dipped in our own batter and deep fried to a golden brown**

BROILED ALASKAN CRAB LEGS
    with drawn butter — THE House Favorite

SEAFOOD PLATTER **— Combination of the above items**

FRESH BATTERED LAKE PERCH

Choice of Soup or Salad & Choice of Potato on Above Dinners

*18-11 This is a sample of
selections from a dinner menu.*

ALF'S PUB

to Define

a la carte menu . . .
dinner menu . . .
dress code . . . entrée . . .
etiquette . . . finger foods . . .
maître d' . . . reservation . . .
tip

to Discuss

1. What is the key to good manners?
2. When should you begin to eat at a meal?
3. Why should heated discussions or arguments be avoided at mealtime?
4. When you are finished eating, where should you put used flatware? Your napkin?
5. If you accidently drop food on the floor, what should you do?
6. What should you do if you don't know how to eat a particular food or use a certain utensil?
7. How should you remove a pit or bone from your mouth?
8. List at least four foods which can be eaten properly with your fingers.
9. When is chicken considered a finger food?
10. What information should you give when making a reservation at a restaurant?
11. What should you do if you are not sure what an item is on a menu?
12. How much is a waiter or waitress usually tipped for good service?
13. If your check at a restaurant totals $10.00, how much would you leave for a 15 percent tip?

to Do

1. Create a skit about awkward situations which can arise at the dinner table. Perform it for the class and have them discuss how they would handle the situation.
2. Demonstrate how to eat some of the difficult foods described in this chapter.
3. Create a game which could be used to teach young children about table manners.
4. Consult an etiquette book in your library for information on how to organize a formal dinner party for six people. What can a host do to make his or her guests comfortable?
5. Collect menus from local restaurants. In class review the terms on the menu. Look up any terms you don't understand. Which restaurants would be considered casual? Which would be considered formal?
6. Create a poster or comic strip illustrating do's and don'ts for diners.

19

Company's coming

What's the secret to giving great parties? After reading this chapter, you will know how planning can make a party a success. You will be able to plan and give a party for family or friends. You will be able to describe ways of creating fun party themes. You will also be able to help guests feel comfortable and to have a good time.

*E*verybody likes a party. It's fun to go to parties, and it's fun to give them. When you entertain, you usually have some purpose in mind. It may be to celebrate a special occasion such as your friend's birthday or your sister's graduation. Or it may be to bring friends or relatives together for a holiday feast. Whatever the reason, the goal of entertaining is to provide enjoyment for your guests and for yourself.

BEGIN WITH PLANNING

Most good parties begin with planning. Planning includes developing a budget, making a guest list, setting a date for the party and sending invitations. Choosing refreshments and decorations is also part of the planning process. When a party is carefully planned, things usually run smoothly. This allows you to enjoy the party along with your guests.

Your budget

One of the first steps in planning a party is to decide how much money you can afford to spend. A great party doesn't have to cost a lot. A dinner based on chicken or a casserole could taste just as good as a more expensive steak dinner. See 19-1. If your budget won't stretch enough to cover a whole meal, plan an after-dinner party and serve dessert or snacks. Cake and punch cost much less than a four-course dinner.

Although food will probably be your biggest expense, you may need room in your budget for nonfood items too. These could include anything from invitations and decorations to rented punch bowls and live entertainment. A sample budget for parties is shown in 19-2.

The guest list

Make a list of people you would like to invite to your party. The amount of money you have to spend may determine how many guests you can entertain. Some people enjoy giving big parties so they can invite all their friends. They plan to spend a lot of time and money on a party. Others prefer simple, casual parties where people can sit around and talk or listen to music. If you aren't comfortable giving a large party, you may wish to invite a smaller group of friends. If you are planning a dinner, you may have to limit your guest list.

The space you have for a party may also affect your guest list. For instance, if you live in a small apartment, you won't be able to invite a large group. People become uncomfortable in overcrowded rooms. If you want to give a party for a larger crowd, consider having it outdoors where there will be more room.

Setting the date

After making the guest list, you are ready to set the date and time for your party. First, check with your family to make sure that your party plans don't conflict with their plans. Also, check to see what is going on in the community. You don't want your party to conflict with other events such as a game or concert.

Invitations

Invitations to a party can be given in several ways. If the party is small, and you are inviting close friends, you may ask them in person or by phone. For special events, it's nice to send written invitations. Most stationery stores have an assortment of printed invitations. But this can add to your expenses,

especially if you are inviting a lot of people. You can always use your imagination to create your own invitations.

Invitations should be received by guests at least one week before the party. An invitation usually includes the date, time, kind of party and place. Directions on how to get to the party may also be included. Many invitations have *R.S.V.P.* or *Regrets Only* written on them. People put R.S.V.P. or Regrets Only on invitations so they will know how many people will be coming. This allows them to plan refreshments more accurately. If you receive an invitation with R.S.V.P., let the host know if you are planning to come. If you receive an invitation with Regrets Only written on it, contact the host only if you will be unable to attend the party.

Refreshments

Refreshments are an important part of any party. What you serve will vary, depending on the kind of party you are planning and the money you have to spend. See 19-3. The refreshments you serve don't have to be expensive or elaborate to be good. But they should be carefully planned so they can be made in advance and served easily. When refreshments are planned carefully, the host has more time to enjoy the party along with his or her guests.

Select refreshments for your party which you know you can prepare well. It's not a good idea to use a new recipe when preparing refreshments for company. Perhaps you could experiment with the recipe by serving it to your family first. If you are planning a dinner party, keep the meal simple. Most people will enjoy a casserole dish served with warm bread and a tossed salad. You could finish the meal by serving fruit tarts or pie. Iced tea is a simple, low cost beverage to prepare for a meal of this type. Beginners should start out with simple meals such as this one. As cooking and hosting skills improve, meals can become a little more complex.

If you are inviting friends for an after dinner party, you can serve snack foods so guests can munch throughout the evening. Or, perhaps you want to invite some friends to a party after a game. Some simple, inexpensive snack foods include popcorn, chips, pretzels, dips, raw vegetables, cheese and crackers. Some parties, such as a New Year's Eve party, may last a long time. You may want to have a buffet table of salads, cold cuts and rolls so guests can help themselves. (Be sure that perishable foods are kept either hot or cold to prevent spoilage or food poisoning.)

For almost any type of informal party, a fun refreshment idea is to serve "make-your-own" sundaes or pizzas. Provide all the toppings for sundaes or pizzas and let your guests create their own variations.

Whatever refreshments you decide to serve,

BUDGET	
ITEM	**COST**
Food and beverages:	
_____	_____
_____	_____
_____	_____
_____	_____
_____	_____
Invitations: _____	_____
Decorations: _____	_____
Entertainment: _____	_____
Miscellaneous items to buy:____	_____
Miscellaneous items to rent:____	_____
TOTAL:_____	

19-2 *Using a budget plan such as this one can help you to decide how much money you can spend on a party.*

EVAPORATED MILK ASSOC.

19-1 *Creamed chicken with noodles, a tossed salad, glazed oranges and chocolate cake make an elegant, yet inexpensive, buffet.*

THEODORE R. SILLS, INC.

19-3 *These simple refreshments are appropriate for a child's party.*

take time to write out the menu. This helps to save time when making a shopping list. It also helps when you are starting to prepare the food.

Decorations

You don't have to have decorations for a party. But carrying out a theme with decorations can be a lot of fun. The decorations can be elaborate or simple, depending on your time and money. If you use a theme, carry it out in the invitations and food as well. For instance, you may use a clown theme for a child's birthday party. The invitations could feature a clown and the birthday cake could be decorated to look like a clown.

For most parties, the refreshment table is usually the focal point for decorations. If you are having a dinner party, place cards, a centerpiece and the food can also carry out the theme.

Other planning tips

When planning a party, you will need to consider other details too. Make sure you have enough glasses and dinnerware. You can rent these items and almost anything else you need for a large party. But that costs money. You may find it less costly to use paper plates and cups. See if you can borrow extra folding chairs and tables from friends.

PUTTING YOUR PLAN INTO ACTION

A well-organized plan is essential for most parties. Your plan should give attention to what can be done in advance. This way you'll have plenty of time for last minute details. To make sure you get everything done, take time to write your plan on paper. An outline of a typical party plan is shown in 19-4. Your list should be as detailed as possible. For instance, the house will need cleaning. You will probably need to buy or make extra ice and store it. You will also need to prepare refreshments and set the table. After you've made the list, decide when and how you will complete each task. Then check off each task as it is finished.

The day of the party you will have to take care of many last minute details. If you have thought through your party plans, you will know exactly what things should be done and when. By the time your guests arrive, everything will be ready for them. The more you get done in advance, the more you'll be able to relax and enjoy your own party.

HOSTING A PARTY

Your main role as host is to make your guests comfortable. Plan to greet your guests at the door and receive their coats. If people don't know each other, introduce them. Check often to see that glasses and platters of food are refilled. When you entertain informally, you may set everything up and encourage your guests to help themselves.

As host you are responsible for the mood of the party. You should plan your party so that you have time to be with your guests. If a guest is being left out of the activity, it is your job to see that the person is included. As guests get ready to leave, you should be on hand to help them with their coats and say good-bye.

PARTY IDEAS

Some people have a special knack for creating clever party themes. Others stick to more traditional themes based on holidays or special occasions. When it comes to planning informal or formal parties, you are only limited by your imagination. Developing a theme through clever use of decorations and food is an art.

Holidays

Many people entertain at holiday time. Relatives often get together on religious holidays such as Easter, Passover, Christmas and Hanukkah. National holidays such as the Fourth of July, Memorial Day and Thanksgiving are times when people gather to celebrate. Throughout the year there are special days that lend themselves easily to party themes. Valentine's Day is a time to carry out a hearts and flowers theme. For St. Patrick's

Day, green paper shamrocks make great decorations. And a little green food coloring in refreshments such as milk shakes and cakes can also help carry out the theme.

It's easy to carry out a Halloween theme. Invitations can be shaped as goblins or pumpkins. Almost any simple refreshment can be adapted to a Halloween theme, 19-5. For additional fun, plan some games that relate to Halloween. You might have a contest to see who can throw the most marshmallows into a pumpkin, or a ghostly treasure hunt.

If you are looking for an enjoyable way to entertain your friends around Christmas, invite them to a "cookie swap." Ask friends to bring several dozen of their favorite type of cookie. Have them also bring copies of the recipe for each guest. As host, you provide the beverages such as fruit punch or hot spiced tea. Everyone then samples the cookies. Each person takes home new recipes and enjoys a good time as well.

Personal occasions

Families and friends often get together to celebrate personal events. Birthdays and anniversaries are the most frequently celebrated events, 19-6. But graduations, christenings,

19-5 Refreshments for Halloween parties can be fun, yet simple.

19-6 Birthday parties are special occasions for people of all ages.

RUBBERMAID, INC.

PARTY PLAN

Theme or purpose: _____

Day: _____

Time: _____

Place: _____

Guest list: _____

_____

_____

_____

Things to buy: _____

Things to rent: _____

Things to borrow: _____

Things to do ahead (purchasing, borrowing, cooking, setting up):

Two weeks before: _____

Week of: _____

Day before: _____

Day of party: _____

Just before guests arrive: _____

19-4 Most parties require careful planning in advance.

confirmations, weddings and bar mitzvahs are all times when families celebrate. Often families hold receptions to honor a graduate or to celebrate a wedding. Receptions can be elaborate affairs or simple get-togethers.

Showers are often given by friends or relatives to celebrate engagements, weddings and births. Usually dessert and a beverage are served at showers, 19-7.

Regional and ethnic parties

For a different approach to a party use a regional or ethnic theme. You can create interesting party themes featuring almost any region of the United States or a foreign country. A "Wild West Night", "A Night on Broadway" or a "Hawaiian Luau" may feature different regions of the United States. A "Mexican Fiesta", a "German Sausage Festival" or an "African Safari Night" are examples of good themes for parties.

Invite your friends to dress in some type of costume. For instance, if the party has a western theme, cowboy hats and boots might be in order. For an African party, batik prints and sarong style dresses are costume possibilities. You can borrow records from the library to play during your party that will further carry out the theme. Use travel posters to decorate the walls. For refreshments, try to choose foods which are staple or popular foods of the region or country, 19-8.

Progressive party

If you and your friends live near each other, you may want to have a *progressive dinner*. You will need to get together in advance to plan it. Each person is responsible for a different course in the meal. The group starts out at one house for the first course. The group then travels from home to home for different courses of the meal until it ends up at the last place for dessert. An advantage to a progressive party is that every one shares in the entertaining responsibilities and expenses.

Brunch

A *brunch* is actually a combination of breakfast and lunch. Usually a brunch is held between 10 a.m. and 2 p.m. Brunch menus can be kept fairly simple. A typical brunch might include fruit punch, scrambled eggs with ham and coffee cake. You may want to serve a more elaborate brunch. Tomato juice, quiche Lorraine (an egg pie), a relish tray, fresh fruit and iced tea may be served. See 19-9. Perhaps your school has a faculty appreciation day. You may wish to invite teachers to your class for brunch.

Come-as-you-are party

A *come-as-you-are party* can be a lot of fun. Invite your friends to come as they are the moment they receive their invitation. Extend your invitations by phone at different times of the day. Whatever your guests are wearing at the time you call is what they must wear to the party. Carry out the theme further by giving prizes for the person who "got caught," "was most together," etc.

FORMAL PARTIES

Sometimes you may want to entertain formally. For instance, you may want to give a dinner party before a formal dance. Formal occasions always require written invitations. Be sure to let your guests know that you are planning a formal party. The type of clothing to be worn is sometimes specified. For instance, the invitation may state *Black Tie*. This means men should wear tuxedos and women should wear dressy gowns.

Food and decorations are usually elaborate at formal parties, 19-10. Usually a seating plan is developed. Often, place cards are set on the table.

IMPROMPTU PARTIES

Most parties are planned in advance. But there will be times when you'll want to invite friends to your home on the spur of the moment. And sometimes people drop by unexpectedly. This type of party is called *impromptu*.

It's not difficult to turn such visits into special occasions if you have refreshments on

19-7 Refreshments can add a
festive touch to any party. This
cake helps to carry out the
theme of a shower.

19-9 Quiche Lorraine makes a
fine entrée for a brunch.

19-8 Foods such as these would
contribute to the theme of a
Chinese party.

19-10 Refreshments for formal
parties are usually elaborate.

hand. Powdered drink mixes such as fruit punch and lemonade are good to have on hand. Popcorn is a snack which can be made in minutes, 19-11. Cookies keep for months in the freezer if they are properly wrapped. Cookies thaw quickly when spread on baking sheets and placed in the oven at a low temperature for several minutes. Chips and raw vegetables can be served with a mayonnaise or yogurt dip flavored with spices or instant broth. Canned sandwich spreads can be used on bread, toast or crackers to make attractive snacks.

PLANNING EVENTS AWAY FROM HOME

Most school and community events are planned and carried out by committees. Each committee is responsible for planning and following through on a specific task. The committees for a school dance might include the following:
• Arrangements (finding location and chaperones)
• Publicity
• Tickets and finance
• Refreshments
• Band
• Entertainment
• Theme/decorations
• Program and favors
• Photography
• Cleanup

When planning events away from home, you will need to use the same planning procedures outlined for entertaining at home. But you will also have some additional work to do. First, you'll have to set a date with the school or the management of the place where the event will be held. At that time, be sure to ask about any special rules regarding the use of the facility.

If you have to rent a place, compare the prices of different places. Check out country clubs, churches, schools, restaurants and hotels to find the best rate. Check to see if you must use special caterers. In some places you will not be able to bring your own food and beverages. Find out what equipment is available for your use and who is responsible for the cleanup. Many times there is an additional charge for some of these items. You should be aware of this early in your planning.

If the party is open to the public, you will also have to make plans for advertising. Posters, flyers and newspaper articles will help to let others know the event is taking place. If you expect a large crowd, make arrangements with the local police to assign someone to be at the event. Your organization will probably have to pay for this security service.

It is important to plan the budget thoroughly, especially if the event is designed to make money. If you are not sure how to develop a budget, check with people who have had experience. Usually they will be glad to help out.

19-11 Fresh popcorn is easy to make when company drops by unexpectedly.

to Define

Black tie . . . brunch . . . come-as-you-are party . . . impromptu party . . . progressive dinner . . . R.S.V.P. . . . theme

to Discuss

1. What does planning a party include?
2. Why should you check with your family before setting a date and time for your party?
3. What should you do if you receive an invitation with R.S.V.P. written on it?
4. What will determine the refreshments you serve at a party? How should they be planned?
5. Why should you write out a menu for refreshments to be served at a party?
6. Why should you plan your party on paper?
7. List at least four themes for parties you might have for family or friends.
8. What is an advantage of a progressive dinner?
9. What type of food and decorations are usually found at formal parties?
10. List at least four refreshment ideas for an impromptu party.
11. What is your main role as host of a party?
12. If a guest is being left out of an activity, what should you do?
13. What special arrangements may be needed if you are planning a party away from home?

to Do

1. Create a display showing different types of homemade party invitations.
2. Write a newspaper article on "How to be a gracious host."
3. Start a collection of recipes which would be easy and inexpensive to prepare for a party.
4. Plan a party to celebrate an event such as a birthday or holiday. Establish a budget and develop a plan for invitations, decorations, refreshments, etc.
5. Create a party theme book showing ideas for invitations, games, decorations, table arrangements and refreshments for various occasions or themes.
6. Sponsor a brunch for teachers on "teacher recognition day." Plan the menu, keeping it simple, so that it can take place during class or before class begins.
7. Organize a party planning service for parents of small children. Assist parents in planning, decorating, entertainment, refreshments and cleanup.

R.C. BIGELOW, INC.

Spiced tea, fresh doughnut "holes" and crisp apples are tasty refreshments which can be served anytime.

Widening food horizons

As your interest in food increases, you may wish to explore various areas related to food.

20

Growing it yourself

How do you grow your own vegetables? After reading this chapter, you will be able to plan, prepare and plant a vegetable garden. You will be able to explain how to care for your garden to insure a good harvest. You will also know the basics of planting an indoor garden.

$\mathcal{Y}$ou can get a great feeling of satisfaction from growing your own vegetables. You can have a lot of fun eating the harvest too. There is nothing like eating a ripe, juicy tomato fresh off the vine. String beans are at their peak in flavor and texture when they are just picked. Homegrown lettuce can be picked right before mealtime for a really fresh salad.

By growing your own vegetables, you can have different varieties of vegetables that aren't always available in the supermarket. Did you know you could grow a special "burpless" cucumber? Some plants are developed for special color effects. For instance, there is a red lettuce that's tasty and colorful in a salad. And have you ever seen yellow beets? Or how about a squash which, when cooked and opened, contains strings of "noodles" inside? Served with butter, cheese and tomato sauce, it's a delicious spaghetti squash. See 20-1.

Many people find that home gardens can save them quite a bit of money. This is especially true if they grow enough vegetables to preserve for the winter months. Vegetables can be enjoyed throughout the winter when they are frozen or canned.

Some people believe that the quality of foods grown and processed at home is better than commercially grown and processed foods. When vegetables are processed at home, people can add seasonings to their own tastes. Some people also prefer foods that are "organically" grown. This means that chemical fertilizers and pesticides were not used in growing the foods.

Whatever the reasons, growing vegetables yourself can be a rewarding experience, 20-2. Gardens, however, involve work and the possibility of failure. You can reduce the risk of failure with careful planning and regular attention to your garden.

PLANNING A VEGETABLE GARDEN

Before you start planting, it is important to plan the garden on paper. Begin planning early in the year. Order seed catalogs and study them to acquaint yourself with the many varieties of vegetables. Seed catalogs are filled with information that will help you choose the varieties which will grow best in your garden, 20-3. Your county extension service can also help you to plan your garden.

If possible, order seeds with a friend. One package of seeds is more than enough for the average family. By ordering with a friend, you can share the seeds, saving money and avoiding waste.

Planning a garden takes some thought. Start planning your garden by asking yourself some basic questions.

20-2 Growing your own vegetables can be a rewarding experience.

20-3 Seed catalogs can give you useful information for planning your garden.

BURPEE SEEDS

20-1 You may wish to grow different varieties of vegetables. This interesting type of squash is called spaghetti squash.

Why are you growing this garden?

How will the vegetables be used? Do you want them for canning, freezing or eating fresh off the vine? The answer to this question will determine the varieties of vegetables you choose. Consult a seed catalog to select the type of vegetable that is best for your purposes. For instance, Italian tomatoes are great for sauces. Beefsteak tomatoes, on the other hand, are good in fresh salads. Some varieties of tomatoes, such as Tiny Tim, are small, ripen sooner than other varieties and can grow in small containers. These are great if you have only a small garden plot.

What should you grow?

There's no reason to grow vegetables that no one will eat. Make a list of the vegetables you and your family like. Plan the garden around your tastes. But once in a while, be adventurous and try something new. You may be pleasantly surprised.

How much space will you need?

You don't need a large garden to provide plenty of fresh vegetables for your family. Tomatoes, eggplants and green peppers are bush plants that require little room. Cucumbers, peas and pole beans are climbers and will grow well along a fence or trellis. Swiss chard, spinach and lettuce plants produce a lot of food, and they don't take up much space. Corn, potatoes, squash and pumpkin are large plants that need more space than other vegetables, 20-4. Even so, because new varieties are constantly being developed, you may find a variety that takes up less space.

Some vegetables are pretty plants and can be grown in a flower garden. You might want to try growing curly leaf lettuce or cabbage beside your marigolds and petunias.

Where should the garden be located?

Sunlight is the most important factor to consider when choosing a location for your garden. Generally, a garden should get sunlight all day. If your garden is shaded part of the time, plant leafy vegetables (like lettuce and spinach) in the shady spots. Devote sunny areas to tomato, eggplant, cucumber and pepper plants. Do not locate the garden under trees. The tree branches would shade the vegetable plants, and the tree roots would deprive the plants of food and moisture.

A level garden plot is better than a sloping one. When it rains, level land holds the rain and absorbs it. If the garden slopes, the rain may run off before much water can be absorbed. Sometimes when rain runs off, good topsoil is taken with it. This process is called *soil erosion*. If your land slopes, you can help prevent soil erosion by planting rows across the slope rather than up and down. The plants which grow across the slope will catch rain water and help keep the topsoil in place.

Where should vegetables be planted?

The best way to plan the placement of vegetables in the garden is to do it on paper first. A pencil, graph paper, seed catalog and list of vegetables you want to grow are the materials you need. See 20-5.

Determine which direction is north. Plant rows in a north/south direction. This way, all the plants will get equal amounts of sunlight.

Draw an outline of the garden to scale on the graph paper. For instance, each square metre (about one square yard) of garden may be equal to four squares on your graph paper. You may want your garden to be five metres (about five yards) long and four metres (about four yards) wide. Thus, the rectangle on the graph paper would be 20 squares by 16 squares.

Arrange the plants according to expected height. Shorter plants should go in the front (the side that gets the most sun). Taller plants should be in the back. This prevents the taller plants from casting shadows over the shorter ones.

Read the planting directions on the seed packages and in the seed catalogs. They will tell you how much space is needed between the rows of plants and between the seeds in each row. The directions will also tell you how deep the seeds should be planted.

Draw the rows and plants on your graph

BURPEE SEEDS

20-4 Some vegetables, such as squash, need a lot of space in which to grow.

20-5 Plan your garden on paper to decide where vegetables should be planted.

paper. When you're ready to plant, use your drawing as a guide. It's a map of your garden.

GETTING THE GARDEN READY

After the heavy rains of early spring, it's time to prepare your garden plot. Pick up a handful of soil. If it is heavy and thick, like mud, it's still too early to plant. When the soil is crumbly and loose in your hand, you can prepare the soil for planting. Successful gardening requires a few basic tools. See 20-6.

Preparing the soil

Clear the area of any rocks. Turn the soil over with a spade. After spading, let the soil stand for a few days. Then rake the garden smooth, 20-7.

Mark the rows for planting. *Stake out* each row as it is drawn on your graph paper plan. To stake out a row, place a wooden stake at each end of the row and tie a string between

them. The string will be your guide for planting a straight row. Follow the directions that come with the seeds to determine how to space the rows. Correct spacing is important so that the plants will grow properly. Make a shallow furrow with the hoe or a sturdy stick. Seeds will be planted in the furrow. See 20-8. Now you're ready to plant.

PLANTING YOUR GARDEN

You will be planting either seeds or seedlings in your garden. *Seedlings* are tiny plants which have already been started indoors. When seedlings are placed into the ground, they are called *transplants*.

Some seeds can be planted directly into the ground in early spring. These are called *cool weather vegetables* because they can withstand cool temperatures (but not frost). Some seeds need more warmth and longer growing periods. These *warm weather vegetables* are

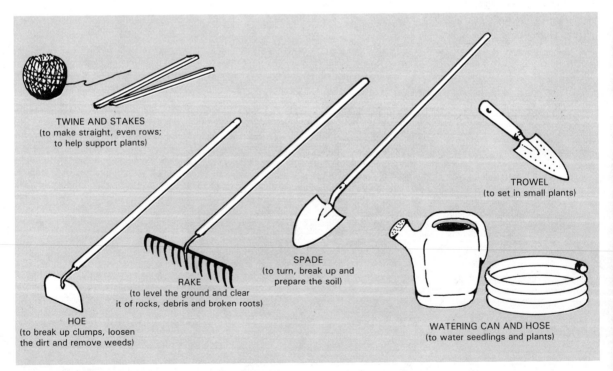

TWINE AND STAKES
(to make straight, even rows;
to help support plants)

TROWEL
(to set in small plants)

SPADE
(to turn, break up and
prepare the soil)

RAKE
(to level the ground and clear
it of rocks, debris and broken roots)

HOE
(to break up clumps, loosen
the dirt and remove weeds)

WATERING CAN AND HOSE
(to water seedlings and plants)

20-6 Gardening usually requires a few basic tools.

often started indoors and then transplanted outside when cool temperatures have passed. Examples of these two types of vegetables are listed in 20-9.

A planting calendar can tell you which plants are cool weather plants and which are warm weather plants. See 20-10. A crop of cool weather vegetables can be started in the early spring. A crop of warm weather vegetables can be planted in late spring. And another cool weather crop can be started in late summer. This *succession gardening* allows you to get the most from your garden.

Some vegetables, such as green beans, can be planted every two weeks for a continuous harvest. The same can be done with lettuce, spinach and radishes. When a harvest is completed, the old plants can be cleared and more seeds can be planted.

It's a good idea to label the stakes at the end of each row with a waterproof marker so you'll know what you have planted in each row of your garden.

Planting seeds outdoors

Before you plant a certain vegetable, consult your planting calendar to be sure the timing is right. After you have staked out the rows and made a shallow furrow, you are ready to place the seeds into the ground. Use the string

20-8 Use a string as a guide for making straight rows. Before planting your seeds, make a shallow furrow in the soil.

20-7 Before planting, you must prepare the soil. Raking makes the garden smooth.

COOL WEATHER VEGETABLES

beets	leeks
broccoli	lettuce
Brussels sprouts	onions
cabbage	parsley
carrots	parsnips
cauliflower	peas
celery	potatoes
Chinese cabbage	radishes
Swiss chard	spinach
chives	turnips

WARM WEATHER VEGETABLES

green beans	peppers
lima beans	pumpkin
corn	summer squash
cucumbers	winter squash
eggplant	tomatoes
cantaloupe	watermelon

20-9 Cool weather vegetables can be planted in early spring. Warm weather vegetables must be planted later, when it is warmer.

as a guide to make a straight row. The proper depth for planting seeds is generally related to the size of the seeds. Small seeds can usually be placed in very shallow furrows and covered with a sprinkling of soil. Large seeds (like beans) should be placed in deeper furrows and covered with dirt. Always read the planting directions on the seed package. Be sure to water the garden thoroughly after the seeds are planted.

Starting seeds indoors

A good time to start seeds is six to eight weeks before you plan to set the plants outside. Seeds need warmth, so put them in a place where the temperature range is 22 to 26°C (72 to 78°F). Seeds also need moisture. They can be started in almost any type of container, as long as there is drainage. Egg cartons, milk cartons and flat boxes are all good. There should be a small hole or holes in the bottom of the container to allow for drainage. Place potting soil in the container and plant the seeds. Cover the seeds with soil, and water thoroughly. Be sure to label the containers so you'll know what you planted.

Keep seedlings warm and away from drafts. Once they have sprouted, it's very important for them to have good light. If the seedlings grow long, thin and weak, they may not be getting enough light. Check them every day to make sure they have enough water. But don't keep them soaked, or they may rot or develop a fungus.

If you are going away for a few days, place a clear plastic bag over the seedlings. This will keep the moisture inside. (You can also do this with regular house plants.) Use a clothespin or a stick to keep the plastic up and away from the plants' leaves. The plants will stay moist for quite a while.

When the seedlings have a good start on growing, it's time to thin out the plants. Take scissors and cut off seedlings that are too crowded. The plants that are left should be far enough apart that their leaves do not touch each other.

Transplanting seedlings into the garden

Seedlings which have been started indoors must be "hardened" before you plant them outside. To do this, place them outside during the day and bring them back inside at night. Do this for a week before transplanting them outside. Hardening helps the plants adjust to their new home outdoors.

SAMPLE PLANTING CALENDAR

APRIL MAY	JUNE JULY	AUGUST	SEPTEMBER	OCTOBER
Plant seeds outdoors:	**Transplant seedlings:**		**Plant seeds outdoors:**	
cool weather vegetables, such as lettuce, cabbage, beets, carrots, peas, radishes, onions, spinach	tomatoes, eggplant, peppers		turnips, beets, parsnips, cabbage, lettuce, broccoli, cauliflower	
	Plant seeds outdoors:			
Start seeds indoors:	warm weather vegetables, such as corn, squash, beans, cucumbers			
tomatoes, eggplant, peppers, (usually 6 to 8 weeks before transplanting outside)				

20-10 This is a sample planting calendar. You may need to modify it according to the region in which you live.

The seedlings are ready to be transplanted when:
1. They have two or more sets of leaves.
2. They have been hardened.
3. Your planting calendar indicates it is the right time to transplant.

The best time to transplant seedlings is on a cloudy day or in the late afternoon. A hot midday sun can wilt the young plants. Be very careful as you transplant seedlings. Their roots and stems are delicate. Plants absorb water and nutrients from the soil through their roots. Damaging the roots may kill the plants.

A spoon is a good tool for gently lifting each seedling out of its container. Keep as much soil on the roots as you can. If you have to hold the plant, hold it by the stem. Place the seedling carefully into a hole and gently push the soil down over the roots. Don't pack the soil down with heavy pressure. Water the plants thoroughly after transplanting.

Some plants do not grow well after they have been transplanted. Examples are cucumber, squash and pumpkin. Other plants, including lettuce, spinach and tomatoes, grow well after being transplanted.

TAKING CARE OF YOUR GARDEN

Once your garden is planted outside, keep it free of weeds. Weeds will rob your vegetable plants of water, nutrients and sunlight. Without water, nutrients and sunlight, your vegetable plants will soon die. Pulling weeds by hand is one way of keeping them under control. This is hard work, and it must be done constantly during the growing season. *Mulching* is a much easier way to control weeds. Place a heavy layer of hay, wood chips, grass clippings or strips of newspaper between rows of plants, 20-11. This heavy layer prevents weeds from growing between the rows of plants.

These organic materials will gradually *degrade* (break down) and become dark, crumbly soil. This breakdown of organic material into soil is called *composting*. Composting is a good, inexpensive way to make excellent soil. Vegetable plants are hungry plants. They need soil rich in nutrients to grow well and yield a good crop. Compost soil is very helpful in keeping the ground light and nourishing.

To make large quantities of rich soil, you can also build a *compost heap*. Pile and wet down leaves, grass clippings, straw, vegetable scraps, eggshells, coffee grounds and newspapers. Bacteria work on these materials, breaking them down to form rich soil. Organic materials should be placed on the heap in layers. Each layer should be about 15 cm (six inches) thick. A few shovelfuls of soil should be added between each layer. Compost

20-11 These tomato plants have been mulched with hay to prevent weeds and to retain moisture in the soil.

heaps may be of any size. They take several weeks or months to develop, depending upon the size of the heap and organic materials used. This rich soil is then transferred to the garden, as needed, to enrich the soil.

While your plants are growing, they will need sunlight, water and food. Plants can get food from the soil. But you can also feed them extra nutrients by using fertilizer. *Fertilizer* is used to make the soil more fertile and productive. It can be purchased in almost any store that sells plants or plant supplies. It's very important to read the directions before using a fertilizer. Too much can ruin your garden. It's also important to distribute fertilizer evenly throughout the garden. Feed your plants early in the morning. Some fertilizers can "burn" the plants if they are applied during the heat of the day.

Water your garden thoroughly between rains. Morning is the best time for this job. Evening waterings can attract insects and encourage fungus growth and plant rot.

Insects are a big problem in most gardens. They can eat every part of a plant and destroy an entire garden. Many gardeners use *pesticides* to control insects and diseases. Pesticides are toxic (poisonous) substances that kill insects and other tiny organisims that cause disease. You can apply them as a spray or a dust.

Remember, pesticides are poisons. Poisons for insects can also harm people and animals. Follow these precautions when you use pesticides:
• Follow all directions carefully.
• Do not spray or dust on windy days.
• Store pesticides out of reach of children and animals. Keep the containers tightly covered.
• Don't throw unused portions down the drain. Pesticides may corrode pipes, or they may contaminate sewage systems or the water supply.
• Wash your hands thoroughly after handling pesticides.
• Wait a few days after spraying or dusting to pick any vegetables.
• Thoroughly rinse the vegetables you pick.

WINDOWSILL GARDENING

If you don't have outside space for a garden, you can have a garden growing in containers near your windows. See 20-12. You can grow lettuce, spinach, radishes, parsley, chives and herbs of all kinds. A box 15 cm deep (about 6 inches) is basically all you need. Tomato plants and root vegetables such as beets and carrots need deeper containers, at least 30 cm (12 inches) deep.

There are many kinds of midget fruits and vegetables you can grow in containers. You can grow them indoors on a windowsill or in a hanging basket. Midget beets, carrots and radishes will do well next to a sunny window.

Many herbs are very easy to grow on the windowsill. They can be planted in any kind of container that has good drainage. They require basic potting soil, adequate water and lots of sunlight. Parsley, sweet basil, chives and tarragon are good choices for a beginning gardener.

Whether you grow tiny or full-sized plants, be sure they get enough sun, water and fertilizer. And be sure they are planted in soil with good drainage. With an indoor garden, you don't have to worry about the weather. You can plant your crops anytime and harvest them throughout the year.

RUBBERMAID, INC.

20-12 You can plant an indoor garden if you don't have space outside.

toDefine

composting . . .
compost heap . . .
cool weather vegetables . . .
degrade . . . fertilizer . . .
mulching . . . pesticides . . .
organic gardening . . .
seedlings . . . soil erosion . . .
stake out . . .
succession gardening . . .
transplants . . .
warm weather vegetables

toDiscuss

1. List at least three reasons people plant vegetable gardens.
2. Why is it a good idea to use a seed catalog when planning your garden?
3. How do you decide what vegetables should be grown in your garden?
4. When planning the location of your garden, what is the most important consideration?
5. Why shouldn't you locate your garden under trees?
6. Why should rows in the garden run north and south?
7. How can seeds be started indoors?
8. Why must seedlings be "hardened" before they are transplanted outdoors?
9. When is the best time to transplant seedlings?
10. What can you do to prevent weeds from getting out of control in the garden?
11. Why is compost soil good for the garden?
12. List at least four safety precautions you should follow when using pesticides.
13. Name at least six foods which could be grown in an indoor garden.

toDo

1. Write for some seed catalogs. Study them to learn which varieties of vegetables are best suited to the climate in your area.
2. Using seed catalogs, plan a small garden for your home or school. (Remember, the garden doesn't have to be large to yield a variety of fresh vegetables.)
3. Invite a county extension agent to your class to discuss home gardening.
4. Collect containers which could be used to grow vegetables on a patio or deck. Visit the school cafeteria to see what is thrown out. You may find large cans and ice cream containers which are deep enough to grow larger plants such as tomatoes or carrots.
5. Create an herb garden in your classroom.
6. Visit a county fair to see the vegetable exhibits. Keep a list of the varieties that seem to take the top prizes. (These are probably the best varieties for your local climate.)
7. Visit a nursery and look at the seedlings available for transplanting. Compare the cost of a garden planted with nursery plants versus one planted with seeds started at home.
8. Demonstrate what happens when seedlings do not get enough light, water or both. Obtain four tomato plant seedlings. Plant 1 should receive light and water. Plant 2 should receive light but no water. Plant 3 should receive water but no light. Plant 4 should receive neither light nor water. Check the seedlings every day. Which plant looks healthy? Write down your results and report them to class.

21

A food career for you

Is a career in food for you?
After reading this chapter, you
will be able to discuss a variety
of careers related to foods. You
will be able to describe careers
related to food including careers
in: food service, marketing,
processing and providing information
about foods.

*C*an you picture yourself as a master chef, a food processing plant manager or a dietitian? These are just a few of the many careers that are related to food.

You may already be familiar with the jobs of waiters, waitresses and grocery store clerks. Many other jobs are related to foods too. For instance, do you know what a nutritionist does? Have you thought about a career in food science, marketing or public relations?

Since all people need food, it's no surprise that so many jobs are somehow related to food. These jobs fall into four main groups.
1. Food service.
2. Marketing food.
3. Processing food.
4. Providing information about food.

FOOD SERVICE

When people think of a career in foods, they often think about the restaurant business first. There are thousands of restaurants in this country. They range from small cafes to fast food chains to fancy restaurants.

Many jobs in restaurants offer opportunities for you to break into the food service business. Without experience, you might begin with a job waiting on or clearing tables. Or you might work in the kitchen of a restaurant on busy evenings and weekends. While the pay is low, you will gain valuable experience in the storage, preparation and service of food.

Another type of food service is *catering*. Some businesses specialize in preparing and serving food for private parties. Many catered events take place on weekends. You might be able to find a part-time job with a caterer while you are a student.

Many institutions have food service operations. School cafeterias, college dining rooms and hospital kitchens all employ food service workers. You may also find a job working in the kitchens of corporation cafeterias or dining rooms. If you live near a large airport, you might work for a company which prepares meals for the airlines. In general, the skills needed in institutional kitchens and dining rooms are very similar to those needed in restaurants.

All food service operations, both institutions and restaurants, employ three basic types of workers: service workers, kitchen workers and management.

Food service workers

Food service workers deal with the public. Service workers include waiters and waitresses who serve food, 21-1. They also include bus persons who clear and set tables. In restaurants where alcoholic beverages are served, bartenders are part of the service staff. Larger restaurants have other service workers, such as cashiers and hosts who handle reservations and seat guests. Some restaurants have a *maître d'* who is in charge of the service in the dining room. A maître d' usually has years of experience in customer service. Often, the maître d' can cook special dishes, such as flaming desserts, at the table and serve them with a flair.

Kitchen workers

In the kitchen of a small restaurant, you may find only one chef and a helper. Large restaurants have a *master chef* and *assistant chefs,* each in charge of a certain aspect of the menu, 21-2. For instance, there might be a pastry chef, a grill chef and a salad chef in addition to the master chef.

Good chefs are well paid and in great demand. It can take years to learn how to cook well. A person may go to school for a few weeks to learn fast food cooking techniques. But master chefs may study and work ten or

TUPPERWARE® HOME PARTIES

21-1 A food service worker may wait on customers at a restaurant.

WESTERN ICEBERG LETTUCE, INC.

21-2 A salad chef creates appetizing salads and relish trays.

more years to be qualified to run a fine gourmet kitchen, 21-3.

A large kitchen also requires many helpers to wash pots and pans, scrape dirty dishes and run the dishwasher. Other people are also needed to help with the preparation of the food. These people may do such jobs as peeling vegetables or slicing bread.

Management

The *restaurant manager* is in charge of the entire operation of a restaurant. (In a small restaurant, the manager is often the owner.) The manager decides whom to hire and what will be served. This person generally makes sure the quality of service is kept at a high level. Controlling costs and making sure the business earns a profit is the responsibility of the manager. Capable restaurant managers are always in demand. A restaurant manager usually has many years of experience in food service. Often this person has a college degree in food service management.

MARKETING FOOD

Marketing food is not simply a matter of selling food to consumers. Research, technology, advertising and distribution are all involved in marketing food. A great number and variety of careers are available in the marketing field. Some occupations deal with developing new food products. Others are involved in selling food in stores.

Developing food products

Have you ever thought about how new food products are developed? A great deal of expense and risk is involved in marketing a new product. In fact, less than one idea out of every thousand actually becomes a product that is sold nationwide.

The development of a food product usually begins by identifying a consumer need. For instance, a food company may think that older people who live alone have a need for inexpensive, nutritious, single-serving main dishes. To test the theory, the food company may hire a *market researcher*. This person would have some background in psychology and statistics. He or she would talk with older people who live alone to see if they would use such main dishes. After interviewing perhaps a hundred older people, the market researcher would report the findings to the food company.

If the market researcher gave an encouraging report, the company would develop several product ideas. They might come up with concepts such as "frozen chicken crêpes" or "stew for one." Next, the market researcher would develop a survey about these product ideas. He or she would survey several thousand older people. The results might show that people seem to prefer one product over another.

Next, the company would produce a small amount of the product that people like best. They would invite older people to taste it in the company's test kitchen. Trained interviewers would observe and record the reactions. The interviewers would note how people responded to the taste, color and size of the portion. If the results were good, the company would probably put a product manager in charge of the new product.

A *product manager* is responsible for developing a new product. The product manager calls on the talents of various people within the company. *Food technologists* decide how the product will be produced, labeled and packaged. *Factory workers* make the product. A sales force is needed to sell the product and make sure the product is properly displayed. *Advertising specialists* plan advertising campaigns using television, radio and newspapers, 21-4.

The new product is tested by selling it in a single city. Market researchers then study how the product is selling. Market researchers find out who is buying the product, who isn't buying the product and why. If the product sells well in the test market, the company may begin selling it on a national basis. You may then finally see it where you shop.

To increase the chances of product success, food companies employ many skilled people on their marketing teams. Members of marketing teams have advanced training in subjects such as home economics, statistics, psychology, packaging and food technology. Product managers usually have a master's degree in business administration.

Selling food in stores

Once food products have been developed, the next marketing step begins. This step involves selling the food to the consumer. There are many jobs related to selling food to the consumer.

When visiting a supermarket, have you noticed the people working there and the various jobs they do? Selling food involves a variety of occupations. For instance, a *stock clerk* receives and counts products delivered to the supermarket. The stock clerk may mark the items and place them on shelves or store them until they are needed. Students can often find part-time jobs as stock clerks.

A good *checker* can make a big difference in a supermarket. A checker with a pleasant personality and who is also accurate, can improve customer relations. Checkers ring up sales and often bag groceries. They know the prices of many products. Some stores hire students to work as checkers after school. Experience working part-time could qualify you for a full-time summer job.

An entry level job in a supermarket, such as being a stock clerk or checker, may lead in other career directions as well. You may be interested in a position with a firm that sells food to supermarkets. Working part-time in the store, you would get a chance to see salespeople. You would get an idea about what their work is like. You may decide that you want to go into sales. Supermarket experience may be an asset when you apply for a job. Your supermarket experience could also help you if you wanted to move into a management position in a supermarket.

In most supermarkets, the store is divided into different departments. Each department has a manager or clerk in charge. For instance, the produce manager is in charge of fresh fruits and vegetables, 21-5. The meat manager supervises the butchers in the meat

CULINARY INSTITUTE

21-3 These students are studying how to become master chefs.

SUNKIST GROWERS, INC.

21-4 Advertising specialists plan advertising campaigns to promote products.

SUNKIST GROWERS, INC.

21-5 This produce manager takes pride in creating an attractive display.

department. Butchers are responsible for cutting up large sides of meat into chops, steaks and roasts. The butcher also weighs and prices the meat before it is put out for sale. The dairy manager is responsible for stocking the dairy case. The dairy case contains milk and milk products, plus other items that need refrigeration such as eggs and refrigerated doughs.

Experience may help you to advance to department manager and eventually store manager. A *store manager* is responsible for what happens in the store. Hiring people, making sure merchandise is properly priced and handling customer complaints are all part of a manager's job. The store manager is also responsible for the operation of the store. For instance, when checkout lines become long, the manager may open another register. A store manager must have a strong business background and be able to deal with people.

Some supermarkets employ home economists. *Supermarket home economists* provide customers with shopping information, 21-6. A supermarket home economist must have a college degree in home economics with training in foods, nutrition and consumer education.

Specialty stores. Experience in a supermarket might lead you to open your own food store. It could be a store specializing in cheese, coffee, meat, fish, candy or health foods. It might even be a bakery. Running your own small business is very challenging. You may be the buyer, salesperson and bookkeeper. The hours are usually much longer than when you are working for someone else. But if you want to be your own boss, the rewards may be worth the effort.

Before opening a food store, you have to know something about your products. For instance, if you wanted to open your own bakery, you would need to know how to bake. (Or, you could hire a professional baker.) To learn about baking, you might take baking courses at a vocational school. Or you might get a job as an *apprentice* in a commercial bakery. An apprentice baker learns on the job by working under an experienced baker. At first, you would be asked to do jobs like carrying bags of flour to the bakers and cleaning the mixers. You would also have a chance to learn how various rolls, cakes and pastries are made. In time, you would learn how to operate the mixers and other equipment. You would also learn the oven temperatures at which products are baked. Eventually, you would become a skilled baker.

You could earn a living by working in a commercial bakery or in a big hotel kitchen. With enough experience, you could start your own bakery. This job is not for everyone. Bakers generally are at work by five o'clock in the morning. Their work requires that they stand up most of the day. In the summer, the kitchen can become very hot. It's a demanding job. But for someone willing to work hard and learn the art of baking, it can be a very satisfying career.

PROCESSING FOOD

Food seldom goes straight from a farm, ranch or orchard to the store where you buy it. Most food is processed in some way — usually canned or frozen. This is done at a processing plant. Even food that is sold fresh, such as produce or meat, may not go straight to the store. Instead, it may go to a center for storage or special packaging and distribution.

In a processing plant, most of the work is done by machines. If the food must be peeled, cored or packed, it is fed into special machines designed to do the task, 21-7. Each machine has an operator to check that the machine is working properly. Attendants watch food as it moves along conveyor belts. They remove any damaged pieces. Quality control is important in a food processing plant. Inspectors check every step of the process. Government inspectors also visit processing plants to make sure the food is being handled under sanitary conditions.

Some employees are assigned to the shipping department. There they receive the food to be processed, maintain the inventory and ship processed food.

Most food processing plants hire people without experience and train them on the job. High school graduates are preferred. A few jobs, such as machine maintenance, would require additional training.

Supervisors at the plant assign workers to their jobs. They also train new employees and oversee workers to make sure everything is running smoothly. Supervisors generally start out as workers and are promoted because they work hard and know the operation.

A *plant manager* is in charge of the processing plant. This person makes major decisions regarding how much food to process and when to buy new equipment. The plant manager also assigns employees' work schedules. How does a person become a plant manager? In some companies supervisors are given special training to become managers. Other companies may require that the manager have a college degree. In a processing plant where the machinery is very complex, a plant manager often must have a degree in engineering.

FOOD INFORMATION

What do home economics teachers, food editors and dietitians have in common? These people all have careers dealing with information about food. If you enjoy working with people and know a lot about food, perhaps you would like a food information career. Education, mass media and dietetics are areas you might consider.

Education

Would you like to teach a foods course like the one you are taking right now? You might enjoy teaching others the skills you are learning. To qualify as a *home economics teacher* in a public school, you need a degree in home economics. In most states, you also need to be a certified teacher. To become certified, you need to take certain education courses and acquire some practice teaching experience.

In addition to formal education, a successful teacher needs certain skills. You would need to be able to demonstrate how to prepare and cook food. Your students would come to your class with different levels of ability. You would have to be able to detect these differences. You would need to work with each student to help him or her get the most from your course. A good teacher is always looking for new ways of teaching the basic information in a course. This makes learning more interesting and meaningful for the students.

You may enjoy teaching adults. There are several types of jobs that might appeal to you.

JEWEL FOOD STORES

21-6 A supermarket home economist is prepared to assist and advise customers about their food purchases.

SUNKIST GROWERS, INC.

21-7 People working in processing plants often operate machines. This machine picks up oranges and places them in crates.

Usually you need some special training to qualify as an instructor. For instance, suppose you wanted to teach home economics, nutrition or marketing at the college level. You would need at least a master's degree in your field. Some colleges and universities require their teachers to have a doctorate. To teach at a school for professional chefs, you would need a combination of training and work experience.

You may be able to earn a living by teaching at a private cooking school or by teaching others in your home. This means you will need to become skilled in one or more aspects of cooking. You do not have to have a college degree to do this. But you will probably need to take special cooking courses.

You may find it interesting to become an *extension home economist*. Usually, one or more home economists are employed in county cooperative extension offices. Extension home economists educate people in the community. They answer questions about food, clothing, money management and other aspects of home and family life. They often develop short courses which are taught throughout the county, 21-8. They also keep homemakers up-to-date by writing newspaper articles and sometimes appearing on radio and television.

An extension home economist has a college degree in home economics. If you like a job with lots of variety, you might enjoy being an extension home economist.

Mass media

Food-related jobs in the media can be exciting and interesting. If you decide to pursue a media career in food, the chances are remote that you will become a television star. But there are many other opportunities available.

For instance, you might become a *food editor* for a newspaper or magazine. It would be your job to research and write interesting articles about food. Before publishing recipes, you might test them out yourself to be sure they work well. You would probably work with a photographer and a food stylist to prepare photographs for your article. A *food stylist* prepares foods to look their best before a camera. There is a special art to preparing foods that look appetizing in a photograph. Special attention must be given to colors and other details so all the elements of a photograph look good together.

Food writers also work in the public relations departments of food companies or for public relations firms. *Public relations* is different from advertising. The goal of the public relations department is to make people aware of various products. Often, they do this by developing new and interesting ways to use food products. For instance, suppose a whipped topping is being promoted. A public relations firm may create a book of recipes using the product. If you work in public relations, you will develop press releases about your clients' products. You will develop special promotions and new ideas for products. Many of the pictures in this textbook were developed for public relations purposes. Public relations people also attend conventions, meetings and press conferences to give information about their clients' products.

Some food writers work independently. They write articles for many different companies rather than working full-time for one company. This is called *free-lancing*. Free-lance writing requires a great deal of self-discipline. No one is there to tell you when to work and to make sure you get your work done.

Communicating about food can be the basis for a very interesting career. To qualify, you must be a good writer. Besides courses in writing and journalism, you need to take courses in food preparation, nutrition and consumer issues. A college degree in home economics would provide a good foundation for entry into this field.

In addition to formal education, success as a food writer requires a high personal interest in food. Do you like to cook? When you eat in a restaurant, do you try new items to see what they are like? If a friend serves a dish you particularly like, do you ask for the recipe and try it yourself? If you want the material you write to sell, it must be of interest to a large number of people. Writing interesting copy is easier if you have a strong, personal interest in the subject.

Dietetics

Dietitians and nutritionists have careers in dietetics. *Dietetics* is the science of applying the principles of nutrition. Depending on where they work, *dietitians* apply principles of nutrition in many different ways. A *nutritionist* is a dietitian with additional training.

In hospitals and nursing homes, dietitians plan meals for patients and staff. Meals must be nutritious and appetizing. The dietitian is always concerned with the special food needs of people with health problems. For instance, patients with heart conditions often require low-sodium diets and must not have salt in their food. Some patients need a bland diet which omits spicy and fatty foods. The dietitian works closely with doctors and nurses to be sure these special food needs are understood and met. Often a dietitian will meet individually with the patient to explain a special diet.

Many dietitians work for government agencies in various health programs. For instance, a local health clinic might offer a program for pregnant women. This program might include sessions led by a dietitian or nutritionist.

A nutritionist can specialize in research, public health, therapeutic diets or food service administration. Like dietitians, nutritionists apply their skills in health care facilities and government agencies. They teach in universities and hospitals. They also work as members of public and private research teams that attempt to find answers to such questions as:

- What causes obesity?
- What happens to children who don't eat properly?
- What role does nutrition play in preventing disease?
- Are synthetic foods nutritionally superior to natural foods?

Dietitians and nutritionists are often employed by various food companies. Public interest in nutrition is growing. Food companies are paying more attention to the nutritional value of their products. Dietitians and nutritionists become involved in product development, package information and consumer information, 21-9.

Perhaps a career in this field sounds interesting to you, but you aren't interested in spending four or more years in college. You may want to attend a vocational school and

WESTCHESTER COUNTY COOPERATIVE EXTENSION

21-8 One of the jobs of an extension home economist is advising county residents about good nutrition.

SUNKIST GROWERS, INC.

21-9 A dietitian or nutritionist may work in the test kitchen of a food company.

take the courses required to qualify as a *dietetic assistant*. Or you could enroll in a two-year program and earn an associate degree as a *dietetic technician*. As a dietetic assistant or technician, you would be assisting dietitians and nutritionists.

WORKING TOWARD YOUR FUTURE CAREER

Perhaps you think you are a long way from the position of "supermarket manager," "master chef" or "food editor." Well, you're right. But people with these jobs once had no more knowledge and experience in their fields than you have right now. They developed their skills with training and experience. You can do the same. If you think you would enjoy a career in foods, make up your mind to qualify. See 21-10.

CULINARY INSTITUTE

21-10 If you enjoy working with food, a career in foods may be for you.

to Define

apprentice . . . catering . . .
dietitian . . .
extension home economist . . .
food editor . . .
food technologist . . .
free-lancing . . .
market researcher . . .
master chef . . .
nutritionist . . .
plant manager . . .
product manager . . .
public relations . . .
restaurant manager . . .
store manager . . .
supermarket home economist

to Discuss

1. List four basic categories of food-related careers.

2. List three basic types of workers in food service.

3. What are the general responsibilities of a restaurant manager?

4. Which people work with a product manager to develop a new product?

5. Name at least two careers in the area of marketing.

6. What kind of training do members of marketing teams have?

7. How can an entry level job in a supermarket lead into other food careers?

8. What type of background should a store manager have?

9. What type of worker might be promoted to the position of supervisor in a food processing plant?

10. Describe at least two careers in the area of food processing.

11. What kind of decisions does a plant manager make?

12. Name at least two careers which deal with providing information about food.

13. What skills should a successful home economics teacher have?

14. What training does an extension home economist have?

15. Give examples of at least three food-related careers in the area of mass media.

16. What types of courses should you take to prepare to become a food writer?

17. Where might a dietitian be employed?

to Do

1. As a class project, compile a list of food-related careers in your community. Make a large chart or bulletin board display showing the types of jobs. You may also wish to include the salary range, training involved and possibilities for advancement.

2. Invite people who work in the food industry to come to class and talk about their careers.

3. Visit a restaurant to learn about restaurant operation. Prepare a list of questions in advance.

4. Contact the food editor of your local newspaper. Discuss how a food article is prepared. Then write an article on some aspect of food. (You may wish to submit it to your school paper.) This will be good experience in the area of journalism.

5. Observe the school cafeteria staff at work preparing and serving lunch and cleaning up. Make a list of the skills they must have. If time permits, discuss institutional food service careers with the staff.

6. Conduct a market research project about the food in your school cafeteria. Prepare a survey and poll students to discover their likes and dislikes regarding the food. Tally your results and attempt to work with the cafeteria staff to modify the food service.

22

The future of food

After reading this chapter, you will be able to list several agricultural and technological developments in the area of foods. You also will be able to discuss present and future trends in food production and how they might improve food supplies for the world.

What will you be eating years from now? Will there be enough food for everyone? Some people today are worried that there will soon be too many people and not enough food. They are afraid that the population will increase at an alarming rate, while the amount of farmland will decrease. They also worry that changes in the weather, which have hurt food crops in the past, will be even worse in the future. But is the future really that gloomy? Let's take a look at the facts and current trends.

HOW FAST IS THE POPULATION GROWING?

Before the industrial period of the 1700's birth rates were very high. But, because of wars, famines, plagues and other disasters, death rates were also high. The result was that the population stayed almost the same.

As industry developed, methods of producing, preserving and shipping food improved. This meant fewer famines to reduce the population. Improved sanitation, medical care and education reduced the threat of plagues and other illness. As a result, death rates dropped. But birth rates continued at the same high rate. These factors caused the population to increase very rapidly.

This trend, however, has begun to reverse. As countries become more industrialized, people, who once lived on farms, have moved to the cities to work in industries. The people remaining on farms must produce more food to feed those in the cities, 22-1

In the cities, large families are considered a disadvantage. It costs more to raise children in the city than in the country. Moreover, in the city children are not needed to help with chores as they were on the farm.

In recent years, the rate of population growth has started to go down in industrialized countries. (Industrialized countries are commonly referred to as developed countries.) It has even started to drop in many developing countries as well. (Developing countries are countries which are striving to become more industrialized.) This does not mean that there are fewer people. The total number of people has continued to increase, but at a slower rate than before.

The end result of all these trends has been a decrease in the population growth rate for much of the world. This decrease has already occurred in a number of industrialized countries, such as the United States, Russia and Japan. It is also taking place in other countries such as China, South Korea, India and Egypt.

WORLD FOOD SOURCES AND HABITS

There are over four billion people in the world today. They eat vast amounts of food each year. They eat fruits, vegetables and other foods. But most of the world's people use grain as the staple food of their diet. Over 70 percent of the world's cropland is used to raise grain, 22-2. The most important grains are rice and wheat, followed by corn, barley, oats and rye.

Grain can be eaten directly or indirectly. It is eaten *directly* as a vegetable or flour product. Grain is eaten *indirectly* by feeding it to animals. From these animals we get meat, milk and eggs. Grains eaten indirectly provide the world's people with almost two-thirds of the kilojoules (Calories) and half of the protein they consume. Listed below are sources of protein for the world's people:

Grains	50%
Legumes (beans, peas)	20%
Animals	25%
Fish	5%

DEERE AND COMPANY

22-1 *Technology will help future farmers to produce enough food to feed more people than ever before. This planter can plant up to 16 rows at a time.*

DEERE AND COMPANY

22-2 *Much of the world's cropland is used to raise grain. Grains are staple foods for most of the world's population.*

In industrialized countries such as the United States, most grains are eaten indirectly in foods such as meat, milk and eggs. Each person in the United States uses an average of about 900 kilograms (2,000 pounds) of grain each year. But only about 170 kilograms (150 pounds) of that is eaten directly in grain products such as cereal or bread. By contrast, people in developing countries may eat as little as 180 kilograms (about 400 pounds) of grain each year. Most of this grain is eaten directly.

The eating habits of people in developing countries are likely to change in the future. As their countries become more industrialized and personal incomes rise, people's eating patterns may change. At first, they will tend to buy more of the same foods they are used to eating. Next, they will begin buying different types of food. Usually, they will add meats, fruits and vegetables to their diets. They will spend more money on pleasure foods, such as cakes and candies. (People in developed countries eat three times as much sugar as people in developing countries. They eat more than four times as much meat, fat and oil. And they eat about six times as much milk and eggs.) The trend is toward a pattern of eating more food and having more varied diets as countries become richer. This will create a need for additional amounts and kinds of food in the future.

TRENDS IN AGRICULTURE

Fortunately, food is a renewable resource. Food is not like coal or oil, which have limited supplies and cannot be restored readily. Wherever the soil and climate permit, food crops can be planted and grown over and over again. Fortunately, too, there are several ways of increasing food production. New technology, new farming methods and high-yielding varieties of plants and animals offer promising solutions. Improvements in these areas have already produced striking results in the United States.

United States farmers now produce one-third more wheat on one-third fewer acres

than in the past, 22-3. The development of *hybrid* corn (a combination of several varieties) has tripled corn yields in recent years. Less than four percent of the total United States population are farmers. Less land and fewer farmers are now needed because production methods have become more efficient.

The United States provides food for its own people. It also produces large surpluses for export to the rest of the world. The United States accounts for 65 percent of the world's grain exports. Agricultural products are one of the United States' major exports.

What makes many farmers in the United States successful? It's true, of course, that the United States has one of the world's largest areas of fertile land. The country also has a good growing climate and adequate rainfall for most of that land. But these advantages have always been present. They do not account for the recent dramatic increase in

USDA

22-3 United States farmers produce more food than ever before, despite a shrinking farm population and use of less land.

316

yields. This dramatic increase in yields is the result of new developments in technology, farming methods and special breeding programs. Many other countries can adapt and build on these developments for their own special needs.

From horse to machine

Many years ago, most farm work in the United States was done by human labor. Then a dramatic change took place. Horse drawn machines took over much of the work formerly done by people, 22-4. Then, gasoline-powered machines replaced horses. The result in both cases was that farmers were able to grow more food than ever before. One farmer could handle much more land. The average size of each farm also increased. This happened as farmers took over the land of neighbors who sold out and moved to the city.

Chemical fertilizers

Most farmers in the United States depend on chemical fertilizers. In recent years, chem-ical fertilizers have increased crop yields by over 50 percent. They have restored fertility to soil that was worn out by intensive farming. In some parts of the world, two to five times more food might be grown if chemical fertilizers were used.

Petroleum is used in the production of chemical fertilizers. Petroleum is also needed to run tractors and other farm machinery. For this reason, the high cost of petroleum is a growing problem to farmers around the world.

Pest control

Every year, up to one-third of the world's food crops are destroyed by pests such as rodents and insects, and by disease and weeds. Pesticides and herbicides have already helped to reduce this loss, 22-5. *Pesticides* are used to kill rodents and insects which can destroy crops. *Herbicides* kill weeds which compete with crops for water, sunlight, fertilizer and space. These methods are effective, but they do pose a threat to the environment.

DEERE AND COMPANY

22-4 Many years ago, most farm work was done with horse drawn machines.

DEERE AND COMPANY

22-5 The use of pesticides and herbicides helps to reduce crop losses due to rodents, insects, disease and weeds.

Other methods are available which pose little or no threat to the environment. For instance, *crop rotation* aids in pest control because it changes and mixes up the conditions which favor certain pests. Natural predators such as birds and some insects can help control the pest population. Weeds can be controlled by using cultivating tractors or hand labor. None of these methods will eliminate all pests and weeds. A combination of techniques is usually necessary, including some use of pesticides and herbicides.

Conserving water

Much of the world's land is too dry for normal farming. Even areas that usually get enough rain may suffer droughts which cause food shortages. New systems are being developed which make farmers more independent of nature's whims.

One system, called *trickle irrigation,* can produce savings of 50 percent or more in both water and energy. The system uses small, "leaky" pipes placed near plants, 22-6. Fertilizer can be added to water as it trickles slowly through the pipes. Both water and fertilizer can be brought to the root system of each plant.

Another way of saving water is through *controlled environment agriculture,* which is now in commercial use. Instead of growing crops in the field, with the risk of frost or drought, crops can be raised in protected enclosures. These enclosures are like greenhouses. Controlled environment agriculture allows farmers to control the amount of moisture, nutrients, light and heat.

Growing crops in a controlled environment in water, instead of soil, is called *hydroponics.* Hydroponics can produce yields 10 to 50 times higher than crops grown in traditional fields. By using the hydroponics method, crops can be grown year-round. Because this method recycles water, it needs only one to five percent as much water as crops grown in fields. Chemical fertilizers in the water are also recycled so that less is needed. This also eliminates the problem of polluting streams, ponds, and lakes with the runoff chemicals.

Another way to save water is to breed plants that use water more efficiently. For instance, plants with small leaves (or none at all, such as the cactus) lose water less rapidly than broadleaf plants.

Improved farm practices

Some improvements in farm practices can greatly increase farm productivity. Agricultural research gives detailed data about such things as how much fertilizer should be used on different crops. Research can also tell the farmer how deep to plow soil or what vitamins should be fed to a calf. Timing is also important. The results of research can help a farmer know when to apply fertilizer to plants for the greatest benefit. Also, based on research, the

USDA

22-6 Irrigation systems are being studied and improved to make the most efficient use of limited water supplies.

farmer will know when and how to use pesticides effectively.

Sometimes improvements are very simple. In the Philippines, a small amount of fertilizer is mixed with soil to form a mud ball. This is placed near the roots of plants. This method increases yields by 30 to 50 percent, compared to the usual method of spreading fertilizer on top of the soil.

Minimum tillage

The *minimum tillage* system skips the practice of plowing the soil before planting, 22-7. With special tools, seeds are planted in a slit in the soil without plowing the field in advance. Herbicides replace the need to use cultivating tractors to keep down weed growth. This saves fuel and the expense of heavy machinery. Minimum tillage also conserves soil, water and fertilizer because by not disturbing the soil, there is less erosion. The system also makes more farming possible on sloping and poorly drained land.

Multicropping

Multicropping involves planting seeds between rows of half-grown crops. When the first crop is harvested, the second is almost grown and ready to be harvested before the growing season ends. Multicropping is useful in areas where land is difficult to clear and in countries which have little good farmland. It enables farmers to get the most from limited acreage. Multicropping could double or even quadruple the amount of food produced in many areas.

Raising more livestock

Meat from livestock is one of the best sources of high-quality protein for people. A lot of meat is eaten in the United States. This is sometimes criticized as a wasteful use of grain. This is because animals such as cattle, sheep and goats use about four kilograms (eight pounds) of grain to produce about one-half kilogram (one pound) of meat. However, these animals also thrive on grass, hay, stalks and leaves left after harvesting a crop. These are products that people either cannot or prefer not to eat.

About two-thirds of the world's farmland is in pasture and meadow. Over half of this land is not suitable for food crops, 22-8. Raising livestock is the only effective use for this land. In developing countries, grazing animals feed almost entirely on wild plants and grass. Even in developed countries, only about 25 percent of animal feed comes from grain.

Animals such as pigs and poultry require

22-7 *This corn was planted using the minimum tillage system. The crop was planted with little or no plowing to break up the soil.*

22-8 *Much of the world's land is not suitable for growing human food crops. Raising livestock is the most effective way to produce food on this kind of land.*

The future of food **319**

less food to raise than animals such as cattle. Poultry and pigs need only about one kilogram (two pounds) of feed to add about one-half kilogram (one pound) of body weight. This feed can include various wastes and by-products, including table scraps. Also some animals can be selected and bred to gain weight on even less feed, 22-9.

Poultry and pigs also breed faster than cows and sheep. Cows, for instance, typically have one calf at a time, whereas pigs have several offspring in one litter. It's now possible to increase the average size of litters even more.

New breeds of animals

Careful selection and crossbreeding have produced animals that are meatier and healthier than in the past. A new breed that holds some promise for the future is the "beefalo." This animal was developed by crossing cattle and buffalo. The beefalo thrives on grass and weeds, and it gains weight twice as fast as beef cattle. The beefalo is healthier than most breeds of cattle and adapts well to rugged land and climates with temperature extremes. It is larger and leaner than beef cattle and contains twice the protein per animal.

High-yielding seed varieties

Recently, high-yielding varieties of seeds have become available to farmers throughout the world. These varieties generally mature earlier, produce more grain, and are more resistant to plant disease. The plants have shorter, stiffer stalks, so that using more fertilizer increases the grain yield rather than the size of the whole plant. High-yielding varieties of seeds are now used in nearly half of the total wheat acreage. High-yielding varieties are also used in almost one-third of the total rice acreage world-wide.

Improvements in handling the harvest

The industry of agriculture is often called *agri-industry*. Agri-industry has done a great deal to increase the amount of food available to feed the world. Technological advances in the food processing industry have provided greater variety, better quality and more convenient food. Before the invention of refrigerators, for instance, many fresh fruits and vegetables could only be eaten while in season. Even then, they were only available in the area in which they were grown.

We now use many frozen foods. They are convenient and are usually of high quality, at economical prices. For instance, food science has developed frozen concentrates that produce fruit juice which tastes similar to fresh juice and costs less.

Refrigerated trucks and freight cars have improved the methods by which food is distributed and stored. Preventing unnecessary losses helps to make more food available. As much as 25 percent of the world's food harvest is lost to rats, insects and fungus before it reaches the table. Improved storage facilities would help many countries keep enough grain to feed their own people without depending upon imports.

NEW FOODS IN YOUR FUTURE

Besides using new methods to grow food, we are likely to be eating many new kinds of food in the future, 22-10. Scientists have already developed wheat, corn, rice, barley, sorghum and even potatoes with a higher protein content. Scientists have crossed wheat and rye to produce "triticale." Triticale is a new, higher protein grain that combines the high yield of wheat with the disease resistance of rye.

New ways are also being found to use items which were once considered by-products or garbage. The seeds from cotton plants are a good example. Years ago, food scientists discovered how to remove the oil from the seeds. Today, cottonseed oil is used in many foods. Scientists are now developing ways to make the high-protein leftovers useful to people.

Farming the sea

The world fish catch now provides only five percent of the total protein people eat. Many fish and other forms of sea life could be farmed and used to feed people or livestock. For instance, millions of *krill,* small, shrimp-like creatures, are available to boost protein supplies. A plentiful supply of high-protein algae could be used for animal feed. Fish and other seafood can be raised and harvested in enclosed bodies of water called *fish farms.*

Engineered foods

Engineered foods are new foods or imitations of old, familiar ones. They may be made with natural or synthetic ingredients. They may include *additives* to increase their acceptance in terms of nutrition, appetite appeal, storage, economy or convenience. Examples of engineered foods are breakfast items that offer concentrated, balanced nutrition in forms that look and taste like cookies.

Synthetic ingredients are produced in a laboratory from materials that wouldn't ordinarily be considered food. All foods are a mixture of chemicals. Oranges, for instance, are a mixture of about 225 chemical compounds. White potatoes are a combination of about 125 chemical compounds. Scientists are able to analyze and separate out useful chemicals in food and duplicate these compounds in a laboratory, 22-11.

USDA

22-10 Scientists are producing many new foods which might be available to you in the future.

USDA

22-11 Scientists analyze and duplicate useful chemicals found in familiar foods to produce new foods.

DEERE AND COMPANY

22-9 Animals such as these are often bred to gain weight quickly on less feed.

For many years, it has been possible to make synthetic vitamins. They are chemically identical to natural vitamins. Vitamin C is a good example. As the demand for vitamin C increased, it became more economical to produce synthetic vitamin C. Many other vitamins are now being *synthesized* (manufactured), as well as flavorings and other food additives. Since the molecular structure of synthetic vitamins is the same as the "real" thing, the body can't tell the difference. This ability to synthesize or duplicate natural ingredients that may be in short supply helps to keep food costs down.

Artificial foods. Artificial foods are made of edible raw materials processed to resemble, or imitate, a familiar food. Coffee whiteners made from food oils are an example. Sometimes artificial foods improve the nutritional quality or decrease the kilojoule (Calorie) content of the products they imitate. Many diet products are technically considered artificial foods.

Fortified foods. Fortified foods have nutrients added to increase their nutritional quality. Bread, milk, cereals and other basic foods are often fortified. The addition of iodine to salt has almost eliminated goiter in the United States. Fortified foods can be adjusted to meet the nutritional needs of specific groups of people, such as infants and pregnant women. Fortifying foods is one way to give people more nutrition without changing their eating habits. Care must be taken, however, not to unbalance the overall nutrient intake of people. Excesses of some nutrients can create more problems than they solve.

Formulated foods. Formulated foods combine nutrients into the proportions needed by a certain group of people. Infant formulas are a good example. Formulated foods are especially useful when people cannot get all the nutrition they need from the usual foods they eat. Formulated foods have been used succesfully to provide protein to children in developing countries.

Meat substitutes. Food technology has made it possible to use plant proteins to make foods that resemble meats in texture, appearance and taste, 22-12. These foods, called meat *analogues* or *textured vegetable protein,* are usually made from soybeans. They can be shaped to resemble many types of meat, and fortified with additional nutrients.

Meat analogues are becoming popular for many reasons. They are often cheaper than meat and contain fewer kilojoules (Calories). The low fat content may better meet the needs of special diets (such as one with little saturated fat). Meat analogues are easier to use for large-scale food preparation because they are easier to handle and are less susceptible to spoilage. They also have less waste because there are no bones or excess fat.

Vegetable proteins are often used as a meat extender. Vegetable proteins can be added to meat products such as hot dogs, ground beef, sausage and casseroles. The protein content is increased and the cost is decreased. Vegetable proteins can also be used to make high-protein beverages and desserts.

Single-cell protein

High-quality protein can also be obtained from one-celled organisms such as bacteria and yeast. These are called *single-cell proteins.* These organisms can be grown on some unusual substances, including crude oil and natural gas. They also thrive on organic waste products. These waste products are not only plentiful, but a nuisance that costs cities millions of dollars for disposal.

The proteins of one-celled organisms contain all of the essential amino acids. This makes them useful for fortifying food. The production of single-cell proteins is much more efficient than producing protein by raising animals or growing grain. Beef calves, for instance, take a month or two to double their weight. Chickens take two to four weeks. But single-cell organisms take just two hours.

Growing single-cell proteins does not depend on the weather since they are grown in "factories." It takes relatively little space and no farmland. There is also little problem with waste disposal, since nearly everything gets used. Growing single-cell proteins is cheaper than producing milk or soybean meal.

Single-cell proteins are used mainly as an ingredient in livestock feed. It's most popular in countries which have to import feed or protein supplements for livestock. For people, single-cell proteins are currently limited to a form of yeast. This yeast is used to fortify processed cereals, pastas, ground meats, baby foods, salad dressings, soups and sweets.

Will people accept new foods?

For technological advances in food production to be beneficial, people must accept new foods. Over 5,000 new products appear on United States supermarket shelves every year. Of these, only about 500 survive. What makes a food acceptable? Taste, appearance, texture, cost, nutrition and convenience are important. But habit is a powerful factor too.

Food tastes and habits change slowly, but they do change. Changing the eating habits of Americans and people throughout the world toward a better and more balanced diet will not happen overnight. It is not enough to make new foods available. People must be educated and enticed into eating them, especially foods that are radically different, such as single-cell protein foods.

GOVERNMENTAL ASSISTANCE TO FARMERS

Technology for increasing agricultural production is available. However, farmers often need governmental assistance before they will be able and willing to use this technology, particularly in developing countries. Governments should be willing to recognize that feeding their people is a major concern. Since money is limited, governments may have to forego spending funds on other projects.

Opening and irrigating the land

In developing countries, most of the farmers own very small plots of land. The government may have to provide money to help open new land and irrigate that land. These tasks require heavy machinery which would be too expensive for the small farmer.

Technical training

New, high-yielding varieties of seeds are useful to farmers only if they are taught how to use them to obtain the best results. The seeds may need to be planted differently than seeds they have been accustomed to using. Governments should make seeds available when they are needed and send technicians to the farms to teach farmers how to grow them. Governments also need to make low-interest loans available to farmers. These low-interest loans will enable the farmers to buy seeds and the necessary equipment.

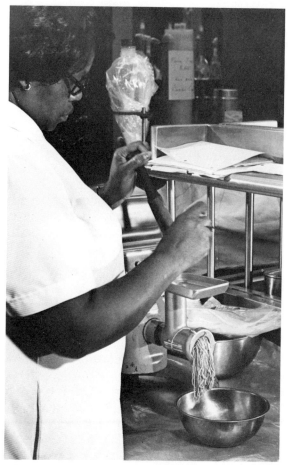

USDA

22-12 Soybeans are often used to produce meat substitutes which resemble meats in texture, appearance and taste.

Markets, storage and distribution systems

Once they have harvested their crops, farmers need to sell the food in order to earn a profit. People living in the cities may want to buy it. But the farmers must have a way to store the food after harvest and then transport it as the market calls for it, 22-13. Farmers need granaries, roads, canals and railroads to handle their surplus food. If farmers think they cannot transport and sell surpluses, they will only produce as much as their families can eat. When farmers do this, they and their families remain poor and the people in the cities remain hungry.

Governments should encourage farmers with policies which will assure them a fair return for their effort. This can be done if the government buys the farmers' grain when the price falls below a certain level. (A good year may produce an abundant crop which drives prices down and can actually hurt farmers.) Another way is to encourage world-wide markets for agricultural products. Very often, a surplus in one area of the world coincides with a shortage in another area. This means that the world price is higher than what the farmer can get locally. World markets help to level out the ups and downs of farm prices. Exports of United States' farm surpluses also help to offset the United States' trade imbalance, which is largely affected by oil imports.

International cooperation

The richer, industrialized countries of the world are becoming more and more aware that the progress of the entire world depends on creating a better fed world. It is more helpful to teach developing countries the techniques for growing their own food than to simply give them food, 22-14. Many interna-

USDA

22-13 After harvest, grain is stored in grain elevators until there is a market demand for it.

tional institutions now exist to lend money to countries at low interest rates. In addition, international research and training centers have been set up for developing and using new technology.

It is possible to solve the problems of feeding the world today and in the future. The knowledge and technology now exist. However, it's not reasonable to expect that the world's resources can support unlimited population growth.

Expanding the world's production of food to its fullest would be very costly in terms of money and other resources. For instance, millions of acres of wilderness would need to be turned over to organized food production. This would affect the ecological balance of vast areas of land. It would endanger animals and plants that live in those wilderness areas. Many of them are already endangered species. Increasing the use of pesticides and chemical fertilizers indefinitely will create serious pollution problems. Most of the world's farmers have small farms. To consolidate these farms would displace many small farmers. This could create serious social problems in rural areas.

During the Industrial Revolution, the English philospher, Thomas Malthus, predicted that the world's population would soon outgrow its food supply. Since then, many things have happened to increase that food supply far beyond anything Malthus imagined possible. The latest example is the "Green Revolution," the introduction of high-yield varieties of seed. Nevertheless, the fact remains that each food increase makes possible an increased population size. This new, larger population is then capable of increasing beyond the available food supply. In addition, it will take more land for houses and cities required by increasing numbers of people. In the United States, much farmland has been transformed into housing, roads and industrial parks needed by an expanding population.

As with the energy crisis, the food situation is serious, but not yet desperate. Solutions are available, if we will adopt them wisely. We must work to keep our population and our appetites within the limits of our renewable resources. Those resources are large and can be increased considerably. But they are not inexhaustible by any means.

USDA

22-14 *International cooperation between developed and developing countries is needed to increase world food production.*

to Define

agri-industry . . .
artificial foods . . .
controlled environment
agriculture . . .
engineered foods . . .
fish farms . . .
formulated foods . . .
fortified foods . . .
herbicides . . . hybrid . . .
hydroponics . . .
meat analogues . . .
minimum tillage. . . .
multicropping . . .
pesticide . . .
single-cell protein . . .
synthesized . . .
synthetic ingredients . . .
textured vegetable protein . . .
trickle irrigation

to Discuss

1. What is the staple food in the diets of most of the world's people?

2. How is grain eaten indirectly?

3. List at least three ways food production could be increased.

4. What makes it possible for the United States to produce large surpluses of food?

5. Why do many farmers depend on chemical fertilizers?

6. List at least three advantages to minimum tillage.

7. Why is eating meat often criticized as a wasteful use of grain? Why is this criticism often invalid?

8. What are two characteristics of animals produced as a result of careful selection and crossbreeding?

9. List at least three advantages to high-yielding varieties of seeds.

10. How does synthesizing or duplicating natural ingredients affect food costs?

11. Name an example of a formulated food.

12. List at least three reasons meat analogues are becoming popular.

13. What can governments do to help small farmers become more productive?

to Do

1. Choose one of the agricultural technologies discussed in this chapter and explore it in more detail (for instance: hydroponics, fish farming, controlled environment agriculture). The agricultural specialists at your county extension office should be a helpful source of information.

2. Go to a supermarket and find two examples of each of the following:
    Artificial food
    Fortified food
    Formulated food
    Meat analogue
Write down the names of the products and compare your list with those of your classmates.

3. Write a report on soybeans and the variety of foods that are made from them.

4. Discuss new food products that your family has adopted in the last year. What foods did they replace?

5. Invite a farmer or county extension agent to your classroom. Discuss with this person the advantages and disadvantages of farming now and in the future.

6. Visit a farm and observe various farming methods. Ask the farmer questions about methods used on his or her farm. Present a report of your visit to class.

7. Collect magazine or newspaper articles dealing with new trends in agriculture and food production. Present this information to your class.

Appendices

Appendix A
Recommended daily dietary allowances

RECOMMENDED DAILY DIETARY ALLOWANCES [a]

Designed for the maintenance of good nutrition of practically all healthy people in the U.S.A.

	Age (years)	Weight (kg)	Weight (lbs)	Height (cm)	Height (in)	Protein (g)	Fat-Soluble Vitamins Vitamin A (μg R.E.)[b]	Vitamin D (μg)[c]	Vitamin E (mg α T.E.)[d]	Water-Soluble Vitamins Vitamin C (mg)	Thiamin (mg)	Riboflavin (mg)	Niacin (mg N.E.)[e]	Vitamin B6 (mg)	Folacin [f] (μg)	Vitamin B12 (μg)	Minerals Calcium (mg)	Phosphorus (mg)	Magnesium (mg)	Iron (mg)	Zinc (mg)	Iodine (μg)
Infants	0.0-0.5	6	13	60	24	kg x 2.2	420	10	3	35	0.3	0.4	6	0.3	30	0.5[g]	360	240	50	10	3	40
	0.5-1.0	9	20	71	28	kg x 2.0	400	10	4	35	0.5	0.6	8	0.6	45	1.5	540	360	70	15	5	50
Children	1-3	13	29	90	35	23	400	10	5	45	0.7	0.8	9	0.9	100	2.0	800	800	150	15	10	70
	4-6	20	44	112	44	30	500	10	6	45	0.9	1.0	11	1.3	200	2.5	800	800	200	10	10	90
	7-10	28	62	132	52	34	700	10	7	45	1.2	1.4	16	1.6	300	3.0	800	800	250	10	10	120
Males	11-14	45	99	157	62	45	1000	10	8	50	1.4	1.6	18	1.8	400	3.0	1200	1200	350	18	15	150
	15-18	66	145	176	69	56	1000	10	10	60	1.4	1.7	18	2.0	400	3.0	1200	1200	400	18	15	150
	19-22	70	154	177	70	56	1000	7.5	10	60	1.5	1.7	19	2.2	400	3.0	800	800	350	10	15	150
	23-50	70	154	178	70	56	1000	5	10	60	1.4	1.6	18	2.2	400	3.0	800	800	350	10	15	150
	51+	70	154	178	70	56	1000	5	10	60	1.2	1.4	16	2.2	400	3.0	800	800	350	10	15	150
Females	11-14	46	101	157	62	46	800	10	8	50	1.1	1.3	15	1.8	400	3.0	1200	1200	300	18	15	150
	15-18	55	120	163	64	46	800	10	8	60	1.1	1.3	14	2.0	400	3.0	1200	1200	300	18	15	150
	19-22	55	120	163	64	44	800	7.5	8	60	1.1	1.3	14	2.0	400	3.0	800	800	300	18	15	150
	23-50	55	120	163	64	44	800	5	8	60	1.0	1.2	13	2.0	400	3.0	800	800	300	18	15	150
	51+	55	120	163	64	44	800	5	8	60	1.0	1.2	13	2.0	400	3.0	800	800	300	10	15	150
Pregnant						+30	+200	+5	+2	+20	+0.4	+0.3	+2	+0.6	+400	+1.0	+400	+400	+150	h	+5	+25
Lactating						+20	+400	+5	+3	+40	+0.5	+0.5	+5	+0.5	+100	+1.0	+400	+400	+150	h	+10	+50

a The allowances are intended to provide for individual variations among most normal persons as they live in the United States under usual environmental stresses. Diets should be based on a variety of common foods in order to provide other nutrients for which human requirements have been less well defined. See text for detailed discussion of allowances and of nutrients not tabulated. See Table III (p. 4) for weights and heights by individual year of age. See Table III (p. 4) for suggested average energy intakes.

b Retinol equivalents. 1 retinol equivalent = 1 μg retinol or 6 μg β-carotene. See text for calculation of vitamin A activity of diets as retinol equivalents.

c As cholecalciferol. 10 μg cholecalciferol = 400 I.U. vitamin D.

d α tocopherol equivalents. 1 mg d-α-tocopherol = 1 α T.E. See text for variation in allowances and calculation of vitamin E activity of the diet as α tocopherol equivalents.

e 1 N.E. (niacin equivalent) is equal to 1 mg of niacin or 60 mg of dietary tryptophan.

f The folacin allowances refer to dietary sources as determined by *Lactobacillus casei* assay after treatment with enzymes ("conjugases") to make polyglutamyl forms of the vitamin available to the test organism.

g The RDA for vitamin B12 in infants is based on average concentration of the vitamin in human milk. The allowances after weaning are based on energy intake (as recommended by the American Academy of Pediatrics) and consideration of other factors such as intestinal absorption; see text.

h The increased requirement during pregnancy cannot be met by the iron content of habitual American diets nor by the existing iron stores of many women; therefore the use of 30 - 60 mg of supplemental iron is recommended. Iron needs during lactation are not substantially different from those of nonpregnant women, but continued supplementation of the mother for 2 - 3 months after parturition is advisable in order to replenish stores depleted by pregnancy.

Food and Nutrition Board, National Academy of Sciences-National Research Council, Revised 1980

Appendix B
U.S. recommended daily allowances

UNITED STATES RECOMMENDED DAILY ALLOWANCES (U.S. RDA)

	UNIT	INFANTS (0-12 MO.)	CHILDREN UNDER 4 YRS.	ADULTS AND CHILDREN 4 OR MORE YRS.	PREGNANT OR LACTATING WOMEN
Vitamin A	IU	1500	2500	5000	8000
Vitamin D	IU	400	400	400	400
Vitamin E	IU	5	10	30	30
Vitamin C	mg	35	40	60	60
Folacin	mg	0.1	0.2	0.4	0.8
Thiamin (B$_1$)	mg	0.5	0.7	1.5	1.7
Riboflavin (B$_2$)	mg	0.6	0.8	1.7	2.0
Niacin	mg	8	9	20	20
Vitamin B$_6$	mg	0.4	0.7	2	2.5
Vitamin B$_{12}$	mcg	2	3	6	8
Biotin	mg	0.05	0.15	0.3	0.3
Pantothenic acid	mg	3	5	10	10
Calcium	g	0.6	0.8	1	1.3
Iron	mg	15	10	18	18
Phosphorus	g	0.5	0.8	1	1.3
Iodine	mcg	45	70	150	150
Magnesium	mg	70	200	400	450
Zinc	mg	5	8	15	15
Copper	mg	0.6	1	2	2.0

g = gram   mg = milligram   mcg = microgram   IU = International unit

Appendix C
Percentages of U.S. RDA

Each individual does not require 100 percent of the U.S. RDA for every nutrient. But at the same time, some individuals require more than 100 percent of certain nutrients during certain stages of the life cycle.

PERCENTAGES OF U.S. RDA

AGE	FOOD ENERGY[1]	PROTEIN[2]	VITAMIN A	VITAMIN C	THIAMIN	RIBO—FLAVIN	NIACIN[3]	CALCIUM	IRON
Years	Calories	Percent of U.S. Recommended Daily Allowance							
Child: 1-3	1300	35	40	70	50	50	30	80	85
Child: 4-6	1800	50	50	70	60	65	35	80	60
Child: 7-10	2400	55	70	70	80	75	50	80	60
Male: 11-14	2800	70	100	75	95	90	55	120	100
Male: 15-18	3000	85	100	75	100	110	55	120	100
Male: 19-22	3000	85	100	75	100	110	60	80	60
Male: 23-50	2700	90	100	75	95	95	45	80	60
Male: 51+	2400	90	100	75	80	90	35	80	60
Female: 11-14	2400	70	80	75	80	80	45	120	100
Female: 15-18	2100	75	80	75	75	85	30	120	100
Female: 19-22	2100	75	80	75	75	85	35	80	100
Female: 23-50	2000	75	80	75	70	75	30	80	100
Female: 51+	1800	75	80	75	70	65	25	80	60
Pregnant	+300[4]	+50[4]	100	100	+20[4]	+20[4]	35	120	100+
Nursing	+500[4]	+35[4]	120	135	+20[4]	+30[4]	35	120	100

[1] Calorie needs differ depending on body composition and size, age, and activity of the person.
[2] U.S. RDA of 65 grams is used for this table. In labeling, a U.S. RDA of 45 grams is used for foods providing high-quality protein, such as milk, meat, and eggs.
[3] The percentage of the U.S. RDA shown for niacin will provide the RDA of niacin if the RDA for protein is met. Some niacin is derived in the body from tryptophan, an amino acid present in protein.
[4] To be added to the percentage for the girl or woman of the appropriate age.

Appendix D   Nutritive values of the edible part of foods

NUTRITIVE VALUES OF THE EDIBLE PART OF FOODS

(Dashes (—) denote lack of reliable data for a constituent believed to be present in measurable amount)

DAIRY PRODUCTS (CHEESE, CREAM, IMITATION CREAM, MILK, RELATED PRODUCTS)

Foods, approximate measures, units, and weight (edible part unless footnotes indicate otherwise) (B)	Grams	Water Per cent (C)	Food energy Calories (D)	Protein Grams (E)	Fat Grams (F)	Saturated (total) Grams (G)	Unsaturated Oleic Grams (H)	Unsaturated Linoleic Grams (I)	Carbohydrate Grams (J)	Calcium Milligrams (K)	Phosphorus Milligrams (L)	Iron Milligrams (M)	Potassium Milligrams (N)	Vitamin A value International units (O)	Thiamin Milligrams (P)	Riboflavin Milligrams (Q)	Niacin Milligrams (R)	Ascorbic acid Milligrams (S)
Butter. See Fats, oils; related products, items																		
Cheese:																		
Cheddar: Cut pieces — 1 oz	28	37	115	7	9	6.1	2.1	.2	Trace	204	145	.2	28	300	.01	.11	Trace	0
Cottage (curd not pressed down): Creamed (cottage cheese, 4% fat): Large curd — 1 cup	225	79	235	28	10	6.4	2.4	.2	6	135	297	.3	190	370	.05	.37	.3	Trace
Small curd — 1 cup	210	79	220	26	9	6.0	2.2	.2	6	126	277	.3	177	340	.04	.34	.3	Trace
Low fat (2%) — 1 cup	226	79	205	31	4	2.8	1.0	.1	8	155	340	.4	217	160	.05	.42	.3	Trace
Uncreamed (cottage cheese dry curd, less than 1/2% fat) — 1 cup	145	80	125	25	1	.4	.1	Trace	3	46	151	.3	47	40	.04	.21	.2	0
Cream — 1 oz	28	54	100	2	10	6.2	2.4	.2	1	23	30	.3	34	400	Trace	.06	Trace	0
Mozzarella, made with— Whole milk — 1 oz	28	48	90	6	7	4.4	1.7	.2	1	163	117	.1	21	260	Trace	.08	Trace	0
Part skim milk — 1 oz	28	49	80	8	5	3.1	1.2	.1	1	207	149	.1	27	180	.01	.10	Trace	0
Parmesan, grated: Ounce — 1 oz	28	18	130	12	9	5.4	2.2	.1	1	390	229	.3	30	200	.01	.11	.1	0
Swiss — 1 oz	28	37	105	8	8	5.0	1.7	.2	1	272	171	Trace	31	240	.01	.10	Trace	0
Pasteurized process cheese: American — 1 oz	28	39	105	6	9	5.6	2.1	.2	Trace	174	211	.1	46	340	.01	.10	Trace	0
Swiss — 1 oz	28	42	95	7	7	4.5	1.7	.1	1	219	216	.2	61	230	Trace	.08	Trace	0
Pasteurized process cheese food, American — 1 oz	28	43	95	6	7	4.4	1.7	.1	2	163	130	.2	79	260	.01	.13	Trace	0
Cream, sweet: Half-and-half (cream and milk) — 1 cup	242	81	315	7	28	17.3	7.0	.6	10	254	230	.2	314	260	.08	.36	.2	2
1 tbsp	15	81	20	Trace	2	1.1	.4	Trace	1	16	14	Trace	19	20	.01	.02	Trace	Trace
Light, coffee, or table — 1 cup	240	74	470	6	46	28.8	11.7	1.0	9	231	192	.1	292	1,730	.08	.36	.1	2
1 tbsp	15	74	30	Trace	3	1.8	.7	.1	1	14	12	Trace	18	110	Trace	.02	Trace	Trace
Whipping, unwhipped (volume about double when whipped): Light — 1 cup	239	64	700	5	74	46.2	18.3	1.5	7	166	146	.1	231	2,690	.06	.30	.1	1
1 tbsp	15	64	45	Trace	5	2.9	1.1	.1	Trace	10	9	Trace	15	170	Trace	.02	Trace	Trace
Heavy — 1 cup	238	58	820	5	88	54.8	22.2	2.0	7	154	149	.1	179	3,500	.05	.26	.1	1
1 tbsp	15	58	80	Trace	6	3.5	1.4	.1	Trace	10	9	Trace	11	220	Trace	.02	Trace	Trace
Cream, sour — 1 cup	230	71	495	7	48	30.0	12.1	1.1	10	268	195	.1	331	1,820	.08	.34	.2	2
1 tbsp	12	71	25	Trace	2	1.6	.6	.1	1	14	10	Trace	17	90	Trace	.02	Trace	Trace
Milk: Fluid: Whole (3.3% fat) — 1 cup	244	88	150	8	8	5.1	2.1	.2	11	291	228	.1	370	310[2]	.09	.40	.2	2
Lowfat (2%): No milk solids added — 1 cup	244	89	120	8	5	2.9	1.2	.1	12	297	232	.1	377	500	.10	.40	.2	2
Milk solids added: No milk solids added — 1 cup	244	90	100	8	3	1.6	.7	.1	12	300	235	.1	381	500	.10	.41	.2	2

(A)	(B)		(C)	(D)	(E)	(F)	(G)	(H)	(I)	(J)	(K)	(L)	(M)	(N)	(O)	(P)	(Q)	(R)	(S)
Milk solids added:																			
Label claim less than 10 g of protein per cup.	1 cup----------------------	245	90	105	9	2	1.5	.6	.1	12	313	245	.1	397	500	.10	.42	.2	2
Label claim 10 or more grams of protein per cup (protein fortified).	1 cup----------------------	246	89	120	10	3	1.8	.7	.1	14	349	273	.1	444	500	.11	.47	.2	3
Nonfat (skim):																			
No milk solids added------	1 cup----------------------	245	91	85	8	Trace	.3	.1	Trace	12	302	247	.1	406	500	.09	.37	.2	2
Buttermilk-------------------	1 cup----------------------	245	90	100	8	2	1.3	.5	Trace	12	285	219	.1	371	[3]80	.08	.38	.1	2
Canned:																			
Evaporated, unsweetened:																			
Whole milk-----------------	1 cup----------------------	252	74	340	17	19	11.6	5.3	0.4	25	657	510	.5	764	[3]610	.12	.80	.5	5
Skim milk------------------	1 cup----------------------	255	79	200	19	1	.3	.1	Trace	29	738	497	.7	845	[4]1,000	.11	.79	.4	3
Sweetened, condensed---------	1 cup----------------------	306	27	980	24	27	16.8	6.7	.7	166	868	775	.6	1,136	[3]1,000	.28	1.27	.6	8
Dried:																			
Cup[7]-----------------------	1 cup----------------------	68	4	245	24	Trace	.3	.1	Trace	35	837	670	.2	1,160	[6]1,610	.28	1.19	.6	4
Milk beverages:																			
Chocolate milk (commercial):																			
Regular----------------------	1 cup----------------------	250	82	210	8	8	5.3	2.2	.2	26	280	251	.6	417	[3]300	.09	.41	.3	2
Lowfat (2%)------------------	1 cup----------------------	250	84	180	8	5	3.1	1.3	.1	26	284	254	.6	422	500	.10	.42	.3	2
Eggnog (commercial)------------	1 cup----------------------	254	74	340	10	19	11.3	5.0	.6	34	330	278	.5	420	890	.09	.48	.3	4
Malted milk, home-prepared with 1 cup of whole milk and 2 to 3 heaping tsp of malted milk powder (about 3/4 oz):																			
Shakes, thick:[8]																			
Chocolate, container, net wt., 10.6 oz.	1 container----------------	300	72	355	9	8	5.0	2,0	.2	63	396	378	.9	672	260	.14	.67	.4	0
Vanilla, container, net wt., 11 oz.	1 container----------------	313	74	350	12	9	5.9	2.4	.2	56	457	361	.3	572	360	.09	.61	.5	0
Milk desserts, frozen:																			
Ice cream:																			
Regular (about 11% fat):																			
Hardened-------------------	1/2 gal--------------------	1,064	61	2,155	38	115	71.3	28.8	2.6	254	1,406	1,075	1.0	2,052	4,340	.42	2.63	1.1	6
	1 cup----------------------	133	61	270	5	14	8.9	3.6	.3	32	176	134	.1	257	540	.05	.33	.1	1
	3-fl oz container----------	50	61	100	2	5	3.4	1.4	.1	12	66	51	Trace	96	200	.02	.12	.1	Trace
Soft serve (frozen custard)	1 cup----------------------	173	60	375	7	23	13.5	5.9	.6	38	236	199	.4	338	790	.08	.45	.2	1
Rich (about 16% fat), hardened.	1/2 gal--------------------	1,188	59	2,805	33	190	118.3	47.8	4.3	256	1,213	927	.8	1,771	7,200	.36	2.27	.9	5
	1 cup----------------------	148	59	350	4	24	14.7	6.0	.5	32	151	115	.1	221	900	.04	.28	.1	1
Ice milk:																			
Hardened (about 4.3% fat)----	1/2 gal--------------------	1,048	69	1,470	41	45	28.1	11.3	1.0	232	1,409	1,035	1.5	2,117	1,710	.61	2.78	.9	6
	1 cup----------------------	131	69	185	5	6	3.5	1.4	.1	29	176	129	.1	265	210	.08	.35	.1	1
Soft serve (about 2.6% fat)	1 cup----------------------	175	70	225	8	5	2.9	1.2	0.1	38	274	202	0.3	412	180	0.12	0.54	0.2	1
Sherbet (about 2% fat)-------	1/2 gal--------------------	1,542	66	2,160	17	31	19.0	7.7	.7	469	827	594	2.5	1,585	1,480	.26	.71	1.0	31
	1 cup----------------------	193	66	270	2	4	2.4	1.0	.1	59	103	74	.3	198	190	.03	.09	.1	4
Milk desserts, other:																			
Custard, baked---------------	1 cup----------------------	265	77	305	14	15	6.8	5.4	.7	29	297	310	1.1	387	930	.11	.50	.3	1
Puddings:																			
From home recipe:																			
Starch base:																			
Chocolate--------------	1 cup----------------------	260	66	385	8	12	7.6	3.3	.3	67	250	255	1.3	445	390	.05	.36	.3	1
Vanilla (blancmange)---	1 cup----------------------	255	76	285	9	10	6.2	2.5	.2	41	298	232	Trace	352	410	.08	.41	.3	2
Tapioca cream------------	1 cup----------------------	165	72	220	8	8	4.1	2.5	.5	28	173	180	.7	223	480	.07	.30	.2	2
From mix (chocolate) and milk:																			
Regular (cooked)---------	1 cup----------------------	260	70	320	9	8	4.3	2.6	.2	59	265	247	.8	354	340	.05	.39	.3	2
Instant------------------	1 cup----------------------	260	69	325	8	7	3.6	2.2	.3	63	374	237	1.3	335	340	.08	.39	.3	2
Yogurt:																			
With added milk solids:																			
Made with lowfat milk:																			
Fruit-flavored[9]----------	1 container, net wt., 8 oz	227	75	230	10	3	1.8	.6	.1	42	343	269	.2	439	[10]120	.08	.40	.2	1
Plain--------------------	1 container, net wt., 8 oz	227	85	145	12	4	2.3	.8	.1	16	415	326	.2	531	[10]150	.10	.49	.3	2
Made with whole milk-------	1 container, net wt., 8 oz	227	88	140	8	7	4.8	1.7	.1	11	274	215	.1	351	280	.07	.32	.2	1
EGGS																			
Eggs, large (24 oz per dozen):																			
Raw:																			
Whole, without shell-------	1 egg----------------------	50	75	80	6	6	1.7	2.0	.6	1	28	90	1.0	65	260	.04	.15	Trace	0
White----------------------	1 white--------------------	33	88	15	3	Trace	0	0	0	Trace	4	4	Trace	45	0	Trace	.09	Trace	0

NUTRITIVE VALUES OF THE EDIBLE PART OF FOODS - Continued

(Dashes (—) denote lack of reliable data for a constituent believed to be present in measurable amount)

| | | | | | | Fatty Acids | | | NUTRIENTS IN INDICATED QUANTITY | | | | | | | | | |
Item No. (A)	Foods, approximate measures, units, and weight (edible part unless footnotes indicate otherwise) (B)		Water (C)	Food energy (D)	Protein (E)	Fat (F)	Saturated (total) (G)	Unsaturated Oleic (H)	Linoleic (I)	Carbohydrate (J)	Calcium (K)	Phosphorus (L)	Iron (M)	Potassium (N)	Vitamin A value (O)	Thiamin (P)	Riboflavin (Q)	Niacin (R)	Ascorbic acid (S)
		Grams	Percent	Calories	Grams	Grams	Grams	Grams	Grams	Grams	Milligrams	Milligrams	Milligrams	Milligrams	International units	Milligrams	Milligrams	Milligrams	Milligrams
	Yolk----------- 1 yolk-----------	17	49	65	3	6	1.7	2.1	.6	Trace	26	86	.9	15	310	.04	.07	Trace	0
	Cooked:																		
	Fried in butter----- 1 egg-----	46	72	85	5	6	2.4	2.2	.6	1	26	80	.9	58	290	.03	.13	Trace	0
	Hard-cooked, shell removed- 1 egg-----	50	75	80	6	6	1.7	2.0	.6	1	28	90	1.0	65	260	.04	.14	Trace	0
	Poached---------- 1 egg-----	50	74	80	6	6	1.7	2.0	.6	1	28	90	1.0	65	260	.04	.13	Trace	0
	Scrambled (milk added) in butter. Also omelet. 1 egg-----	64	76	95	6	7	2.8	2.3	.6	1	47	97	.9	85	310	.04	.16	Trace	0
	FATS OILS; RELATED PRODUCTS																		
	Butter:																		
	Regular (1 brick or 4 sticks per lb):																		
	Tablespoon (about 1/8 stick). 1 tbsp-----	14	16	100	Trace	12	7.2	2.9	.3	Trace	3	3	Trace	4	[11]430	Trace	Trace	Trace	0
	Pat (1 in square, 1/3 in high; 90 per lb). 1 pat-----	5	16	35	Trace	4	2.5	1.0	.1	Trace	1	1	Trace	1	[11]150	Trace	Trace	Trace	0
	Whipped (6 sticks or two 8-oz containers per lb).																		
	Tablespoon (about 1/8 stick). 1 tbsp-----	9	16	65	Trace	8	4.7	1.9	.2	Trace	2	2	Trace	2	[11]290	Trace	Trace	Trace	0
	Fats, cooking (vegetable shortenings). 1 cup-----	200	0	1,770	0	200	48.8	88.2	48.4	0	0	0	0	0	---	0	0	0	0
	1 tbsp-----	13	0	110	0	13	3.2	5.7	3.1	0	0	0	0	0	---	0	0	0	0
	Lard---------- 1 cup-----	205	0	1,850	0	205	81.0	83.8	20.5	0	0	0	0	0	0	0	0	0	0
	1 tbsp-----	13	0	115	0	13	5.1	5.3	1.3	0	0	0	0	0	0	0	0	0	0
	Margarine:																		
	Regular (1 brick or 4 sticks per lb):																		
	Tablespoon (about 1/8 stick)- 1 tbsp-----	14	16	100	Trace	12	2.1	5.3	3.T	Trace	3	3	Trace	4	[11]470	Trace	Trace	Trace	0
	Pat (1 in square, 1/3 in high; 90 per lb). 1 pat-----	5	16	35	Trace	4	.7	1.9	1.1	Trace	1	1	Trace	1	[12]170	Trace	Trace	.1	0
	Soft, two 8-oz containers per lb. 1 container-----	227	16	1,635	1	184	32.5	71.5	65.4	Trace	53	52	.4	59	[12]7,500	.01	.08	.1	0
	1 tbsp-----	14	16	100	Trace	12	2.0	4.5	4.T	Trace	3	3	Trace	4	[12]470	Trace	Trace	Trace	0
	Whipped (6 sticks per lb):																		
	Stick (1/2 cup)---- 1 stick-----	76	16	545	Trace	61	11.2	28.7	16.7	Trace	18	17	.1	20	[12]2,500	Trace	.03	Trace	0
	Tablespoon (about 1/8 stick)- 1 tbsp-----	9	16	70	Trace	8	1.4	3.6	2.1	Trace	2	2	Trace	2	[11]310	Trace	Trace	Trace	0
	Oils, salad or cooking:																		
	Corn------------- 1 cup-----	218	0	1,925	0	218	27.7	53.6	125.1	0	0	0	0	0	---	0	0	0	0
	1 tbsp-----	14	0	120	0	14	1.7	3.3	7.8	0	0	0	0	0	---	0	0	0	0
	Olive------------ 1 cup-----	216	0	1,910	0	216	30.7	154.4	17.7	0	0	0	0	0	---	0	0	0	0
	1 tbsp-----	14	0	120	0	14	1.9	9.7	1.1	0	0	0	0	0	---	0	0	0	0
	Peanut----------- 1 cup-----	216	0	1,910	0	216	37.4	98.5	67.0	0	0	0	0	0	---	0	0	0	0
	1 tbsp-----	14	0	120	0	14	2.3	6.2	4.2	0	0	0	0	0	---	0	0	0	0
	Safflower-------- 1 cup-----	218	0	1,925	0	218	20.5	25.9	159.8	0	0	0	0	0	---	0	0	0	0
	1 tbsp-----	14	0	120	0	14	1.3	1.6	10.0	0	0	0	0	0	---	0	0	0	0
	Soybean oil, hydrogenated (partially hardened). 1 cup-----	218	0	1,925	0	218	31.8	93.1	75.6	0	0	0	0	0	---	0	0	0	0
	Salad dressings:																		
	Commercial:																		
	Blue cheese:																		
	Regular--------- 1 tbsp-----	15	32	75	1	8	1.6	1.7	3.8	1	12	11	Trace	6	30	Trace	.02	Trace	Trace
	French:																		
	Regular--------- 1 tbsp-----	16	39	65	Trace	6	1.1	1.3	3.2	3	2	2	.1	13	---	---	---	---	---
	Italian:																		
	Regular--------- 1 tbsp-----	15	28	85	Trace	9	1.6	1.9	4.7	1	2	1	Trace	2	Trace	Trace	Trace	Trace	---
	Mayonnaise------- 1 tbsp-----	14	15	100	Trace	11	2.0	2.4	5.6	Trace	3	4	.1	5	40	Trace	.01	Trace	---
	Mayonnaise type:																		
	Regular--------- 1 tbsp-----	15	41	65	Trace	6	1.1	1.4	3.2	2	2	4	Trace	1	30	Trace	Trace	Trace	---

(A)	(B)	(C)	(D)	(E)	(F)	(G)	(H)	(I)	(J)	(K)	(L)	(M)	(N)	(O)	(P)	(Q)	(R)	(S)
Tartar sauce, regular --- 1 tbsp	14	34	75	Trace	8	1.5	1.8	4.1	1	3	4	.1	11	30	Trace	Trace	Trace	Trace
Thousand Island:																		
Regular--- 1 tbsp	16	32	80	Trace	8	1.4	1.7	4.0	2	3	3	.1	18	50	Trace	Trace	Trace	Trace
Low calorie (10 Cal per tsp)--- 1 tbsp	15	68	25	Trace	2	.4	.4	1.0	2	3	3	.1	17	50	Trace	Trace	Trace	Trace
From home recipe:																		
Cooked type[13]--- 1 tbsp	16	68	25	1	2	.5	.6	.3	2	14	15	.1	19	80	.01	.03	Trace	Trace
FISH, SHELLFISH, MEAT, POULTRY; RELATED PRODUCTS																		
Fish and shellfish:																		
Clams:																		
Raw, meat only--- 3 oz	85	82	65	11	1	—	—	—	2	59	138	5.2	154	90	.08	.15	1.1	8
Crabmeat (white or king), canned, not pressed down. 1 cup	135	77	135	24	3	—	—	—	1	61	246	1.1	149	—	.11	.11	2.6	—
Fish sticks, breaded, cooked, frozen (stick, 4 by 1 by 1/2 in). 1 fish stick or 1 oz	28	66	50	5	3	—	—	—	2	3	47	.1	—	0	.01	.02	.5	—
Haddock, breaded, fried[14]--- 3 oz	85	66	140	17	5	1.4	2.2	1.2	5	34	210	1.0	296	—	.03	.06	2.7	2
Ocean perch, breaded, fried[14]--- 1 fillet	85	59	195	16	11	2.7	4.4	2.3	6	28	192	1.1	242	—	.10	.10	1.6	—
Oysters, raw, meat only (13–19 medium Selects). 1 cup	240	85	160	20	4	1.3	.2	.1	8	226	343	13.2	290	740	.34	.43	6.0	—
Salmon, pink, canned, solids and liquid. 3 oz	85	71	120	17	5	.9	.8	.1	0	[15]167	243	.7	307	60	.03	.16	6.8	—
Sardines, Atlantic, canned in oil, drained solids. 3 oz	85	62	175	20	9	3.0	2.5	.5	0	372	424	2.5	502	190	.02	.17	4.6	—
Scallops, frozen, breaded, fried, reheated. 6 scallops	90	60	175	16	8	—	—	—	—	—	—	—	—	—	—	—	—	—
Shrimp:																		
Canned meat--- 3 oz	85	70	100	21	1	.1	.1	Trace	1	98	224	2.6	104	50	.01	.03	1.5	—
French fried[16]--- 3 oz	85	57	190	17	9	2.3	3.7	2.0	9	61	162	1.7	195	70	.03	.07	2.3	—
Tuna, canned in oil, drained solids. 3 oz	85	61	170	24	7	1.7	1.7	.7	0	7	199	1.6	—	70	.04	.10	10.1	—
Tuna salad[17]--- 1 cup	205	70	350	30	22	4.3	6.3	6.7	7	41	291	2.7	—	590	.08	.23	10.3	2
Meat and meat products:																		
Bacon, (20 slices per lb, raw), broiled or fried, crisp. 2 slices	15	8	85	4	8	2.5	3.7	.7	Trace	2	34	.5	35	0	.08	.05	.8	—
Beef,[18] cooked:																		
Cuts braised, simmered or pot roasted:																		
Lean and fat (piece, 2 1/2 by 2 1/2 by 3/4 in). 3 oz	85	53	245	23	16	6.8	6.5	.4	0	10	114	2.9	184	30	.04	.18	3.6	—
Lean only--- 2.5 oz	72	62	140	22	5	2.1	1.8	.2	0	10	108	2.7	176	10	.04	.17	3.3	—
Ground beef, broiled:																		
Lean with 10% fat--- 3 oz or patty 3 by 5/8 in	85	60	185	23	10	4.0	3.9	.3	0	10	196	3.0	261	20	.08	.20	5.1	—
Lean with 21% fat--- 2.9 oz or patty 3 by 5/8 in	82	54	235	20	17	7.0	6.7	.4	0	9	159	2.6	221	30	.07	.17	4.4	—
Roast, oven cooked, no liquid added:																		
Relatively fat, such as rib:																		
Lean and fat (2 pieces, 4 1/8 by 2 1/4 by 1/4 in). 3 oz	85	40	375	17	33	14.0	13.6	.8	0	8	158	2.2	189	70	.05	.13	3.1	—
Lean only--- 1.8 oz	51	57	125	14	7	3.0	2.5	.3	0	6	131	1.8	161	10	.04	.11	2.6	—
Relatively lean, such as heel of round:																		
Lean and fat (2 pieces, 4 1/8 by 2 1/4 by 1/4 in). 3 oz	85	62	165	25	7	2.8	2.7	.2	0	11	208	3.2	279	10	.06	.19	4.5	—
Steak:																		
Relatively fat-sirloin, broiled:																		
Lean and fat (piece, 2 1/2 by 2 1/2 by 3/4 in). 3 oz	85	44	330	20	27	11.3	11.1	.6	0	9	162	2.5	220	50	.05	.15	4.0	—
Lean only--- 2.0 oz	56	59	115	18	4	1.8	1.6	.2	0	7	146	2.2	202	10	.05	.14	3.6	—
Relatively lean-round, braised:																		
Lean and fat (piece, 4 1/8 by 2 1/4 by 1/2 in). 3 oz	85	55	220	24	13	5.5	5.2	.4	0	10	213	3.0	272	20	.07	.19	4.8	—
Lean only--- 2.4 oz	68	61	130	21	4	1.7	1.5	.2	0	9	182	2.5	238	10	.05	.16	4.1	—
Beef, canned:																		
Corned beef--- 3 oz	85	59	185	22	10	4.9	4.5	.2	0	17	90	3.7	—	—	.01	.20	2.9	—
Corned beef hash--- 1 cup	220	67	400	19	25	11.9	10.9	.5	24	29	147	4.4	440	—	.02	.20	4.6	—
Beef, dried, chipped--- 2 1/2-oz jar	71	48	145	24	4	—	—	—	0	14	287	3.6	142	—	.05	.23	2.7	0
Beef and vegetable stew--- 1 cup	245	82	220	16	11	4.9	4.5	.2	15	29	184	2.9	613	2,400	.15	.17	4.7	17

NUTRITIVE VALUES OF THE EDIBLE PART OF FOODS - Continued

(Dashes (—) denote lack of reliable data for a constituent believed to be present in measurable amount)

	Foods, approximate measures, units, and weight (edible part unless footnotes indicate otherwise)	Water	Food energy	Protein	Fat	Fatty Acids — Saturated (total)	Fatty Acids — Unsaturated Oleic	Fatty Acids — Unsaturated Linoleic	Carbohydrate	Calcium	Phosphorus	Iron	Potassium	Vitamin A value	Thiamin	Riboflavin	Niacin	Ascorbic acid
(A)	(B)	(C)	(D)	(E)	(F)	(G)	(H)	(I)	(J)	(K)	(L)	(M)	(N)	(O)	(P)	(Q)	(R)	(S)
		Per-cent	Cal-ories	Grams	Grams	Grams	Grams	Grams	Grams	Milli-grams	Milli-grams	Milli-grams	Milli-grams	Inter-national units	Milli-grams	Milli-grams	Milli-grams	Milli-grams
	Chop suey with beef and pork (home recipe). 1 cup. 250 g	75	300	26	17	8.5	6.2	.7	13	60	248	4.8	425	600	.28	.38	5.0	33
	Heart, beef, lean, braised. 3 oz. 85 g	61	160	27	5	1.5	1.1	.6	1	5	154	5.0	197	20	.21	1.04	6.5	1
	Lamb, cooked: Chop, rib (cut 3 per lb with bone), broiled:																	
	Lean and fat. 3.1 oz. 89 g	43	360	18	32	14.8	12.1	1.2	0	8	139	1.0	200	—	.11	.19	4.1	—
	Lean only. 2 oz. 57 g	60	120	16	6	2.5	2.1	.2	0	6	121	1.1	174	—	.09	.15	3.4	—
	Leg, roasted:																	
	Lean and fat (2 pieces, 4 1/8 by 2 1/4 by 1/4 in). 3 oz. 85 g	54	235	22	16	7.3	6.0	.6	0	9	177	1.4	241	—	.13	.23	4.7	—
	Lean only. 2.5 oz. 71 g	62	130	20	5	2.1	1.8	.2	0	9	169	1.4	227	—	.12	.21	4.4	—
	Shoulder, roasted:																	
	Lean and fat (3 pieces, 2 1/2 by 2 1/2 by 1/4 in). 3 oz. 85 g	50	285	18	23	10.8	8.8	.9	0	9	146	1.0	206	—	.11	.20	4.0	—
	Lean only. 2.3 oz. 64 g	61	130	17	6	3.6	2.3	.2	0	8	140	1.0	193	—	.10	.18	3.7	—
	Liver, beef, fried[20] (slice, 6 1/2 by 2 3/8 by 3/8 in). 3 oz. 85 g	56	195	22	9	2.5	3.5	.9	5	9	405	7.5	323	[2]45,390	.22	3.56	14.0	23
	Pork, cured, cooked: Ham, light cure, lean and fat, roasted (2 pieces, 4 1/8 by 2 1/4 in).[22] 3 oz. 85 g	54	245	18	19	6.8	7.9	1.7	0	8	146	2.2	199	0	.40	.15	3.1	—
	Luncheon meat: Boiled ham, slice (8 per 8-oz pkg.). 1 oz. 28 g	59	65	5	5	1.7	2.0	.4	0	3	47	.8	—	0	.12	.04	.7	—
	Canned, spiced or unspiced: Slice, approx. 3 by 2 by 1/2 in. 1 slice. 60 g	55	175	9	15	5.4	6.7	1.0	1	5	65	1.3	133	0	.19	.13	1.8	—
	Pork, fresh,[18] cooked: Chop, loin (cut 3 per lb with bone), broiled:																	
	Lean and fat. 2.7 oz. 78 g	42	305	19	25	8.9	10.4	2.2	0	9	209	2.7	216	0	.75	0.22	4.5	—
	Lean only. 2 oz. 56 g	53	150	17	9	3.1	3.6	.8	0	7	181	2.2	192	0	.63	.18	3.8	—
	Roast, oven cooked, no liquid added: Lean and fat (piece, 2 1/2 by 2 1/2 by 3/4 in). 3 oz. 85 g	46	310	21	24	8.7	10.2	2.2	0	9	218	2.7	233	0	.78	.22	4.8	—
	Lean only. 2.4 oz. 68 g	55	175	20	10	3.5	4.1	.8	0	9	211	2.6	224	0	.73	.21	4.4	—
	Shoulder cut, simmered: Lean and fat (3 pieces, 2 1/2 by 2 1/2 by 1/4 in). 3 oz. 85 g	46	320	20	26	9.3	10.9	2.3	0	9	118	2.6	158	0	.46	.21	4.1	—
	Lean only. 2.2 oz. 63 g	60	135	18	6	2.2	2.6	.6	0	8	111	2.3	146	0	.42	.19	3.7	—
	Sausages (see also Luncheon meat (items 190-191)): Bologna, slice (8 per 8-oz pkg.). 1 slice. 28 g	56	85	3	8	3.0	3.4	.5	Trace	2	36	.5	65	—	.05	.06	.7	—
	Braunschweiger, slice (6 per 6-oz pkg.). 1 slice. 28 g	53	90	4	8	2.6	3.4	.8	1	3	69	1.7	—	1,850	.05	.41	2.3	—
	Brown and serve (10-11 per 8-oz pkg.), browned. 1 link. 17 g	40	70	3	6	2.3	2.8	.7	Trace	—	—	—	—	—	—	—	—	—
	Devilled ham, canned. 1 tbsp. 13 g	51	45	2	4	1.5	1.8	.4	0	1	12	.3	—	0	.02	.01	.2	—
	Frankfurter (8 per 1-lb pkg.), cooked (reheated). 1 frankfurter. 56 g	57	170	7	15	5.6	6.5	1.2	1	3	57	.8	—	—	.08	.11	1.4	—
	Pork link (16 per 1-lb pkg.), cooked. 1 link. 13 g	35	60	2	6	2.1	2.4	.5	Trace	1	21	.3	35	0	.10	.04	.5	—
	Salami: Cooked type, slice (8 per 8-oz pkg.). 1 slice. 28 g	51	90	5	7	3.1	3.0	.2	Trace	3	57	.7	—	—	.07	.07	1.2	—
	Veal, medium fat, cooked, bone removed: Cutlet (4 1/8 by 2 1/4 by 1/2 in), braised or broiled. 3 oz. 85 g	60	185	23	9	4.0	3.4	.4	0	9	196	2.7	258	—	.06	.21	4.6	—

FRUITS AND FRUIT PRODUCTS

(A)	(B)	Grams	(C)	(D)	(E)	(F)	(G)	(H)	(I)	(J)	(K)	(L)	(M)	(N)	(O)	(P)	(Q)	(R)	(S)
Rib (2 pieces, 4 1/8 by 2 1/4 by 1/4 in), roasted.	3 oz	85	55	230	23	14	6.1	5.1	.6	0	10	211	2.9	259	—	.11	.26	6.6	—
Poultry and poultry products:																			
Chicken, cooked:																			
Breast, fried,[23] bones removed, 1/2 breast (3.3 oz with bones).	2.8 oz	79	58	160	26	5	1.4	1.8	1.1	1	9	218	1.3	—	70	.04	.17	11.6	—
Drumstick, fried,[23] bones removed (2 oz with bones).	1.3 oz	38	55	90	12	4	1.1	1.3	.9	Trace	6	89	.9	—	50	.03	.15	2.7	—
Half broiler, broiled, bones removed (10.4 oz with bones).	6.2 oz	176	71	240	42	7	2.2	2.5	1.3	0	16	355	3.0	483	160	.09	.34	15.5	—
Chicken, canned, boneless----	3 oz	85	65	170	18	10	3.2	3.8	2.0	0	18	210	1.3	117	200	.03	.11	3.7	3
Chicken a la king, cooked (home recipe).	1 cup	245	68	470	27	34	2.7	14.3	3.3	12	127	358	2.5	404	1,130	.10	.42	5.4	12
From home recipe----	1 cup	250	78	255	31	10	2.4	3.4	3.1	10	58	293	2.5	473	280	.08	.23	4.3	10
Turkey, roasted, flesh without skin:																			
Dark meat, piece, 2 1/2 by 1 5/8 by 1/4 in.	4 pieces	85	61	175	26	7	2.1	1.5	1.5	0	—	—	2.0	338	—	.03	.20	3.6	—
Light meat, piece, 4 by 2 by 1/4 in.	2 pieces	85	62	150	28	3	.9	.6	.7	0	—	—	1.0	349	—	.04	.12	9.4	—
Light and dark meat: Chopped or diced----	1 cup	140	61	265	44	9	2.5	1.7	1.8	0	11	351	2.5	514	—	.07	.25	10.8	—
Apples, raw, unpeeled, without cores): 3 1/4 in diam. (about 2 per lb with cores).	1 apple	212	84	125	Trace	1	—	—	—	31	15	21	.6	233	190	.06	.04	.2	8
Applejuice, bottled or canned[24]---	1 cup	248	88	120	Trace	Trace	—	—	—	30	15	22	1.5	250	—	.02	.05	.2	2[52]
Applesauce, canned: Sweetened----	1 cup	255	76	230	1	Trace	—	—	—	61	10	13	1.3	166	100	.05	.03	.1	3[52]
Unsweetened----	1 cup	244	89	100	Trace	Trace	—	—	—	26	10	12	1.2	190	100	.05	.02	.1	2[52]
Apricots: Raw, without pits (about 12 per lb with pits).	3 apricots	107	85	55	1	Trace	—	—	—	14	18	25	.5	301	2,890	.03	.04	.6	11
Canned in heavy sirup (halves and sirup).	1 cup	258	77	220	2	Trace	—	—	—	57	28	39	.8	604	4,490	.05	.05	1.0	10
Dried: Uncooked (28 large or 37 medium halves per cup).	1 cup	130	25	340	7	1	—	—	—	86	87	140	7.2	1,273	14,170	.01	.21	4.3	16
Apricot nectar, canned----	1 cup	251	85	145	1	Trace	—	—	—	37	23	30	.5	379	2,380	.03	.03	.5	36[26]
Avocados, raw, whole, without skins and seeds: California, mid- and late-winter (with skin and seed, 3 1/8-in diam.; wt., 10 oz).	1 avocado	216	74	370	5	37	5.5	22.0	3.7	13	22	91	1.3	1,303	630	.24	.43	3.5	30
Florida, late summer and fall (with skin and seed, 3 5/8-in diam.; wt., 1 lb).	1 avocado	304	78	390	4	33	6.7	15.7	5.3	27	30	128	1.8	1,836	880	.33	.61	4.9	43
Banana without peel (about 2.6 per lb with peel).	1 banana	119	76	100	1	Trace	—	—	—	26	10	31	.8	440	230	.06	.07	.8	12
Blackberries, raw----	1 cup	144	85	85	2	1	—	—	—	19	46	27	1.3	245	290	.04	.06	.6	30
Blueberries, raw----	1 cup	145	83	90	1	1	—	—	—	22	22	19	1.5	117	150	.04	.09	.7	20
Cantaloup. See Muskmelons (item 271).																			
Cherries: Sour (tart), red, pitted, canned, water pack.	1 cup	244	88	105	2	Trace	—	—	—	26	37	32	.7	317	1,660	.07	.05	.5	12
Sweet, raw, without pits and stems.	10 cherries	68	80	45	1	Trace	—	—	—	12	15	13	.3	129	70	.03	.04	.3	7
Cranberry juice cocktail, bottled, sweetened.	1 cup	253	83	165	Trace	Trace	—	—	—	42	13	8	.8	25	Trace	.03	.03	.1	81[27]
Cranberry sauce, sweetened, canned, strained.	1 cup	277	62	405	Trace	1	—	—	—	104	17	11	.6	83	60	.03	.03	.1	6
Dates: Whole, without pits----	10 dates	80	23	220	2	Trace	—	—	—	58	47	50	2.4	518	40	.07	.08	1.8	0
Fruit cocktail, canned, in heavy sirup.	1 cup	255	80	195	1	Trace	—	—	—	50	23	31	1.0	411	360	.05	.03	1.0	5
Grapefruit: Raw, medium, 3 3/4-in diam. (about 1 lb 1 oz):																			

NUTRITIVE VALUES OF THE EDIBLE PART OF FOODS - Continued

(Dashes (—) denote lack of reliable data for a constituent believed to be present in measurable amount)

Foods, approximate measures, units, and weight (edible part unless footnotes indicate otherwise) (A)	(B)	Grams	Water (C) Per cent	Food energy (D) Cal ories	Pro tein (E) Grams	Fat (F) Grams	Satu rated (total) (G) Grams	Oleic (H) Grams	Lino leic (I) Grams	Carbo hydrate (J) Grams	Calcium (K) Milli grams	Phos phorus (L) Milli grams	Iron (M) Milli grams	Potas sium (N) Milli grams	Vitamin A value (O) Inter national units	Thiamin (P) Milli grams	Ribo flavin (Q) Milli grams	Niacin (R) Milli grams	Ascorbic acid (S) Milli grams
Pink or red	1/2 grapefruit with peel[28]	241	89	50	1	Trace	—	—	—	13	20	20	.5	166	540	.05	.02	.2	44
White	1/2 grapefruit with peel[28]	241	89	45	1	Trace	—	—	—	12	19	19	.5	159	10	.05	.02	.2	44
Canned, sections with sirup	1 cup	254	81	180	2	Trace	—	—	—	45	33	36	.8	343	30	.08	.05	.5	76
Grapefruit Juice:																			
Raw, pink, red, or white	1 cup	246	90	95	1	Trace	—	—	—	23	22	37	.5	399	(2[9])	.10	.05	.5	93
Canned, white:																			
Unsweetened	1 cup	247	89	100	1	Trace	—	—	—	24	20	35	1.0	400	20	.07	.05	.5	84
Sweetened	1 cup	250	86	135	1	Trace	—	—	—	32	20	35	1.0	405	30	.08	.05	.5	78
Frozen, concentrate, unsweetened: Diluted with 3 parts water by volume.	1 cup	247	89	100	1	Trace	—	—	—	24	25	42	.2	420	20	.10	.04	.5	96
Grapes, European type (adherent skin), raw:																			
Thompson Seedless	10 grapes	50	81	35	Trace	Trace	—	—	—	9	6	10	.2	87	50	.03	.02	.2	2
Tokay and Emperor, seeded types	10 grapes[30]	60	81	40	Trace	Trace	—	—	—	10	7	11	.2	99	60	.03	.02	.2	2
Grapejuice:																			
Canned or bottled	1 cup	253	83	165	1	Trace	—	—	—	42	28	30	.8	293	—	.10	.05	.5	[25]Trace
Frozen concentrate, sweetened: Diluted with 3 parts water by volume.	1 cup	250	86	135	1	Trace	—	—	—	33	8	10	.3	85	10	.05	.08	.5	[31]10
Lemon, raw, size 165, without peel and seeds (about 4 per lb with peels and seeds).	1 lemon	74	90	20	1	Trace	—	—	—	6	19	12	.4	102	10	.03	.01	.1	39
Lemon Juice:																			
Raw	1 cup	244	91	60	1	Trace	—	—	—	20	17	24	.5	344	50	.07	.02	.2	112
Limejuice:																			
Raw	1 cup	246	90	65	1	Trace	—	—	—	22	22	27	.5	256	20	.05	.02	.2	79
Muskmelons, raw, with rind, without seed cavity:																			
Cantaloup, orange-fleshed (with rind and seed cavity, 5-in diam., 2 1/3 lb).	1/2 melon with rind[33]	477	91	80	2	Trace	—	—	—	20	38	44	1.1	682	9,240	.11	.08	1.6	90
Honeydew (with rind and seed cavity, 6 1/2-in diam., 5 1/4 lb).	1/10 melon with rind[33]	226	91	50	1	Trace	—	—	—	11	21	24	.6	374	60	.06	.04	.9	34
Oranges, all commercial varieties, raw:																			
Whole, 2 5/8-in diam., without peel and seeds (about 2' 1/2 per lb with peel and seeds).	1 orange	131	86	65	1	Trace	—	—	—	16	54	26	.5	263	260	.13	.05	.5	66
Sections without membranes	1 cup	180	86	90	2	Trace	—	—	—	22	74	36	.7	360	360	.18	.07	.7	90
Orange Juice:																			
Raw, all varieties	1 cup	248	88	110	2	Trace	—	—	—	26	27	42	.5	496	500	.22	.07	1.0	124
Canned, unsweetened	1 cup	249	87	120	2	Trace	—	—	—	28	25	45	1.0	496	500	.17	.05	.7	100
Frozen concentrate: Diluted with 3 parts water by volume.	1 cup	249	87	120	2	Trace	—	—	—	29	25	42	.2	503	540	.23	.03	.9	120
Papayas, raw, 1/2-in cubes	1 cup	140	89	55	1	Trace	—	—	—	14	28	22	.4	328	2,450	.06	.06	.4	78
Peaches:																			
Raw:																			
Whole, 2 1/2-in diam., peeled, pitted (about 4 per lb with peels and pits).	1 peach	100	89	40	1	Trace	—	—	—	10	9	19	.5	202	[34]1,330	.02	.05	1.0	7
Sliced	1 cup	170	89	65	1	Trace	—	—	—	16	15	32	.9	343	[35]2,260	.03	.09	1.7	12
Canned, yellow-fleshed, solids and liquid (halves or slices):																			
Sirup pack	1 cup	256	79	200	1	Trace	—	—	—	51	10	31	.8	333	1,100	.03	.05	1.5	8
Water pack	1 cup	244	91	75	1	Trace	—	—	—	20	10	32	.7	334	1,100	.02	.07	1.5	7
Dried:																			
Uncooked	1 cup	160	25	420	5	1	—	—	—	109	77	187	9.6	1,520	6,240	.02	.30	8.5	29
Cooked, unsweetened, halves and juice.	1 cup	250	77	205	3	1	—	—	—	54	38	93	4.8	743	3,050	.01	.15	3.8	5

Item No. (A)

NUTRIENTS IN INDICATED QUANTITY

Fatty Acids

(A)	(B)	g	(C)	(D)	(E)	(F)	(G)	(H)	(I)	(J)	(K)	(L)	(M)	(N)	(O)	(P)	(Q)	(R)	(S)
Frozen, sliced, sweetened:																			
Cup	1 cup	250	77	220	1	Trace	—	—	—	57	10	33	1.3	310	1,630	.03	.10	1.8	[35]103
Pears:																			
Raw, with skin, cored:																			
Bartlett, 2 1/2-in diam. (about 2 1/2 per lb with cores and stems).	1 pear	164	83	100	1	1	—	—	—	25	13	18	.5	213	30	.03	.07	.2	7
Bosc, 2 1/2-in diam. (about 3 per lb with cores and stems).	1 pear	141	83	85	1	1	—	—	—	22	11	16	.4	83	30	.03	.06	.1	6
D'Anjou, 3-in diam. (about 2 per lb with cores and stems).	1 pear	200	83	120	1	1	—	—	—	31	16	22	.6	260	40	.04	.08	.2	8
Canned, solids and liquid, sirup pack, heavy (halves or slices).	1 cup	255	80	195	1	1	—	—	—	50	13	18	.5	214	10	.03	.05	.3	3
Pineapple:																			
Raw, diced	1 cup	155	85	80	1	Trace	—	—	—	21	26	12	.8	226	110	.14	.05	.3	26
Canned, heavy sirup pack, solids and liquid:																			
Crushed, chunks, tidbits	1 cup	255	80	190	1	Trace	—	—	—	49	28	13	.8	245	130	.20	.05	.5	18
Slices and liquid:																			
Medium	1 slice; 1 1/4 tbsp liquid.	58	80	45	Trace	Trace	—	—	—	11	6	3	.2	56	30	.05	.01	.1	4
Pineapple juice, unsweetened, canned.	1 cup	250	86	140	1	Trace	—	—	—	34	38	23	.8	373	130	.13	.05	.5	[27]80
Plums:																			
Raw, without pits:																			
Japanese and hybrid (2 1/8-in diam., about 6 1/2 per lb with pits).	1 plum	66	87	30	Trace	Trace	—	—	—	8	8	12	.3	112	160	.02	.02	.3	4
Canned, heavy sirup pack (Italian prunes), with pits and liquid:																			
Cup	1 cup	272	77	215	1	Trace	—	—	—	56	23	26	2.3	367	3,130	.05	.05	1.0	5
Prunes, dried, "softenized," with pits:																			
Uncooked	4 extra large or 5 large prunes.[36]	49	28	110	1	Trace	—	—	—	29	22	34	1.7	298	690	.04	.07	.7	1
Prune juice, canned or bottled	1 cup	256	80	195	1	Trace	—	—	—	49	36	51	1.8	602	—	.03	.03	1.0	5
Raisins, seedless:																			
Cup, not pressed down	1 cup	145	18	420	4	Trace	—	—	—	112	90	146	5.1	1,106	30	.16	.12	.7	1
Raspberries, red:																			
Raw, capped, whole	1 cup	123	84	70	1	1	—	—	—	17	27	27	1.1	207	160	.04	.11	1.1	31
Rhubarb, cooked, added sugar:																			
From raw	1 cup	270	63	380	1	Trace	—	—	—	97	211	41	1.6	548	220	.05	.14	.8	16
Strawberries:																			
Raw, whole berries, capped	1 cup	149	90	55	1	1	—	—	—	13	31	31	1.5	244	90	0.04	0.10	0.9	88
Tangerine, raw, 2 3/8-in diam., size 176, without peel (about 4 per lb with peels and seeds).	1 tangerine	86	87	40	1	Trace	—	—	—	10	34	15	.3	108	360	.05	.02	.1	27
Watermelon, raw, 4 by 8 in wedge with rind and seeds[37] (1/16 of 32 2/3-lb melon, 10 by 16 in).	1 wedge with rind and seeds	926	93	110	2	1	—	—	—	27	30	43	2.1	426	2,510	.13	.13	.9	30

GRAIN PRODUCTS

(A)	(B)	g	(C)	(D)	(E)	(F)	(G)	(H)	(I)	(J)	(K)	(L)	(M)	(N)	(O)	(P)	(Q)	(R)	(S)
Bagel, 3-in diam.: Water	1 bagel	55	29	165	6	2	.2	.6	.4	30	8	41	1.2	42	0	.15	.11	1.4	0
Barley, pearled, light, uncooked	1 cup	200	11	700	16	2	.3	.8	.8	158	32	378	4.0	320	0	.24	.10	6.2	0
Biscuits, baking powder, 2-in diam. (enriched flour, vegetable shortening): From home recipe	1 biscuit	28	27	105	2	5	1.2	2.0	1.2	13	34	49	.4	33	Trace	.08	.08	.7	Trace
Dry, grated	1 cup	100	7	390	13	5	1.0	1.6	1.4	73	122	141	3.6	152	Trace	.35	.35	4.8	Trace
Soft. See white bread																			
Breads: Slice (18 per loaf)	1 slice	25	35	65	2	1	.1	.2	.2	13	22	32	.5	34	Trace	.08	.06	.8	Trace
French or vienna bread, enriched:[38] Slice: French (5 by 2 1/2 by 1 in)	1 slice	35	31	100	3	1	.2	.4	.2	19	15	30	.8	32	Trace	.14	.08	1.2	Trace
Vienna (4 3/4 by 4 by 1/2 in)	1 slice	25	31	75	2	1	.2	.3	.2	14	11	21	.6	23	Trace	.10	.06	.8	Trace

NUTRITIVE VALUES OF THE EDIBLE PART OF FOODS - Continued

(Dashes (—) denote lack of reliable data for a constituent believed to be present in measurable amount)

Item No. / Foods, approximate measures, units, and weight (edible part unless footnotes indicate otherwise) (A) (B)	Grams	Water (C) Percent	Food energy (D) Calories	Protein (E) Grams	Fat (F) Grams	Fatty Acids — Saturated (total) (G) Grams	Fatty Acids — Unsaturated Oleic (H) Grams	Fatty Acids — Unsaturated Linoleic (I) Grams	Carbo-hydrate (I) Grams	Calcium (K) Milligrams	Phos-phorus (L) Milligrams	Iron (M) Milligrams	Potas-sium (N) Milligrams	Vitamin A value (O) International units	Thiamin (P) Milligrams	Ribo-flavin (Q) Milligrams	Niacin (R) Milligrams	Ascorbic acid (S) Milligrams
Italian bread, enriched:																		
Slice, 4 1/2 by 3 1/4 by 3/4 in. — 1 slice	30	32	85	3	Trace	Trace	Trace	.1	17	5	23	.7	22	0	.12	.07	1.0	0
Raisin bread, enriched:[38]																		
Slice (18 per loaf) — 1 slice	25	35	65	2	1	.2	.3	.2	13	18	22	.6	58	Trace	.09	.06	.6	Trace
Rye Bread:																		
American, light (2/3 enriched wheat flour, 1/3 rye flour):																		
Slice (4 3/4 by 3 3/4 by 7/16 in) — 1 slice	25	36	60	2	Trace	Trace	Trace	.1	13	19	37	.5	36	0	.07	.05	.7	0
Pumpernickel (2/3 rye flour, 1/3 enriched wheat flour):																		
Slice (5 by 4 by 3/8 in) — 1 slice	32	34	80	3	Trace	.1	Trace	.2	17	27	73	.8	145	0	.09	.07	.6	0
White bread, enriched:[38]																		
Soft-crumb type:																		
Slice (18 per loaf) — 1 slice	25	36	70	2	1	.2	.3	.3	13	21	24	.6	26	Trace	.10	.06	.8	Trace
Slice (22 per loaf) — 1 slice	20	36	55	2	1	.2	.2	.2	10	17	19	.5	21	Trace	.08	.05	.7	Trace
Slice (24 per loaf) — 1 slice	28	36	75	2	1	.2	.3	.3	14	24	27	.7	29	Trace	.11	.07	.9	Trace
Slice (28 per loaf) — 1 slice	24	36	65	2	1	.2	.3	.2	12	20	23	.6	25	Trace	.10	.06	.8	Trace
Cubes — 1 cup	30	36	80	3	1	.2	.3	.3	15	25	29	.8	32	Trace	.12	.07	1.0	Trace
Crumbs — 1 cup	45	36	120	4	1	.3	.5	.5	23	38	44	1.1	47	Trace	.18	.11	1.5	Trace
Firm-crumb type:																		
Slice (20 per loaf) — 1 slice	23	35	65	2	1	.2	.3	.3	12	22	23	.6	28	Trace	.09	.06	.8	Trace
Loaf, 2 lb — 1 loaf	907	35	2,495	82	34	7.7	11.8	10.4	455	871	925	22.7	1,097	Trace	3.60	2.20	30.0	Trace
Slice, toasted — 1 slice	23	24	75	2	1	.2	.3	.3	14	26	28	.7	33	Trace	.09	.06	.9	Trace
Whole-wheat bread:																		
Soft-crumb type:[38]																		
Slice (16 per loaf) — 1 slice	28	36	65	3	1	1	.2	.2	14	24	71	.8	72	Trace	.09	.03	.8	Trace
Firm-crumb type:[38]																		
Slice (18 per loaf) — 1 slice	25	36	60	3	1	.1	.2	.3	12	25	57	.8	68	Trace	.06	.03	.7	Trace
Breakfast cereals:																		
Hot type, cooked:																		
Corn (hominy) grits, degermed: Enriched — 1 cup	245	87	125	3	Trace	Trace	Trace	.1	27	2	25	.7	27	[40]Trace	.10	.07	1.0	0
Farina, quick-cooking, enriched — 1 cup	245	89	105	3	Trace	Trace	Trace	.1	22	[41]147	[41]113	(42)	25	0	.12	.07	1.0	0
Oatmeal or rolled oats — 1 cup	240	87	130	5	2	.4	.8	.9	23	22	137	1.4	146	0	.19	.05	.2	0
Wheat, rolled — 1 cup	240	80	180	5	1	—	—	—	41	19	182	1.7	202	0	.17	.07	2.2	0
Ready-to-eat:																		
Bran flakes (40% bran), added sugar, salt, iron, vitamins — 1 cup	35	3	105	4	1	—	—	—	28	19	125	15.6	137	1,650	.41	.49	4.1	12
Bran flakes with raisins, added sugar, salt, iron, vitamins — 1 cup	50	7	145	4	1	—	—	—	40	28	146	16.9	154	2,350	.58	.71	5.8	18
Corn flakes: Plain, added sugar, salt, iron, vitamins — 1 cup	25	4	95	2	Trace	—	—	—	21	(43)	9	0.6	30	1,180	.29	.35	2.9	9
Sugar-coated, added salt, iron, vitamins — 1 cup	40	2	155	2	Trace	—	—	—	37	1	10	1.0	27	1,880	.46	.56	4.6	14
Corn, puffed, plain, added sugar, salt, iron, vitamins — 1 cup	20	4	80	2	1	—	—	—	16	4	18	2.3	—	940	.23	.28	2.3	7
Oats, puffed, added sugar, salt, minerals, vitamins — 1 cup	25	3	100	3	1	—	—	—	19	44	102	2.9	—	1,180	.29	.35	2.9	9
Rice, puffed: Plain, added iron, thiamin, niacin — 1 cup	15	4	60	1	Trace	—	—	—	13	3	14	.3	15	0	.07	.01	.7	0
Presweetened, added salt, iron, vitamins — 1 cup	28	3	115	1	0	—	—	—	26	3	14	[49]1.1	43	1,250	.38	.43	5.0	[45]15
Wheat flakes, added sugar, salt, iron, vitamins — 1 cup	30	4	105	3	Trace	—	—	—	24	12	83	([53])	81	1,410	.35	.42	3.5	11
Wheat, puffed: Plain, added iron, thiamin, niacin — 1 cup	15	3	55	2	Trace	—	—	—	12	4	48	.6	51	0	.08	.03	1.2	0

Food	Measure	(B)	(C)	(D)	(E)	(F)	(G)	(H)	(I)	(J)	(K)	(L)	(M)	(N)	(O)	(P)	(Q)	(R)	(S)
Presweetened, added salt, iron, vitamins.	1 cup	38	3	140	3	Trace	—	—	—	33	7	52	[4]1.6	63	1,680	.50	.57	6.7	[4]520
Wheat, shredded, plain	1 oblong biscuit or 1/2 cup spoon-size biscuits.	25	7	90	2	1	—	—	—	20	11	97	.9	87	0	.06	.03	1.1	0
Wheat germ, without salt and sugar, toasted.	1 tbsp	6	4	25	2	1	—	—	—	3	3	70	.5	57	10	.11	.05	.3	1
Cake icings. See Sugars and Sweets																			
Cakes made from cake mixes with enriched flour:[46]																			
Angelfood: Piece, 1/12 of cake	1 piece	53	34	135	3	Trace	—	—	—	32	50	63	.2	32	0	.03	.08	.3	0
Coffeecake: Piece, 1/6 of cake	1 piece	72	30	230	5	7	2.0	2.7	1.5	38	44	125	1.2	78	120	.14	.15	1.3	Trace
Cupcakes, made with egg, milk, 2 1/2-in diam.: Without icing	1 cupcake	25	26	90	1	3	.8	1.2	.7	14	40	59	.3	21	40	.05	.05	.4	Trace
Devil's food with chocolate icing: Piece, 1/16 of cake	1 piece	69	24	235	3	8	3.1	2.8	1.1	40	41	72	1.0	90	100	.07	.10	.6	Trace
Cupcake, 2 1/2-in diam	1 cupcake	35	24	120	2	4	1.6	1.4	.5	20	21	37	.5	46	50	.03	.05	.3	Trace
Gingerbread: Piece, 1/9 of cake	1 piece	63	37	175	2	4	1.1	1.8	1.1	32	57	63	.9	173	Trace	.09	.11	.8	Trace
White, 2 layer with chocolate icing: Piece, 1/16 of cake	1 piece	71	21	250	3	8	3.0	2.9	1.2	45	70	127	.7	82	40	.09	.11	.8	Trace
Yellow, 2 layer with chocolate icing: Piece, 1/16 of cake	1 piece	69	26	235	3	8	3.0	3.0	1.3	40	63	126	.8	75	100	.08	.10	.7	Trace
Cakes made from home recipes using enriched flour:[47]																			
Boston cream pie with custard filling: Piece, 1/12 of cake	1 piece	69	35	210	3	6	1.9	2.5	1.3	34	46	70	.7	[48]61	140	.09	.11	.8	Trace
Fruitcake, dark: Slice, 1/30 of loaf	1 slice	15	18	55	1	2	.5	1.1	.5	9	11	17	.4	74	20	.02	.02	.2	Trace
Plain, sheet cake: Without icing: Whole cake (9-in square)	1 cake	777	25	2,830	35	108	29.5	44.4	23.9	434	497	793	8.5	[48]614	1,320	1.21	1.40	10.2	2
Piece, 1/9 of cake	1 piece	86	25	315	4	12	3.3	4.9	2.6	48	55	88	.9	[48]68	150	.13	.15	1.1	Trace
With uncooked white icing: Piece, 1/9 of cake	1 piece	121	21	445	4	14	4.7	5.5	2.7	77	61	91	.8	[47]74	240	.14	.16	1.1	Trace
Pound:[49] Slice, 1/17 of loaf	1 slice	33	16	160	2	10	2.5	4.3	2.3	16	6	24	.5	20	80	.05	.06	.4	0
Spongecake: Piece, 1/12 of cake	1 piece	66	32	195	5	4	1.1	1.3	.5	36	20	74	1.1	57	300	.09	.14	.6	0
Cookies made with enriched flour:[50][51]																			
Brownies with nuts: Home-prepared, 1 3/4 by 1 3/4 by 7/8 in: From home recipe	1 brownie	20	10	95	1	6	1.5	3.0	1.2	10	8	30	.4	38	40	.04	.03	.2	Trace
From commercial recipe	1 brownie	20	11	85	1	4	.9	1.4	1.3	13	9	27	.4	34	20	.03	.02	.2	Trace
Frozen, with chocolate icing,[52] 1 1/2 by 1 3/4 by 7/8 in.	1 brownie	25	13	105	1	5	2.0	2.2	.7	15	10	31	.4	44	50	.03	.03	.2	Trace
Chocolate chip: Commercial, 2 1/4-in diam., 3/8 in thick.	4 cookies	42	3	200	2	9	2.8	2.9	2.2	29	16	48	1.0	56	50	.10	.17	.9	Trace
From home recipe, 2 1/3-in diam.	4 cookies	40	3	205	2	12	3.5	4.5	2.9	24	14	40	.8	47	40	.06	.06	.5	Trace
Fig bars, square (1 5/8 by 1 5/8 by 3/8 in) or rectangular (1 1/2 by 1 3/4 by 1/2 in).	4 cookies	56	14	200	2	3	.8	1.2	.7	42	44	34	1.0	111	60	.04	.14	.9	Trace
Gingersnaps, 2-in diam., 1/4 in thick.	4 cookies	28	3	90	2	2	.7	1.0	.6	22	20	13	.7	129	20	.08	.06	.7	0
Macaroons, 2 3/4-in diam., 1/4 in thick.	2 cookies	38	4	180	2	9	—	—	—	25	10	32	.3	176	0	.02	.06	.2	0
Oatmeal with raisins, 2 5/8-in diam., 1/4 in thick.	4 cookies	52	3	235	3	8	2.0	3.3	2.0	38	11	53	1.4	192	30	.15	.10	1.0	Trace
Plain, prepared from commercial chilled dough, 2 1/2-in diam., 1/4 in thick.	4 cookies	48	5	240	2	12	3.0	5.2	2.9	31	17	35	0.6	23	30	0.10	0.08	0.9	0
Sandwich type (chocolate or vanilla), 1 3/4-in diam., 3/8 in thick.	4 cookies	40	2	200	2	9	2.2	3.9	2.2	28	10	96	.7	15	0	.06	.10	.7	0

NUTRITIVE VALUES OF THE EDIBLE PART OF FOODS - Continued

(Dashes (—) denote lack of reliable data for a constituent believed to be present in measurable amount)

NUTRIENTS IN INDICATED QUANTITY

Foods, approximate measures, units, and weight (edible part unless footnotes indicate otherwise) (B)	(grams)	Water (C) Per cent	Food energy (D) Calories	Protein (E) Grams	Fat (F) Grams	Fatty Acids Saturated (total) (G) Grams	Unsat. Oleic (H) Grams	Unsat. Linoleic (I) Grams	Carbohydrate (J) Grams	Calcium (K) Milligrams	Phosphorus (L) Milligrams	Iron (M) Milligrams	Potassium (N) Milligrams	Vitamin A value (O) International units	Thiamin (P) Milligrams	Riboflavin (Q) Milligrams	Niacin (R) Milligrams	Ascorbic acid (S) Milligrams
Vanilla wafers, 1 3/4-in diam., 1/4 in thick. — 10 cookies	40	3	185	2	6	—	—	—	30	16	25	.6	29	50	.10	.09	.8	0
Cornmeal: Whole-ground, unbolted, dry form. — 1 cup	122	12	435	11	5	.5	1.0	2.5	90	24	312	2.9	346	[5,6]620	.46	.13	2.4	0
Degermed, enriched: Cooked — 1 cup	240	88	120	3	Trace	Trace	.1	.2	26	2	34	1.0	38	[5]140	.14	.10	1.2	0
Crackers:[38] Graham, plain, 2 1/2-in square — 2 crackers	14	6	55	1	1	.3	.5	.3	10	6	21	.5	55	0	.02	.08	.5	0
Rye wafers, whole-grain, 1 7/8 by 3 1/2 in. — 2 wafers	13	6	45	2	Trace	—	—	—	10	7	50	.5	78	0	.04	.03	.2	0
Saltines, made with enriched flour. — 4 crackers or 1 packet	11	4	50	1	1	.3	.5	.4	8	2	10	.5	13	0	.05	.05	.4	0
Doughnuts, made with enriched flour:[38] Cake type, plain, 2 1/2-in diam., 1 in high. — 1 doughnut	25	24	100	1	5	1.2	2.0	1.1	13	10	48	.4	23	20	.05	.05	.4	Trace
Yeast-leavened, glazed, 3 3/4-in diam., 1 1/4 in high. — 1 doughnut	50	26	205	3	11	3.3	5.8	3.3	22	16	33	.6	34	25	.10	.10	.8	0
Macaroni, enriched, cooked (cut lengths, elbows, shells): Firm stage (hot) — 1 cup	130	64	190	7	1	—	—	—	39	14	85	1.4	103	0	.23	.13	1.8	0
Tender stage: Cold macaroni — 1 cup	105	73	115	4	Trace	—	—	—	24	8	53	.9	64	0	.15	.08	1.2	0
Hot macaroni — 1 cup	140	73	155	5	1	—	—	—	32	11	70	1.3	85	0	.20	.11	1.5	0
Macaroni (enriched) and cheese: From home recipe (served hot)[38,bb] — 1 cup	200	58	430	17	22	8.9	8.8	2.9	40	362	322	1.8	240	860	.20	.40	1.8	Trace
Muffins made with enriched flour:[38] From home recipe: Blueberry, 2 3/8-in diam., 1 1/2 in high. — 1 muffin	40	39	110	3	4	1.1	1.4	.7	17	34	53	.6	46	90	.09	.10	.7	Trace
Bran — 1 muffin	40	35	105	3	4	1.2	1.4	.8	17	57	162	1.5	172	90	.07	.10	1.7	Trace
Corn (enriched degermed cornmeal and flour), 2 3/8-in diam., 1 1/2 in high. — 1 muffin	40	33	125	3	4	1.2	1.6	.9	19	42	68	.7	54	[5,7]120	.10	.10	.7	Trace
Plain, 3-in diam., 1 1/2 in high. — 1 muffin	40	38	120	3	4	1.0	1.7	1.0	17	42	60	.6	50	40	.09	.12	.9	Trace
Noodles (egg noodles), enriched, cooked. — 1 cup	160	71	200	7	2	—	—	—	37	16	94	1.4	70	110	.22	.13	1.9	0
Noodles, chow mein, canned. — 1 cup	45	1	220	6	11	—	—	—	26	—	—	—	—	—	—	—	—	—
Pancakes, (4-in diam.):[38] Plain: Made from home recipe using enriched flour. — 1 cake	27	50	60	2	2	.5	.8	.5	9	27	38	.4	33	30	.06	.07	.5	Trace
Made from mix with enriched flour, egg and milk added. — 1 cake	27	51	60	2	2	.7	.7	.3	9	58	70	.3	42	70	.04	.06	.2	Trace
Pies, piecrust made with enriched flour, vegetable shortening (9-in diam.): Apple: Sector, 1/7 of pie — 1 sector	135	48	345	3	15	3.9	6.4	3.6	51	11	30	.9	108	40	.15	.11	1.3	2
Banana cream: Sector, 1/7 of pie — 1 sector	130	54	285	6	12	3.8	4.7	2.3	40	86	107	1.0	264	330	.11	.22	1.0	1
Blueberry: Sector, 1/7 of pie — 1 sector	135	51	325	3	15	3.5	6.2	3.6	47	15	31	1.4	88	40	.15	.11	1.4	4
Cherry: Sector, 1/7 of pie — 1 sector	135	47	350	4	15	4.0	6.4	3.6	52	19	34	.9	142	590	.16	.12	1.4	Trace
Custard: Sector, 1/7 of pie — 1 sector	130	58	285	8	14	4.8	5.5	2.5	30	125	147	1.2	178	300	.11	.27	.8	0
Lemon meringue: Sector, 1/7 of pie — 1 sector	120	47	305	4	12	3.7	4.8	2.3	45	17	59	1.0	60	200	.09	.12	.7	4

(A)	(B)	(C)	(D)	(E)	(F)	(G)	(H)	(I)	(J)	(K)	(L)	(M)	(N)	(O)	(P)	(Q)	(R)	(S)
Mince:																		
Sector, 1/7 of pie	1 sector	135	365	3	16	4.0	6.6	3.6	56	38	51	1.9	240	Trace	.14	.12	1.4	1
Peach:																		
Sector, 1/7 of pie	1 sector	135	345	3	14	3.5	6.2	3.6	52	14	39	1.2	201	990	.15	.14	2.0	4
Pecan:																		
Sector, 1/7 of pie	1 sector	118	495	6	27	4.0	14.4	6.3	61	55	122	3.7	145	190	.26	.14	1.0	Trace
Pumpkin:																		
Sector, 1/7 of pie	1 sector	130	275	5	15	5.4	5.4	2.4	32	66	90	1.0	208	3,210	.11	.18	1.0	Trace
Pizza (cheese) baked, 4 3/4-in sector; 1/8 of 12-in pie.[19]	1 sector	60	145	6	4	1.7	1.5	0.6	22	86	89	1.1	67	230	0.16	0.18	1.6	4
Popcorn, popped:																		
Plain, large kernel	1 cup	6	25	1	Trace	Trace	.1	.2	5	1	17	.2	—	—	—	.01	.1	0
With oil (coconut) and salt added, large kernel.	1 cup	9	40	1	2	1.5	.2	.2	5	1	19	.2	—	—	—	.01	.2	0
Pretzels, made with enriched flour:																		
Dutch, twisted, 2 3/4 by 2 5/8 in.	1 pretzel	16	60	2	1	—	—	—	12	4	21	.2	21	0	.05	.04	.7	0
Thin, twisted, 3 1/4 by 2 1/4 by 1/4 in.	10 pretzels	60	235	6	3	—	—	—	46	13	79	.9	78	0	.20	.15	2.5	0
Stick, 2 1/4 in long	10 pretzels	3	10	Trace	Trace	—	—	—	2	1	4	Trace	4	0	.01	.01	.1	0
Rice, white, enriched:																		
Instant, ready-to-serve, hot	1 cup	165	180	4	Trace	Trace	Trace	Trace	40	5	31	1.3	—	0	.21	(59)	1.7	0
Long grain:																		
Cooked, served hot	1 cup	205	225	4	Trace	.1	.1	.1	50	21	57	1.8	57	0	.23	.02	2.1	0
Parboiled:																		
Cooked, served hot	1 cup	175	185	4	Trace	.1	.1	.1	41	33	100	1.4	75	0	.19	.02	2.1	0
Rolls, enriched:[38]																		
Commercial:																		
Brown-and-serve (12 per 12-oz pkg.), browned.	1 roll	26	85	2	2	.4	.7	.5	14	20	23	.5	25	Trace	.10	.06	.9	Trace
Cloverleaf or pan, 2 1/2-in diam., 2 in high.	1 roll	28	85	2	2	.4	.6	.4	15	21	24	.5	27	Trace	.11	.07	.9	Trace
Frankfurter and hamburger (8 per 11 1/2-oz pkg.).	1 roll	40	120	3	2	.5	.8	.6	21	30	34	.8	38	Trace	.16	.10	1.3	Trace
Hard, 3 3/4-in diam., 2 in high.	1 roll	50	155	5	2	.4	.6	.5	30	24	46	1.2	49	Trace	.20	.12	1.7	Trace
Hoagie or submarine, 11 1/2 by 3 by 2 1/2 in.	1 roll	135	390	12	4	.9	1.4	1.4	75	58	115	3.0	122	Trace	.54	.32	4.5	Trace
From home recipe:																		
Cloverleaf, 2 1/2-in diam., 2 in high.	1 roll	35	120	3	3	.8	1.1	.7	20	16	36	.7	41	30	.12	.12	1.2	Trace
Spaghetti, enriched, cooked:																		
Firm stage, "al dente," served hot.	1 cup	130	190	7	1	—	—	—	39	14	85	1.4	103	0	.23	.13	1.8	0
Tender stage, served hot.	1 cup	140	155	5	1	—	—	—	32	11	70	1.3	85	0	.20	.11	1.5	0
Spaghetti (enriched) in tomato sauce with cheese:																		
From home recipe	1 cup	250	260	9	9	2.0	5.4	.7	37	80	135	2.3	408	1,080	.25	.18	2.3	13
Spaghetti (enriched) with meat balls and tomato sauce:																		
From home recipe	1 cup	248	330	19	12	3.3	6.3	.9	39	124	236	3.7	665	1,590	.25	.30	4.0	22
Waffles, made with enriched flour, 7-in diam.:[38]																		
From home recipe	1 waffle	75	210	7	7	2.3	2.8	1.4	28	85	130	1.3	109	250	.17	.23	1.4	Trace
From mix, egg and milk added	1 waffle	75	205	7	8	2.8	2.9	1.2	27	179	257	1.0	146	170	.14	.22	.9	Trace
Wheat flours:																		
All-purpose or family flour, enriched:																		
Sifted, spooned	1 cup	115	420	12	1	.2	.1	.5	88	18	100	3.3	109	0	.74	.46	6.1	0
Unsifted, spooned	1 cup	125	455	13	1	.2	.1	.5	95	20	109	3.6	119	0	.80	.50	6.6	0
Cake or pastry flour, enriched, sifted, spooned.	1 cup	96	350	7	1	.1	.1	.3	76	16	70	2.8	91	0	.61	.38	5.1	0
Self-rising, enriched, unsifted, spooned.	1 cup	125	440	12	1	.2	.1	.5	93	331	583	3.6	—	0	.80	.50	6.6	0
Whole-wheat, from hard wheats, stirred.	1 cup	120	400	16	2	.4	.2	1.0	85	49	446	4.0	444	0	.66	.14	5.2	0
LEGUMES (DRY), NUTS, SEEDS; RELATED PRODUCTS																		
Almonds, shelled:																		
Slivered, not pressed down (about 115 almonds).	1 cup	115	690	21	62	5.0	42.2	11.3	22	269	580	5.4	889	0	.28	1.06	4.0	Trace

NUTRITIVE VALUES OF THE EDIBLE PART OF FOODS - Continued

(Dashes (—) denote lack of reliable data for a constituent believed to be present in measurable amount)

NUTRIENTS IN INDICATED QUANTITY

Item No. (A)	Foods, approximate measures, units, and weight (edible part unless footnotes indicate otherwise) (B)	Water (C) Per-cent	Food energy (D) Cal-ories	Pro-tein (E) Grams	Fat (F) Grams	Fatty Acids Saturated (total) (G) Grams	Unsaturated Oleic (H) Grams	Unsaturated Linoleic (I) Grams	Carbo-hydrate (J) Grams	Calcium (K) Milli-grams	Phos-phorus (L) Milli-grams	Iron (M) Milli-grams	Potas-sium (N) Milli-grams	Vitamin A value (O) Inter-national units	Thiamin (P) Milli-grams	Ribo-flavin (Q) Milli-grams	Niacin (R) Milli-grams	Ascorbic acid (S) Milli-grams
	Beans, dry:																	
	Common varieties as Great Northern, navy, and others:																	
	Cooked, drained:																	
	Great Northern —— 1 cup	69	210	14	1	—	—	—	38	90	266	4.9	749	0	.25	.13	1.3	0
	Pea (navy) —— 1 cup	69	225	15	1	—	—	—	40	95	281	5.1	790	0	.27	.13	1.3	0
	Red kidney —— 1 cup	76	230	15	1	—	—	—	42	74	278	4.6	673	10	.13	.10	1.5	—
	Lima, cooked, drained —— 1 cup	64	260	16	1	—	—	—	49	55	293	5.9	1,163	—	.25	.11	1.3	—
	Blackeye peas, dry, cooked (with residual cooking liquid) —— 1 cup	80	190	13	1	—	—	—	35	43	238	3.3	573	30	.40	.10	1.0	—
	Brazil nuts, shelled (6-8 large kernels) —— 1 oz	5	185	4	19	4.8	6.2	7.1	3	53	196	1.0	203	Trace	.27	.03	.5	—
	Cashew nuts, roasted in oil —— 1 cup	5	785	24	64	12.9	36.8	10.2	41	53	522	5.3	650	140	.60	.35	2.5	—
	Coconut meat, fresh:																	
	Piece, about 2 by 2 by 1/2 in —— 1 piece	51	155	2	16	14.0	.9	.3	4	6	43	.8	115	0	.02	.01	.2	1
	Shredded or grated, not pressed down —— 1 cup	51	275	3	28	24.8	1.6	.5	8	10	76	1.4	205	0	.04	.02	.4	2
	Filberts (hazelnuts), chopped (about 80 kernels) —— 1 cup	6	730	14	72	5.1	55.2	7.3	19	240	388	3.9	810	—	.53	—	1.0	Trace
	Lentils, whole, cooked —— 1 cup	72	210	16	Trace	—	—	—	39	50	238	4.2	498	40	.14	.12	1.2	0
	Peanuts, roasted in oil, salted (whole, halves, chopped) —— 1 cup	2	840	37	72	13.7	33.0	20.7	27	107	577	3.0	971	—	.46	.19	24.8	0
	Peanut butter —— 1 tbsp	2	95	4	8	1.5	3.7	2.3	3	9	61	.3	100	—	.02	.02	2.4	0
	Peas, split, dry, cooked —— 1 cup	70	230	16	1	—	—	—	42	22	178	3.4	592	80	.30	.18	1.8	—
	Pecans, chopped or pieces (about 120 large halves) —— 1 cup	3	810	11	84	7.2	50.5	20.0	17	86	341	2.8	712	150	1.01	.15	1.1	2
	Sunflower seeds, dry, hulled —— 1 cup	5	810	35	69	8.2	13.7	43.2	29	174	1,214	10.3	1,334	70	2.84	.33	7.8	—
	Walnuts:																	
	Black:																	
	Chopped or broken kernels —— 1 cup	3	785	26	74	6.3	13.3	45.7	19	Trace	713	7.5	575	380	.28	.14	.9	—
	Persian or English, chopped (about 60 halves) —— 1 cup	4	780	18	77	8.4	11.8	42.2	19	119	456	3.7	540	40	.40	.16	1.1	2
	Cake icings:																	
	Boiled, white:																	
	Plain —— 1 cup	18	295	1	0	0	0	0	75	2	2	Trace	17	0	Trace	0.03	Trace	0
	Uncooked:																	
	Chocolate made with milk and butter —— 1 cup	14	1,035	9	38	23.4	11.7	1.0	185	165	305	3.3	536	580	.06	.28	.6	1
	White —— 1 cup	11	1,200	2	21	12.7	5.1	.5	260	48	38	Trace	57	860	Trace	.06	Trace	Trace
	Candy:																	
	Caramels, plain or chocolate —— 1 oz	8	115	1	3	1.6	1.1	.1	22	42	35	.4	54	Trace	.01	.05	.1	Trace
	Chocolate:																	
	Milk, plain —— 1 oz	1	145	2	9	5.5	3.0	.3	16	65	65	.3	109	80	.02	.10	.1	Trace
	Semisweet, small pieces (50 per oz) —— 1 cup or 6-oz pkg	1	860	7	61	36.2	19.8	1.7	97	51	255	4.4	553	30	.02	.14	.9	0
	Chocolate-coated peanuts —— 1 oz	1	160	5	12	4.0	4.7	2.1	11	33	84	.4	143	Trace	.10	.05	2.1	Trace
	Fondant, uncoated (mints, candy corn, other) —— 1 oz	8	105	Trace	1	.3	.3	.1	25	4	2	.3	—	0	Trace	Trace	Trace	0
	Fudge, chocolate, plain —— 1 oz	8	115	1	3	1.3	1.4	.6	21	22	24	.3	42	Trace	.01	.03	.1	Trace
	Gum drops —— 1 oz	12	100	Trace	Trace	—	—	—	25	2	Trace	.1	1	0	0	Trace	Trace	0
	Hard —— 1 oz	1	110	0	Trace	—	—	—	28	6	2	.5	1	0	0	0	0	0
	Marshmallows —— 1 oz	17	90	1	Trace	—	—	—	23	5	2	.5	2	0	0	Trace	Trace	0
	Chocolate-flavored beverage powders (about 4 heaping tsp per oz):																	
	Honey, strained or extracted —— 1 tbsp	17	65	Trace	0	0	0	0	17	1	1	.1	11	0	Trace	.01	.1	Trace
	Jams and preserves —— 1 tbsp	29	55	Trace	Trace	—	—	—	14	4	2	.2	18	Trace	Trace	.01	Trace	Trace
	—— 1 packet	29	40	Trace	Trace	—	—	—	10	3	1	.1	12	Trace	Trace	Trace	Trace	Trace
	Jellies —— 1 tbsp	29	50	Trace	Trace	—	—	—	13	4	1	.3	14	Trace	Trace	.01	Trace	Trace
	—— 1 packet	29	40	Trace	Trace	—	—	—	10	3	1	.2	11	Trace	Trace	Trace	Trace	1
	Sirups:																	
	Chocolate-flavored sirup or topping:																	
	Thin type —— 1 fl oz or 2 tbsp	32	90	1	1	.5	.3	Trace	24	6	35	.6	106	Trace	.01	.03	.2	0
	Fudge type —— 1 fl oz or 2 tbsp	25	125	2	5	3.1	1.6	.1	20	48	60	.5	107	60	.02	.08	.2	Trace

(A)	(B)	(C)	(D)	(E)	(F)	(G)	(H)	(I)	(J)	(K)	(L)	(M)	(N)	(O)	(P)	(Q)	(R)	(S)
Molasses, cane:																		
Light (first extraction)	1 tbsp	24	50	—	—	—	—	—	13	33	9	.9	183	—	.01	.01	Trace	—
Blackstrap (third extraction)	1 tbsp	24	45	—	—	—	—	—	11	137	17	3.2	585	—	.02	.04	.4	—
Sorghum	1 tbsp	23	55	—	—	—	—	—	14	35	5	2.6	—	—	—	.02	Trace	—
Table blends, chiefly corn, light and dark	1 tbsp	24	60	0	0	0	0	0	15	9	3	.8	1	0	0	0	0	0
Sugars:																		
Brown, pressed down	1 cup	2	820	0	0	0	0	0	212	187	42	7.5	757	0	.02	.07	.4	0
White:																		
Granulated	1 cup	1	770	0	0	0	0	0	199	0	0	.2	6	0	0	0	0	0
	1 tbsp	1	45	0	0	0	0	0	12	0	0	Trace	Trace	0	0	0	0	0
	1 packet	1	23	0	0	0	0	0	6	0	0	Trace	Trace	0	0	0	0	0
Powdered, sifted, spooned into cup.	1 cup	1	385	0	0	0	0	0	100	0	0	.1	3	0	0	0	0	0

VEGETABLE AND VEGETABLE PRODUCTS

(A)	(B)	(C)	(D)	(E)	(F)	(G)	(H)	(I)	(J)	(K)	(L)	(M)	(N)	(O)	(P)	(Q)	(R)	(S)
Asparagus, green:																		
Cooked, drained:																		
Cuts and tips, 1 1/2- to 2-in lengths:																		
From raw	1 cup	94	30	3	Trace	—	—	—	5	30	73	.9	265	1,310	.23	.26	2.0	38
From frozen	1 cup	93	40	6	Trace	—	—	—	6	40	115	2.2	396	1,530	.25	.23	1.8	41
Spears, 1/2-in diam. at base:																		
From raw	4 spears	94	10	1	Trace	—	—	—	2	13	30	.4	110	540	.10	.11	.8	16
From frozen	4 spears	92	15	2	Trace	—	—	—	2	13	40	.7	143	470	.10	.08	.7	16
Beans:																		
Lima, immature seeds, frozen, cooked, drained:																		
Thick-seeded types (Fordhooks)	1 cup	74	170	10	Trace	—	—	—	32	34	153	2.9	724	390	.12	.09	1.7	29
Thin-seeded types (baby limas)	1 cup	69	210	13	Trace	—	—	—	40	63	227	4.7	709	400	.16	.09	2.2	22
Snap:																		
Green:																		
Cooked, drained:																		
From raw (cuts and French style)	1 cup	92	30	2	Trace	—	—	—	7	63	46	.8	189	680	.09	.11	.6	15
From frozen:																		
Cuts	1 cup	92	35	2	Trace	—	—	—	8	54	43	.9	205	780	.09	.12	.5	7
French style	1 cup	92	35	2	Trace	—	—	—	8	49	39	1.2	177	690	.08	.10	.4	9
Canned, drained solids (cuts)	1 cup	92	30	2	Trace	—	—	—	7	61	34	2.0	128	630	.04	.07	.4	5
Yellow or wax:																		
Cooked, drained:																		
From raw (cuts and French style)	1 cup	93	30	2	Trace	—	—	—	6	63	46	.8	189	290	.09	.11	.6	16
From frozen (cuts)	1 cup	92	35	2	Trace	—	—	—	8	47	42	.9	221	140	.09	.11	.5	8
Canned, drained solids (cuts)	1 cup	92	30	2	Trace	—	—	—	7	61	34	2.0	128	140	.04	.07	.4	7
Beans, mature. See Beans, dry and Blackeye peas, dry																		
Bean sprouts (mung):																		
Raw	1 cup	89	35	4	Trace	—	—	—	7	20	67	1.4	234	20	.14	.14	.8	20
Beets:																		
Cooked, drained, peeled:																		
Whole beets, 2-in diam.	2 beets	91	30	1	Trace	—	—	—	7	14	23	.5	208	20	.03	.04	.3	6
Diced or sliced	1 cup	91	55	2	Trace	—	—	—	12	24	39	.9	354	30	.05	.07	.5	10
Canned, drained solids:																		
Whole beets, small	1 cup	89	60	2	Trace	—	—	—	14	30	29	1.1	267	30	.02	.05	.2	5
Diced or sliced	1 cup	89	65	2	Trace	—	—	—	15	32	31	1.2	284	30	.02	.05	.2	5
Broccoli, cooked, drained:																		
From raw:																		
Stalk, medium size	1 stalk	91	45	6	1	—	—	—	8	158	112	1.4	481	4,500	.16	.36	1.4	162
Stalks cut into 1/2-in pieces	1 cup	91	40	5	Trace	—	—	—	7	136	96	1.2	414	3,880	.14	.31	1.2	140
From frozen:																		
Stalk, 4 1/2 to 5 in long	1 stalk	91	10	1	Trace	—	—	—	1	12	17	.2	66	570	.02	.03	.2	22
Chopped	1 cup	92	50	5	1	—	—	—	9	100	104	1.3	392	4,810	.11	.22	.9	105
Brussels sprouts, cooked, drained:																		
From raw, 7-8 sprouts (1 1/4- to 1 1/2-in diam.)	1 cup	88	55	7	1	—	—	—	10	50	112	1.7	423	810	.12	.22	1.2	135
From frozen	1 cup	89	50	5	Trace	—	—	—	10	33	95	1.2	457	880	.12	.16	.9	126
Cabbage:																		
Common varieties:																		
Raw:																		
Coarsely shredded or sliced	1 cup	92	15	1	Trace	—	—	—	4	34	20	0.3	163	90	0.04	0.04	0.2	33

NUTRITIVE VALUES OF THE EDIBLE PART OF FOODS - Continued

(Dashes (—) denote lack of reliable data for a constituent believed to be present in measurable amount)

Item No. (A)	Foods, approximate measures, units, and weight (edible part unless otherwise indicated) (B)	(grams)	Water (C) Percent	Food energy (D) Calories	Protein (E) Grams	Fat (F) Grams	Fatty Acids Saturated (total) (G) Grams	Unsaturated Oleic (H) Grams	Linoleic (I) Grams	Carbohydrate (J) Grams	Calcium (K) Milligrams	Phosphorus (L) Milligrams	Iron (M) Milligrams	Potassium (N) Milligrams	Vitamin A value (O) International units	Thiamin (P) Milligrams	Riboflavin (Q) Milligrams	Niacin (R) Milligrams	Ascorbic acid (S) Milligrams
	Finely shredded or chopped-- 1 cup	90	92	20	1	Trace	—	—	—	5	44	26	.4	210	120	.05	.05	.3	42
	Cooked, drained-- 1 cup	145	94	30	2	Trace	—	—	—	6	64	29	.4	236	190	.06	.06	.4	48
	Red, raw, coarsely shredded or sliced. 1 cup	70	90	20	1	Trace	—	—	—	5	29	25	.6	188	30	.06	.04	.3	43
	Carrots: Raw, without crowns and tips, scraped:																		
	Whole, 7 1/2 by 1 1/8 in, or strips, 2 1/2 to 3 in long. 1 carrot or 18 strips	72	88	30	1	Trace	—	—	—	7	27	26	.5	246	7,930	.04	.04	.4	6
	Cooked (crosswise cuts), drained 1 cup	155	91	50	1	Trace	—	—	—	11	51	48	.9	344	16,280	.08	.08	.8	9
	Cauliflower: Raw, chopped-- 1 cup	115	91	31	3	Trace	—	—	—	6	29	64	1.3	339	70	.13	.12	.8	90
	Cooked, drained: From raw (flower buds)-- 1 cup	125	93	30	3	Trace	—	—	—	5	26	53	.9	258	80	.11	.10	.8	69
	From frozen (flowerets)-- 1 cup	180	94	30	3	Trace	—	—	—	6	31	68	.9	373	50	.07	.09	.7	74
	Celery, Pascal type, raw: Stalk, large outer, 8 by 1 1/2 in, at root end. 1 stalk	40	94	5	Trace	Trace	—	—	—	2	16	11	.1	136	110	.01	.01	.1	4
	Pieces, diced-- 1 cup	120	94	20	1	Trace	—	—	—	5	47	34	.4	409	320	.04	.04	.4	11
	Collards, cooked, drained: From raw (leaves without stems)- 1 cup	190	90	65	7	1	—	—	—	10	357	99	1.5	498	14,820	.21	.38	2.3	144
	From frozen (chopped)-- 1 cup	170	90	50	5	1	—	—	—	10	299	87	1.7	401	11,560	.10	.24	1.0	56
	Corn, sweet: Cooked, drained: From raw, ear 5 by 1 3/4 in- 1 ear[61]	140	74	70	2	1	—	—	—	16	2	69	.5	151	[62]310	.09	.08	1.1	7
	From frozen: Ear, 5 in long-- 1 ear[61]	229	73	120	4	1	—	—	—	27	4	121	1.0	291	[62]440	.18	.10	2.1	9
	Kernels-- 1 cup	165	77	130	5	1	—	—	—	31	5	120	1.3	304	[62]580	.15	.10	2.5	8
	Canned: Cream style-- 1 cup	256	76	210	5	2	—	—	—	51	8	143	1.5	248	[62]840	.08	.13	2.6	13
	Whole kernel: Vacuum pack-- 1 cup	210	76	175	5	1	—	—	—	43	6	153	1.1	204	[62]740	.06	.13	2.3	11
	Wet pack, drained solids-- 1 cup	165	76	140	4	1	—	—	—	33	8	81	.8	160	[62]580	.05	.08	1.5	7
	Cowpeas. See Blackeye peas.																		
	Cucumber slices, 1/8 in thick (large, 2 1/8-in diam.; small, 1 3/4-in diam.): With peel-- 6 large or 8 small slices	28	95	5	Trace	Trace	—	—	—	1	7	8	.3	45	70	.01	.01	.1	3
	Dandelion greens, cooked, drained-- 1 cup	105	90	35	2	1	—	—	—	7	147	44	1.9	244	12,290	.14	.17	—	19
	Endive, curly (including escarole), raw, small pieces. 1 cup	50	93	10	1	Trace	—	—	—	2	41	27	.9	147	1,650	.04	.07	.3	5
	Kale, cooked, drained: From raw (leaves without stems and midribs). 1 cup	110	88	45	5	1	—	—	—	7	206	64	1.8	243	9,130	.11	.20	1.8	102
	Lettuce, raw: Butterhead, as Boston types: Leaves-- 1 outer or 2 inner or 3 heart leaves.	15	95	Trace	Trace	Trace	—	—	—	Trace	5	4	.3	40	150	.01	.01	Trace	1
	Crisphead, as Iceberg: Wedge, 1/4 of head-- 1 wedge	135	96	20	2	Trace	—	—	—	4	27	30	.7	236	450	.08	.08	.4	8
	Pieces, chopped or shredded-- 1 cup	55	96	5	Trace	Trace	—	—	—	2	11	12	.3	96	180	.03	.03	.2	3
	Looseleaf (bunching varieties including romaine or cos), chopped or shredded pieces. 1 cup	55	94	10	1	Trace	—	—	—	2	37	14	.8	145	1,050	.03	.04	.2	10
	Mushrooms, raw, sliced or chopped-- 1 cup	70	90	20	2	Trace	—	—	—	3	4	81	.6	290	Trace	.07	.32	2.9	2
	Mustard greens, without stems and midribs, cooked, drained. 1 cup	140	93	30	3	1	—	—	—	6	193	45	2.5	308	8,120	.11	.20	.8	67
	Okra pods, 3 by 5/8 in, cooked-- 10 pods	106	91	30	2	Trace	—	—	—	6	98	43	.5	184	520	.14	.19	1.0	21
	Onions: Mature: Raw: Chopped-- 1 cup	170	89	65	3	Trace	—	—	—	15	46	61	.9	267	[65]Trace	.05	.07	.3	17
	Cooked (whole or sliced), drained. 1 cup	210	92	60	3	Trace	—	—	—	14	50	61	.8	231	[65]Trace	.06	.06	.4	15

(A)	(B)	(C)	(D)	(E)	(F)	(G)	(H)	(I)	(J)	(K)	(L)	(M)	(N)	(O)	(P)	(Q)	(R)	(S)
Young green, bulb (3/8 in diam.) and white portion of top.	6 onions	30	88	15	Trace	Trace	—	—	—	3	12	12	.2	69	Trace	.02	.01	.1	8
Parsley, raw, chopped	1 tbsp	4	85	Trace	Trace	Trace	—	—	—	Trace	7	2	.2	25	300	Trace	.01	Trace	6
Parsnips, cooked (diced or 2-in lengths).	1 cup	155	82	100	2	1	—	—	—	23	70	96	.9	587	50	.11	.12	.2	16
Peas, green: Canned:																		
Whole, drained solids	1 cup	170	77	150	8	1	—	—	—	29	44	129	3.2	163	1,170	.15	.10	1.4	14
Strained (baby food)	1 oz (1 3/4 to 2 tbsp)	28	86	15	1	Trace	—	—	—	3	3	18	.3	28	140	.02	.03	.3	3
Frozen, cooked, drained	1 cup	160	82	110	8	Trace	—	—	—	19	30	138	3.0	216	960	.43	.14	2.7	21
Peppers, hot, red, without seeds, dried (ground chili powder, added seasonings).	1 tsp	2	9	5	Trace	Trace	—	—	—	1	5	4	.3	20	1,300	Trace	.02	.2	Trace
Peppers, sweet (about 5 per lb, whole), stem and seeds removed:																		
Raw	1 pod	74	93	15	1	Trace	—	—	—	4	7	16	.5	157	310	.06	.06	.4	94
Cooked, boiled, drained	1 pod	73	95	15	1	Trace	—	—	—	3	7	12	.4	109	310	.05	.05	.4	70
Potatoes, cooked:																		
Baked, peeled after baking (about 2 per lb, raw).	1 potato	156	75	145	4	Trace	—	—	—	33	14	101	1.1	782	Trace	.15	.07	2.7	31
Boiled (about 3 per lb, raw):																		
Peeled after boiling	1 potato	137	80	105	3	Trace	—	—	—	23	10	72	.8	556	Trace	.12	.05	2.0	22
Peeled before boiling	1 potato	135	83	90	3	Trace	—	—	—	20	8	57	.7	385	Trace	.12	.05	1.6	22
French-fried, strip, 2 to 3 1/2 in long:																		
Prepared from raw	10 strips	50	45	135	2	7	1.7	1.2	3.3	18	8	56	.7	427	Trace	.07	.04	1.6	11
Frozen, oven heated	10 strips	50	53	110	2	4	1.1	.8	2.1	17	5	43	.9	326	Trace	.07	.01	1.3	11
Hashed brown, prepared from frozen.	1 cup	155	56	345	3	18	4.6	3.2	9.0	45	28	78	1.9	439	Trace	.11	.03	1.6	12
Mashed, prepared from— Raw:																		
Milk added	1 cup	210	83	135	4	2	.7	.4	Trace	27	50	103	.8	548	40	.17	.11	2.1	21
Milk and butter added	1 cup	210	80	195	4	9	5.6	2.3	0.2	26	50	101	0.8	525	360	0.17	0.11	2.1	19
Potato chips, 1 3/4 by 2 1/2 in oval cross section.	10 chips	20	2	115	1	8	2.1	1.4	4.0	10	8	28	.4	226	Trace	.04	.01	1.0	3
Potato salad, made with cooked salad dressing.	1 cup	250	76	250	7	7	2.0	2.7	1.3	41	80	160	1.5	798	350	.20	.18	2.8	28
Pumpkin, canned	1 cup	245	90	80	2	1	—	—	—	19	61	64	1.0	588	15,680	.07	.12	1.5	12
Radishes, raw (prepackaged) stem ends, rootlets cut off.	4 radishes	18	95	5	Trace	Trace	—	—	—	1	5	6	.2	58	Trace	.01	.01	.1	5
Sauerkraut, canned, solids and liquid.	1 cup	235	93	40	2	Trace	—	—	—	9	85	42	1.2	329	120	.07	.09	.5	33
Southern peas. See Blackeye peas																		
Spinach:																		
Raw, chopped	1 cup	55	91	15	2	Trace	—	—	—	2	51	28	1.7	259	4,460	.06	.11	.3	28
Cooked, drained: From raw	1 cup	180	92	40	5	1	—	—	—	6	167	68	4.0	583	14,580	.13	.25	.9	50
From frozen: Chopped	1 cup	205	92	45	6	1	—	—	—	8	232	90	4.3	683	16,200	.14	.31	.8	39
Leaf	1 cup	190	92	45	6	1	—	—	—	7	200	84	4.8	688	15,390	.15	.27	1.0	53
Squash, cooked:																		
Summer (all varieties), diced, drained.	1 cup	210	96	30	2	Trace	—	—	—	7	53	53	.8	296	820	.11	.17	1.7	21
Winter (all varieties), baked, mashed.	1 cup	205	81	130	4	1	—	—	—	32	57	98	1.6	945	8,610	.10	.27	1.4	27
Sweetpotatoes: Cooked (raw, 5 by 2 in; about 2 1/2 per lb):																		
Baked in skin, peeled	1 potato	114	64	160	2	1	—	—	—	37	46	66	1.0	342	9,230	.10	.08	.8	25
Candied, 2 1/2 by 2-in piece	1 piece	105	60	175	1	3	2.0	.8	.1	36	39	45	.9	200	6,620	.06	.04	.4	11
Canned: Solid pack (mashed)	1 cup	255	72	275	5	1	—	—	—	63	64	105	2.0	510	19,890	.13	.10	1.5	36
Vacuum pack, piece 2 3/4 by 1 in.	1 piece	40	72	45	1	Trace	—	—	—	10	10	16	.3	80	3,120	.02	.02	.2	6
Tomatoes:																		
Raw, 2 3/5-in diam. (3 per 12 oz pkg.).	1 tomato[66]	135	94	25	1	Trace	—	—	—	6	16	33	.6	300	1,110	.07	.05	.9	[67]28
Canned, solids and liquid	1 cup	241	94	50	2	Trace	—	—	—	10	[68]14	46	1.2	523	2,170	.12	.07	1.7	41
Tomato catsup	1 cup	273	69	290	5	1	—	—	—	69	60	137	2.2	991	3,820	.25	.19	4.4	41
	1 tbsp	15	69	15	Trace	Trace	—	—	—	4	3	8	.1	54	210	.01	.01	.2	2
Tomato juice, canned: Cup	1 cup	243	94	45	2	Trace	—	—	—	10	17	44	2.2	552	1,940	.12	.07	1.9	39

NUTRITIVE VALUES OF THE EDIBLE PART OF FOODS - Continued

(Dashes (—) denote lack of reliable data for a constituent believed to be present in measurable amount)

Foods, approximate measures, units, and weight (edible part unless footnotes indicate otherwise) (B)	Grams	Water (C)	Food energy (D)	Protein (E)	Fat (F)	Fatty Acids Saturated (total) (G)	Unsaturated Oleic (H)	Linoleic (I)	Carbohydrate (J)	Calcium (K)	Phosphorus (L)	Iron (M)	Potassium (N)	Vitamin A value (O)	Thiamin (P)	Riboflavin (Q)	Niacin (R)	Ascorbic acid (S)
	Grams	Percent	Calories	Grams	Grams	Grams	Grams	Grams	Grams	Milligrams	Milligrams	Milligrams	Milligrams	International units	Milligrams	Milligrams	Milligrams	Milligrams
Turnips, cooked, diced -- 1 cup	155	94	35	1	Trace	—	—	—	8	54	37	.6	291	Trace	.06	.08	.5	34
Turnip greens, cooked, drained:																		
From raw (leaves and stems) -- 1 cup	145	94	30	3	Trace	—	—	—	5	252	49	1.5	—	8,270	.15	.33	.7	68
From frozen (chopped) -- 1 cup	165	93	40	4	Trace	—	—	—	6	195	64	2.6	246	11,390	.08	.15	.7	31
Vegetables, mixed, frozen, cooked -- 1 cup	182	83	115	6	1	—	—	—	24	46	115	2.4	348	9,010	.22	.13	2.0	15
MISCELLANEOUS ITEMS																		
Beverages, carbonated, sweetened, nonalcoholic:																		
Carbonated water -- 12 fl oz	366	92	115	0	0	0	0	0	29	—	—	—	—	0	0	0	0	0
Cola type -- 12 fl oz	369	90	145	0	0	0	0	0	37	—	—	—	—	0	0	0	0	0
Fruit-flavored sodas and Tom Collins mixer -- 12 fl oz	372	88	170	0	0	0	0	0	45	—	—	—	—	0	0	0	0	0
Ginger ale -- 12 fl oz	366	92	115	0	0	0	0	0	29	—	—	0	0	0	0	0	0	0
Root beer -- 12 fl oz	370	90	150	0	0	0	0	0	39	—	—	0	0	0	0	0	0	0
Chocolate:																		
Bitter or baking -- 1 oz	28	2	145	3	15	8.9	4.9	.4	8	22	109	1.9	235	20	.01	.07	.4	0
Semisweet, see Candy, chocolate																		
Gelatin, dry -- 1 7-g envelope	7	13	25	6	Trace	0	0	0	0	—	—	—	—	—	—	—	—	—
Gelatin dessert prepared with gelatin dessert powder ard water -- 1 cup	240	84	140	4	0	0	0	0	34	—	—	—	—	—	—	—	—	—
Mustard, prepared, yellow -- 1 tsp or individual serving pouch or cup	5	80	5	Trace	Trace	—	—	Trace	Trace	4	4	.1	7	—	—	—	—	—
Olives, pickled, canned:																		
Green -- 4 medium or 3 extra large or 2 giant.[69]	16	78	15	Trace	2	.2	1.2	Trace	Trace	8	2	.2	7	40	—	—	—	—
Ripe, Mission -- 3 small or 2 large[69]	10	73	15	Trace	2	.2	1.2	Trace	Trace	9	1	.1	2	10	Trace	Trace	—	—
Pickles, cucumber:																		
Dill, medium, whole, 3 3/4 in long, 1 1/4-in diam. -- 1 pickle	65	93	5	Trace	Trace	—	—	—	1	17	14	.7	130	70	Trace	.01	Trace	4
Fresh-pack, slices 1 1/2-in diam., 1/4 in thick. -- 2 slices	15	79	10	Trace	Trace	—	—	—	3	5	4	.3	—	20	Trace	Trace	Trace	1
Sweet, gherkin, small, whole, about 2 1/2 in long, 3/4-in diam. -- 1 pickle	15	61	20	Trace	Trace	—	—	—	5	2	2	.2	—	10	Trace	Trace	Trace	1
Soups:																		
Canned, condensed:																		
Prepared with equal volume of milk:																		
Cream of chicken -- 1 cup	245	85	180	7	10	4.2	3.6	1.3	15	172	152	0.5	260	610	0.05	0.27	0.7	2
Cream of mushroom -- 1 cup	245	83	215	7	14	5.4	2.9	4.6	16	191	169	.5	279	250	.05	.34	.7	1
Tomato -- 1 cup	250	84	175	7	7	3.4	1.7	1.0	23	168	155	.8	418	1,200	.10	.25	1.3	15
Prepared with equal volume of water:																		
Beef broth, bouillon, consomme. -- 1 cup	240	96	30	5	0	0	0	0	3	Trace	31	.5	130	Trace	Trace	.02	1.2	—
Beef noodle -- 1 cup	240	93	65	4	3	.6	.7	.8	7	7	48	1.0	77	50	.05	.07	1.0	Trace
Clam chowder, Manhattan type (with tomatoes, without milk). -- 1 cup	245	92	80	2	3	.5	.4	1.3	12	34	47	1.0	184	880	.02	.02	1.0	—
Cream of chicken -- 1 cup	240	92	95	3	6	1.6	2.3	1.1	8	24	34	.5	79	410	.02	.05	.5	Trace
Cream of mushroom -- 1 cup	240	90	135	2	10	2.6	1.7	4.5	10	41	50	.5	98	70	.02	.12	.7	Trace
Split pea -- 1 cup	245	85	145	9	3	1.1	1.2	.4	21	29	149	1.5	270	440	.25	.15	1.5	1
Tomato -- 1 cup	245	91	90	2	2	.4	.4	1.0	16	15	34	.7	230	1,000	.05	.05	1.2	12
Vegetable beef -- 1 cup	245	92	80	5	2	—	—	—	10	12	49	.7	162	2,700	.05	.05	1.0	—
Dehydrated:																		
Bouillon cube, 1/2 in -- 1 cube	4	4	5	1	Trace	—	—	—	Trace	—	—	—	4	—	—	—	—	—
Mixes:																		
Unprepared:																		
Onion -- 1 1/2-oz pkg	43	3	150	6	5	1.1	2.3	1.0	23	42	49	.6	238	30	.05	.03	.3	6
White sauce, medium, with enriched flour. -- 1 cup	250	73	405	10	31	19.3	7.8	.8	22	288	233	.5	348	1,150	.12	.43	.7	2
Yeast:																		
Baker's, dry, active -- 1 pkg	7	5	20	3	Trace	—	—	—	3	3	90	1.1	140	Trace	.16	.38	2.6	Trace

1 Vitamin A value is largely from beta-carotene used for coloring.
2 Applies to product without added vitamin A.
3 Applies to product without added vitamin A added.
4 Applies to product with added vitamin A. Without added vitamin A, value is 20 International Units (I.U.).
5 Yields 1 qt of fluid milk when reconstituted according to package directions.
6 Applies to product with added vitamin A.
7 Weight applies to product with label claim of 1 1/3 cups equal 3.2 oz.
8 Applies to products made from thick shake mixes and that do not contain added ice cream. Products made from milk shake mixes are higher in fat and usually contain added ice cream.
9 Content of fat, vitamin A, and carbohydrate varies. Consult the label when precise values are needed for special diets.
10 Applies to product made with milk containing no added vitamin A.
11 Based on year-round average.
12 Based on average vitamin A content of fortified margarine. Federal specifications for fortified margarine require a minimum of 15,000 International Units (I.U.) of vitamin A per pound.
13 Fatty acid values apply to product made with regular-type margarine.
14 Dipped in egg, milk or water, and breadcrumbs; fried in vegetable shortening.
15 If bones are discarded, value for calcium will be greatly reduced.
16 Dipped in egg, breadcrumbs, and flour or batter.
17 Prepared with tuna, celery, salad dressing (mayonnaise type), pickle, onion, and egg.
18 Outer layer of fat on the cut was removed to within approximately 1/2 in of the lean. Deposits of fat within the cut were not removed.
19 Crust made with vegetable shortening and enriched flour.
20 Regular-type margarine used.
21 Value varies widely.
22 About one-fourth of the outer layer of fat on the cut was removed. Deposits of fat within the cut were not removed.
23 Vegetable shortening used.
24 Also applies to pasteurized apple cider.
25 Applies to product with added ascorbic acid. For value of product with added ascorbic acid, refer to label.
26 Applies to product without added ascorbic acid.
27 Based on product with label claim of 45% of U.S. RDA in 6 fl oz.
28 Based on product with label claim of 100% of U.S. RDA in 6 fl oz.
29 For white-fleshed varieties, value is about 20 International Units (I.U.) per cup; for red-fleshed varieties, 1,080 I.U.
30 Weight includes seeds. Without seeds, weight of the edible portion is 57 g.
31 Applies to product without added ascorbic acid. With added ascorbic acid, based on claim that 6 fl oz of reconstituted juice contain 45% or 50% of the U.S. RDA, value in milligrams is 108 or 120 for a 6-fl oz can (item 258), 36 or 40 for 1 cup of diluted juice.
32 For products with added thiamin and riboflavin but without added ascorbic acid, values in milligrams would be 0.60 for thiamin, 0.80 for riboflavin, and trace for ascorbic acid. For products with only ascorbic acid added, value varies with the brand. Consult the label.
33 Weight includes rind.
34 Represents yellow-fleshed varieties. For white-fleshed varieties, value is 50 International Units (I.U.) for 1 peach, 90 I.U. for 1 cup of slices.
35 Value represents products with added ascorbic acid. For products without added ascorbic acid, value in milligrams is 116 for a 10-oz container, 103 for 1 cup.
36 Weight includes pits.
37 Weight includes rind and seeds. Without rind and seeds, weight of the edible portion is 426 g.
38 Made with vegetable shortening.
39 Applies to product made with white cornmeal. With yellow cornmeal, value is 150 International Units (I.U.).
40 Applies to white varieties. For yellow varieties, value is 30 International Units (I.U.).
41 Applies to products that do not contain di-sodium phosphate. If di-sodium phosphate is an ingredient, value is 162 mg.
42 Value may range from less than 1 mg to about 8 mg depending on the brand. Consult the label.
43 Applies to product with the brand. Consult the label.
44 Value varies with the brand. Consult the label.
45 Applies to product with added ascorbic acid. Without added ascorbic acid, value is trace.
46 Excepting angelfood cake, cakes were made from mixes containing vegetable shortening; icings, with butter.
47 Excepting spongecake, vegetable shortening used for cake portion; butter, for icing. If butter or margarine used for cake portion, vitamin A values would be higher.
48 Applies to product made with a sodium aluminum-sulfate type baking powder. With a low-sodium type baking powder containing potassium, value would be about twice the amount shown.
49 Equal weights of flour, sugar, eggs, and vegetable shortening.
50 Products are commercial unless otherwise specified.
51 Made with enriched flour and vegetable shortening except for macaroons which do not contain flour or shortening.
52 Icing made with butter.
53 Applies to yellow varieties; white varieties contain only a trace.
54 Contains vegetable shortening and butter.
55 Made with corn oil.
56 Made with regular margarine.
57 Applies to product made with yellow cornmeal.
58 Made with enriched degermed cornmeal and enriched flour.
59 Product may or may not be enriched with riboflavin. Consult the label.
60 Value varies with the brand. Consult the label.
61 Weight includes cob.
62 Based on yellow varieties. For white varieties, value is trace.
63 Weight includes refuse of outer leaves and core. Without these parts, weight is 163 g.
64 Weight includes core. Without core, weight is 539 g.
65 Value based on white-fleshed varieties.
66 Weight includes cores and stem ends. Without these parts, weight is 123 g.
67 Based on year-round average. For tomatoes marketed from November through May, value is about 12 mg; from June through October, 32 mg.
68 Applies to product without calcium salts added. Value for products with calcium salts added may be as much as 63 mg for whole tomatoes, 241 mg for cut forms.
69 Weight includes pits.
70 Value may vary from 6 to 60 mg.

Appendix E
Metric information

Although the United States is coming closer to a complete metric conversion, consumers will not have to throw away the recipes or kitchen measuring tools now being used. Conventional recipes will still be measured in the customary cups, tablespoons and teaspoons. But for metric recipes, metric measures will be needed.

In home kitchens, volume measurements will be used for almost all foods. Foods which are commonly measured by weight, such as potatoes, coffee, apples and meat, however, will be measured in grams.

COMMON MEASURES

Metric	Conventional	Metric	Conventional
1 mL	1/4 teaspoon	50 mL	1/4 cup
2 mL	1/2 teaspoon	125 mL	1/2 cup
5 mL	1 teaspoon	250 mL	1 cup
15 mL	1 tablespoon	500 mL	2 cups
25 mL	1/8 cup	1000 mL	1 quart

OVEN THERMOSTAT MARKINGS

deg. C	deg. F	deg. C	deg. F
100	200	190	375
120	250	200	400
140	275	220	425
150	300	230	450
160	325	240	475
180	350	260	500

CONVERSION FACTORS

LENGTH

	Multiply by	
millimetres to inches		0.039
centimetres to inches		0.394
inches to millimetres		25.40
inches to centimetres		2.540

WEIGHT

	Multiply by	
grams to ounces		0.035
grams to pounds		0.002
kilograms to pounds		2.2
ounces to grams		28.350
pounds to grams		454
pounds to kilograms		0.454

LIQUID MEASURE

	Multiply by	
millilitres to ounces		0.034
litres to pints		2.1
litres to quarts		1.056
litres to gallons		0.264
ounces to millilitres		29.573
pints to litres		0.473
quarts to litres		0.946
gallons to litres		3.785

ENERGY

	Multiply by	
kilocalorie to kilojoule		4.184
kilojoule to kilocalorie		0.239

TEMPERATURE

Fahrenheit to Celsius: degree $C = 5/9 \times (F - 32)$ Celsius to Fahrenheit: degree $F = (9/5 \times C) + 32$

USEFUL MEASURES

3 teaspoons = 1 tablespoon	1 cup = 8 fluid ounces
4 tablespoons = 1/4 cup	1 cup = 1/2 pint
5 1/3 tablespoons = 1/3 cup	2 cups = 1 pint
8 tablespoons = 1/2 cup	4 cups = 1 quart
10 2/3 tablespoons = 2/3 cup	4 quarts = 1 gallon
12 tablespoons = 3/4 cup	8 quarts = 1 peck
16 tablespoons = 1 cup	4 pecks = 1 bushel

Cooking utensils such as saucepans and casseroles will be measured in litres rather than quarts. Baking utensils such as cake pans, cookie sheets and pie plates will be measured in centimetres.

UTENSIL	METRIC MEASURE	COVENTIONAL MEASURE
Saucepan	1 L 2 L 3 L	1 quart 2 quart 3 quart
Skillet	15 cm 25 cm 30 cm	6 in. 10 in. 12 in.
Baking or cake pan	20 cm by 5 cm 23 cm by 5 cm 33 cm by 21 cm by 5 cm	8 in. by 2 in. 9 in. by 2 in. 13 in. by 9 in. by 2 in.
Cookie sheet	41 cm by 28 cm 46 cm by 30 cm	16 in. by 11 in. 18 in. by 12 in.
Jelly roll pan	39 cm by 27 cm by 2.5 cm	15 1/2 in. by 10 1/2 in. by 1 in.
Loaf pan	19 cm by 10 cm by 6 cm 23 cm by 13 cm by 8 cm	7 1/2 in. by 3 3/4 in. by 2 1/4 in. 9 in. by 5 in. by 3 in.
Round cake pan	20 cm by 4 cm 23 cm by 4 cm	8 in. by 1 1/2 in. 9 in. by 1 1/2 in.
Pie plate	20 cm by 3 cm 23 cm by 3 cm	8 in. by 1 1/4 in. 9 in. by 1 1/4 in.
Tube pan	25 cm by 10 cm	10 in. by 4 in.
Casserole	1 L 1.5 L 2 L 3 L	1 quart 1 1/2 quart 2 quart 3 quart
Custard cup	200 mL	6 ounces

Glossary

A

additives: substances added to foods to improve their nutritional value, color, flavor, texture, storage life, etc.

agri-business: the industry of agriculture.

a la carte menu: a menu with each item priced separately.

all-purpose flour: a flour composed of both hard and soft wheats that is generally good for all cooking purposes.

American Gas Association (AGA) star: a seal on gas appliances which indicates that the appliance meets safety and performance standards of the AGA.

amino acid: organic compounds which combine to form protein molecules.

amphetamines: drugs which stimulate the nervous system; "uppers" (slang).

apprentice: a person who learns on the job by working under an experienced person.

artificial foods: foods made from edible raw materials, but processed to imitate or resemble familiar foods.

au gratin: sprinkled with grated cheese and heated until the cheese is melted.

B

bake: to cook food in an oven.

baking chocolate: unsweetened chocolate used in cooking.

baking powder: a leavening agent composed of baking soda and a dry acid powder that begins to produce carbon dioxide as soon as it is mixed with a liquid.

baking soda: a leavening agent that begins to produce carbon dioxide when mixed with an acidic ingredient.

barbecue: a picnic where food is cooked outdoors. To cook foods over hot coals or in the oven with a special sauce.

basal metabolism: the energy needed by the body at rest to sustain basic life functions.

Basic Four Food Groups: a simple-to-use guide for assuring adequate nutrition based on grouping foods according to their main nutrient contributions. The Food Groups are: Milk and Milk Products; Fruits and Vegetables; Grain Products; and Meat and other Protein Sources.

baste: to spoon or brush liquid over food several times while it is cooking.

batch feed disposer: a type of food waste disposer designed to grind food in certain amounts.

batter: a flour and liquid mixture that is thin enough to be poured.

beat: to combine ingredients using a fast motion which adds air to the mixture and makes the mixture smooth.

beef: meat from mature cattle.

behavior modification: changing behavior, especially habit patterns, using a system that rewards change.

beriberi: a disease caused by a deficiency of thiamin (vitamin B_1). Symptoms affect the nervous system, causing weakness, weight loss, and deterioration of the muscles.

biscuit method: a method of combining ingredients: the fat is cut into the dry ingredients; then a small amount of liquid is mixed in forming a dough

black tea: a major type of tea, produced by fermenting tea leaves.

black tie: a formal occasion when men are expected to wear tuxedos and women should wear dressy gowns.

blanching: the process of treating fruits and vegetables by dipping them into boiling water for a few seconds.

blistering: the formation of small pockets of air in an empty pie shell as it is baking. This may be prevented by pricking the pastry before baking.

boil: to cook in a liquid at a temperature high enough so that the liquid bubbles.

boiled frosting: a light, fluffy frosting made by boiling a sweet, sticky mixture, cooling it, and folding it into stiffly beaten egg whites.

botulism: food poisoning caused by Clostridium botulinum.

bouquet garni: a French term for a small cheesecloth bag containing herbs and other seasonings that will be used to flavor dishes being cooked.

braise: a form of simmering foods slowly in a small amount of liquid in a covered pot.

bran: thin layers of a fibrous substance that cover a kernel of grain.

bread: to dip food in liquid such as beaten egg or

milk and then roll it in crumbs made from bread, crackers or some type of cereal.

bread flour: a special flour made from hard wheat. It produces strong gluten, which is desirable in baking yeast breads.

broil: to cook uncovered under a direct source of heat.

broiler-fryer: a tender, medium-sized chicken that can be prepared by almost any cooking method.

brown: to cook food quickly at a high temperature until the surface becomes brown.

brown sugar: a type of sugar that has a light or dark brown color due to the molasses left over in the sugar refining process.

brunch: a meal served between 10 a.m. and 2 p.m. that is a combination of breakfast and lunch.

buffet service: food is set out on a table so that guests can serve themselves.

built-in: an appliance which has been built into a wall or counter.

butter: a common fat made by churning cream.

butter cream frosting: a creamy frosting made from confectioner's sugar, butter or margarine, milk, and a flavoring such as vanilla.

C

caffeine: a stimulant found in coffee and tea.

cake flour: a flour made from soft wheat that produces cakes with a fine, tender texture.

Calorie: a unit for measuring heat production; the customary unit used to measure the energy supplied by food. One Calorie is equal to about 4 kilojoules.

capon: a young, desexed male chicken, larger than a broiler-fryer.

carbohydrate: a nutrient group composed of sugars, starches and fiber.

carotene: a yellow pigment found in many fruits and vegetables that can be converted by vitamin A in the body.

catering: a type of food service. The act of conducting a business specializing in preparing and serving food at private parties and special events.

centerpiece: decorations used as the center of interest on a dinner table.

cereal: in general, any grain used for food; also a common breakfast food made from grain.

chiffon cake: a basic type of cake resembling a foam cake, but containing fat.

cholesterol: a complex, fat-like substance.

chop: to cut food into small, uneven pieces.

circulating air system: a system which moves air in a refrigerator, freezer or convection oven.

cleanup center: the counter and cabinets around the kitchen sink where dishes are washed and foods are prepared for cooking.

clear liquid diet: a convalescent diet based on "clear" liquids such as broths, fruit drinks, gelatin and tea. Its purpose is to provide nourishment without irritating the digestive system.

Clostridium botulinum: bacteria which produce deadly toxins. Found in canned foods which have not been properly processed.

Clostridium perfringens: toxin-producing bacteria found in meat, poultry and other high protein foods which can cause food poisoning. Occurs most often when foods are not kept at the proper temperature for a period of time.

coagulate: the transformation of protein from a loose, jelly-like substance into a firm substance.

cocoa: a powder made from chocolate, with some of the cocoa butter removed.

coldpack cheese: cheeses made by blending shredded natural cheeses.

collagen: a protein substance that holds cells together.

come-as-you-are party: a party where each person dresses in the same clothing they were wearing at the moment they received the invitation.

compromise service: a meal where appetizers, soups, and desserts are dished out in the kitchen and the main course is served by the host at the table.

compost heap: a pile of organic matter of various types (such as grass clippings, vegetable scraps, egg shells, etc.) left to decompose and form a rich soil-like material that can be used as fertilizer.

composting: the process of making and using a compost heap.

condensation: a process by which steam changes to water as seen when droplets of water collect on the inside of a container as its contents cool.

condiment: something that adds a flavor accent to food, such as mustard, catsup, salad dressing, etc.

confectioner's sugar: a fine, powdery sugar made by grinding granulated sugar.

connective tissue: a tissue composed mostly of protein that "connects," or holds, the muscle cells in meat together.

continental service: a waiter or waitress brings each person a plate of food.

continuous cleaning oven: an oven with specially coated walls. The coating causes food spatters and spills to be burned away over a period of time as the oven is used.

continuous feed disposer: a type of food waste disposer into which food is fed continuously once the switch has been turned on.

controlled environment agriculture: growing crops in protected enclosures, such as green houses.

convalescent: a person recovering from illness or surgery.

convection oven: an oven which uses a circulating air system to cook food.

convenience products: food products in forms where some or all of the preparation has been done for you.

cooking center: the kitchen area including the range where food is cooked.

cool weather vegetables: vegetables whose seeds can be planted outdoors in the early spring because they can withstand cool temperatures.

core: to remove the center (pits or hard fibers) from fruits.

cost per serving: the price of one portion of a certain food.

cover: an individual place setting which includes flatware, glassware and linens needed by one person.

cream: to combine fat such as butter and sugar by beating until the mixture is light and fluffy; the fat portion of milk.

creole: a style of cooking popular around New Orleans that combines French, Spanish, African and American Indian influences.

crispers: special compartments in refrigerators which are used to store produce.

crumb crust: a crust made from a crumb mixture loosely held together with some kind of fat.

crustaceans: term for many kinds of shellfish with segmented bodies that have legs and crust-like shells with joints.

cube: to cut food into evenly shaped cubes 1 cm (1/2 inch) or larger.

culture: the knowledge, beliefs and traditions shared by a group of people.

cultured buttermilk: a thickened milk with a tangy flavor made by adding lactic acid bacteria to low-fat or skim milk.

curdled: describes milk in which small, soft lumps of milk solids have separated out from milk or a milk mixture.

cut in: to blend solid fat and flour using a pastry blender, a fork or two knives.

D

deep-fat fry: to cook in hot fat until the food becomes brown. Use enough fat so food will float.

defrost: to remove frost which has collected around the refrigerator's cooling system.

degrade: to break down.

dehydration: removal or loss of a substantial amount of water.

dehydrator: an appliance that provides a controlled drying atmosphere.

dice: to cut food into evenly shaped cubes smaller than 1 cm (1/2 inch).

dietitian: a person who has a degree in dietetics.

dinner menu: a menu with prices that include entrée, appetizer, salad and dessert.

dinnerware: a term which includes plates, cups, saucers and bowls.

diuretics: substances that stimulate urine production.

dough: a flour and liquid mixture thick enough to handle, knead, roll, etc.

dovetail: a method of working in such a way so that while one task is in progress, you can be working on something else.

dredge: to cover food with a dry ingredient such as flour or sugar.

dress code: a policy which specifies what people should wear.

dressed fish: fish that has had all waste removed except bones.

dry heat cooking methods: methods of cooking without adding liquid, including broiling, baking or roasting, frying, etc. These methods are appropriate for tender cuts of meat, tender poultry, and any fish or shellfish.

dry measures: utensils used to measure dry ingredients.

dry milk: a shelf-stable milk product made by removing the water from milk.

E

earthenware: material used to make dinnerware which is less expensive than fine china.

elastin: a type of connective tissue that accounts for some of the toughness in meats and is affected very little by cooking.

emulsifier: an agent that stabilizes an emulsion, preventing the liquids from separating.

emulsion: a liquid mixture of two liquids that do not combine with each other. In an emulsion, tiny droplets of one liquid float around in the other liquid.

endosperm: the large, starchy portion of a grain kernel.

engineered foods: new foods, or imitations of old ones, made with natural or synthetic ingredients.

English service: the host serves food at the table and guests pass plates around table until each person has been served.

enriched: the addition of thiamin, riboflavin, niacin and iron to a food according to a specific formula prescribed by federal law.

entrée: the main course.

espresso: a strong, dark, Italian coffee brewed by a special method, usually served in small cups.

essential amino acid: an amino acid necessary for life and health that must be supplied by the diet.

etiquette: social rules and customs held by a group of people.

evaporated milk: milk that has been concentrated by removing about half of the water and then sealed and sterilized in cans to preserve the product.

expiration date: a type of open dating that indicates the last date a product should be used or eaten.

extension home economist: a home economist employed by county cooperative extension offices.

extracts (flavor): the oils and flavors essences of certain foods (such as vanilla beans), usually dissolved in alcohol.

F

fad diet: a diet which is popular for a short time. Most often, fad diets are restrictive in the foods the dieter is permitted to eat, and they tend to be nutritionally unbalanced.

family service: serving food by passing serving dishes clockwise around the table so people can serve themselves.

fasting: going without food; eating little or nothing.

fat: a nutrient group that supplies concentrated energy; also the form in which the body stores excess energy.

fat-soluble vitamin: a vitamin that will dissolve in fat. Vitamins A, D, E and K are fat-soluble.

fertilizer: a substance added to soil to enrich it and make it more productive.

fiber: a complex carbohydrate that cannot be di-

gested by the human body, but is useful in helping to remove body wastes.

finger foods: foods that may be eaten properly with your fingers.

fine china: material used to make dinnerware. The most expensive form of dinnerware.

fish farms: enclosed bodies of water in which fish and other seafood can be raised and harvested.

fish fillets: pieces of fish cut lengthwise, along the backbone.

fish steaks: pieces of fish cut crosswise, through the backbone.

flatware: a term used to refer to knives, forks and spoons.

flavor enhancer: an ingredient that brings out other flavors in food without adding any flavor of its own. MSG (monosodium glutamate) is the most common example.

flute: to pinch and shape dough to create a decorative pattern, usually applied to the rim of a pie shell.

foam cake: a light, foamy type of cake made with beaten egg whites and no fat.

foamy stage: egg whites beaten to a bubbly, but still liquid stage.

fold: a gentle way of adding an ingredient to a light, airy mixture so that the mixture remains light.

food allergies: sensitivity to foods which can result in illness.

food co-ops: an organization of consumers established to buy food in large quantities and distribute it to their group's members at favorable prices.

food editor: a person whose job is to research and write articles about food.

food storage center: the area in and around the refrigerator-freezer including cabinets and counter space where food is stored.

food technologist: a person who decides how a product will be produced, labeled and packaged.

formulated foods: foods that combine nutrients into the exact proportions needed by a certain group of people, such as formulas for feeding babies.

fortified: describes a product that has had nutrients added to improve its nutritional value.

fortified foods: foods to which nutrients have been added to improve their nutritional quality.

freezer burn: food drying out on the surface because it has been improperly wrapped for freezing.

freshness date: a type of open dating that estimates the last date the product will be at peak quality or freshness.

fruit drink: fruit juice with added sugar and water.

fruit juice: the natural liquid which is found in fruit.

full liquid diet: a convalescent diet based on foods that are liquid or that will liquify at body temperature. This type of diet is often prescribed as a transition from a clear liquid diet to a soft diet.

full warranty: a seller's promise that a product will work properly and be free from defects. The product will be repaired or replaced free of charge if it does not work properly.

G

garnishes: decorations used on food.

gelatinization: a process that occurs when a starch is mixed with a liquid and heated, causing the starch to swell and thicken into a sticky mass.

generic brand: a brand characterized by very plain packaging and only required labeling information, sometimes called a "no-brand" brand.

germ: the part of a grain kernel that would produce a new plant if it were allowed to sprout.

glass ceramic: a material used to make dinnerware which is stronger than earthenware, stoneware and ironstone.

glassware: glasses of many shapes and styles.

glucose: a common simple sugar; the basic fuel used by the body.

gluten: a stretchy substance which gives structure to baked goods. It is formed when the proteins in flour are moistened and kneaded.

goiter: a condition in which the thyroid gland enlarges, caused by a deficiency of iodine.

grades: guides to the quality of a product, generally based on the appearance of the food.

grate: to rub food on a grating tool producing small bits of food.

grease: to spread a thin layer of shortening over the inside of a cooking utensil (casserole, baking dish.)

green tea: a major type of tea made from unfermented tea leaves.

H

habit: an act or behavior repeated so often that it becomes almost automatic.

half and half: a cream product containing about 12 percent milk fat.

head space: a space left at the top of a container so that food can expand during canning or freezing.

heating element: coils of wire on electric ranges which heat up and produce heat when the range is turned on.

heavy whipping cream: a cream product containing about 38 percent milk fat.

herbicide: a poison used to kill weeds.

herbs: leaves of plants such as basil, thyme and rosemary used to season foods.

homogenized milk: milk that has been processed so that the milk fat is broken up into fine particles and dispersed throughout the milk.

hybrid: a combination of several plant varieties to produce specific desired characteristics.

hydroponics: growing crops in water within a controlled environment, such as a greenhouse.

I

ice cream: a frozen dessert or snack made from milk, sugar, stabilizers, and various flavorings.

ice milk: a frozen dessert or snack similar to ice cream, but containing less fat.

impromptu party: a party which is not planned in advance.

in season: the time of harvest for a fresh fruit or vegetable.

inspection: a check to insure that a food product is free from disease organisms and safe to eat, and was processed under sanitary conditions.

instant freeze-dried coffee: a type of instant coffee made by drying frozen brewed coffee.

iron-deficiency anemia: a condition caused by a deficiency of iron in the diet. Symptoms include a tired, rundown feeling and a pale look.

ironstone: material used to make dinnerware which is stronger than earthenware.

J

julienne: to cut foods in long thin strips.

K

kernels: the seeds of a cereal grain.

kilojoule: the basic metric unit used to measure all forms of energy, roughly equivalent to 0.25 Calorie.

knead: a special technique for handling dough which involves a push-fold-turn motion.

kneading: the manipulation of dough with a fold-push-turn action, important to developing the gluten in bread dough.

kosher: permitted by, or in compliance with, Jewish religious laws.

L

lactating: describes a female who is producing milk for feeding an infant.

lamb: meat that comes from sheep less than a year old.

lard: a hard cooking fat made from the fatty tissue of pork.

leavening agent: a substance that produces bubbles inside a baked product to make it rise.

legumes: edible seeds that grow in a pod, including a variety of hard beans, split peas, and lentils.

limited warranty: a seller's promise that a product will work properly and be free from any defects. It will be repaired or replaced, but you might be charged for repairs or shipping.

liquid measures: utensils used to measure liquid ingredients.

low-fat milk: milk which contains only about 2 percent milk fat.

M

maître d': the person in charge of the dining room staff.

malnutrition: condition caused by lack of nourishment, either in terms of quality or quantity.

marbling: small streaks of fat found in meat, usually a sign that the meat will be tender and juicy.

margarine: a common household fat made from vegetable oils or a combination of vegetable oils and animal fat.

marinate: to let food stand in a seasoned acid liquid. Foods are marinated to enhance flavor and/or make foods more tender.

market researcher: a person who conducts research to learn about consumer needs and wants.

mash: to crush food until it has a smooth texture.

master chef: a chef who has studied with accomplished chefs for many years to gain skill in preparing food.

meat analogues: imitation meats generally produced by special processing of vegetable proteins.

meat extenders: ingredients that can be added to ground meat or processed meats to create more servings.

melamine: a type of plastic used to make dinnerware.

menu: a list of the specific foods to be served at a meal.

meringue: a sweet, foamy mixture of beaten egg whites and sugar.

metabolism: the overall process of breaking down and using food in the body for energy, tissue building, or regulation of body functions.

microwave oven: an oven which produces microwaves for cooking food.

microwaves: high frequency energy waves often used to cook food.

milk chocolate: sweetened chocolate with milk and vanilla added, popular as a candy as well as in cooking.

mince: to cut food into very tiny pieces.

mineral: nutrient group composed of simple elements of nature that are essential for life and health.

minimum tillage: planting seeds in a slit in the ground instead of tilling (plowing and cultivating) the soil.

mix: a general term for combining or blending ingredients.

mixing center: the area of the kitchen where tools for mixing and baking are stored.

moist heat methods: methods of cooking that include liquids to provide a moist cooking environment.

molasses: a syrupy product that is a by-product of sugar refining. It varies from a light brown syrup with a mild flavor to a dark, rather bitter syrup.

mollusks: shellfish with hard outer shells that may be either one piece or two pieces hinged together.

muffin method: a method of combining ingredients: the dry ingredients are mixed in one bowl, the liquid ingredients in another, and the two are combined by stirring the liquid mixture into a "well" made in the center of the dry mixture.

mulching: loose material such as hay, strips of newspaper or wood chips placed around plants to help control weed growth.

multicropping: planting new seeds between the rows of half-grown crops to increase the total yield from the land.

N

name brand: a well-known, widely advertised

brand.

natural cheese: cheeses that are usually cured (aged) to allow for flavor development. They may or may not be ripened to develop distinct flavor characteristics.

neighborhood stores: relatively small stores conveniently located in a neighborhood, usually characterized by a friendly atmosphere and personal service.

night blindness: condition caused by a lack of vitamin A in which the eyes have difficulty adjusting to changing light conditions.

nutrient density: the kind and amount of nutrients supplied by a food in relation to the kilojoules (Calories).

nutrition: the science of food and how it is used in the body.

nutritionist: a dietitian with additional training.

O

obesity: a condition in which a person's weight is 20 percent (or more) greater than the ideal weight for that person.

one dish meals: foods from several food groups that are combined and cooked in one pot.

oolong tea: a major type of tea, made by partly fermenting tea leaves.

open dating: dates on products that can be read and understood easily by consumers.

open stock: a term used which means each piece of tableware can be purchased individually.

organic foods: foods grown or produced without chemical fertilizers or pesticides.

organic gardening: gardening without the use of chemical fertilizers or pesticides.

osmosis: the passage of liquids through a membrane to equalize the solutions on either side of the membrane.

oxidation: a chemical reaction in which oxygen combines with a fuel substance. This process makes it possible for the body to obtain energy from food.

P

pack date: a type of open dating that shows when a product was packed or produced.

panbroil: to cook meat in an uncovered skillet, pouring off extra fat as it builds up.

panfry: to cook food in an uncovered skillet adding fat.

pare: to cut away the skin with a knife or peeler.

pareve: in Orthodox Judaism, foods which are neither meat nor dairy foods.

pasta: the whole range of macaroni and noodle products made from durum wheat flour.

pasteurized: processed by a heat treatment to kill harmful bacteria.

pasteurized process cheese: a soft blend of shredded natural cheeses heated to prevent further flavor development.

pasteurized process cheese food: a product similar to pasteurized process cheese except that it is softer, more moist, milder in flavor, and lower in fat.

pasteurized process cheese spread: a product similar to pasteurized process cheese food except that is has less fat and more moisture, making it even softer and easier to spread.

pellagra: a disease caused by a deficiency of niacin (a B vitamin). It affects the skin, nervous system and digestive tract.

perishable: likely to spoil or decay quickly if not stored properly, especially without refrigeration.

pesticide: a chemical substance applied to plants to kill insects and other garden pests.

pilot light: a tiny flame which ignites a gas burner when the control is turned on.

place setting: a complete table service for one person.

planning center: the area of the kitchen containing desk and telephone and cookbooks where meals are planned.

plant manager: a person in charge of a processing plant.

poach: to cook food in hot or simmering liquid so the food can float.

polyunsaturated fat: a fat molecule capable of holding additional hydrogen atoms. Most oils are composed of polyunsaturated fat.

pork: meat from hogs.

potpie: a main dish made by filling a pie shell with a thick stew of gravy, meat and vegetables.

poultry: birds such as chickens, turkeys and ducks that are raised for food.

preparation plan: a plan indicating the time it takes to prepare and cook each item on the menu.

preserve: to minimize or prevent loss or spoilage.

pressure cooker: an air-tight pot that cooks with steam under pressure, thereby increasing the temperature and decreasing the cooking time.

processed fish: fish that has been processed in some way (such as canning, smoking, salting, marinating) to preserve it.

processing time: the time canned food must be heated.

produce: fresh fruits and vegetables.

product manager: a person responsible for developing a new product.

progressive dinner: a dinner party which is planned so that each course is eaten at a different home.

protein: a major nutrient group that supplies the basic building materials for body cells and for many substances involved in controlling body processes.

public relations: the art of making people aware of information.

pull date: a type of open dating used primarily by the store that indicates the last date the product should be on display for sale.

Q

quality control: controlling the cost of food by purchasing food of a specific quality.

quantity control: controlling the cost of food by limiting portion size.

quick breads: term that refers to a number of breads using a fast-working leavening agent (rather than yeast) to make them rise.

R

Recommended Dietary Allowances (RDA's): a table of levels of intake recommended for each of several nutrients in order to maintain good health for most of the population.

Regrets Only: often written on invitations to instruct the person invited to contact the host if he or she is unable to attend an event.

reservation: reserves a table for you.

restaurant manager: a person in charge of the entire operation of a restaurant.

rickets: a condition of severe bone deformity caused by a deficiency of vitamin D.

roast: to cook meats or poultry in an oven.

roasting chicken: a young female chicken, larger than a broiler-fryer. Roasting chickens have a high meat yield in relation to bone.

Rock Cornish game hen: the smallest type of chicken available.

royal frosting: a thick frosting used to make flowers and other fancy decorations on a cake.

R.S.V.P.: stands for "please reply" in French. Is put on invitations so the host will know how many guests to expect.

Russian service: a waiter or waitress brings a platter of food to the table and serves each person individually.

S

Salmonella: a type of bacteria found in the intestines of human beings and animals. Also found in meat, poultry, eggs and dairy products. Can cause food poisoning.

saturated fat: a fat molecule that is filled to capacity with hydrogen atoms. Saturated fat is usually found in solid food fats.

saute: to cook food in a small amount of hot fat.

scald: to heat milk to just below the boiling point. Also means to dip food into boiling water for a few seconds.

scorch: to burn.

score: to make slashes through the outer edge of fat on meat. This prevents meat from curling as it cooks.

scrape: to remove the outer skin of food by rubbing with the sharp edge of a knife.

scurvy: the disease caused by a deficiency of vitamin C; symptoms include bleeding gums, bruises, sores, and deterioration of body tissues.

sear: to brown meat.

seedling: a tiny plant sprouted indoors.

self-cleaning oven: an oven which cleans itself using a very high temperature when the dial is set to clean.

self-rising flour: a type of flour that includes salt and a leavening agent.

semi-sweet chocolate: a blend of unsweetened chocolate and sugar, usually sold in bars or small chips for cooking.

service sets: matching flatware including place settings and serving pieces.

serving center: the area of the kitchen near the range where food is served.

sherbet: a frozen dessert made with sugar, milk solids, water and flavorings (usually fruit juices).

shish kebab: small chunks of meat (traditionally lamb) roasted on skewers.

shortened cake: a basic type of cake containing fat and using a quick leavening agent such as baking soda or baking powder; also called a "butter cake".

shortening: a solid, white, all-fat product usually made by hydrogenating vegetable oils, widely used in baking and frying.

shred: to cut food into very narrow strips.

silver plate: a term used for flatware which is made from metal which is covered with a thin coating of silver.

simmer: to cook in liquid at a temperature below boiling.

single-cell protein: protein obtained from one-celled organisms such as bacteria and yeast, useful for fortifying foods.

skim milk: milk that contains less than 1 percent milk fat.

skin: a film that may form on the surface of milk being heated. It is composed of milk solids that have separated out and risen to the top.

slice: to cut food into flat pieces.

small measures: utensils used to measure small amounts of liquid and dry ingredients.

soft diet: a special diet consisting of easily digested food with little or no fiber, often prescribed as a transition between liquid diets and regular diets. This type of diet is also used by people with chewing difficulties or digestive problems.

soft peak stage: egg whites beaten to the point where they will stand up in soft, shiny, white peaks.

soil erosion: a gradual loss of topsoil, often carried away by the runoff of rain that could not be absorbed quickly enough by the ground.

soul food: cuisine developed by blacks and poor whites in the rural South, using inexpensive foods.

sour cream: a smooth, thick, slightly sour product made by adding lactic acid bacteria to light cream.

soybean: a nutritious, versatile legume that can be used to make a number of very different foods, including cooking oil, flour, snack products, soy sauce and imitation meats.

specialty shops: food stores specializing in a particular type of food, such as butcher shops, bakeries, and health food stores.

spices: seasonings made from the bark, root, fruit or bud of certain plants, such as black pepper, cinnamon, allspice, etc.

stainless steel: metal used to make flatware.

stake out: to mark off a row to be planted, using two stakes and a string.

standard of identity: a legal description of a product listing the ingredients that must be included in order for the product to use the standard name; a product which meets the standard of identity is not required to list all ingredients on its label.

Staphylococcus aureus (Staph): bacteria found in the throat, nose or skin of healthy people that can cause food poisoning.

staple foods: (1) food and ingredients that are used frequently in a household and usually kept on hand; (2) the main foods eaten by a people of a region or ethnic group.

starch: a type of carbohydrate unit composed of many units of simple sugars joined together.

status: position or rank, usually associated with respect and admiration.

steam: to cook food in a covered container or a rack so that steam cooks the food.

steamer: a cooking utensil used for cooking foods by steam.

sterling silver: metal, often used for flatware, which contains at least 92.5 percent silver.

stew: a form of simmering food covered with liquid in a large pot.

stewing hen: a mature chicken that needs to be cooked by a moist heat method.

stiff peak stage: egg whites beaten to the point where they will stand upright in shiny, white peaks.

stir: to move a spoon in a circle to mix ingredients.

stir-frying: a cooking method in which small pieces of food are fried quickly, usually in a wok.

stoneware: durable, heavy dinnerware which is less formal than fine china.

store brand: a brand promoted by a certain store or chain of stores.

store manager: a person responsible for what happens in a store.

sugar: a simple type of carbohydrate. Sugars include sucrose, fructose, and glucose, among others.

supermarket home economist: a person who has a college degree in home economics with training in foods, nutrition and consumer education. Provides customers with shopping information.

supermarkets: large stores offering a wide variety of foods under various brands, as well as an assortment of non-food items.

sweetened condensed milk: a canned milk product made by adding a large amount of sugar to evaporated milk.

synthesized: produced artificially.

synthetic ingredients: food substances produced in a laboratory from materials that wouldn't ordinarily be considered "foods". Synthetic vitamins and flavorings are common examples.

syrup: a thick, sweet liquid.

T

table linens: a term which includes tablecloths, place mats and napkins.

tarnish: discoloration of silver caused by exposure to air and certain foods.

textured vegetable protein: protein obtained from plants that has been processed to give it a texture, usually to imitate another food (such as meat).

theme: an idea which can be used in decorations, invitations, entertainment food, and costumes.

thermostat: a control which regulates the temperature.

tip: money left by customers to express thanks for good service.

toxin: a poison like substance created by bacteria.

trace element: a mineral needed only in tiny amounts to maintain life and good health.

transplants: seedlings that have been transplanted from a container into the ground.

Trichinella spiralis: a tiny worm sometimes found in pork that can cause a serious illness called trichinosis.

trickle irrigation: a method of watering crops using "leaky" pipes that allow water to trickle into the ground around plants.

triple-plated: a term used for silver plated flatware which has three coats of silver over the base metal.

U

underweight: weighing less than is desirable.

Underwriter's Laboratories (UL) seal: a seal on electrical appliances which indicates the appliance meets safety standards.

unit price: the cost of a convenient unit of measure (dozen, kilogram, litre, etc.) of a product, useful in comparison shopping.

United States Recommended Dietary Allowances (U.S. RDA's): A simplified table of dietary recommendations derived from the detailed RDA tables, used by the federal government as the standard for nutritional labeling purposes.

Universal Product Code (UPC): a series of numbers translated into lines and bars, which appears now on most supermarket products designed for use with computerized checkout systems.

unsaturated fat: a fat molecule capable of holding slightly more hydrogen atoms than it presently holds.

V

variety meats: the edible organs of animals, such as brains, heart, liver, etc.

veal: a mild-flavored meat that comes from young cattle.

vegetarian diet: a diet based on foods that come from plants. Some vegetarians also include dairy products and eggs in their diets.

vitamin: a chemical compound needed in very small amounts for life, growth and good health.

W

warm weather vegetables: vegetables whose seeds require more warmth and longer growing periods than cool-weather vegetables. These seeds are often started indoors and transplanted when cool weather has passed.

water: a basic fluid composed of hydrogen and oxygen, essential to life; a major component of most foods.

water-soluble vitamin: a vitamin that will dissolve in water. The water-soluble vitamins are vitamin C and all of the B-vitamins.

whip: a very fast form of beating which adds air to a mixture.

whole milk: milk which contains all of the milk fat (at least 3.5 percent) normally found in milk as it comes from the cow.

wok: a special cooking pan widely used in Oriental cooking, with sides that slope down in the middle.

work triangle: a triangle formed by points created in a kitchen arrangement (placement) of the refrigerator, sink and range.

Y

yeast breads: term that refers to a number of breads and rolls leavened with yeast.

yogurt: a smooth, thickened dairy product made by adding special bacteria to milk. It is sold plain or flavored with fruit or other flavoring ingredients.

Index